NOT FOUND

Perspecta 56
The Yale Architectural Journal

7 INTRODUCTION

21 THE UNSUSTAINABLE SUBLIME
Esther M. Choi

31 REFUSE//REPOSE: FRAMING THREE SCENES
Andrew Economos Miller

44 CRYPTIC DESIGN
Theo Deutinger, Christopher Clarkson

50 EN-ACTORS AT THE VESSEL: NEOLIBERALISM, QUEER FAILURE, AND CRIP REFUSAL
M.C. Overholt, Alex Whee Kim

58 SENTIENT VOLUMES AND THE WORK OF ARAKAWA AND GINS
Dana Karwas

74 ZOMBIE PERSPECTIVE
David Freeland, Brennan Buck

95 PROCESS REMOVAL AND THE INVISIBLE FACTORY
Nina Rappaport

104 BANKING ON HISTORY: 'ROTHSCHILD STYLE' ARCHITECTURE AND THE MAKING OF INTERNATIONAL FINANCE
David Sadighian

120 ELEPHANT IN THE ROOM AND OTHER FABLES
DESIGN EARTH

134 SIX THESES ON ARCHITECTURE AND OBFUSCATION
Marianela D'Aprile, Douglas Spencer

144 ZOMBIES AND GHOSTS
Matthew Soules

157 VIAL ACTS
feminist architecture collaborative

166 ARCHITECTURE UNSEEN: DOROTHEA LANGE AND THE AMERICAN VERNACULAR
Linda Gordon

190 NOTES ON OBFUSCATION
APRDELESP, Xavier Nueno Guitart

196 HYPERHOMOGENEITY; OR ATTENTION WITHIN THE BACKGROUND
Michael Young

206 DRAWINGS NOT FOUND
Ashley Bigham, Erik Herrmann

214 FROM CAMOUFLAGE TO MEMORY: PROJECTIVE DRAWING AND THE ILLUSION OF SPACE
Jerome Tryon

223 DOMINO SUGAR FACTORY, OR, WHAT IS A REAL PHOTOGRAPH?
Noah Kalina

236 AID THEATER: ON RUSSIAN HUMANITARIAN AID OPERATIONS AS SOVEREIGNTY MARKERS IN UKRAINE
Lukas Pauer

250 YOU'VE JUST BEEN FUCKED BY PSYOPS
Trevor Paglen

273 CONTRIBUTORS

277 IMAGE CREDITS

279 ACKNOWLEDGMENTS

INTRODUCTION

Architecture is the perfect form of camouflage. As buildings recede into the background of everyday life, the myriad forces that shape our natural, social, and political landscapes hide in plain sight. Embedded within the spatial and material organizations of the built environment are ideas of value, hierarchy, and control that tilt the ground and influence perception in the name of endless competing interests.

Operating across multiple scales and mediums, architectural camouflage gives familiar form to obscure objectives. Design transforms and encodes our shared environments, from domestic domains to digital territories, through its material practices, aesthetics, and discourses. Immanent in the periphery, architecture's images are internalized as forms for understanding and reshaping the world. Camouflage, in turn, dwells in the architecture of our collective subconscious.

Latent within architecture's deceptions is a profound capacity to reflect the elusive intentions and surreal ambiguities of our ecological entanglements. In masking hierarchies and shifting sensitivities to what escapes perception, architecture can engender vital questions around the agency and significance of its world-making practices. Mediating with and within the background, architecture can awaken new modes of attention to material and social layers previously unimagined or hidden and engage directly with the mirrored frameworks that define reality.

This issue of *Perspecta* considers the complexities and potentialities of architectural concealment, obfuscation, and mimicry; of the power inherent in architecture's expanding capacity as media. In the veiled extents of our physical and digital worlds, what is still not found?

Guillermo Acosta Navarrete
Gabriel Gutierrez Huerta

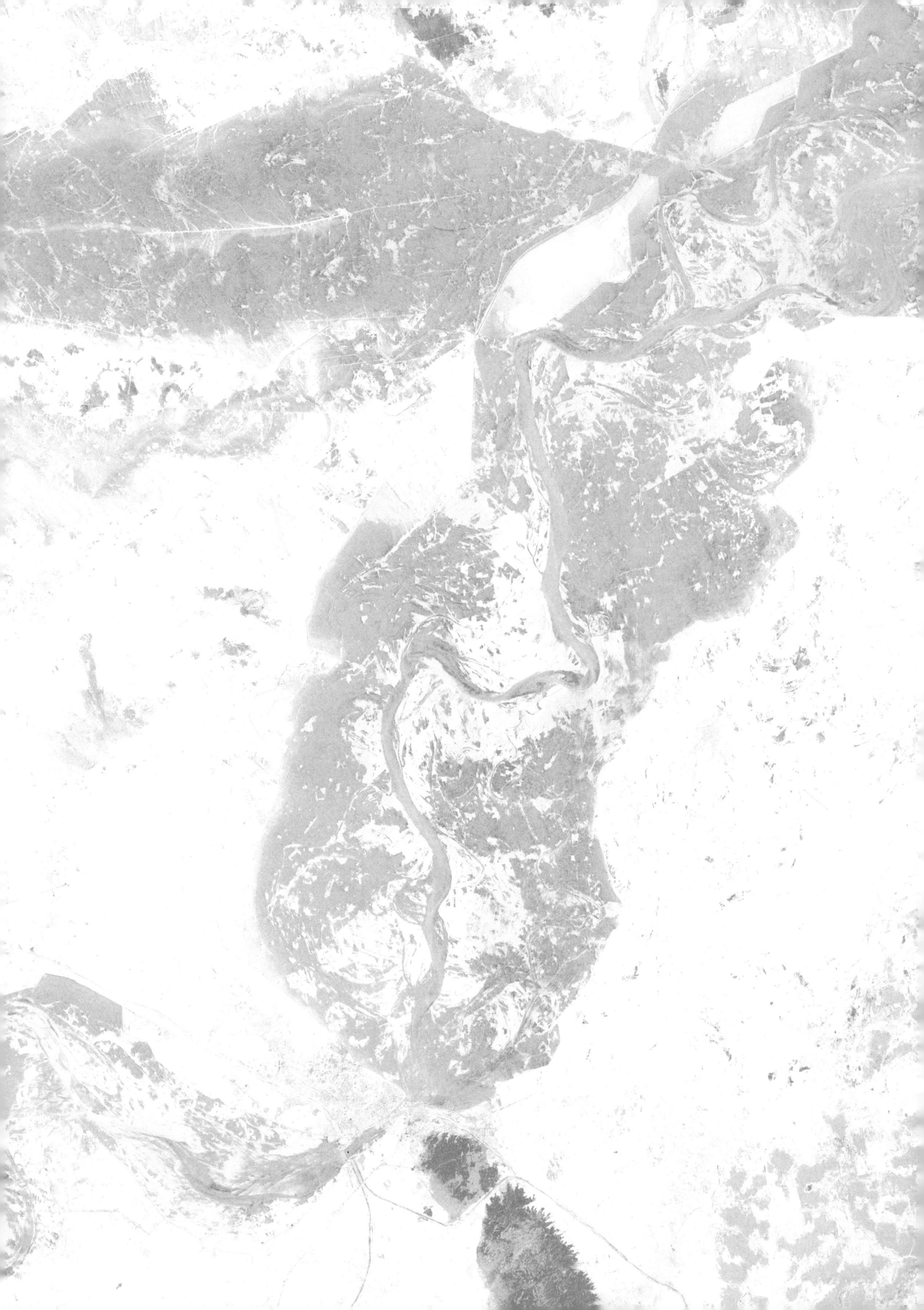

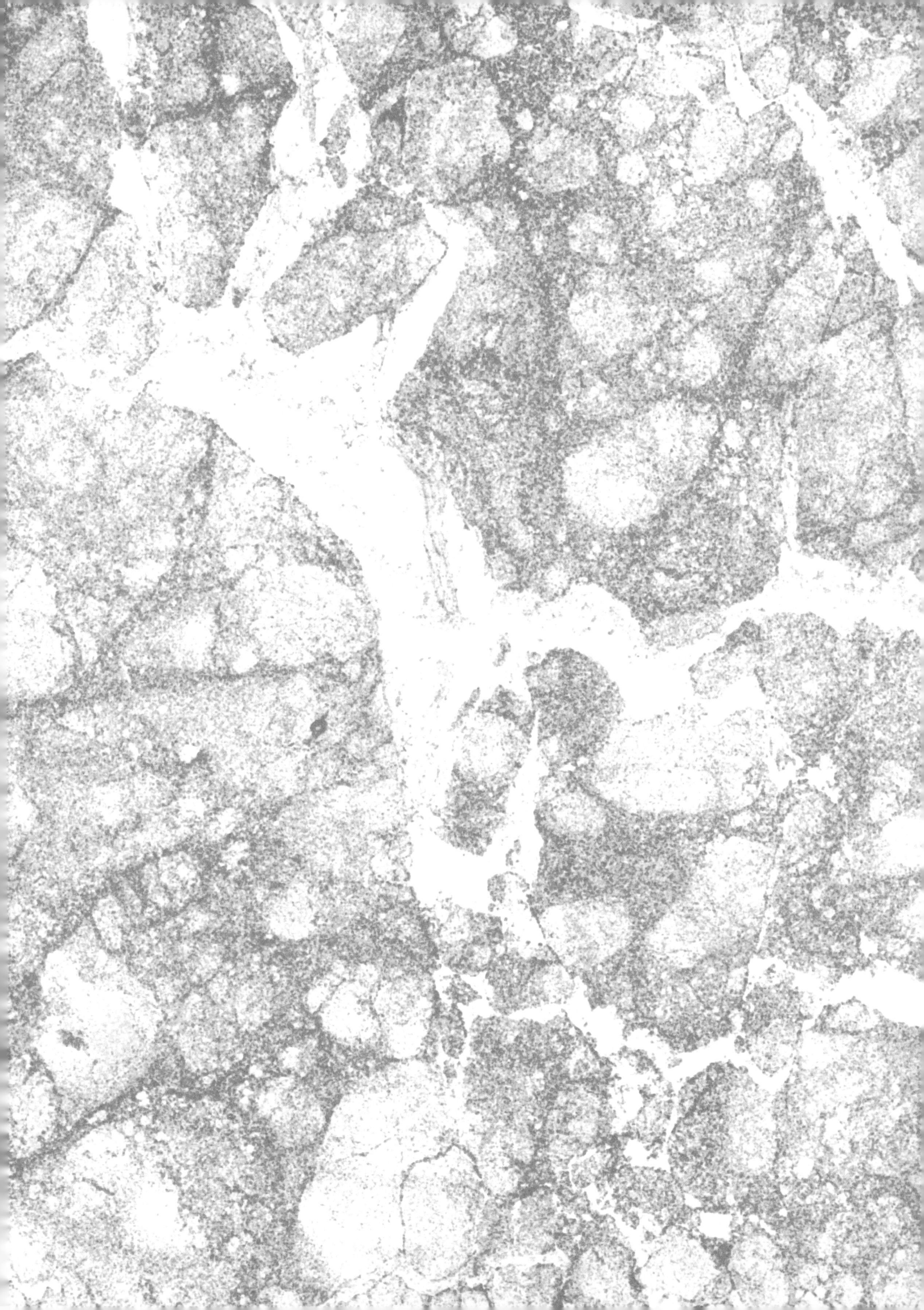

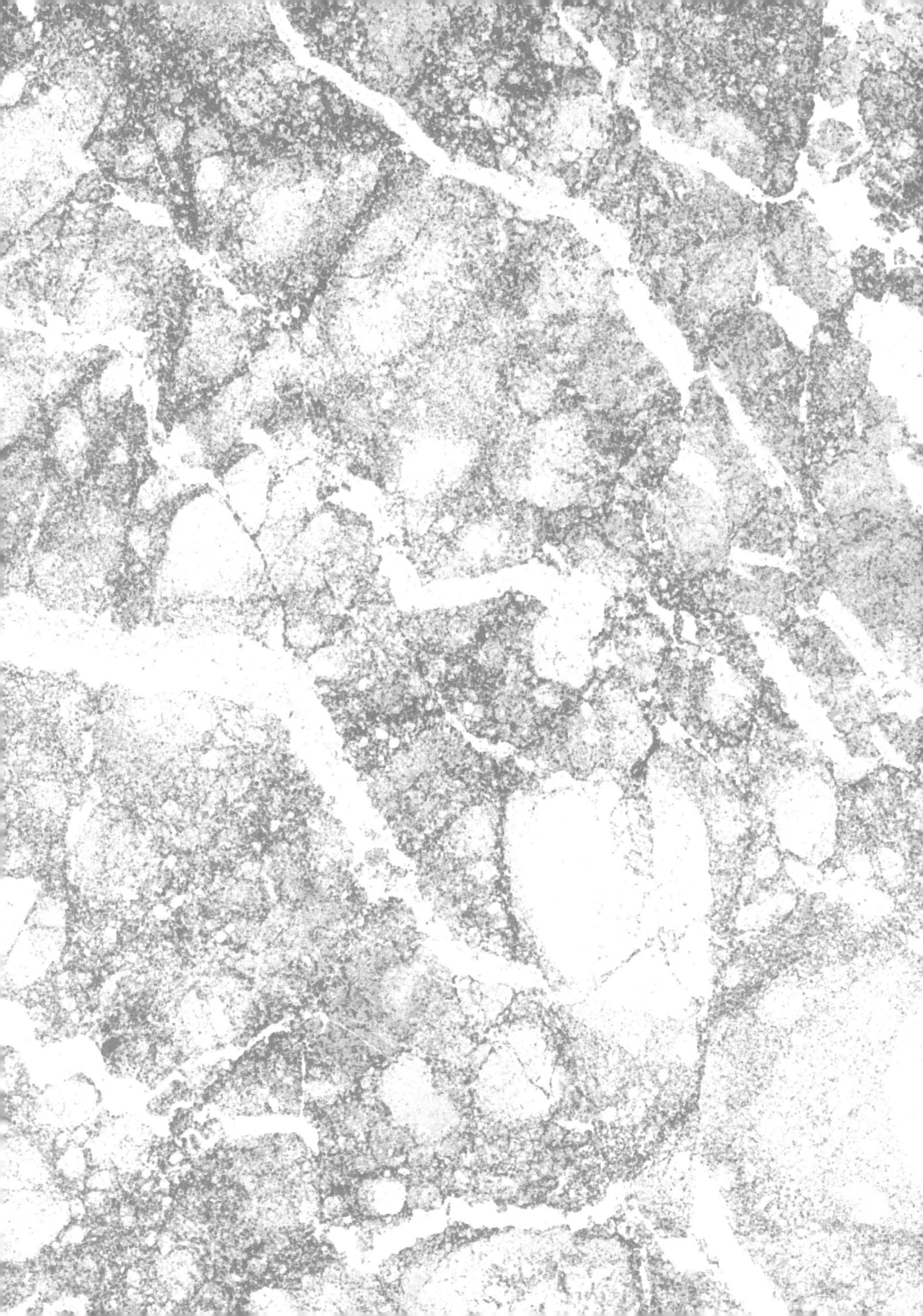

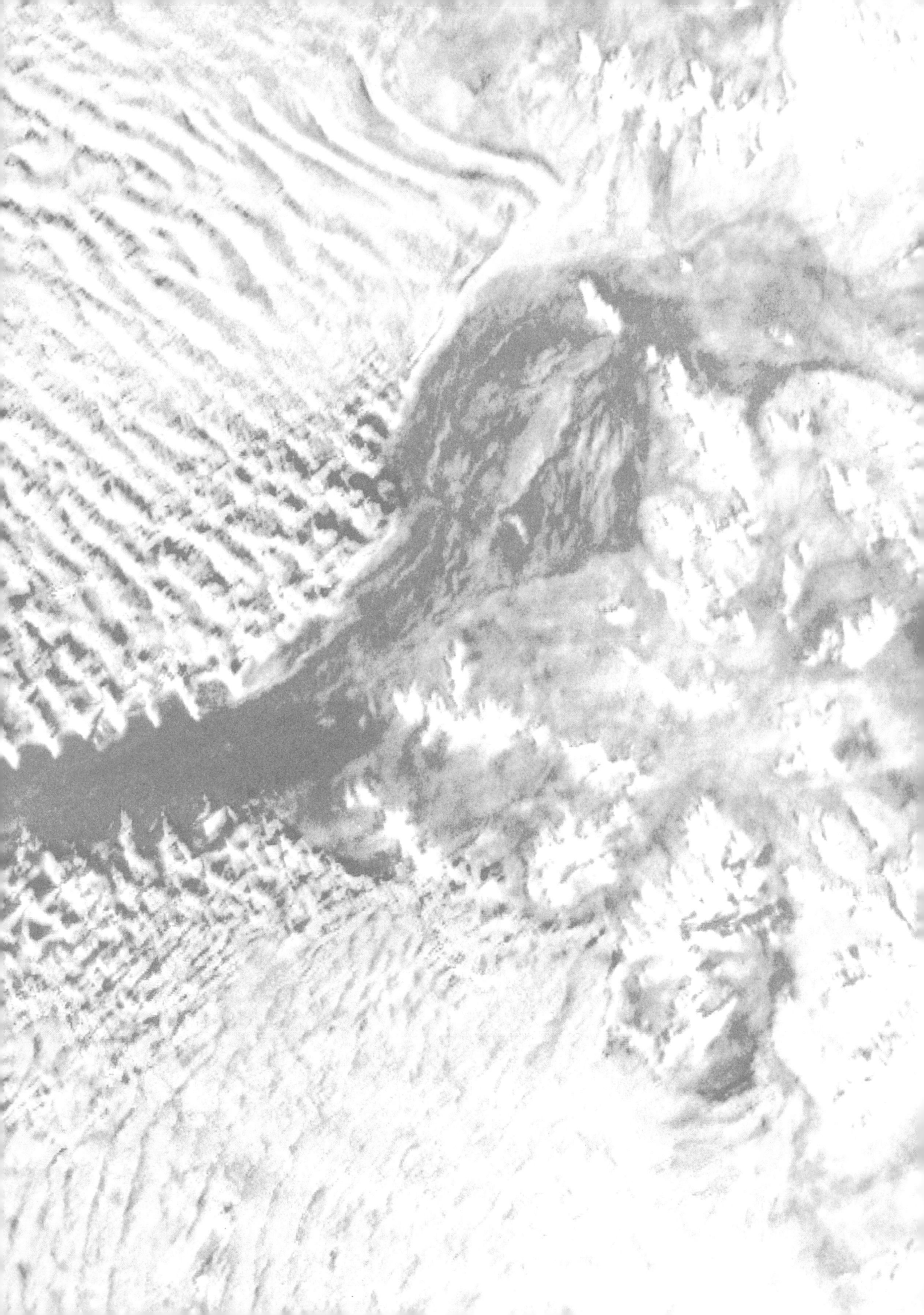

> The irrationality of a thing is no argument against its existence, rather a condition of it.
> —Friedrich Nietzsche[1]

One minute and eighteen seconds into the documentary *This Changes Everything*, Canadian journalist Naomi Klein poses the question, "Is it really possible to be bored by the end of the world?"[2] She pauses as if caught in a riddle. The film cuts from an image of a landscape to the punctum of a defenseless forest engulfed in flames. The pictures are all too common; we have seen them before. But for some reason these horrific depictions of vast destruction most often conjure feelings of deadness rather than action. Amid the endless apocalyptic forecasts issued by scientists, a kind of intellectual numbness consumes the imagination when the topic of sustainability is raised. It is a tragic paradox that cataclysmic ecological extermination elicits, of all things, bathos [Fig. 1, 2].

It seems illogical that mass extinction would evoke apathy. Given that it is *the* defining existential issue of our time, why has the impending annihilation of the human race elicited a half-hearted response, particularly from the interdisciplinary fields of the built environment—disciplines devoted specifically to world-making? Political ecology should have become a central lens through which to define the ethics of these fields' governing institutions and professional protocols at least a decade ago in industrialized nations. Yet we find innumerable contradictions that betray any resolve toward this goal. In conferences, technocratic conversations about environmentalism operate as pretexts for formal opportunism and biophilic fetishism. In universities, courses teaching carbon-intensive design perpetuate a touristic and colonial model of "parachuting" students to exotic locales to "research" and project their imaginations upon other contexts. In corporate offices, industry-sanctioned protocols for decarbonization are touted alongside an unquestioned loyalty to the use of concrete in building design. Meanwhile the ethical and relational potentialities of reimagining the world through empathy has been reduced to LEED certification and the banal accounting of carbon credits. A rational, insurgent response to this emergency is yet to be found.

Yet the lack of drastic action in response to climate change by these fields should come as no surprise. The cynical (or realistic) among us would argue that the unwillingness to commit to a new paradigm of practice led by objectives other than those tethered to neoliberal ideologies and financial gain is merely typical behavior for these professions' most powerful and influential people. Consider the dodgy greenwashing techniques employed by corporations to market their approaches to the built environment. One of the professions' most prestigious honors for "sustainable" architectural research and production, the Holcim Award, is funded by the world's largest aggregates producer, Holcim (formerly LafargeHolcim), which has been charged with innumerable environmental and human-rights offenses worldwide.[3] Indeed these disciplines' will-less and wordless inertia toward the adoption of serious and drastic actions to realize climate recuperation points to a death beyond that of the world's ecosystems—that of cultural production, whose industries are so unmoored from ethical principles and alienated from the conditions of the world that it often acquiesces to economic fatalism and denial.

While hopelessness is one reasonable explanation for inaction toward climate breakdown, the complexity and magnitude of the dilemma may be another.[4] Consider the wildfires in Australia that dominated the news cycle in early 2020, resulting in the deaths of an estimated one billion animals. Let the vast, intricate scales of social relations, local and international economies, material extractions, perfunctory environmental policies, and propaganda narratives unfurl in your mind alongside images of plant and animal life being decimated in wildfires. Picture also the unethical decisions, backroom handshakes, industry lobbies, undisclosed contracts, and financial dealings that led to this increasingly common phenomenon. Then observe as the immensity of the whole situation spirals back down to you in the here and now. If you live in the United States, as I do, consider any number of the $10.1 billion Australian imports that arrived in this country in the past couple of years, which we likely consumed and benefited from unknowingly.[5] We can reasonably assume that these products were connected in one way or another to Australia's top three environmentally depleting exports: Iron ore, coal, and gas. The parallax between the titanic tangle of systems and processes implicated in the consumption of the banal products you and I enjoy on a daily basis—derived explicitly from capitalism's powerful grip on the matrix of life—could be described as "the unsustainable sublime."

From antiquity the sublime has been characterized as an aesthetic experience that elicits a range of contradictory emotions. Yet since the advent of industrialization in the eighteenth century, shock-induced incapacitation has been one of its defining effects. In his 1757 treatise on aesthetics, Edmund Burke theorized the sublime as an experience of indeterminacy that effects an irrational state of astonishment in the soul, producing "some degree of horror."[6] In the face of a sense of danger posed by the infinite and unknowable, the mind's ability to reason is immobilized, along with its capacity for imagination and discernment. The shock of the sublime experience bypasses language itself. Burke issues a reminder of a maxim that rulers have long heeded: "No emotion effectually robs the mind of all its powers of acting and reasoning as fear."[7] This is precisely the sublime's affective power: It "anticipates our reasonings, and hurries us on by an irresistible force."[8]

Because of its power to elicit stupefaction, the sublime has challenged and inspired artists, writers, and philosophers since Longinus.[9] Although it has long been studied and practiced as an aesthetic theory and topic of philosophical inquiry associated with the marvels of nature, the articulation of empire within Britain and the United States, and the effects of industrialization manifested in the history of landscape painting,[10] of particular importance to our discussion is when the trope of the sublime as a broader cultural practice has imparted a sense of inevitability and grandeur to the project of modernization along with its political worldviews and goal of successive "improvement."[11] In this way I hope to propose that better understanding the affective operations of the sublime in three instances outside the landscape tradition—that is, decoding the sublime's material configurations, orchestration of systems, and signatures of feeling—might offer a means to decipher the inner contours of our present moment, when one finds oneself "too much inside the streams of contemporary happening to chart their flow and volume," as George Kubler wrote.[12]

1. CONVENIENCE

Literary scholar Bruce Robbins used the analogy of "the sweatshop sublime" in the early 2000s to describe the moment in which one is overcome by the immobilizing realization that one is participating in an immense web of social exploitation.[13] He narrates how a vortex of seemingly invisible processes and relations collide into the scale of a single commodity: The ordinary teakettle. "To contemplate one's kettle," Robbins writes, is to "suddenly realize, first, that one is the beneficiary of an unimaginably vast and complex social whole" and that one's mindless, daily rituals benefit "from the daily labor of the kettle- and electricity-producing workers, much of it unpleasant and under-remunerated."[14] And finally, there is a third realization:

Figures 1, 2. *This Changes Everything*, directed by Avi Lewis (Toronto, Ontario: Louverture Films, Klein Lewis Productions, 2015).

Figure 3. Roz Chast, "One Morning, While Getting Dressed," *New Yorker*, November 29, 1999.

"That this moment of consciousness will not be converted into action."[15]

Robbins offers another example in the form of a *New Yorker* cartoon by Roz Chast entitled "One morning, while getting dressed [Fig. 3]."[16] The cartoon depicts two different consumer reactions to the hidden systems of sweatshop exploitation that enable the ecstasy of convenience in the West. "One morning, while getting dressed," he writes, "you either do or do not examine the label of your shirt. If you do, you either do or do not realize the conditions of life under which this shirt was, or perhaps was not, produced."[17] The linchpin of this epiphanic grasp of reality is the low stakes of such a discovery. "But whether your thoughts linger or not, whether the shirt turns out to have been made in Mexico or Thailand or the US, the result is the same, the same as if you had not examined the label. All lines converge in the end on the same box: You put on the shirt and forget about it."[18]

From shirts to teakettles, the emotional cycle Robbins sketches in each of his examples of the sweatshop sublime follows the same pattern: There is "a moment of insight accompanied by a surge of power" that jumps in scales from the personal to the planetary. Yet the moment of recognizing this world economic system "of notoriously inconceivable magnitude and interdependence" is not framed as an outward reaction of relational interconnection.[19] Rather this system "that brings goods from the ends of the earth … to satisfy your slightest desire" ultimately enables an embarrassingly self-serving worldview.[20] Not surprisingly, this insight results in paralysis. "Your sudden, heady access to the global scale is not access to a commensurate power of

Figure 4. Jean-François Lyotard, "The Sublime and the Avant-Garde," *Artforum* 22, no. 8 (April 1984): 36–43.

action on the global scale," Robbins continues. "You have a cup of tea or coffee. You get dressed. Just as suddenly, just as shockingly, you are returned to yourself in all your everyday smallness."[21] Acknowledging the consequences of one's actions produces an incapacitation spurred not only by the horrific realization of one's participation in social exploitation but by one's acquiescence to it.

Robbins's examples point to another significant aspect of the sublime's blueprint. Understood as a verb rather than a noun or adjective, *sublime* describes a pattern of gradual, imperceptible changes that lead toward a particular goal of production.[22] The French [*sublimer*] and Latin [*sublimare*] roots of the term signify the conversion of something lowly and menial into something more refined and of greater value.[23] Likewise the process of sublimation—in which a solid is intentionally turned into a vapor and back into a solid so as to create a cultivated product—echoes the sweatshop sublime's vast orchestration of incremental extractions for unidirectional rather than reciprocal gain. The sweatshop sublime's diffuse "nature" or constitution, which blurs its extractive framework, is crucial for converting subjectivities, materials, and energies into consumables for select audiences. Such tactics of diversion are essential to ensuring that little effort, thought, or reflection takes place during the process of consumption. Yet as Robbins's analysis suggests, in this late stage of hypercapitalism it no longer seems necessary to obscure these dangers, privations, or deficiencies to guarantee a consumer's sense of satisfaction with the process. Benefiting from a bankrupt system quells any desire to change it.

2. IMPERVIOUSNESS

In the early 1980s Jean-François Lyotard turned to the appearance of the sublime in Western avant-garde art. He sensed a correspondence between the tropes of avant-garde art and the overwhelming feeling of indeterminacy that characterized modernity's so-called aftermath. In his words, the sublime was "perhaps the only mode of artistic sensibility to characterize the modern."[24] A crucial aspect of the sublime experience, Lyotard observed, is that it creates a feeling that something is perpetually out of grasp [Fig. 4].[25]

Abiding by Ezra Pound's adage "Artists are the antennae of the race," Lyotard turned his analysis to the cultural cacophony of what would be referred to as the "post-medium condition" that emerged after Abstract Expressionism. The indeterminacy of the mediums, métiers, and convoluted meanings of artistic expression seemed to mirror the ineffability of hypercapitalism. He suggested that "a collusion" was taking place between capitalism and the avant-garde. The sense of things being out of grasp, Lyotard realized, was caused by the changing machinations of the market. He writes, "There is something of the sublime in capitalist economy. It is not academic, it is not physiocratic, *it denies nature*. It is, in a sense, an economy regulated by an Idea—infinite wealth or power. It does not provide any example of nature that might verify this Idea. In subordinating science through technologies, it only succeeds in making reality appear increasingly intangible, subject to doubt, instead."[26] For Lyotard this sublime disorder was not merely the by-product of diminishing moral standards eroded by the

Figure 5. Barnett Newman, *Vir Heroicus Sublimis*, 1950–51. Oil on canvas, 7 feet 11 ⅜ inches × 17 feet 9 ¼ inches.

market; rather confusion seemed to be a deliberate intention of the market. Signification and systems of relations had become pirated by hypercapitalism, producing eclectic and incompatible combinations of meaning. "One thinks one is expressing the spirit of the moment," he notes, "whereas one is merely reflecting the spirit of the marketplace."[27]

While studying Barnett Newman's monumental avant-garde canvases, Lyotard came to the realization that the artist sought to accentuate the viewer's experience of the present moment by staging an immersive, sublime encounter. This emphasis on "nowness" rendered an experience of abstraction by pushing the viewer toward a condition of excessive interiority outside of history. Newman's paintings encouraged a subjectivity so removed from the temporal, spatial and social relations of the phenomenal world that the viewer's immediate, and highly individual, response to his work could find articulation only in the bounded perimeter of the (artwork's) surface effects.

Such a position offered freedom for Newman: To evaluate an experience through the singular criterion of one's experiential faculties was to be liberated from social responsibility and the baggage of tradition. In his essay "The Sublime Is Now," Newman suggested that American art produced in "a time without a legend or mythos that can be called sublime" could focus on creating experiences of exaltation without recourse to the pictorial legacies of European Modernism. "We do not need the obsolete props of an outmoded and antiquated legend," he argued. "We are freeing ourselves of the impediments of memory, association, nostalgia, legend, myth, or what have you, that have been the devices of Western European painting. ... The image we produce is the self-evident one of revelation, real and concrete, that can be understood by anyone who will look at it without the nostalgic glasses of history."[28]

Patterns of consumerism mirrored the ahistorical instantaneity advocated by Newman, exacerbated by the rapid expansion of the culture industry and its entanglements with global markets. Writing at the same time as Lyotard, Paul Virilio theorized that speed itself had become the very basis of technological society, producing a culture of acceleration that compressed perceptions of distance and duration.[29] Virilio also noted that fear had a close relationship to speed.[30] The velocity of the global marketplace led to what Fredric Jameson referred to as the "effacement of the traces of production," rendering the social, environmental, and economic relations required for the production of capital even more unequal and difficult to untangle.[31]

Newman's attempt to transform aesthetic experience into an abstract nonentity—that is, *the absence* of something actual—was akin to positioning cultural production in a vacuum. His position assumed a refusal to recognize an event and its viewing subject (that is, *who* possessed the advantaged position to experience this work) in relation to broader historical and political forces. Similar impulses are evident in Newman's painting *Vir Heroicus Sublimis* (1950–51), loosely translated as "Man, heroic and sublime," in which he proposed that one's encounter with painting (or cultural products more broadly) could not only eclipse social relationships but replace them altogether [Fig. 5].[32] Thus the sublime feeling, or "out of grasp-ness," that Lyotard identified in avant-garde abstraction was not merely a pictorial denial of figuration. Rather it was a rejection of the idea that things produced within reality that, in turn, structure reality are the by-products of systems of relations. Newman's desire, in particular, heralded *a deliberately severed experience* of the world as a celebration of the artistic connoisseur's (typically privileged) isolation.

3. INEVITABILITY

Writing about the history of the "technological sublime" in the mid-1960s, historian Leo Marx observed that, by the eighteenth century, rapid industrialization had rendered the belief in continuous progress an irrefutable prophecy in Western nations. By the nineteenth century the machine's agential power seemed to exceed even human capability. The rhetoric of the technological sublime elicited terror and respect by virtue of this fact.[33] Inventions like steam power seemed to defy not only the laws of nature but also commonly held beliefs about space and time as well as the "great law of the universe" that tethered human labor to consumption in a holistic relationship.[34] By extension, those who contributed to the development of technology's "progress" were valorized as intellectual heroes since the technological project was a mechanism imbued, unquestioningly, with social virtue. By the mid-nineteenth century the technological sublime seemed to surpass even the magisterial power of nature. According to historian Perry Miller, "the 'reality' of the revolution had even this early created a sublimity so vast as to make the astronomers' sublime seem pallid."[35]

Yet it is important to remember that the technological sublime has been, from its foundations, a colonial and imperialist enterprise. "Progress" for the commodity frontier relied on the notion of "taming" an uncultivated, virgin landscape in the so-called New World while presupposing that it was uninhabited and ready for the taking. Leo Marx notes that "the backwardness of the country [gave] the progressive impulse an electric charge."[36] Creating an ideological and aesthetic framework in which nature and its brute laborers were characterized as dumb, receptive, invisible, and expendable was a precondition for promoting

Figure 6. John Gast, *American Progress*, 1873.

the success of technology's sublime disciplinary and economic power. A British writer of the mid-nineteenth century referred to technology as a colonial tool for castigating savage barbarism and cultivating civility and stature; it enabled the "transition from a wild and barbarous condition to that of the most elaborate civilization ... [not] gradual, but instantaneous."[37] Technology's mastery over nature and humanity was viewed as an expression of superior, instrumental reason.[38]

It is no coincidence that theories of biological and cultural evolution gained traction alongside the development of the technological sublime, not only in American and European scientific circles but in popular culture as well. At the turn of the century Darwinian philosophies of biologism extended evolutionary principles to all facets of life—the concepts of ecology and Social Darwinism are two offshoots of this philosophical outlook. These scientific theories and rules solidified the bonds between disparate phenomena, providing the semblance of an underlying logical and continuous structure to the world's natural, cultural, social, political, and even technological patterns. Theories of biological, cultural, and social evolution offered an explanation to justify social injustice through development narratives, rendering human civility analogous with "advanced" forms of colonial expansion in the West. In this sense modernization functioned both as a settler colonial metaphor and reality, further imbuing a sense of *super*-natural evolutionary inevitability to the goal of "improvement."

The belief in technological progress was further incentivized by the "democratic" belief that elevating one's conditions, dominion, and rank is a legitimate birthright [Fig. 6].[39] This is precisely the rationale behind the expansionist manifest destiny of the United States. It is significant that historians such as Leo Marx and David E. Nye refer to the technological sublime as a particularly (white) American cultural practice since technological advancement became inextricable from the nation's broader imperialist motives. The image of the technological sublime was synonymous with the imagination, transcendence, and opportunity associated with the ubiquity of the Anglo-American empire.[40]

Yet ideas, words, and images did not alone yield the technological sublime. Sociotechnical instruments and infrastructures engineered to dominate forms of human and more-than-human life have linked the exploitation of unceded Indigenous lands with the dehumanized labor of Black, Indigenous, and other People of Color as the biopower required for these takeovers. Take, for instance, Eli Whitney's 1794 invention of the cotton gin (a machine that split cotton seeds from fibers), which rendered the mass exploitation of both cotton fields *and* Black slavery profitable industries for white Americans. Consider also the "railroad colonialism" that took place across North America and became the linchpin for myths characterizing the American imagination: Patriotic extraordinariness, an inherent right to land, and a belief in free-market expansion [Fig. 7].[41] From the eighteenth century to the present day the technological sublime has demonstrated its unwavering commitment to territorialization, expendability, and growth at all costs in the form of toxic water infrastructures, pipelines for oil and gas, prisons, borders, and dams.

For Winona LaDuke and Deborah Cowen such infrastructures of extraction serve the "Wiindigo economy" (named after the predatory, cannibalistic creature of Anishinaabe legend) and form the backbone of settler colonial nation-building and futurity.[42] In their words, "At the center of the Wiindigo's violence and distribution is infrastructure's seemingly banal and technical world. … Infrastructure is the *how* of settler colonialism, and the settler colony is where the Wiindigo runs free."[43] The reverberations between Leo Marx's historical analysis of the technological sublime and LaDuke and Cowen's Wiindigo infrastructure are patent. Consider how the interdisciplinary industries of the built environment—responsible for the unregulated technological imperialism of the "new frontier" with their unrelenting devotion to technological growth and capital accumulation—still reflect a yearning for Schumpeterian creative destruction. These signs of "progress" lend an illusion of inevitability to the process, akin to a machine that cannot be toppled.

4. SENTIENCE

What these object lessons in sublimity suggest is that the impasse of climate recuperation is not due to the sheer physical breadth of these increasingly frequent natural disasters. Nor is it due to the extensive marshaling of resources required for the realizable goal of environmental repair. Instead the feeling of being powerless to act is caused by hypercapitalism's artful subterfuge of inflicting unusually large amounts of harm for concentrated profit in ways that are persistent, gradual, and subliminal. Nye is correct to remind us that Edmund Burke's version of the sublime reinforced the idea that human beings react to particular configurations of terror in *habitual* ways [Fig. 8].[44] The unsustainable sublime is a cultural practice with a proven track record of setting in motion domino sequences of spectacular brutality.

A more contemporary technique of producing a sense of sublime alienation, along the lines of what Fredric Jameson defined as "hallucinatory exhilaration," is the creation of semantic confusion.[45] It is analogous to Barnett Newman's advocacy of the privileged observer's withdrawal as a form of embodied abstraction. For this reason cognitive dissonance is one of neoliberalism's preferred strategies. In his analysis of the pandemonium following the financial crisis, economic historian Philip Mirowski observed that neoliberal thought had become so expansive as a "theory of everything" that any conflicting position was taken up as evidence by its believers that testified to its validity.[46] Obscurity is necessary to producing a sense of danger and a state of immobility.

Yet as Edmund Burke also pointed out, the sublime has a direct connection to power.[47] Indeed he knew that the sublime could be used as a political tool.[48] Although culture has often acted as the unsustainable sublime's alibi, perhaps we can reclaim its stature. Bruce Robbins points out that, in the *Critique of Judgment*, Immanuel Kant focuses so much on aesthetics "not because he wants to defend rationality but precisely because he can see that the rational community he desires will never come about by means of submission to rationality. … Kant's aesthetics can be read as his political theory, a theory rendered necessary by the political insufficiencies of Reason."[49] Other philosophers of the sublime have argued that aesthetics is a tool that we, as cultural practitioners, have at our disposal in the *absence* of reason. For example, Lyotard argues, "The arts … in a quest for intense effects, can and must overlook mimetic models that are merely beautiful, and must test their limits through surprising, difficult, shocking combinations. Shock is, par excellence, the evidence of (something) happening, rather than nothing at all. It is suspended privation."[50]

If obscuring the injurious dynamics of global capital in the late twentieth and twenty-first centuries is one of the largest reasons for our push toward planetary ecological collapse, what would it take to make such transactions and relationships more onerous, more difficult to consume, and more transparent? Nye points out that the sublime comprises a complex system of views that no single image can convey.[51] We might look to anthropologist Anna Lowenhaupt Tsing's "Patchy Anthropocene"—an analytic tool set based on (landscape) structures, intersectional and unequal relationships, patterns, and systems thinking—to guide our understanding of the complex spatial, scalar, and temporal relations and assemblages that comprise multispecies worlds.[52] Importantly, Tsing and her coauthors suffuse their proposal with a sense of hope that steers away from the singular, universal, and scalable utopias of green capitalism, ecomodernism, and Big Tech—what they refer to as "versions of this revived modernist hope for capitalism and humanity to reinvent itself in a 'greener' and 'better' form in the face of crisis and disruption."[53] Thus a tactical rebuttal of dismantling the cultural operations of the unsustainable sublime may necessitate operating in deliberately minor, fragmentary, incremental, and "behind-the-scenes" ways.

Likewise, what might a cultural praxis that pushes against the privileged separation of subjectivity Newman sought to harness through the medium of painting look and feel like? If political inaction is the result of a disembodied "split" from the conditions, processes, and sources of life, how might cultural workers take small yet obstinate steps to reorient the flows and protocols of our cultural practices to reenergize the affective resonance of such fractures and reduce harm? As a rebuttal to the violence of Wiindigo infrastructure, LaDuke and Cowen offer us the concept of *alimentary infrastructures:* Mechanisms of care that are "life-generating in their design, finance, and effects" and can mobilize social, spiritual, and ecological changes toward a decolonialized future.[54] The authors remind us too that "physical and affective infrastructures are one and the same."[55] Central to the project of colonialism are not only physical systems but also "infrastructures of feeling"[56]—socially reproduced material systems comprised of ideas, beliefs, and emotions that generate racism and white supremacy, which "sanction the extension of the means of life to some, often through their withdrawal from others."[57] If infrastructures are neutral, how might we use our imagination—the greatest political instrument we have, described by Jedediah Purdy as "intensely practical"—to produce new tools, affects, assemblages, systems, and platforms in the service of life?[58] To pose such questions is to question cultural production's allegiance to the project of modernization, often couched in material and spatial approaches, social practices, and histories that purport to be ecological and socially responsible through "technological transcendence,"[59] or optical rather than structural and transformational measures. For this reason we need to address the caustic colonial belief structures that underwrite the narratives, feelings, protocols, and cultural tropes associated with aesthetic and technological production. Otherwise we run the risk of allowing culture to continue to advance the disintegrated vision of economic fatalism—and its corresponding false sense of abject powerlessness—required to perpetuate the unsustainable sublime.

Figure 7. Chinese laborers at work with pick and shovel wheelbarrows and one-horse dump carts filling in under the long-secret town trestle which was originally built in 1865 on the Present Souther Pacific Railroad lines of Sacramento. The picture was taken in 1877 and shows the crude construction methods in use when the first railroad was built across the Sierra Nevada Mountains.

Figure 8. John Martin, *The Great Day of His Wrath*, ca. 1851.

1. Friedrich Nietzsche, "Aph. 515," *Human, All Too Human: A Book for Free Spirits* (1878), trans. R. J. Hollingdale (Cambridge, UK: Cambridge University Press, 1996), 182.
2. *This Changes Everything*, directed by Avi Lewis (Toronto: Louverture Films, Klein Lewis Productions, 2015).
3. See Queensland Parliament, "Overview of Holcim Breaches," November 6, 2010, https://documents.parliament.qld.gov.au/tableoffice/tabledpapers/2010/5310T2432.pdf. The file of offenses was presented in the Queensland Parliament by Robert Messenger, a member of the Legislative Assembly, in response to a proposed Holcim quarry development near two coastal communities in Australia, despite the protests of constituents. Messenger states, "In 2010 Holcim was fined $280,000 in Western Australia for blasting into a heritage zone containing Indigenous rock art up to 10,000 years old; in 2008 Colombia fined Holcim $424,000 for fixing prices in 2005; and in 2006 it was fined in India for failing to comply with takeover regulations during the acquisition of associated cement companies. The EPA also classes Holcim as a high-priority violator after the Ada, Oklahoma, cement plant was fined $321,000 in 2005 for violating its pollution limits more than 1,000 times in a single year. And the sorry list goes on." See Queensland Parliament, "Speech by Robert Messenger extracted from Hansard of Friday, 11 June 2010," https://documents.parliament.qld.gov.au/speeches/spk2010/Robert%20Messenger%20spk%20Burnett%202010_06_11_56.pdf.
4. Kant referred to this sense of vastness ad infinitum as the "mathematical sublime." Immanuel Kant, *Critique of Judgment* (1790; Oxford, UK: Oxford University Press, 2007), 81–87.
5. Statistic from 2018, https://ustr.gov/countries-regions/southeast-asia-pacific/australia.
6. "The passion caused by the great and the sublime in nature, when those causes operate most powerfully, is astonishment; and astonishment is that state of the soul, in which all its motions are suspended, with some degree of horror." Edmund Burke, *A Philosophical Inquiry into the Origin of Our Ideas of the Sublime and Beautiful: With an Introductory Discourse Concerning Taste, and Several Other Additions* (London: Thomas McLean, 1823), 73.
7. Burke, *Philosophical Inquiry*, 74.
8. Burke, *Philosophical Inquiry*, 74.
9. See Longinus, *On the Sublime*, trans. James A. Arieti and John M. Crossett (New York: E. Mellen Press, 1985).
10. See for instance, Andrew Wilton and T. J. Barringer, eds. *American Sublime: Landscape Painting in the United States, 1820–1880* (Princeton, NJ: Princeton University Press, 2002); and Vittoria Di Palma, *Wasteland: A History* (New Haven, CT: Yale University Press, 2014).
11. David E. Nye reminds us that it is important to remember that these objects (and their interpretations) are socially constructed and not predestined phenomena. Culture is the upshot of conditions of possibility and an active agent that can further perpetuate these very conditions. David E. Nye, *American Technological Sublime* (Cambridge, MA: MIT Press, 2016), 3.
12. George Kubler, *The Shape of Time: Remarks on the History of Things* (New Haven, CT: Yale University Press, 1962), 27.
13. Bruce Robbins, "The Sweatshop Sublime," *PMLA* 117, no. 1 "Special topic: Mobile Citizens, Media States" (January 2002): 84–97.
14. Robbins, "Sweatshop Sublime," 84.
15. Robbins, "Sweatshop Sublime," 84.
16. Roz Chast, "One Morning While Getting Dressed," *New Yorker*, November 29, 1999.
17. Robbins, "Sweatshop Sublime," 85.
18. Ibid.
19. Ibid.
20. Ibid.
21. Ibid.
22. See also Nye, *American Technological Sublime*, 4.
23. *Merriam-Webster*, s.v. "sublime," accessed August 9, 2020, https://www.merriam-webster.com/dictionary/sublime.
24. Jean-François Lyotard, "The Sublime and the Avant-Garde," *Artforum*, April 1984, 38. See also Jean-François Lyotard, "Presenting the Unpresentable: The Sublime," *Artforum*, April 1982, 64–70.
25. Lyotard, "Sublime and the Avant-Garde," 36.
26. Lyotard, "Sublime and the Avant-Garde," 43.
27. Lyotard, "Sublime and the Avant-Garde," 43. (Italics are the author's own.)
28. Barnett Newman, "The Sublime Is Now," *Tiger's Eye* 1, no. 6 (December 15, 1948): 53; reprinted in *Barnett Newman: Selected Writings and Interviews*, ed. John P. O'Neill (Berkeley, CA: University of California Press, 1992), 173.
29. See Paul Virilio, *Speed and Politics: An Essay on Dromology*, trans. Mark Polizzotti (New York: Columbia University Press, 1977).
30. Paul Virilio, *The Administration of Fear*, trans. Ames Hodges (Los Angeles: Semiotext(e), 2012), 21.
31. Fredric Jameson, *Postmodernism; or, The Cultural Logic of Late Capitalism* (Durham, NC: Duke University Press, 1991), 314–15.
32. Barnett Newman in "Interview with David Sylvester," in *Barnett Newman*, 254–58.
33. Leo Marx, *The Machine in the Garden: Technology and the Pastoral Ideal in America* (New York: Oxford University Press, 1964), 198.
34. Marx, *Machine in the Garden*, 199.
35. Perry Miller, *The Life of the Mind in America from the Revolution to the Civil War* (New York: Harcourt Brace Jovovich, 1965), 309.
36. Marx, *Machine in the Garden*, 203.
37. Marx, *Machine in the Garden*, 199.
38. Nye, *American Technological Sublime*, 8.
39. Marx, *Machine in the Garden*, 204.
40. Marx, *Machine in the Garden*, 206.
41. See Manu Karuka, *Empire's Tracks: Indigenous Nations, Chinese Workers, and the Transcontinental Railroad* (Oakland, CA: University of California Press, 2019). See also Winona LaDuke and Deborah Cowen's discussion of the Canadian Pacific Railway in "Beyond Wiindigo Infrastructure," *South Atlantic Quarterly* 119, no. 2 (April 2020): 243–68.
42. LaDuke and Cowen, "Beyond Wiindigo," 249.
43. LaDuke and Cowen, "Beyond Wiindigo," 244–45.
44. Nye, *American Technological Sublime*, 6.
45. Jameson, *Postmodernism*, 33.
46. Philip Mirowski, *Never Let a Serious Crisis Go to Waste: How Neoliberalism Survived the Financial Meltdown* (New York: Verso, 2013).
47. Burke, *Philosophical Inquiry*, 85.
48. Consider, for instance, Burke's evocation of sublime terror in his speeches to sway public opinion in the late eighteenth century. Nida Sajid, "In 'Savage' Company: Sublime Aesthetics and the Colonial Imagination," *European Legacy* 24 no. 1 (January 2, 2019): 25–45.
49. Robbins, "Sweatshop Sublime," 95.
50. Lyotard, "Sublime and the Avant-Garde," 40.
51. Nye, *American Technological Sublime*, 11.
52. See Anna Lowenhaupt Tsing, Andrew S. Mathews, and Nils Bubandt, "Patchy Anthropocene: Landscape Structure, Multispecies History, and the Retooling of Anthropology," *Current Anthropology* 60, no. S20 (August 2019): 186–97.
53. Tsing, Mathews, and Bubandt, "Patchy Anthropocene," 192.
54. LaDuke and Cowen, "Beyond Wiindigo," 245–46.
55. LaDuke and Cowen, "Beyond Wiindigo," 262.
56. Ruth Wilson Gilmore, *Golden Gulag: Prisons, Surplus, Crisis, and Opposition in Globalizing California* (Berkeley, CA: University of California Press, 2007).
57. Wilson Gilmore, *Golden Gulag*.
58. Jedediah Purdy, *After Nature* (Cambridge, MA: Harvard University Press, 2015), 7.
59. Tsing, Mathews, and Bubandt, "Patchy Anthropocene," 192.

> All conventional scholarly work is written in the implied first person. Under the mask of objectivity, "I am interested in" becomes "The focus of this study is." The following chapters make no pretense at objectivity: They represent the residue of my self, my cultural condition, my passion (love and hate) for architecture. The non-neutrality of language and history and architecture.
> —Jennifer Bloomer, *Architecture and the Text*[1]

Words borrowed to begin an essay. An exposed cut, the trajectories of thought kept in sight. Refusing the backbreaking labor and catastrophic energy expended to fashion thought and matter as if they spontaneously apparated from the world they were taken from. Instead the fragment: Words, matter, body, and becoming all found in the trash heap.

> The cardinal ruse of theoreticians resides, generally, in the presentation of the result of their deliberations such that the process of deliberation is no longer apparent.—Tiqqun, *Preliminary Materials for a Theory of the Young Girl*[2]

The structure of this essay is that of a designed pile. Two words, *refuse* and *repose*, repeated within three frames—labor, waste, and action—each paired with a scene: An island, a courtyard, and a gallery. Within each frame those two words are given new definitions that muddy their meanings and reveal that they too comprise excessive piles of significance borrowed from disparate fields and cobbled together into a mess of a practice.

> Benjamin's 1928 treatise on allegory, *The Origin of German Tragic Drama* ... was conceived as a tissue of quotations whose logic derived from an emblematic armature ... One of the predominant characteristics of Benjamin's construction of allegory is a slippage of the boundary between visual and verbal criteria.—Jennifer Bloomer[3]

Surrounding the frame and the scene is the field: Words and work by others loosely piled up like Friedrich Nietzsche and Manfredo Tafuri's stones, a quarry of the already worked and cast aside.

> Today, with every new bit of knowledge, one has to stumble over words that are petrified and hard as stones, and one will sooner break a leg than a word.—Friedrich Nietzsche, "Daybreak"[4]

These quote-stones acknowledge that thought does not happen in a vacuum. The work and thought presented in this essay should be considered within its particular context. It is a result of that particular context: A temporary academic context, a half-abandoned geographic context, and a confused embodiment—*my self, my cultural condition, my passions.* This field is no flat plane. Shot through with power differentials, the voices that get recorded, the words that become stones, and the branding tools that reinscribe action into labor can only represent the apparatus that validates them. Reduce, Reuse, Recycle, or Preserve the Academy; Preserve the Work Regime; Preserve Capital.

> The choice to expose these elements in all their incompleteness, in their contingent original state, in their ordinary excess, knowing that if polished, hollowed out, and given a good trim they might together constitute an altogether presentable doctrine, we have chosen trash theory.—Tiqqun[5]

Nor can the personal and the professional be pulled apart. The same power structures that construct the field manifest in the body in the violence between immaterial image and wet matter. The body of work is the work of the body, and vice versa.

> This chasmic body cannot be articulated in terms of the binary opposites that structure thought and language. Never "proper, clean, neat, or tidy," the body is inescapably transgressive … [sperm, menstrual blood, urine, fecal matter, vomit, tears, sobs, screams, cries, and laughter].—Mark C. Taylor, Alterity[6]

And so the value of allegory as a device: An excessive pile of architectural excrement. A way of working and thinking that makes obsolete the binary distinctions distributed by the state. A method to destabilize both the hermeneutic circle of analysis and the corporate annulus of toothless recycling, turning part and whole into pits and holes.

> The promise of Benjaminian allegory … the crossing of female and male, of the excremental (the dirty, the bloody) and the precious (the divine). … The point of X change.—Jennifer Bloomer[7]

FRAME ONE: LABOR (ACADEMIC)

Hannah Arendt echoed Karl Marx in describing labor as the "eternal natural necessity between man and nature," but defined labor as limited to the cyclical activity of subsistence. She delaminates this activity from work by arguing that labor leaves no lasting impact. Undone by the prominence of industrial agriculture and animal husbandry within the culprits of climate change, this idea of a split between labor and work is unnecessarily romantic. Subsistence leaves marks. Even Arendt's vaunted political speech is captured and transmitted as content for the maintenance and growth of capital. Rather than delimit activity based on romantic notions, as Arendt does, the following definitions assume the full capture of labor and its surplus by capital.

> The State does not give power to the intellectuals or conceptual innovators; on the contrary, it makes them a strictly dependent organ with an autonomy that is only imagined yet is sufficient to divest those whose job it becomes simply to reproduce or implement all of their power.—Gilles Deleuze and Félix Guattari, A Thousand Plateaus[8]

Definition One: Refuse. To *refuse* the act of labor is the worker's main instrument of power. But this agency can be enacted only collectively: The individual refusal of labor ends in a prolonged, wasted martyrdom. Collective refusal, on the other hand, is one of the few acts of inaction capable of producing mass change. It is a "productive" cessation.

> The State's response was to take over management of the construction sites, merging all the divisions of labor in the supreme distinction between the intellectual and the manual, the theoretical and the practical, modeled upon the difference between "governors" and the "governed."—Gilles Deleuze and Félix Guattari, A Thousand Plateaus[9]

The Renaissance convention of differentiating the drawing from the building arts marks the naturalization of hylomorphic metaphysics through the modern division of labor in architecture. The dichotomy between form and matter is pulled apart and distributed between the bourgeois and proletariat in a mimicry of Roman architecture. It should be sufficient to note that this strict divide between architect and builder appeared most prominently at the birth of the Roman Empire—Vitruvius wrote his books specifically for Augustus—and with the rise of modern Western imperialism during the Italian Renaissance. The distribution of form as thought and matter as labor is mystified by academic discourses that limit the architect's purview to formal matters, further reducing it to cheap shape. The purpose of the imperialist Western form of architecture is purely to define and distribute increasingly deskilled labor in order to gain external control over the historically difficult construction site.

> The weapon of workers' know-how gave way to the weapon of presumed prescriptive knowledge. A chiasmus: At the construction site the know-how declines, resulting in deskilling and deeper subordination of the work-force; knowing emigrates, distancing itself more and more from doing, and draws more power and aura into capital.—Sergio Ferro, Concrete as Weapon[10]

> It can be said not only that there is no longer a need for skilled or qualified labor, but also that there is a need for unskilled or unqualified labor, for a dequalification of labor.—Gilles Deleuze and Félix Guattari, A Thousand Plateaus[11]

This conflict between the intellectually severed categories of form and matter carries through all of the discipline's tools. From the immaterial social technology of labor and the slippery metaphysics of digital software to the physical tools of construction and the plug-and-play materiality of commodified building materials, there is no critical use of the given tools, only the collective refusal to pick them up.

> The very general primacy of the collective and machinic assemblage over the technical element applies generally, for tools as for weapons. Weapons and tools are consequences.—Gilles Deleuze and Félix Guattari[12]

Definition Two: Repose. To *repose* on the job is subterfuge. It is the sixth cigarette break: The intentional inactivity of the collective on the level of the individual. To *repose* within the framework of labor is an individual rejection of the subjectivizing power of the work regime. It is an embodied refusal of Max Weber's Protestant work ethic, and Luc Boltanski and Eve Chiapello's concept of creative labor.

> The work regime is inseparable from an organization and development of Form, corresponding to which is the formation of the subject.—Gilles Deleuze and Félix Guattari[13]

The privileged half of the hylomorphic split and the tool of architecture—form—appears as the principal instrument for disciplining the worker. Form as command shapes the thoughts and bodies of workers toward immaterial ideals, just as it shapes space. It thus contains all architectures that disavow autonomous "form" while retaining its management

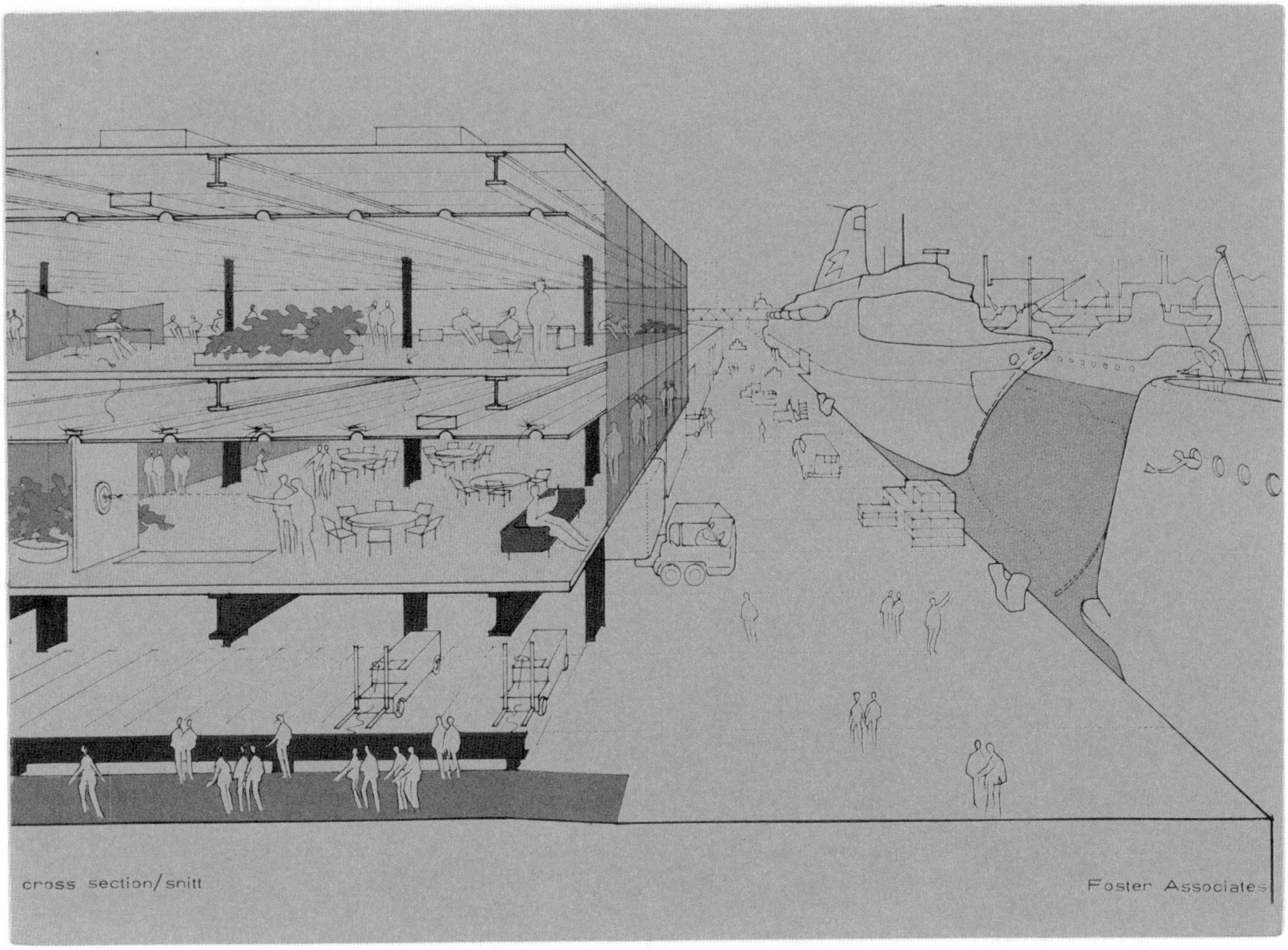

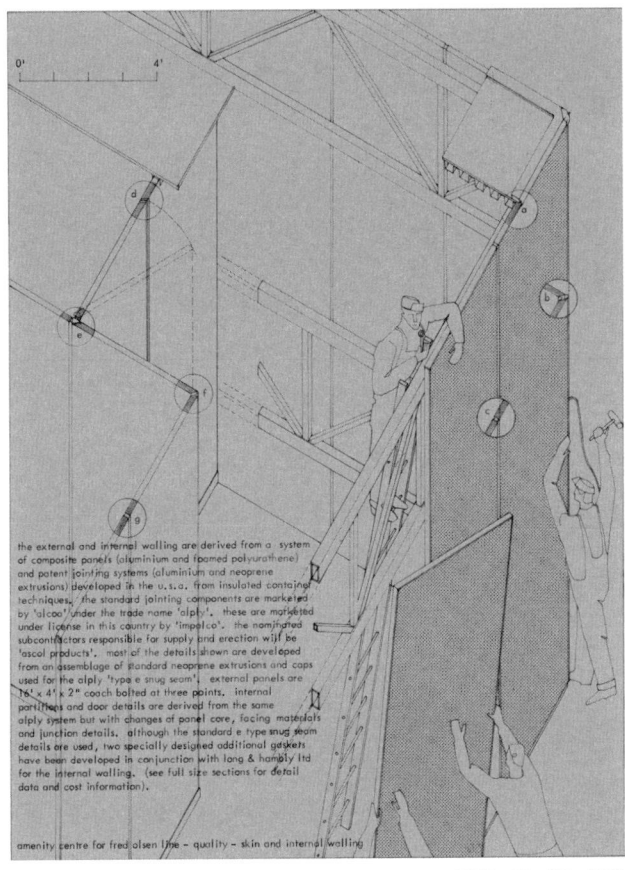

Fred Olsen Amenities Centre, Foster Associates, Millwall, UK, 1968.

structure and subjectivization. Thus naturalizing labor-based identity forms as eternal forms of stagnant being: Architect, designer, worker. Individual *repose* looks toward Herman Melville for its escape.

> I would prefer to be left alone here," said Bartleby, as if offended at being mobbed in his privacy. "That's the word, Turkey," said I—"that's it." "Oh, prefer? oh yes—queer word.—Herman Melville, "Bartleby the Scrivener"[14]

SCENE ONE: TWO ISLANDS

From 1968 through 1975, Foster Associates (renamed Foster + Partners in 1999) engaged in a thorough reinvention of the Norwegian Fred Olsen Shipping Company with the aim of transforming the corporate giant from a banana-producing freight company to a sleek passenger ferry service. This relationship resulted in the production of six speculative and built projects, beginning with a passenger terminal at Millwall Docks and ending seven years later in an unrealized development study for the small island of La Gomera, in the Canary Islands. The collaboration spanned the industrial and commercial processes from production to transport through the nascent neoliberal market. The first and last of the projects stand out for their intentional reshuffling of the production process of the tourism industry, engaging class, labor, and ecology in ways that anticipated certain typologies of contemporary architecture.

Fred Olsen Amenities Centre, Foster Associates, Millwall, UK, 1968.

Photographs from La Gomera taken by the Foster + Associates team, 1974-75.

> Capitalism has to fix space (in immovable structures of transport and communication nets, as well as in built environments of factories, roads, houses, water supplies, and other physical infrastructures) in order to overcome space (achieve a liberty of movement through low transport and communication costs).—David Harvey, "Globalization and the Spatial Fix"[15]

The dockworkers project, initiated in 1968, aimed to produce a space that flattened the distinction between white-collar office worker and blue-collar laborer. Foster Associates proposed a single shared building. As in the Big Tech offices of today, floor-plan flexibility was key to allow for various recreational activities, from games and reading to a gallery space for the display of art from Olsen's private collection.[16] The project comprised integrated workforces, simulated and representational elements, and "high-performance" facade systems (features that would later become signatures of the firm's work), while the ideas about worker edification and recreation as well as the shift from centralized viewing to internal surveillance became key aspects of the neoliberal office. Here architecture is a tool for the reforging of the animating "spirit" of capitalism. In the case of the Fred Olsen Amenities Centre, the expansion of bounds of architecture to include the social collective of dockworkers produced not only a shift in the ideological reservations of the managerial classes but also in the ideology of blue-collar workers toward consumption and "high-brow" behaviors and fears. While the project was under development, white-collar management resisted the inclusion of the dockers. As Foster cites: "How can we possibly have the dockers in the same building? They're dirty, they swear, the secretaries will walk out."[17] As the project finished, attitudes shifted. By the end it was the dockworkers keeping others out. When asked about new services outside of the building for truck drivers, they responded: "The drivers are dirty people; they can't come in here."[18] While this instance records a localized reinscription of social groups, the global shift in the position of the English worker from production to consumption at the birth of neoliberalism is made clear in the material available at the Amenities Center and in a proposal for a travel agency advertising trips to the Canary Islands on Olsen Cruise Lines.

> Consumer capitalism was not born automatically from industrial technologies capable of the production of standardized commodities. It is also a cultural and social construction that required the education of consumers.—Gilles Lipovetsky, *The Paradoxical Happiness*[19]

Seven years after construction of the Millwall building, Foster Associates would begin studies for tourism development on La Gomera. This project shifted the scale of the collaborative projects from architectural structures within an industrial system to the design of the system itself. The team proposed to have the local "surplus labor population" pair vernacular masonry forms with imported green technologies for solar, wind, and water capture and management to create a "restored" ecosystem that would attract tourism to the island. This strategy shifted the focus from a literal specific form to the generalized application of labor across an island, a change only in scale from the status quo.

> The result was a very, very deliberately high energy concept—high energy in terms of manpower. The challenge here was as to how you used the labour force, how you created a building industry, how you actually found work for people to do.
> —Norman Foster[20]

Whereas the Amenities Center worked toward the resubjectivization of individual workers, the La Gomera Study expanded the role of architecture in the definition and distribution of construction labor on a new scale. Together they reveal the global economic shuffling of the neoliberal turn and mark architecture's continued place at the forefront of labor control.

FRAME TWO: WASTE (GEOGRAPHIC)

> The fairest Cosmos is merely a rubbish-heap poured out at random.—Heraclitus[21]

Definition One: Refuse. Matter at the end of its life, ripped from the earth for exchange and now allowed to return past the final point of sale. Distributed across the surface of the earth in order to be removed from the view of some and forced into the lives of others.

> Dirt is matter out of place.—Mary Douglas, *Purity and Danger*[22]

Mary Douglas's dirt is both socially constructed and material. Waste is defined and distributed through social boundaries. In the contemporary condition this means that waste is commodified and transported in reverse through neocolonial networks. Just as each life is valued differently, so its relationship to waste material is defined. As sacrifice zones are marked for extraction, so are they marked for dumping.

Definition Two: Repose. Repose is the quality of the trash pile. All waste storage facilities, especially those for mine tailings, are designed to support a particular material's angle of repose—the slope at which it rests. For general human refuse it is approximately 30 degrees. Waste is the thought and unthought, contained and leaking—matter rejecting an application of form accounted for but not given to. It is the space where matter is allowed to assert itself once again as it finally exits the circuits of exchange and enters our blood.

> In the process of decay, and in it alone, the events of history shrivel up and become absorbed in the setting.—Walter Benjamin, *The Origin of German Tragic Drama*[23]

At the same time waste is the disciplining condition of material in repose. The firm hand guiding production and recycling discourse toward reinvestment leads down a widening gyre toward the stilted distribution of capital and the inevitable equalization of flow through violence. Recycling is the form of "getting it back to work."

> Human activity transforming the world augments the mass of living matter with supplementary apparatuses, composed of an immense quantity of inert matter, which considerably increases the resources of available energy.—Georges Bataille, *The Accursed Share*[24]

Architecture and spatial control form the backbone of these ever-expanding technical apparatuses that perform the same capture applied to labor on the nonhuman biosphere. On a global frame, much of the Western built environment requires this garbage outflow to maintain an ideologically driven view of a "standard of living." It is important to recognize the violence required to maintain this way of life, in the context of both resource extraction and waste exportation. Rather than the circle of toothless recycling that aims to put the tail of the snake farther down the throat of capital, Refuse//Repose is reconstruction in a line—a line of flight, a line of escape. It is an intentional reinscription of the line that divides waste and

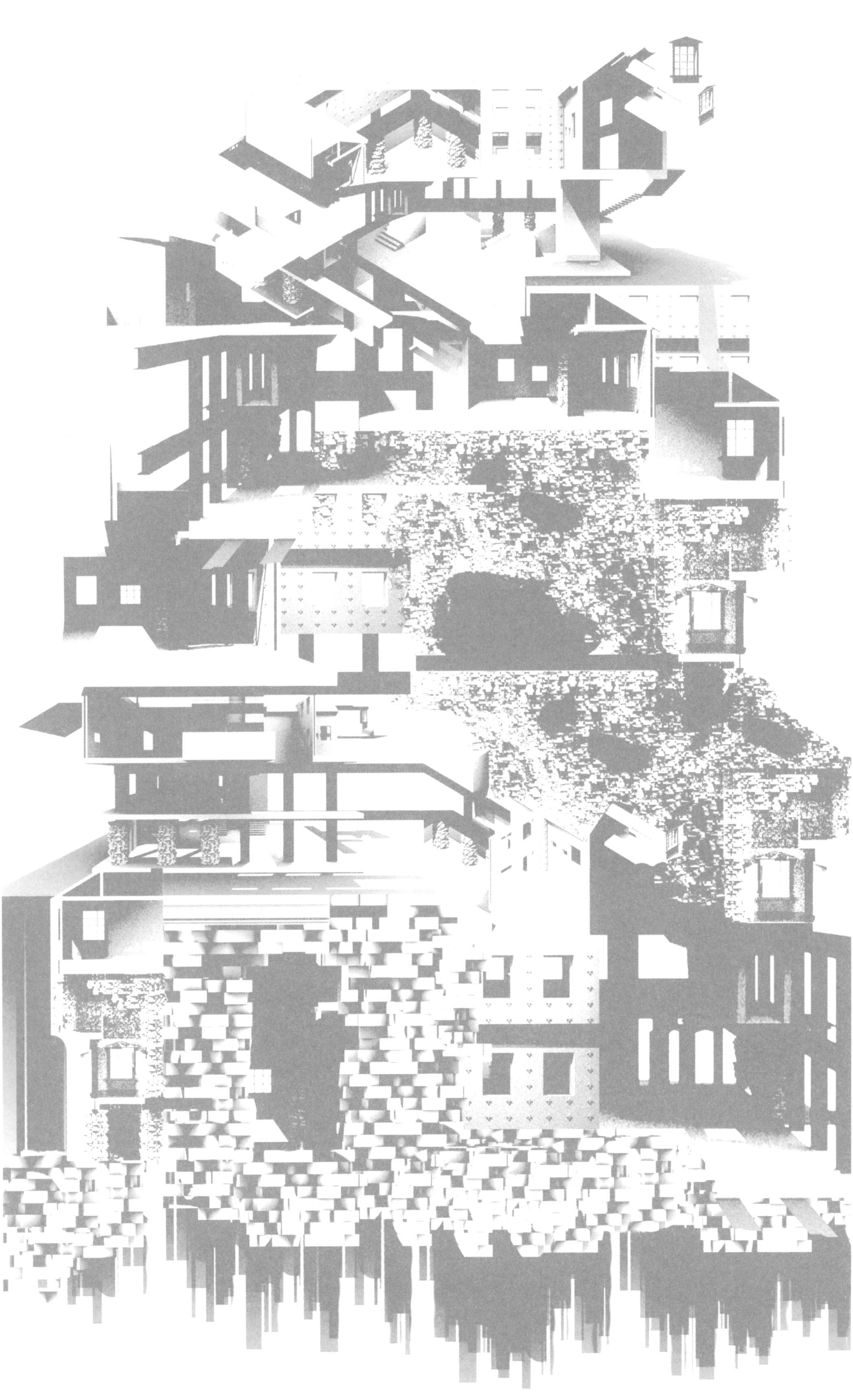

An Apartment in Vienna, Andrew Economos Miller. Advanced Design Studio: Vienna —Another Day in the City, Prof. David Gissen, Yale School of Architecture, Fall 2019.

wasteful, a desire to take hold of the social context of waste delineation and redraw it over the geographies of domination.

SCENE TWO: A COURTYARD

Interior of an urban block in Vienna. Debris is carted through the streets from demolition sites and junkyards across the city and thrown into heaps. Within these encrusted piles are carved niches, caves, and corridors allowing for another form of habitation.

> It is made from parts found or stolen, appropriated, plagiarized; things then twisted, deformed, manipulated so as to join readily to their neighbors. It concerns neighbors and spatial relations, not sequences of events and causes and effects. It is, in a sense, like Gilles Deleuze and Félix Guattari's description of the construction that vandals stealing from the museum make with the stolen bits.
> —Jennifer Bloomer[25]

As the growing pile allows new forms of living within, it keeps the old without. Borrowing the barricades of the revolutionary twentieth century, inhabitants reclaim the power of urban edges against the smooth flow of capital. Bricks become blocks. As a collective practice, this construction inverts the hylomorphic distinction between form and matter. There is no homogenous material and no possibility of planning for a particular materiality when things are used as they reach the site. This critical shift in attitude immediately subverts the political position of the architect. It must be collective.

> The spirit of revolution covered with its cloud this summit where rumbled that voice of the people which resembles the voice of God; a strange majesty was emitted by this titanic basket of rubbish. It was a heap of filth and it was Sinai.
> —Victor Hugo, Les Miserables[26]

FRAME THREE: ACTION (EMBODIED)

The meaningful introduction of (unprocessed) waste material into the production process of architecture requires an immediate shift in the form of architectural labor. Cutting against the modern industrial tendency toward "material" as a commodity that deskills labor to better control construction from off-site, waste's difficult materiality shifts power back to the direct location of action. Since architectural objects result from specific modes of production, they implicated in those modes of production.

> Only the ideal beings of a society, those who have the authority to order and prohibit, can strictly speaking be expressed in architectural form. And so the great monuments raise themselves before us like levees, countering all troubling elements with the logic of majesty and authority.—Georges Bataille, "The Critical Dictionary"[27]

This type of practice forces things to be found in the making rather than a priori and places design on the site, where it can be questioned. It also marks a shift, hopefully, from what Deleuze and Guattari call a royal science into the nomad sciences, which they identify most prominently in architecture as the Gothic.

> Royal science is inseparable from a "hylomorphic" model implying both a form that organizes matter and a matter prepared for the form; it has often been shown that this schema derives less from technology or life than from a society divided into governors and governed, and later, intellectuals and manual laborers.—Deleuze and Guattari[28]

What grows out of these frames are artifacts from worlds oriented around different economics and divisions of labor: A practice of making projects about the making of projects. Both definitions presume action on already existing conditions and turn the social tools of defining waste back on capital to be applied to artifacts of colonial and capitalist lifeways, such as the American suburban home.

Definition One: Re-fuse. Re-fuse is an act of transformation. It implies the return of fragments to a previous shape—but a "previous whole" is not necessary. Re-fusing can also imply the reconfiguration of existing things into new forms. What is necessary for re-fusing is a multiplicity of objects. It is impossible to re-fuse a single thing. It is chimeric.

> The destructive character is young and cheerful. For destroying rejuvenates in clearing away the traces of our own age; it cheers because everything cleared away means to the destroyer a complete reduction, indeed eradication, of her own condition.—Walter Benjamin, "The Destructive Character"[29]

Definition Two: Re-pose. Re-pose is a strategy of casual beauty. For Jennifer Bloomer it is connected to the feminine and the lazy allure of the odalisque, her repose. Re-pose is the lackadaisical cousin to re-fuse. Re-pose does not require permanent transformation.

> They make a [MINOR ARCHITECTURE]: They collect the tools of capitalist culture—mass production machinery of all sorts, washing machines, vacuum cleaners, and stoves—and make of them a great allegorical dumping ground, a petrified landscape, which they set on fire.—Jennifer Bloomer[30]

Both of these terms require acting on a world that already exists and eschewing the false neutrality of empty paper or infinite digital space.

> The ground-level plane of the Gothic journeyman is opposed to the metric plane of the architect, which is on paper and off-site.—Deleuze and Guattari[31]

The presumption that all material is heterogeneous and the choice of debris and waste as a material base requires a shift in the distribution of design agency more similar to the Gothic division of labor than the modern. The construction of a Gothic church operated on two levels: Doctrine and labor. Unlike the theoretically distributed design agency of modern architecture, which "allows multivocality" in the built environment (a myth that mystifies the class homogeneity of architects), the doctrinal plan (the Latin cross form of the cathedral) is clear in its connection to power—both the collective power of religion and the institutional power of the church. Within this political frame, the labor power of the stonemasons and other craftspeople asserted itself in terms of both class action and design agency as detail and problem solving were distributed through the whole working body.

> One does not represent, one engenders and traverses.—Deleuze and Guattari[32]

This politicization of the plan reveals that the contemporary distribution of design agency, seemingly "without politics," is only the political form of architecture in the society of bourgeois individualism and imperial economics. We should understand architecture instead as a vast social function that requires the involvement of multiple collectives. This

Refuse//Repose, Andrew Economos
Miller, The Armstrong Gallery,
Kent State University, 2023.

isn't an argument for the recentralization of authority within architectural planning but for a direct collective engagement within it.

> Opportunities for minor architectures emerge when the soul of a society is understood as more than a singularity, when—though a major soul constructs—minor souls await opportunities to de(con)struct.—Jill Stoner, *Toward a Minor Architecture*[33]

Together the difficult materiality of waste, the communalization of the plan, and the distribution of design agency within an explicitly politicized structure set the tone for the third scene.

> Architecture not in a capsule, but in a soup.
> —Jennifer Bloomer[34]

SCENE THREE: A GALLERY

A single white room divided into three and then into three again. Twenty-one eight-by-three-foot panels. A system designed for weight and an average arm's length rather than any formal connection. The three-room system shades from empty to full, past to future, and clear to unstable: A design intent in a construction that rejects design intent.

> A strange combination of nature and history. ... A profusion of emblems ... grouped around a figural center.—Walter Benjamin, *The Origin of German Tragic Drama*[35]

Labor. The organization of labor to fill the gallery mimicked Gothic tracery. By stabilizing the plan as twenty-one frames, we were able to design the exhibition as a process over time rather than setting out a fixed plan and then executing. The panels were produced by marking the ground with their dimensions and laying out the found objects within the implied frame. This meant that each panel was designed somewhat divorced from the others, at the whim of what we had, and with different attitudes for each.

Refuse//Repose, Andrew Economos
Miller, The Armstrong Gallery,
Kent State University, 2023.

42   REFUSE//REPOSE: FRAMING THREE SCENES

Waste. The material for the gallery was scavenged from a wide variety of sites across northeast Ohio and western Pennsylvania. These sites tended to fit into three categories: Primary, secondary, and tertiary.

Primary salvage was found either in repose or on a site of active demolition. These objects tended to be more degraded than the others as the immediate effluvium of our waste processes. The sites included home demolitions in Warren, Ohio; abandoned dumping grounds in the Grand River Valley, and buried woodsheds.

Secondary salvage was sold in piles from salvage yards, still degraded but passing an eye test for reusability. It is cheap, midsize, and good for filler: Corrugated metal and wood panels, for example.

Tertiary salvage is gussied up. Meeting standards for majoritarian recycling and reuse, it is gentrified garbage sold at a premium. Its recognizable pieces—tables, shelves, and pews—are easily slotted back into the circuit of commodity exchange.

> The superimposition of the chronological and the achronological—form and process, perhaps—is crucial to the concept of allegory.
> —Jennifer Bloomer[36]

Action. While process is the critical lens through which to view the contents of the gallery, the institutional framework of a fellowship is organized around form as its major tool. Within this context the exhibition uses narrative to advantage. The three rooms created by the panels evolve from frame to object, mimicking the temporal process of the project in space and revealing the higher-level narrative about structure and content. This line of rooms is held on its open end by the gravel pile and a retaining wall that mimics the spacing and closes with a degraded materiality that evokes the birth and death of architecture. All of the material was once unformed matter and will be so again.

Within this larger framework each panel tells its own self-contained story. Of the twenty-one panels six are empty frames and the rest designed by a small group and shaped by the whims of the trash pile on a particular Saturday. Some panels deconstruct the typical rooms of an American home while others work through the matter of larger obsolete social formations. Some speak of the historical body through labor while others speak of the desired futures of body production. Some reach across their edges to work together while others are shyer. For example, the two panels in the center room—set against the back wall with symmetrical pieces holding misshapen tools between them—are named Beverly and Ellie, after the twins in David Cronenberg's *Dead Ringers*. The structure allows a space for individuals and teams to work through their desires one at a time rather than funneling a misshapen "social intent" through a single bourgeois author.

The major intention of this practice is to produce new forms of social technology around building that allow for explicit politicization of spatial production—those that simultaneously raise large-scale decisions above the individual and lower the stakes of entry into design for the nonprofessional. As a fragment of a larger project, the gallery explores this as a kind of role-play within the framework of an academic fellowship. By establishing the organizational strategy early, the team could freely play within the framework as predetermined. In that way the frames, as much as the gallery itself, became sites for design and contextual production.

This work allows for design to become smaller, less heroic, and more multivocal. It shifts the collective gaze toward material in salvage yards and teaches new ways of looking at the stuff left behind. One becomes accustomed to the tool very quickly, and the exhibition labor structure allows for a process of epistemological development to occur during production rather than *a priori*.

1. Jennifer Bloomer, *Architecture and the Text: The (S)crypts of Joyce and Piranesi* (New Haven, CT: Yale University Press, 1993), 1.
2. Tiqqun, *Preliminary Materials for a Theory of the Young Girl*, trans. Ariana Reines (Los Angeles: Semiotext(e), 2012), 21.
3. Bloomer, *Architecture and Text*, 10.
4. Friedrich Nietzsche, "Daybreak," in *Opere*, vol. 5, book 1 (Cambridge, UK: Cambridge University Press, 1982), 40.
5. Tiqqun, *Young Girl*, 20.
6. Mark C. Taylor, *Alterity* (Chicago: University of Chicago Press, 1987), 126.
7. Bloomer, *Architecture and Text*, 46.
8. Gilles Deleuze and Félix Guattari, *A Thousand Plateaus: Capitalism and Schizophrenia* (Minneapolis, MN: University of Minnesota Press, 1987), 368.
9. Deleuze and Guattari, *Thousand Plateaus*, 368.
10. Sergio Ferro, *Concrete as Weapon*, trans. Alice Fiuza and Silke Kapp, www.tf-tk.com, 19.
11. Deleuze and Guattari, *Thousand Plateaus*, 368.
12. Deleuze and Guattari, *Thousand Plateaus*, 398.
13. Deleuze and Guattari, *Thousand Plateaus*, 400.
14. Herman Melville, "Bartleby the Scrivener: A Story of Wall Street," in *The Piazza Tales* (New York: Modern Library, 1996), 17.
15. David Harvey, "Globalization and the Spatial Fix," *Geographische Revue* 2 (2001), 25.
16. David Jenkins, "Fred Olsen Amenities Centre" in *Norman Foster Works* I, ed. David Jenkins (Munich: Prestel Publishing, 2003), 155.
17. Jenkins, "Fred Olsen," 157.
18. Jenkins, "Fred Olsen," 157.
19. Gilles Lipovetsky, *The Paradoxical Happiness: Essay on Hyperconsumptive Society* (Paris: Gallimard, 2009), 24. Translated and quoted in Sayak Valencia, *Gore Capitalism* (Pasadena, CA: Semiotext(e), 2018), 71.
20. Typed transcript of a lecture by Norman Foster at the AIA International Conference in London in 1977, Norman
21. Heraclitus, Fragment CXXV. James Hastings, ed., *Encyclopaedia of Religion and Ethics*, vol. 6 (New York: C. Scribner's Sons, 1908), 592.
22. Mary Douglas, *Purity and Danger: An Analysis of the Concepts of Pollution and Taboo* (London, Routledge, 1996), 36.
23. Walter Benjamin, *The Origin of German Tragic Drama* (London: Verso, 1998), 179.
24. Georges Bataille, *The Accursed Share: An Essay on General Economy*, trans. Robert Hurley (New York: Zone Books, 1949), 36.
25. Bloomer, *Architecture and Text*, 15.
26. Victor Hugo, *Les Miserables* (Boston: Little, Brown and Company, 1887), 6.
27. Georges Bataille, "The Critical Dictionary," trans. Dominic Faccini, *October* 60 (1992), 25.
28. Deleuze and Guattari, *Thousand Plateaus*, 369.
29. Walter Benjamin, "The Destructive Character," in *Reflections*, trans. Edmund Jephcott (New York: Harcourt Brace Jovanovich, 1978), 301.
30. Bloomer, *Architecture and Text*, 34.
31. Deleuze and Guattari, *Thousand Plateaus*, 368.
32. Deleuze and Guattari, *Thousand Plateaus*, 364.
33. Jill Stoner, *Toward a Minor Architecture* (Cambridge, MA: MIT Press, 2012), 6–7.
34. Bloomer, *Architecture and Text*, 102.
35. Benjamin, *Tragic Drama*, 167 and 188.
36. Bloomer, *Architecture and Text*, 21.

To camouflage something is to conceal it within its surroundings by way of disguise. This process requires extreme adaptiveness to a specific context and extreme indifference to one's own appearance. This ecological process by which the boundaries of distinct organisms are blurred to appear as indistinct parts of their surroundings is called crypsis.[1] Animals like the chameleon and octopus, for example, transform themselves by way of cryptic coloration, which allows them to blend in with their surroundings. This ability has been developed by some as an antipredator adaptation (to hide), and by some as a predation strategy (to hide and attack). As such, evaluating this process demands an understanding of the organism being hidden as well as its environment.

Our collective, The Department, has identified a phenomenon of intellectual and creative camouflage as "cryptic design." As a case study we examined the United Arab Emirates (UAE) to extrapolate how forms of camouflage are used to mask autocratic ideologies for political and economic gain—benefiting not only an authoritarian regime but also those nation states that depend on a stable relationship with the country.[2]

In 2021 The Department was commissioned by an EU-based publisher to contribute to a book titled *50U*, a "celebratory document" for the UAE's 50th birthday. We were aware that the book was commissioned by someone in the UAE and, given the UAE's controversial stance on freedom of expression, that whatever we produce might be sensitive to the client.[3] As authors based in the EU we take for granted that critique, honesty, and freedom of expression are permitted in our work, if not encouraged and demanded. Yet in our experience collaborating on this book we have discovered that this is in fact a privileged position. The request for a "celebratory" contribution was in fact a camouflaged demand for cryptic design. For that reason we find it important to examine the process of creating this document, what it tells us about the client-author power dynamic, and how this process applies to practices of the built environment as well.

We were asked to provide a visual essay of the country, along with a timeline of its development since 1971 and projected into the future. We began our work in August 2021, creating an all-encapsulating depiction of the economic, political, and cultural climate of the UAE today and across time. The deadline for publication was December 2, 2021 (the date of birthday celebration). Throughout the process we were in discussion with the editors, showing them the illustrations of the political structure and other interesting discoveries we had made concerning the country. The response was one of excitement and curiosity. It turned out, however, that this was not how the UAE wants to present itself to the world—or rather how it wanted European authors to present the country to the world.[4] After the publishers had completed the copyediting and everything seemed ready for publication, the book was forwarded on to a third-party editor in the UAE, who checked our work for "inaccuracies and matters of government sensitivity." On November 1, 2021, with one month to go, our publisher sent us an ominous email: "The UAE seems to have become more sensitive than we already knew." A succinct example of this sensitivity was the removal of the term Persian Gulf, to be replaced with Arabian Gulf in any illustrations.[5] The contention surrounding the nomenclature of the Gulf is perhaps the clearest example of an attempt to redefine an internationally and historically accepted term. The publisher was now encumbered with the task of asking us—and certainly other authors—to reword, remove, and alter elements of our contribution.

Suddenly the publishers had a book riddled with items flagged as unacceptable for publication. So while they negotiated with us about the requested removal of certain unflattering information about the UAE, 200 copies of a smaller version of the book had already been printed with all offensive contributions (such as our own) removed, in order to be released on time for the UAE birthday celebration.

Upon hearing of the demand to remove information about the country's treatment of the Bidoon minority population,[6] its persecution of journalists, and its border disputes with Saudi Arabia, among other things, we were appalled and honestly quite aggravated. It became apparent that a respected group of European researchers, book designers, editors, and publishers were expected to produce a "celebratory" document that was complimentary of the UAE as if its regime had no part in the production of the book.[7] A reader would not expect that money has so much to do with the truthfulness of what's written, especially with so many respected authors. Ultimately this type of publication is an advertisement, a form of propaganda, but there isn't a disclaimer saying, "This is a paid sponsorship by the UAE, cleaned of possible insults to our leader."[8]

The "insults" or rectifications, as the example of disputing the name Persian Gulf shows, go from the level of changing internationally agreed-upon terminology to—as in the case of information about border disputes—altering officially confirmed history and contemporary events.[9]

Feeling unable to present a holistic investigation of the country, we retracted our contribution. However this experience gave us insight into one of the ways a regime can deploy cultural camouflage to encrypt a nation's history and polish its contemporary image. We were fortunate enough to be in a position to remove ourselves from the publication since we were not financially dependent on it. But the publisher, editor, and designer of the book were suddenly caught between authors expecting an honorarium and clients expecting a book. Is it really possible to drop an entire publication just days, or even weeks, before its release when employees' contracts are at stake? After all, people depend on an income from their work, and the client is often the one responsible for how the work will appear. This is a conventional relationship, especially within architectural practice, where the client's needs, desires, and taste heavily dictate architectural decisions (and often rightfully so). Yet there may be reason to ask to what extent that relationship remains ethical. Ultimately the removal and/or adaptation of what we wrote for publication is essentially infringing on our intellectual property to suit the client's wishes.

After what we have experienced as authors, we wonder how much of a blind eye you need to feign as an architect working in a country like the UAE. Much more visible than a celebratory publication, architecture lends itself well to being used as a propaganda tool. Buildings stand in public spaces for all the world to see. In fact the Dubai skyline is one giant marketing stunt that makes use of Western architects such as Adrian Smith and, soon, Santiago Calatrava to convey an aesthetic image of a liberal (Western) democracy.

The very nature of Modern architecture, especially the International Style, is the absence of any culturally specific ornament or significance; consequently it has become significant to all. As the Modernist sign or design is beyond any tribe, kingdom, or nation, it has become supracultural and global.

Through its ubiquity and appeal to the masses, modern design (and architecture) is delinked from modern achievements like democracy, human rights, and scientific truth. To be successful the icons and products of global mass culture must be beyond any ideological, religious, or humanitarian standards. The smartphone, the electric car, and the iconic skyscraper are equally infused with a certain glitz and glamour that people, corporations, and nations want to associate themselves with. The global aesthetic has emerged as an environment in which states can effectively hide. This lack of culturally significant ornament and focus on massing and the masses is not an icon that means nothing, but rather it has become a symbol for sameness —a form of crypsis.

It is no wonder the lure of cosmopolitan sheen has made glass-and-steel high-rise urban planning a global phenomenon. With the contemporary rise of "starchitects" it has become easier than ever for autocratic states to purchase architectural icons—often in the hope that a new building might generate the so-called "Bilbao effect" experienced as a result of Frank Gehry's Guggenheim Museum. The problem with this is not so much that autocratic states are buying architecture from high-profile architects; they have every right to do so. But by creating iconic buildings with the branding of the architect they draw attention away from where we ought to be looking. The focus becomes the aesthetics of the building and the name of the architect rather than the function it serves, the person who commissioned it, or the way in which it was constructed.

Everybody knows and celebrates Rem Koolhaas's CCTV building, but it isn't often acknowledged that it houses Communist China's main agency for disseminating propaganda. Zaha Hadid's Heydar Aliyev Center has become known simply as an architectural masterwork, but if you want to see it you have to go to Baku. Today we too easily ignore the fact that it was built at the request of the Azeri dictator, Ilham Aliyev, and named after his father, a former dictator and KGB chief.[10] Qatar was the focus of a recent scandal regarding the deaths of migrant workers in the construction of buildings for the FIFA 2022 World Cup. Yet the fact that two of the eight stadiums were designed by none other than Foster and Partners and Zaha Hadid Architects with AECOM seemed to escape attention.[11, 12] What responsibility do architects have for the way buildings are constructed or the functions they serve—or for accepting a project commissioned by an ethically dubious client in the first place?

Most recently Saudi Arabia's NEOM project has caught the world's attention with its sleek space-age mystique. The price we pay for such a project is not only $500 billion but also the occasional life of a Huwaitat tribesman. Dozens are being sent to prison, gunned down, or sentenced to execution when protesting against the megacity development.[13] Under the rule of Mohammed bin Salman the rate of executions in the country has almost doubled.[14] Architects confirmed to be working on this project are currently limited to Zaha Hadid Architects, AECOM, UNStudio, Aedas, LAVA, Bureau Proberts, and Mecanoo.[15] These firms are designing a section of the project titled Trojena, which offers year-round skiing—outdoors in the desert. Once again, one must ask: What responsibility do we hold as architects when we decide to design something like this for someone like that—which is so blatantly unconscionable? The ubiquity of iconic contemporary architecture, which is the base for its global success story (it could have been a failure!), is rooted in its generic appearance. On one side is the structure and shape—novel but universal forms such as gherkins, shells, sails, and needles were known all over the globe before they reappeared as skyscrapers—but there is also the architect as an individual with a certain education and hopefully a clear vision for the future of the world. The architect has (or at least should have) an opinion on democracy, human rights, and scientific truth. Yet how does this align with the ideas of the client, the liberty of the people that live in the country, or even the neighborhood of the building? This is where the little crack in the facade of the system emerges—the architect as a person, as a human being, whether star or not.

If foreign workers are being exploited to the extent that the European Parliament is calling on member states to boycott the Dubai Expo, citing the country's human-rights violations, one must get the feeling that there is something wrong.[16] But for clients with so much money it is possible to realize absurd and exciting design commissions coveted by architects, who in turn depend on the capital that these clients have to offer. Designed by architect Adrian Smith of Skidmore, Owings & Merrill, the Burj Khalifa stands regally at 828 meters tall, of which 244 meters is unusable space—so-called "vanity height"—constructed as a spire at the top just for the purpose of reaching the title of tallest building.[17] In order to accomplish this, construction workers from South Asia worked 12-hour shifts in 6-day workweeks. The average construction worker is paid a meager $175 per month, with the first two months of income commonly suspended along with their passport. Surrounded by barbed-wire fencing with a guard post at each entrance, the labor camps built for these sites function more like prisons.[18] In 2006 human-rights organizations found cover-ups of construction-related deaths from heat stroke, exhaustion, and suicide.[19] The Indian consulate in Dubai stated that at least two Indian expats committed suicide per week in 2011.[20]

But what can you do as an architect when you realize in the middle of a project that your client is involved in silencing journalists and treating workers like slaves? What can you do when you realize your building is being constructed by forced labor? The ethical thing to do would be to pull out, but then you are running the risk of ruining your entire practice. You probably shouldn't engage in business with such a client at all, and surely, knowing all of this, you wouldn't—so how does it happen in the first place? For starters, how does an architect evaluate the practices they're engaged with, not only in the UAE but anywhere in the world? The architect may not be directly responsible for the things that are happening to construction workers or where the money is coming from, yet architects are intricately involved in all of these circumstances, conscious of them or not.

The use of cryptic design by contemporary autocracies is a strategic decision. With the expansion of the global stage and the Western reliance on oil exports from Gulf nations, gas from Russia, and goods from China, it has become necessary to feel like we are not doing business with the enemy. It is important to believe that these governments are in some sense similar to the liberal democracies we love so much. Autocratic regimes understand very well that buying their products is more palatable for Western consumers if their abusive practices are kept out of sight. In this way we in the West can live the illusion of a sustainable, democratic, and equal society, and profit from the abusive practices that take place elsewhere.

Soviet Communism came with a very distinct architectural language and a clear view on urban design for the empire. Yet today's autocracies are mostly bare of any ideology. What seems to be a flaw at first sight is a boon for despots. Joseph Stalin and Fidel Castro showed off in military uniforms, and Chairman Mao dressed in a Zhongshan suit (later called the Mao suit) to make a statement for proletarian unity. Today's tyrants—Xi Jinping, Vladimir Putin, Viktor Orbán, and Recep Erdogan—come in business suits and ties, blending in with their democratic colleagues from around the world. This uniform is the perfect camouflage to mask their true undemocratic practices. That the West was so surprised by Putin's invasion of the Ukraine is proof of the effectiveness of the disguise (hide and attack through cryptic design), despite the fact that Russia had already illegally annexed Crimea in 2014 and had leveled cities in Chechnya over two wars, as well as interfering in the Syrian civil war. None of this was new information; but it was comfortably "condemned" and then forgotten so that business could continue as usual.

Leaders like Dubai's Mohammed bin Rashid Al Maktoum are commonly dressed in a thawb, or kandura as it's called in the UAE, a long white robe commonly worn in Arabic cultures. When the sheik is traveling, however, he can be seen sporting a business suit and even a top hat for black-tie events, as a sort of combat uniform for global politics. And while the UAE scores a meager 18/100 points from Freedom House, they call their form of governance

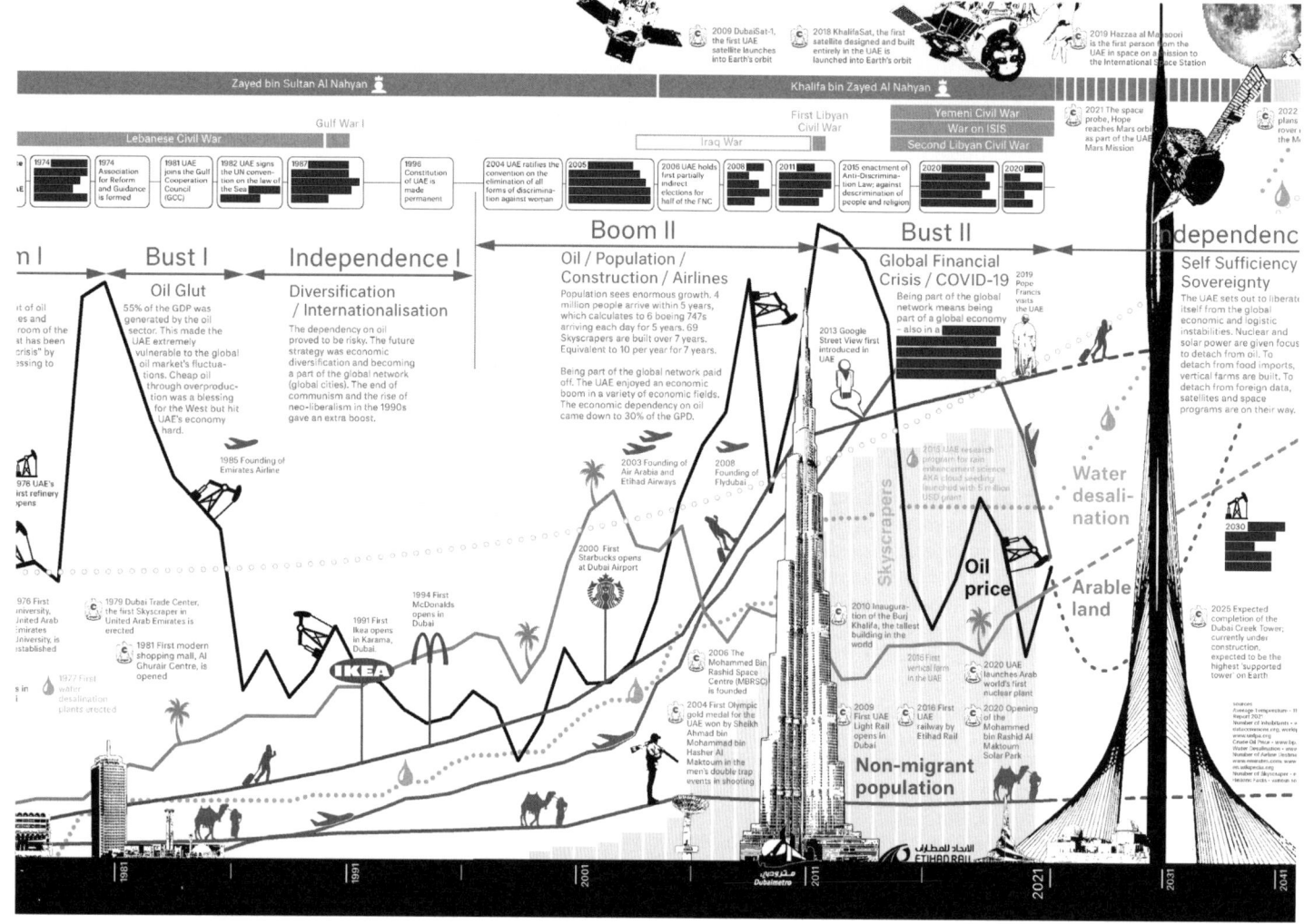

Fragment from the timeline "To Another 50 Years of Independence"

CENSORED INFORMATION

1974 — Treaty of Jeddah, ceding land to Saudi Arabia; not ratified by UAE

1982 — ...but does not ratify it

1987 — Penal code enacted, making adultery punishable by stoning (death sentence)

2005 — Sharia law is adopted as Personal Status Law—flogging, amputation and stoning are legal punishments

2008 — UAE offers Comoros passports to Bidoons

2011 — UAE resumes death penalty after a 3 year suspension

2020 — criminalisation of honour killings, ease of alcohol ban and allowing unmarried cohabitation

2020 — The UAE recognizes Israel

also in a — downturn. It felt humiliating for the proud and independent people of the UAE to be at the mercy of others.

2030 — Predicted depletion of Dubai's off-shore oil reserves

CENSORED INFORMATION

① Overlapping claim by UAE and Iran (Greater & Lesser Tunbs and Abu Musa Islands)

② Persian >> Arabian

③ Neutral zone

④ Disputed Saudi Arabia / UAE Border since 1974 Treaty of Jeddah

The United Arab Emirates is the world's 7th largest crude oil producer and holds the 7th largest natural gas reserves. One of the seven emirates alone, Abu Dhabi, is blessed with 94% of both the UAE's oil and gas reserves: Roughly 98 billion barrels of oil, and an estimated 5.7 trillion cubic meters of natural gas. Border disputes exist between the UAE and Saudi Arabia since 1974, coinciding with the Zarrara oil field; as well as with Iran since 1971, involving three islands and their exclusive economic zone overlapping large natural gas reserves. It was under the condition that the other emirates backed Ras Al-Kaimah's claim to these islands that it joined the United Arab Emirates in 1972. Diversification of the country's economy has brought Oil's contribution to the GDP from 66% at its peak in 1975 to 30% in 2018.

The nation's incredible wealth of oil and gas have made the rest of the world reliant on them; and as such the country has enjoyed a very rapid increase in power and esteem. The oil fields are representative of power concentration, and not only internationally. Oil blessed Abu Dhabi dominates the government with its Emir presiding over the country. As a Federal Monarchy, his first-born son will succeed him. The NGO freedomhouse.org ranks the UAE as "not free" country rewarding it with only 17 out of 100 points (same as Chad and Sudan). Equally bad is its 131 ranking in the World Press Freedom Index. Very minimal criticism of the regime by journalists or bloggers like Ahmed Mansoor is likely to lead to charges with the possibility of long jail terms and mistreatment in prison.

- Oil pipeline
- Gas pipeline
- - - Gas pipeline under construction
- Oil refinery
- Oil field
- Gas field
- Exclusive Economic Zone (EEZ) Border
- - - Unsettled marine borders
- .... Inter-emirate marine boundary
- Exclusive Economic Zone (EEZ)
- Territorial seas (12 nm)
- Internal waters
- Disputed islands—Iran / UAE
- Disputed territories

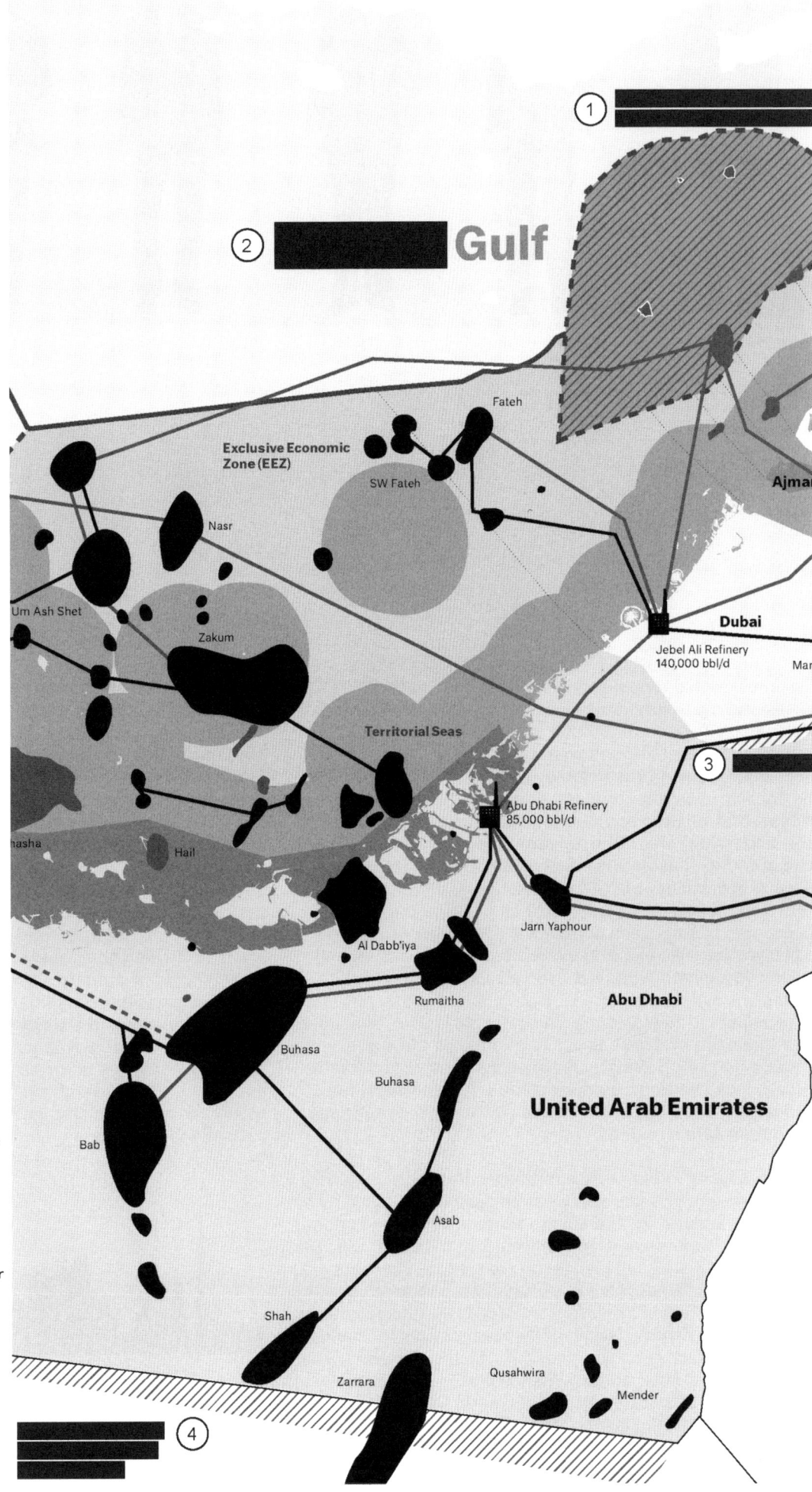

Fragment from the illustration "Oil and Politics"

THEO DEUTINGER, CHRISTOPHER CLARKSON

BASHAR AL-ASSAD	VLADIMIR PUTIN	XI JINPING	RECEP TAYYIP ERDOGAN	OLAF SCHOLZ	JOE BIDEN
President of Syria	President of Russia	President of China	President of Turkey	Prime Minister of Germany	President of the USA
meeting Sheikh Mohamed, President of U.A.E.	meeting Kim Jong Un, leader of North Korea	at the BRIC meeting in South Africa	meeting Ukraine's President Volodymyr Zelensky	at the Munich Security Conference	meeting Israel's Prime Minister Benjamin Netanyahu
19/03/2023	13/09/2023	23/08/2023	07/07/2023	20/02/2023	20/09/2023

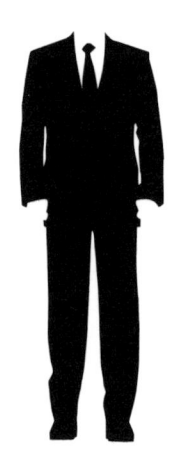

a "federal constitution." Russia calls itself a "federal semipresidential republic, and Turkey refers to itself a "democratic parliamentary republic." Freedom House rates Russia and Turkey 16/100 and 32/100, respectively, in terms of the level of freedom of their citizens.

What works in the fields of media and fashion can also be applied to architecture and urbanism. All modern forms of representation have adopted the parlance of cryptic design; the military uniform, once an earnest symbol of discipline and authority, has become the business suit; wars are called special operations; and autocracies are given official names that belie their true nature—and all of these things are concocted behind glass curtain walls. Architecture has been employed for millennia to denote the power of empires and rulers. Today architecture is used also as a cultural veil to obscure a regime's atrocities. The Modernist glass-and-steel skyscrapers of New Moscow City, Istanbul Levent, Shanghai, and Dubai are exclamation marks of pride on the skylines of those countries. Some are designed by Western architects; others look like they could have been. The cosmopolitan reflection of the Big Apple serves as the ideal camouflage for authoritarian regimes.

People walking in the streets of these cities are engulfed by an illusion of a liberal society. Yet protesters are regularly hit by water cannons, journalists are sentenced to life in prison, opposition leaders are jailed, poisoned, or fall out of windows, and people seeking independence are sent to reeducation camps. The collapse of icon-saturated Soviet Communism in the 1990s, heralded as victory for democracy and capitalism by the Western World, simply forced autocracies to change strategy. Military uniforms, classical architecture, and public executions lost their appeal. What seems to be an expanding list of democratic states around the world has actually seen a steady democratic decline, with 38 percent of the global population living in countries labeled as "not free" and only 20 percent living in countries with the classified as "free" by the Freedom House.[21] Cryptic design and infiltration became part of the new "if you can't beat them, join them" strategy. To hide behind the iconography of your enemy has proven to be much more effective than showing your true intentions.

As we have come to learn in the past few years with the Trump presidency in the United States, simply lying is a highly effective political tool. Call a tank a teapot, and you muddy the waters of what a tank means and what to do when someone offers you tea. Present yourself as a businessman with a shiny high-rise and you gain the status of a success story from New York's Fifth Avenue, regardless of how you got there in the first place.

The iconography of modernity, democracy, and freedom of speech turned into an invisibility coat for despots and autocrats. We in the West have to learn to question and distrust our own imagery to uncover wrongdoings and bad intentions, both abroad and closer to home. More importantly, we should learn to act as humans, not simply as architects or authors. The ability to make an ethically informed decision relies on understanding the ecologies of our practices and the occasions when cryptic design is in effect: The business suit offers political camouflage for the autocrat as an international leader; the skyline acts as cultural camouflage by mimicking the image of a global cosmopolitan city; and the book provides intellectual camouflage that shapes the discourse surrounding a nation.

Dubai skyline

New York City skyline

1. In nature, crypsis is the ability of an animal or a plant to avoid observation or detection by other living organisms using methods including camouflage, mimicry, nocturnality, and a subterranean lifestyle. Crypsis can involve visual, olfactory (with pheromones), or auditory concealment.
2. The globalized world in which we now live has generated global interdependencies between nation states. Resources, workforce, and capital are however unevenly distributed. In order for nations to survive (economically) they depend on beneficial relations with other countries, even at times if their political ideologies are at odds.
3. The UAE is ranked 138 out of 180 countries in the World Freedom Press index of 2022. Reporters without Borders, the institution that compiles the listing, describes the legal framework of the country as follows: "The constitution guarantees freedom of expression, but under a 1980 federal law the authorities can censor media content deemed to be overly critical of policies, the ruling families, religion, or the economy. Journalists are also targeted under the 2012 cybercrime law, which was updated in 2021. In addition, spreading 'rumors', especially about COVID-19, is punishable by a prison sentence as well as a fine." RSF (Reporters without Borders), "United Arab Emirates," https://rsf.org/en/country/united-arab-emirates.
4. Yasser bin Khedia, who commissioned the book, explained that he "cooperated with a work team in the Netherlands as well as in the UAE to produce the book, and choose the characters who will put their experience at work, in addition to taking a group of articles that were written about the country, especially those [that] documented the achievements of the UAE and were outside it." Yasser bin Khedia, "50 U is just the beginning of a long Emirati story," interview, Teller Report, June 29, 2022, https://www.tellerreport.com/life/2022-06-28-yasser-bin-khedia--%E2%80%9C50-u%E2%80%9D-is-just-the-beginning-of-a-long-emirati-story.HyxPZbbtcq.html.
5. Both terms are correct and in use; sometimes this part of the sea is also called the Gulf of Basra. The U.S. National Geospatial-Intelligence Agency (NGA) lists Persian Gulf as the conventional name, along with 16 variants, and we decided to go with that as the most commonly used term. We do not object to the use of Arabian Gulf; we just believe it is at the author's discretion to decide which words are used, and since the book is aimed at an international audience the most popular and internationally conventional name should be used. See "Persian Gulf naming dispute," Wikimedia Foundation, accessed August 31, 2023, https://en.wikipedia.org/wiki/Persian_Gulf_naming_dispute.
6. The book has since been published and distributed globally. The blurb describes how "over a period of just fifty years, they [the UAE] have witnessed the transformation of a partly nomadic, partly town-based community into a globally active metropolitan society." However it omits the fact that descendants of these "partly nomadic" people, the Bedouin, still exist as stateless nationals within the UAE. While official statistics place the number of Bidoon people at 10,000, other estimates have been much higher. This second-class ethnic minority cannot acquire UAE citizenship or nationality because, as a formerly nomadic people, they are not eligible for what is called a "family book," tracing familial heritage in an Emirate since before 1925. In 2008 the UAE government implemented a deal with the Comoros that allows Bidoon people to acquire a nonrenewable passport but does not grant nationality. Diala Alqadi, "'The Door that Cannot Be Closed': Citizens Bidoon Citizenship in the United Arab Emirates" (Honors thesis, Trinity College of Arts and Sciences, Duke University, 2015).
7. The colophon states that the book was commissioned by Yasser bin Khedia, who is a businessman and not a member of the ruling royal family of the UAE. Yet the book was intended to be a gift to sheikh Hamdan bin Rashid Al Maktoum, who passed away before it was completed. Bin Khedia, "950 U is just the beginning."
8. The book's new website does acknowledge funding by DP World (an Emirati multinational logistics company) and A.R.M. Holding (a Dubai-based Investment company, whose group chairman is sheik Ahmed bin Rashid Al Maktoum, a member of Dubai's ruling family). Project50U, "50U 50 Years United Arab Emirates," accessed August 31, 2023, https://project50u.ae.
9. Aside from the nomenclature of the Persian Gulf, these are very real historical and contemporary facts that are being redacted or totally ignored. It is a form of censorship that cannot be seen simply as an editorial decision but rather as a political act.
10. Hrag Vartanian, "Is Contemporary Architecture a PR Panacea for Autocrats? Western Architectural Ethics & Undemocratic Nations," Brookyn Rail, September 2008, https://brooklynrail.org/2008/09/artseen/is-contemporary-architecture-a-pr-panacea-for-autocrats.
11. Niamh McIntyre and Pete Pattisson, "Revealed: 6,500 migrant workers have died in Qatar since World Cup awarded," The Guardian, last modified March 18, 2021, https://www.theguardian.com/global-development/2021/feb/23/revealed-migrant-worker-deaths-qatar-fifa-world-cup-2022.
12. Lizzie Crook, "Dezeen's guide to the 2022 FIFA World Cup Qatar stadium architecture," last modified November 15, 2022, Dezeen, https://www.dezeen.com/2022/11/15/2022-fifa-world-cup-qatar-stadium-architecture.
13. AFP, "UN rights experts denounce planned Saudi executions of megacity opponents," The Guardian, last modified May 3, 2023, https://www.theguardian.com/world/2023/may/03/un-rights-experts-denounce-planned-saudi-executions?CMP=Share_AndroidApp_Other.
14. Martin Chulov, "Rate of Executions in Saudi Arabia almost doubles under Mohammed bin Salman," The Guardian, last modified February 1, 2023, https://www.theguardian.com/world/2023/feb/01/executions-in-saudi-arabia-almost-double-under-mohammed-bin-salman.
15. Tom Ravenscroft, "Everything you need to know about Saudi mega-project Neom," Dezeen, last modified February 14, 2023, https://www.dezeen.com/2023/02/14/neom-guideline-saudi-arabia.
16. Al Jazeera, "EU Parliament urges UAE to free imprisoned human rights activists," last modified September 17, 2021, https://www.aljazeera.com/news/2021/9/17/eu-parliament-urges-uae-to-free-imprisoned-human-rights-activists.
17. The Guardian, "Vanity Height."
18. "According to the Emirates Centre for Human Rights, foreign migrant workers make up roughly 90 percent of the country's labor force, many of them held in conditions akin to indentured servitude. Passports are confiscated, debt bondage to employers is common, and working conditions are appalling. Workers interviewed by Al Jazeera said they earn between $102 and $325 a month, live in cramped rooms with a multitude of other men, and are denied annual leaves by their employers." Shaheen Pasha, "Dubai's towering skyscrapers are built by a 'horrifically exploitative labor system,'" Quartz, last modified May 27, 2013, https://qz.com/88278/dubais-towering-skyscrapers-are-built-by-a-horrifically-exploitative-labor-system.
19. Ghaemi, "Building Towers, Cheating Workers."
20. Malik, "Dubai's Skyscrapers."
21. Sarah Repucci and Amy Slipowitz, "The Global Expansion of Authoritarian Rule," Freedom House, https://freedomhouse.org/report/freedom-world/2022/global-expansion-authoritarian-rule.

Image of the Vessel at Hudson Yards. Designed by Heatherwick Studio (2019).

INTRODUCTION

Since its opening in March of 2019, The Vessel at Hudson Yards (HY) has borne the brunt of critique—perhaps the most scathing of these indictments have called the structure part and parcel of a global system of neoliberal capital.[1] Neoliberalism, so-called, is less a codified theory than it is an overlapping, occasionally contradictory set of beliefs that generally hold at their core the "primacy of the market for governing human affairs."[2] It is often cited as the motivator for global financial deregulation and neocolonial extractive capital, but it even operates as an individualistic ethos of risk-assuming entrepreneurialism or able-bodied exceptionalism. Due in part to this many-headed, multiscalar presence, neoliberalism is hard to pin down—after all, Rajesh Venugopal writes, "Neoliberalism is everywhere, but at the same time, nowhere."[3] Architectural historian Reinhold Martin proposes a reverse reading of neoliberalism through its material instantiations. The built environment, Martin claims, "is a system of coding, a 'rationality' compatible with the much-referenced 'neoliberal rationality,' a set of material-representational relations—practices—active at all scales and therefore susceptible to decoding with the right tool kit."[4]

Indeed, as one such spatial product of neoliberal (ir)rationality, the Vessel—a veritable jungle gym of 154 flights of stairs—demonstrates the political and aesthetic properties of neoliberalism in interplay. While many have critiqued the Vessel as a representation of capital accumulation, in this essay we will also consider the structure as an enactor of neoliberalism in its production of a delimited, embodied notion of agency predicated on extractive and exclusionary conditions of participation in the public sphere.

THE VESSEL: *ENACTING* NEOLIBERALISM

The Vessel, designed by British firm Heatherwick Studio, sits at the center of HY, a partially completed mixed-used development on the western edge of New York City (NYC) that aims to collapse programs of business, retail, housing, and leisure into a freely circulating playground of luxurious economic activity. HY is funded in significant part through public-private partnership (P3), an oft-cited hallmark of neoliberal urban development policy, and approximately $5.7 billion worth of public bonds and taxes are tied into the development's budget.[5] As such, the public is granted permission—or rather, in the interest of economic activity, extended an "invitation,"[6]—to move freely through the privately-owned plaza. However, the terms and conditions of that accessibility are established, surveilled, and policed by the property's developers, Related Companies (RC).

As a condition of P3, RC was obligated to channel these public funds to neighborhoods with high unemployment rates, a task that they eventually colluded with government agencies to evade through economic gerrymandering.[7] Taken at face value, it may seem absurd that the state would undermine its own regulatory oversight of the private sector, but ultimately this move would purportedly earn them $500 million in city taxes. This self-reflexive, self-validating circulatory system of planning and financing that enabled the development of HY makes clear its economic relationship to neoliberalism. Even the Vessel itself—designed in London, prefabricated in Italy, moved across international waters by a German shipping firm, and finally assembled in the US—is a product of loosely regulated globalized commerce. However, not only is the Vessel organized *by* neoliberal systems, the structure is itself an organizer of space that codes its subjects under a neoliberal cultural framework. This is not simply to say that the Vessel symbolically represents neoliberal ideals. We argue that the structure operates performatively—that it *enacts* neoliberalism.

One such performative capacity of the Vessel is best examined by placing the project in the lineage of performance media that has become increasingly popular: Immersive theater. Like neoliberalism, immersive theater is a loosely defined term. Generally, Adam Alston describes it as "theatre that surrounds audiences within an aesthetic space in which they are…free to move and/or participate."[8] It is a model of theater in which the screen—the fourth wall—of the theater envelops the spectators, bringing them into an environmental stage as free-moving participants with some agency to influence or curate their personal experience of the production. For example, in Punchdrunk's NYC-based *Sleep No More*, mobile audience members individually sequence the play's narrative by navigating a building-scale diegetic environment. The interlocking assemblage of stairways that constitutes the Vessel's central experience can be described similarly—the structure conditions each visitor to direct and perform their own experiential narrative by making decisions enabled by each intersecting stair—to climb up or down, to move left or right, along an Escher-esque, vertically lifted labyrinth.

But as with a labyrinth, "free" navigation is not in fact enabled, but *required* and delimited by the Vessel. In video games, user agency is often similarly constructed with neoliberal values in mind. Games, as compared to primarily linear media like film and literature, generally allow their players to enact narratives rather than merely observe them, which suggests a kind of freedom of multilinear choice. As the entrepreneurial, risk-taking player makes decisions or overcomes particular obstacles, they affect the game's narrative outcomes. But freedom and narrative empowerment are in fact conditioned by the coded rules that envelop one's experience of the game. As Daniel Muriel and Garry Crawford explain:

> [Under neoliberalism,] freedom and control…are not opposing pairs; they are an inseparable part of a new formula of handling and defining realities. [They] are, therefore, essential to understand agency in contemporary society, which can be extended to the social universe that emerges around video games.[9]

Similarly, through its elevated, spiraling network of stairs and views, the Vessel brings a greater freedom of movement and vision to an otherwise flat plaza, but it cannot be ignored that the plaza and Vessel are privately-owned spaces tied with the terms and conditions that limit the possible activity of the visiting subject. Alston presents a similar critique of immersive theater, claiming that experience may be:

> …Narcissistic in character, bolstered by receiving the fruits of one's own participatory effort… Audiences are likely to find themselves functioning as something more than an audience, either as a character cast within a given world, or as some kind of hyper-self.[10]

Indeed, in exchange for participatory agency, immersive theater outsources the labor of protagonistic performance from actor to audience. The spectator is upgraded to the role of protagonist. *Sleep No More* retells the story of *Macbeth*, but with most of the dialogue stripped from the scripts, the production is hardly Shakespearean in its demands on its actors. They become what might be described as non-playable characters (NPCs) in video game parlance—environmental figures who are, as Olivia Turnbull describes, "merely supporting characters [that] facilitate the participant's own starring role"[11] as spectator-made-protagonist. The Vessel employs the same strategies of neoliberal rationality. Though the Vessel does not have paid

Anti-Stairs Club Lounge gathering at the Vessel, Hudson Yards (2019). Organized by Finnegan Shannon.

actors on site, visitors quickly, and without compensation, assume both the roles of performer and consumer. To enable this, the Vessel invites its spectator-protagonists to take on yet another element of agential choice and labor—the work of performing, producing, and consuming a circulatory economy of shared social images.

THE CIRCULATORY IMAGE ECONOMY OF THE VESSEL

One pointed question is often asked of the Vessel: *What is its purpose?* A stair, however, certainly has a function—according to Umberto Eco, it denotes "a possibility of going up."[12] Implicit in such a denotation is a destination. A stair serves a transitive function—one goes up *to* somewhere. However, the supposed terminus of the Vessel—its top level—offers little more than any other vantage point within the structure. In fact, all views offered by the Vessel are equally self-reflexive; this sculptural centerpiece of HY sits below its neighbors, all part of the same HY development. Rather than offering an endpoint, the landings at the top of each set of stairs pose an infinite tree of receding decisions—up, down, right, left—and in turn, these choices fold recursively into a game of *circulation* rather than upward mobility. Bernard Suits' definition of gameplay as "the voluntary attempt to overcome unnecessary obstacles,"[13] is appropriate here. Notably, Suits makes no mention of a reward or goal, only a conditioned act. Following that definition, one's circulation through the obstacle, the Vessel's meandering stairs, is itself the purpose.

In her analysis of Frank Gehry Architects' Fondation Louis Vuitton, Joan Ockman writes that many contemporary buildings "are above all about *circulation*...[and] their privileged spaces are zones of movement: Stairs, escalators, ramps, transparent elevators." As "allegorical reflexes of the larger system, ...[these] buildings absorb and introject its currencies into their own aesthetic economy... everything gets swept up by and flows with the current: Money, goods, art, images, people."[14] At the Vessel, tourists are just as swept up into the flow of the structure's physical circulatory system as they are into the economy of images that surround, reinforce, and perpetuate it. A quick perusal of the Vessel's Instagram presence offers a window into this digital economy. A visitor arrives at the Vessel, a self-proclaimed "[instant] social media phenomenon [and] insistently interactive monument."[15] Somewhere around or inside the structure, they take a photograph of themselves with the Vessel in the background. This image is shared and geotagged on Instagram, where the most highly trending images tend toward those featuring well-dressed, well-lit, well-exercised bodies. The Vessel and HY explicitly encourage social media interaction; inviting would-be social media influencers to use hashtags like "@TheVesselNYC" or "#HelloHudsonYards" for a chance to have their images reposted by the complex's own accounts. In turn, popular posts circulate extensively to other spectators-to-be, who are then encouraged to visit the Vessel and document their experience, indefinitely perpetuating its image economy. Along the way, the Vessel amasses cultural currency, bringing a consistent flow of consumer traffic through HY, where many of the tenants, such as Equinox Hotel and VaynerX, are companies at least partially owned by RC or its founder, Stephen Ross. Through the myriad, interconnected systems in which it reveals its circulatory nature, the Vessel is a performative demonstration of a "culture of circulation."[16]

Though this "stairway to nowhere"[17] is a signature structure of its own time, it does have precedents. In Miami's Fontainebleau Hotel, architect Morris Lapidus installed what he reportedly called, "the staircase to nowhere." According to Alice T. Friedman, it was originally "placed against an oversized Piranesian photomural, which created a theatrical backdrop for guests descending to the lobby"[18] from an otherwise needless mezzanine. In the TV series *Marvelous Mrs. Maisel*, the titular character, a comic, excitedly points out these stairs to her manager, saying, "It's there just so that ladies can walk down in their finest gowns and everyone can watch them."[19] At first it seems as though she is making fun of the stairs, but in actuality, Mrs. Maisel is excited to walk down it herself. This narcissistic impulse for "a dramatic entrance"[20] is not a new phenomenon, having been accounted for by architects past, but with the advent of social media it is now "the [image of experience], with its mobility and increasing online availability, rather than experience per se which seems to possess lasting currency."[21]

With each image cycle of performance, production, and consumption, the spectator-protagonist reifies their embodied "gameplay" of circulation through the Vessel into a digital, transmissible object that itself circulates in the image economy. As Yasmin Ibrahim writes, "In this age of the screen,...[we] capture ourselves on the move, making the self both a subject and object of production and consumption online."[22] Ibrahim's cogent description of this image economy resonates with a phenomenon of immersive theater noted by Agnès Silvestre, where the proximity of performers to their audience reconfigures their relationship to "mirror that of consumer to advertisement." Silvestre interviews a cast member who supposes that, in this proximity, "audiences... 'project onto [the] characters a version of themselves they'd like to be, a lover they'd like to have, a life they'd like to live.'"[23] At the Vessel, this work is yet again outsourced to the spectator-protagonists, whose digital labor collectively assembles a reflexive marketing network that disseminates curated images of their selves.

This environment of curated selves[24] circulating around the Vessel engenders a culture of "cruel optimism," an affective subject-object relationship coined by Lauren Berlant wherein "something you desire is actually an obstacle to your flourishing."[25] The image economy of the Vessel promotes a conventional "fantasy of the good life,"[26] where able-bodied, heteronormative subjects quite literally promote the idea of vertical mobility aboard a Vessel moored in the midst of a monumental consumer capital complex. Both in this physical presence at the center of this consumer complex and in the social media platforms on which this image economy circulates, the Vessel siphons an incredible sum of money toward what McKenzie Wark has called "the vectoralist class,"[27] for whom capital value is not only accrued through the production of objects—here the users and their data—but also in the management and control of their circulation. RC itself capitalizes on the vectoral flows of spectator-protagonists that move through the Vessel and its commercial surroundings—this consistent circulation of bodies assures its vital place in the NYC fabric, pumping both cultural currency that powers real estate value and consumerism like an economic mitochondrion.

Meanwhile, the spectator-protagonist assumes all the precarity of free agency as a would-be influencer scraping together a virtual, untethered currency of likes and follows in exchange for self-images that project an unreal, heteronormative ideal. Further still, the embodied game of circulating through the Vessel, its central purpose, celebrates physical movement as a central value of the public sphere. In the aforementioned promotional video, Heatherwick himself declares that the Vessel is "extremely interactive—but properly—using your physicality," while enthusiastically gripping his legs,[28] making quite clear that the project's entire aesthetic proposition, this culture of circulation, wholly excludes people with mobility limitations.

from point A to point B, it instead develops a game of spatial circulation. And while RC and its fellow vectoral capitalists have an active interest in enticing ludic participation for the purposes of data extraction and cultural currency, this section argues that they also have a unique interest in re-inscribing the able-bodied, heterosexual subject as the normative member of the public through the production of difference. As Alston notes, though the opportunity for participation is doled out in spaces like the Vessel, it "is often unevenly distributed."[30]

In his book *Crip Theory*, Robert McRuer suggests that, in addition to being defined by privatization and deregulation, neoliberalism can be understood as a cultural system against which both "embodied and sexual identities have been imagined and composed over the past quarter century."[31] Reflecting on the etymology of "homosexual" and "disabled," McRuer demonstrates how both categories are formulated as oppositional to a normative condition; in the Oxford English Dictionary (OED), "heterosexual" is defined as the opposite of "homosexual" and "ability" is defined as a state of being free from "disability," revealing how certain subject positions are foundationally signed as deviant or "other." Such a proposition is understood spatially at the Vessel, where circulation via stairs is further inscribed as the normative mode of participation through the presence

Anti-Stairs Club Lounge gathering at the Vessel, Hudson Yards (2019). Organized by Finnegan Shannon.

DIS/ABILITY, SEXUALITY, AND "CHOICE" AT THE VESSEL

On December 23, 2019, the U.S Attorney's Office in the Southern District of New York declared the Vessel to be in violation of the Americans with Disabilities Act (ADA) of 1990. While designed to provide access to the Vessel for a broader array of bodies, the elevator, the Attorney's Office alleged, only allowed individuals with disabilities to access three of the Vessel's 80 platforms. Needless to say, lateral movement around the structure was, and remains, impossible for non-bipedal users. In response, RC made a commitment to install a new platform lift that will "allow individuals with disabilities to enjoy 360-degree views from the Vessel's top level."[29] But, as we have explored above, views were never the primary object of desire at the Vessel. Abandoning the expected semiotic performance of the staircase as a vector

of an opposite, insufficient mechanism of circulation—the elevator. While this "othering" at the Vessel certainly produces a distinction between "normal" and "abnormal"—or widely encouraged and merely accommodated—modes of circulation, it also produces a more nefarious distinction between different kinds of bodies, namely between those that can be separated into the socially constructed categories of "abled" and "disabled."

In addition to being defined by its opposite, ability is defined in the OED as the "ability to work." Rooted in the logic of late industrial capitalism, ability signifies what McRuer suggests is the obligatory nature of able-bodiedness in now neoliberal capitalism: The notion that one is "free to sell one's labor but not free to do anything else" effectively translates to "free to have an able body but not particularly free to have anything else."[32] In other words, in a system where freedom is conditioned on labor, and labor is conditioned on so-called "ability," the idea of choice may be advertised to the subject with disabilities (e.g., the choice between elevator or stairs), but it does not actually exist. Able-bodiedness, in this way, becomes a prerequisite for the neoliberal subject's full participation in the public sphere.

The neoliberal proposition of choice is not limited to physical spaces like the Vessel, but it is also present in digital game mechanics. In *The Sims* series, for example, players are endowed with the authorial power of identity creation—everything from the avatar's race, gender, hairstyle, breast and buttocks size, to personality can be determined by the player. Authorial decision making in *The Sims* extends to the environmental: Players can design the game-world and the kind of house their avatars will reside in—the latter capability has spawned a whole genre of digital architectural design practice and utopic fantasy. In games like *Grand Theft Auto*, Muriel and Crawford remind us, dialogue options and other choice-based actions allow players to manipulate character relationships and narrative outcomes.[33] Such examples demonstrate the medium's capacity to endow the player with a sense of agency, even when the structure of choices in their games remain pre-constructed and necessarily limiting.

While such agency can be understood as an emancipatory framework, the kind of bounded agency suggested in these games is simultaneously reflective of a neoliberal practice of down-shifting liability—one that allows for both the divestment of responsibility on the part of the state or the corporation (the designer)—and the reassignment of that responsibility to the individual. As a result, subjects playing video games not only participate in structures that confer neoliberal values, but they also, often unknowingly, (1) reproduce "ideas of freedom that can be found in the neoliberal rationale" and (2) co-sign the idea that "should they exert themselves, they will be able to achieve their goals, or else they will fail due to their own deficiencies or lack of effort."[34] Similarly, when HY visitors post images at the Vessel with "@theVesselNYC," they are both participating within a mediated, circulatory system underwritten by neoliberal values *and* reproducing those values within the global, digital forum of Instagram.

This paradigm demonstrates how the dual operation of neoliberalism described throughout this paper is re-inscribed in the question of ability. It supports the design of public spaces that value ableism *and* casts the burden of a disabled subject's inability to comply with capitalist labor regimes and the existing manifestation of digital and physical environments onto that very subject. In essence, at the Vessel, subjects with "noncompliant bodies" bear the brunt of the failures of its design.[35] Though legislation like the ADA has transformed the built environment in positive ways over the last thirty years, inequitable structures like the Vessel continue to emerge in our public spaces; and while the addition of a new platform lift might provide an avenue for disabled visitors to interact with the Vessel, it ultimately only provides one pre-scripted narrative vector. As Lisa Duggan astutely notes, in neoliberalism, "diversity" and "tolerance" may be supported in narrow terms, but radical inclusion and participation are not.[36]

FAILURE: QUEERING & CRIPPING SPATIAL PRACTICES

Neoliberal spaces like the Vessel not only present illusory, and often impossible, choices to users, but they can also be difficult to evade altogether; to quote disability activist and scholar Kevin Gotkin: "How to refuse stairs is no simple process."[37] What possibilities for activism exist against the backdrop of a neoliberal system that seems to both inundate and ooze from the environments we collectively inhabit? We turn to both "queer" and "crip" theories in this final section to understand how *queering* and *cripping* spatial practices become liberative modes of resisting hegemony and living otherwise. While queerness represents sexual identity that falls outside of the category of "heterosexuality," it also signifies "a way of being, doing, and desiring *differently*."[38] In this way, queerness becomes a mode of engaging with the world, and *queering* an active practice of appropriating, subverting and reimagining heterosexist identity formations. "Cripping," Carrie Sandahl argues, is similarly constructed to "queering" because:

> Both queering and cripping expose the arbitrary delineation between normal and defective and the negative social ramifications of attempts to homogenize humanity, and both disarm what is painful with wicked humor, including camp.[39]

As we have explored, the idea that certain bodies—namely queer and disabled bodies—will "fail" to comply with ableist and heterosexist spatial scripts has become naturalized in neoliberal design practices. But what if the very idea of *failing* could be queered and cripped to productive ends? Ruberg suggests that queering video games, and in turn queering *failure* in video games, has long been central to the development of alternative LGBTQ+ digital practices:

> Players bring...queerness with them when they choose to play in ways that a game did not intend. In such moments, queer play resists and repurposes games for alternative desires; it upends the normative logics that structure the game and transform it into a space for testing the boundaries of pleasure, identity, and agency.[40]

In this formulation, one possibility for queer play is to seek out failure, however it might be creatively defined within the context of a particular game. Ruberg gives us examples of fantastic, pleasurable failures within her own queer gameplaying practices—from wandering around the streets of *Grand Theft Auto* and avoiding the game's prompt to advance through the narrative via heist schemes and pointed interactions with other characters; to spending more time dancing with other characters than engaging them in an expected sword-fight in *Nidhogg*.⁴¹

Failure, Ruberg cautions, can move toward neoliberal scripts by playing right into their hand, or it can move against the grain of those very scripts. Failing toward a game system involves failing in a way that is expected or encouraged by the game—here Ruberg gives the example of falling down the stairs in *Stair Dismount*, thus enacting the presupposed purpose of the game—whereas failing *against* a game means resisting "formations of control predictability, and homogeneity."⁴² At the Vessel, a similar distinction between genres of failure holds. For a disabled subject, failing *toward* the Vessel might mean accepting its bifurcated circulatory system by taking the elevator, while failing *against* the Vessel could be practiced through an outright rejection of circulation in favor of alternative place-making practices.

PERFORMING THE JOY OF REFUSAL: ANTI-STAIRS CLUB LOUNGE

In April of 2019, a disabilities activist group under the moniker "Anti-Stairs Club Lounge" put the practice of failing *against* the Vessel into action. Clad in neon orange hats, the group convened at the base of the Vessel to engage in peaceful, joyful protest—sharing conversation, resting on custom-designed anti-stairs pillows, and signing a playfully subversive pledge emblazoned with the words: "As long as I live, I will not go up a single step of the Vessel." In addition to creating a non-ableist space by creating an accessible, though ephemeral, "lounge" in HY, the group also imagined and demanded a different form of public space, calling for the same construction budget of the Vessel ($150 million) to be awarded for the creation of a permanent Anti-Stairs Club Lounge. Participants also created an alternative digital space for activism instead of advertisement, flooding Instagram with images captioned with "#antistairsclublounge."

The artist at the helm of the Anti-Stairs Club Lounge, Finnegan Shannon, commissioned photographer Maria Baranova to document the event, whose portfolio of experience is primarily in performance art and theater photography. This is not by accident—*The Anti-Stairs Club Lounge* is simultaneously a collective work of activism and embodied performance meant to be on display. In an interview with *The Creative Independent,* Finnegan states that, as with most protests, the project was motivated by collective anger, and that they "wanted it to be a chance to be together in that frustration and anger."⁴³ But at the same time, one of the most striking elements seen in Baranova's photographs of the *Anti-Stairs Club Lounge at the Vessel* is the choreographic performance of sheer joy and contagious conviviality expressed by the event participants in community. In this expression, the participants show that to refuse the Vessel and Hudson Yards—ergo, to refuse the so-called "good life"—is not to lack or be disenfranchised, but is in fact to afford pleasurable "luxury" in itself. As Lynne Segal writes of the emancipatory potency of collective joy:

> Moments of joy usually break down the distances between people, bringing us together at least with those able to share the same delight. Such collective sentiment explains joy's traditional ties with things that are larger, better and more exciting than we are individually. How could there not be a certain delight and freedom in escaping that gloomy tyrant—ourselves—forever brooding over or blocking out our own feelings of failure, shortcomings, neediness, neglect or isolation?⁴⁴

Reading Segal's psychological analysis of joy against the political backdrop of Berlant's "cruel optimism," one can see in the images of the *Anti-Stairs Club Lounge* a defensive inversion of alienating "failure, shortcomings, neediness" brought about by the individualistic, ableist exclusivity of the good life into a pleasurable freedom through the collective act of refusing the good life's toxic invitation.

These practices of resistance, which in many ways reflect the queer game-playing practices that Ruberg describes, can also be understood as unique examples of *cripping* the public sphere. Here, McRuer's and Aimi Hamraie's account of the "do-it-yourself curb cut" proves a useful reference point. As Hamraie notes, the legend of the DIY curb cut in disability activism harkens back to the late 1960s, when disability activists around the United States took sledgehammers to street curbs that proved barriers to accessibility in urban spaces.[45] The curb cut reminds us that (1) material barriers to access and equality are everywhere in the material world and (2) that disability activists have always been both active agents in the formation of a more equitable built environments and designers of projected futures. Indeed, cripping has always been both a theoretical and spatial practice, shaping a "necessary openness to the accessible public cultures we might yet inhabit."[46] The Anti-Stairs Club Lounge community is embedded in this remarkable lineage of activism, and yet is distinctly of its time as it rejects the Vessel's exploitation of visitors' labor and hetero-ableist exclusivity in favor of radical inclusion and collective activism.

Though their work of space-making is markedly different than that of Heatherwick studio or RC, activists like the Anti-Stairs Club Lounge should themselves be considered spatial practitioners—designers of the built environment—as well. In his ethnographic work on the digital platform *Second Life*, Tom Boellstorff similarly asks how disabled players occupy the subject position of "entrepreneur." In a neoliberal context, entrepreneurship, Boellstorff notes, is "presumed to be constituted through risk and individual productivity," and is therefore "part of a cultural framework that narrowcasts dependency, mutuality, and collaboration."[47] Yet through their participation in *Second Life*, many users with disabilities subvert this notion of entrepreneurship, producing user-generated content not with the intention of profit but rather with an appetite for teamwork, generous exchange of resources, and the making of new social bonds. In this way, they not only refigure the definition of entrepreneurship, but also challenge the capitalist and ableist assumptions that underpin its narrow definition in the first place. Similarly, members of the Anti-Stairs Club Lounge project occupy the subject position of "spatial practitioner," and in doing so, they challenge its associations with an array of neoliberal values. Activists like these offer a blueprint for expanding modes of spatial practice that privilege collaboration instead of privatization, mutual aid instead of economic exploitation, and a culture of collectivity in lieu of a culture of circulation.

CONCLUSION

As we have explored throughout this paper, the culture of circulation propelled by the Vessel is powered by a basic desire for performance, visibility, and shared experience—in short, a desire for access to a cultural commons. However, in order to sustain the self-reflexive economy of this circulatory culture, such environments distribute this access unevenly, perpetuating an affective relation of "cruel optimism." Simultaneously, this uneven distribution inculcates an ideal neoliberal subjectivity of individualistic opportunism, undercutting the collective solidarity that is necessary for a meaningful and equitable commons.

In response to this paradigm, activist spatial practices like the Anti-Stairs Club Lounge effectively "curb-cut" their way through the neoliberal constructs of a circulatory culture. This is not to say that they wholly "overturn" or replace neoliberalism, but rather they prove useful methodologies for investing in systems of mutuality that neoliberalism attempts to delegitimize and destabilize. Indeed, the Anti-Stairs Club Lounge directly reclaims and redistributes this cultural commons by declaring that the only barrier to accessing their club lounge—a term intentionally loaded with overtones of exclusivity—is radical inclusivity.

POSTSCRIPT

Since our research for this article commenced in early 2020, four individuals committed suicide at the Vessel. The last death occurred even after safety-motivated security measures were implemented at the project site. This has led to the indefinite closure of the structure. In the aftermath, the Vessel's social media accounts have been removed, diminishing its digital presence in the image economy for which it was built. We join calls by disability activists and community stakeholders to demolish the Vessel. What comes in its wake must be accompanied by a forceful critique of the conditions of the Vessel's emergence: The privatization of public space, the siphoning of government funding from projects that could benefit low income communities toward the benefit of real estate companies, and the many forms of violence and exclusion inherent in its architectural and political organization.

Authors' note: This article was published in an issue of *Imago: Studi di Cinema e Media* titled "Narrative Architectures: Bodies, Spaces, Technologies in Contemporary Media Experience" in the Fall of 2021 (issue 22). The essay was originally titled "En-actors at the Vessel: Architecture, Neoliberalism, and Queer/Crip Refusal." We have made minor revisions to the article to make its structure more legible to an architectural audience and to expand on the activism of the Anti-Stairs Club Lounge. Much of the verb tense used in the article reflects the moment at which it was originally written and published—when the Vessel was still frequented by tourists prior to its indefinite closure for public use.

1. Michael Kimmelman, "Hudson Yards is Manhattan's Biggest, Newest, Slickest Gated Community. Is This the Neighborhood New York Deserves?," *The New York Times* online, March 14, 2019, https://www.nytimes.com/interactive/2019/03/14/arts/design/hudson-yards-nyc.html.
2. Kenny Cupers, Catharina Gabrielsson, and Helena Mattsson, eds., "Introduction: Undead Neoliberalisms," in *Neoliberalism on the Ground: Architecture and Transformation from the 1960s to the Present* (Pittsburgh: University of Pittsburgh Press, 2020), 3.
3. Rajesh Venugopal, "Neoliberalism as concept," *Economy and Society* 44, no. 2 (April 2015): 165.
4. Reinhold Martin, "Epilogue: Neoliberalism and Architecture, Backward," in *Neoliberalism on the Ground*, 409.
5. Bridget Fisher and Flávia Leite, "The Cost of New York City's Hudson Yards Redevelopment," (Working Paper, The New School for Social Research, 2018) 27.
6. Hudson Yards, "Introducing The Vessel," YouTube Video, 1:42, September 14, 2016, https://www.youtube.com/watch?v=OLG3uTmceCE.
7. Kirston Capps, "The Hidden Horror of Hudson Yards Is How It Was Financed," *Bloomberg City Lab*, April 12, 2019, https://www.bloomberg.com/news/articles/2019-04-12/the-visa-program-that-helped-pay-for-hudson-yards.
8. Adam Alston, "Audience Participation and Neoliberal Value: Risk, agency and responsibility in immersive theatre," *Performance Research* 18, no. 2 (June 2013): 128.
9. Daniel Muriel and Garry Crawford, "Video Games and Agency in Contemporary Society," *Games and Culture* 15, no. 2 (March 2020): 147.
10. Alston, 131.
11. Olivia Turnbull, "It's All about You: Immersive Theatre and Social Networking," *Journal of Contemporary Drama in English* 4, no. 1 (May 2016): 158.
12. Umberto Eco, "Function and Sign: The Semiotics of Architecture," in *Rethinking Architecture: A Reader in Cultural Theory* ed. Neil Leach (London: Routledge, 1997), 176.
13. Bernard Suits, *The Grasshopper: Games, Life, and Utopia* (Toronto: University of Toronto Press, 1978), 41.
14. Joan Ockman, "Circulation System," in *The Building*, ed. José Aragüez (Zurich: Lars Muller, 2016), 234.
15. Paul Goldberger, Jeff Chu, and Sarah Medford, *The Story of New York's Staircase* (Munich: Prestel, 2019), 101.
16. Benjamin Lee and Edward LiPuma, "Cultures of Circulation: The Imaginations of Modernity," in *Public Culture* 14, no. 1 (January 2002): 192.
17. Ted Loos, "A $150 Million Stairway to Nowhere on the Far West Side," *The New York Times*, September 14, 2016, https://www.nytimes.com/2016/09/15/arts/design/hudson-yards-own-social-climbing-stairway.html.
18. Alice T. Friedman, *American Glamour and the Evolution of Modern Architecture* (New Haven, CT: Yale University Press, 2010), chap. 4, https://www.aaeportal.com/?id=-15079.
19. Marvelous Mrs. Maisel, "It's Comedy or Cabbage," *Amazon video*, 55:54, https://www.amazon.com/gp/video/detail/B082355JC7.
20. Morris Lapidus, *An Architecture of Joy* (Miami, FL: E. A. Seemann, 1979), 164.
21. Alice T. Friedman, "American Glamour 2.0: architecture, spectacle, and social media," *Consumption Markets & Culture* 20, no. 6 (April 2017), 578.
22. Yasmin Ibrahim, *Production of the 'Self' in the Digital Age* (London: Palgrave Macmillan, 2018), 2.
23. Agnès Silvestre, "Punchdrunk and the Politics of Spectatorship," *Culturebot*, November 14, 2012, https://www.culturebot.org/2012/11/14997/punch-drunk-and-the-politics-of-spectatorship.
24. Ibrahim, 2.
25. Lauren Berlant, *Cruel Optimism* (Durham, NC: Duke University Press, 2011), 1.
26. Ibid., 1.
27. McKenzie Wark, *Capital is Dead: Is This Something Worse?* (Verso Books, 2019), 11.
28. Hudson Yards, "The Vessel."
29. Geoffrey S. Berman, United States Department of Justice, United States Attorney, Southern District of New York, *Manhattan U.S. Attorney Announces Agreement With Related Companies To Increase Accessibility Of The Vessel In Hudson Yards*, press release, December 23, 2019, https://www.justice.gov/usao-sdny/pr/manhattan-us-attorney-announces-agreement-related-companies-increase-accessibility.
30. Alston, 133.
31. Robert McRuer, *Crip Theory* (New York and London, New York University Press, 2006), 2.
32. McRuer, 8.
33. Muriel and Crawford, 148-149.
34. Ibid., 152.
35. Joel Sanders, "Non-Compliant Bodies: Social Equity and Public Space," (presentation, AIANY Diversity and Inclusion Committee, Center for Architecture, New York, NY, May 23, 2017). https://vimeo.com/277353899.
36. Lisa Duggan, *The Twilight of Equality?: Neoliberalism, Cultural Politics, and the Attack on Democracy*. Boston: Beacon Press, 2003: 21.
37. Kevin Gotkin, "Stair Worship: Heatherwick's Vessel," *The Avery Review*, no.33 (2018), accessed online: http://www.averyreview.com/issues/33/stair-worship.
38. Bonnie Ruberg, *Video Games Have Always Been Queer* (New York and London: NYU Press, 2019), 6.
39. Carrie Sandahl, "Queering the Crip or Cripping the Queer?: Intersections of Queer and Crip Identities in Solo Autobiographical Performance," *GLQ: A Journal of Lesbian and Gay Studies* 9, no. 1-2 (2003), 37.
40. Ruberg, 17-18.
41. Ruberg, 145-147.
42. Derek A. Burrill, "Queer Theory, the Body, and Video Games," in *Queer Game Studies*, ed. Bonnie Ruberg and Adrienne Shaw (Minneapolis: University of Minnesota Press, 2017), 31.
43. Finnegan Shannon, "On community, protest, and public space," Interview by Amelia Brod, *The Creative Independent*, March 19, 2020, https://thecreativeindependent.com/people/artist-shannon-finnegan-on-community-protest-and-public-space.
44. Lynne Segal, *Radical Happiness: Moments of Collective Joy* (London: Verso, 2018), ebook.
45. Aimi Hamraie, *Building Access: Universal Design and the Politics of Disability* (Minneapolis: University of Minnesota Press, 2017), 95.
46. McRuer, 35.
47. Tom Boellstorff, "The opportunity to contribute: disability and the digital entrepreneur," *Information, Communication & Society* 22, no. 4 (2019): 484.

Note: Please use the spaces provided in this article to reorient as a way to transcend time.

In a large sunlit room at the Reversible Destiny Foundation in the Brooklyn Navy Yard, founded by Arakawa and Madeline Gins, the soft-spoken projects manager shared a curious anecdote. In a subdued tone of voice, ST Luk recounted how a visiting researcher had succumbed to the staggering array of materials, experiencing a cascade of panic attacks that forced an abrupt halt and eventual end to their curatorial project. They never returned to the foundation. A cup of water, offered in kindness, punctuated this unsettling narrative.

Arakawa and Gins are known to the public mostly for built architectural work such as *Site of Reversible Destiny—Yoro Park* in Gifu Prefecture, Japan, considered their masterpiece; the Krebs cycle-inspired *Bioscleave House (Lifespan Extending Villa)*, on Long Island, recently off the list for sale;[1] *Reversible Destiny Lofts—Mitaka (In Memory of Helen Keller)*, notable in pop culture for the episode in the HBO series *Girls* where Shoshanna freaks out in Tokyo; the *Biotopological Scale-Juggling Escalator*, traversing Comme des Garçons to Prada at the Dover Street Market New York; and the cylindrical, gravity-defying *Ubiquitous Site, Nagi's Ryoanji, Architectural Body* in Japan, their first built work.

Yet their work extends much further—and across a variety of disciplines. Arakawa and Gins established the Reversible Destiny Foundation[2] to promote their philosophy through the mediums of art, architecture, and writing. While contradictions are in some sense intrinsic to their work, one tenet of their practice, reflected by the name of the foundation, was that mortality could be fought, delayed, and even undone. They devoted their artistic practice to this principle, especially in terms of rethinking the connections between architectural environments and the human body.

A visit to the Reversible Destiny Foundation offers a panorama of this effort, as well as the lives bound up in the collaboration. One can unearth Arakawa and Gins's early work in reels of 16mm films that daringly deviated from prescriptive norms—including scenes from *For Example* (1971), portraying a child masquerading as an inebriated urchin on the streets of the Lower East Side in the early 1970s. There are file boxes from their Houston Street studio brimming with bric-a-brac, including a classic Coca-Cola glass that Gins grabbed from the shelf in the studio, tilted on its side, and incorporated into the architectural model for Dover Street Market, which she and her studio staff worked on for months. Most memorable was the topographical tableau of lavatorial layers, where a top-view rendering shows one bathroom ingeniously offset (double bathroom!) within another. Their work is an architectural palindrome traversing the dimensions of form and function—but also space and time. They provided a personal lens on their own relationship with mortality in pieces like the *spacetimemassenergy wave hello*, showing two people waving over a chasm.

INSTRUCTIONS: *Stop, look left, look right, then wave to your future self from the past.*

Their ideas reveal a synthesis of offsets, countermeasures, and time delays that accumulate into a pedagogical theater

8 REASSEMBLING

AN INVESTIGATION OF THE ELEMENTS OF REASSEMBLY AND OF THE POSSIBLE APPLICATIONS OF THESE IN ORDER TO CHANGE USAGE

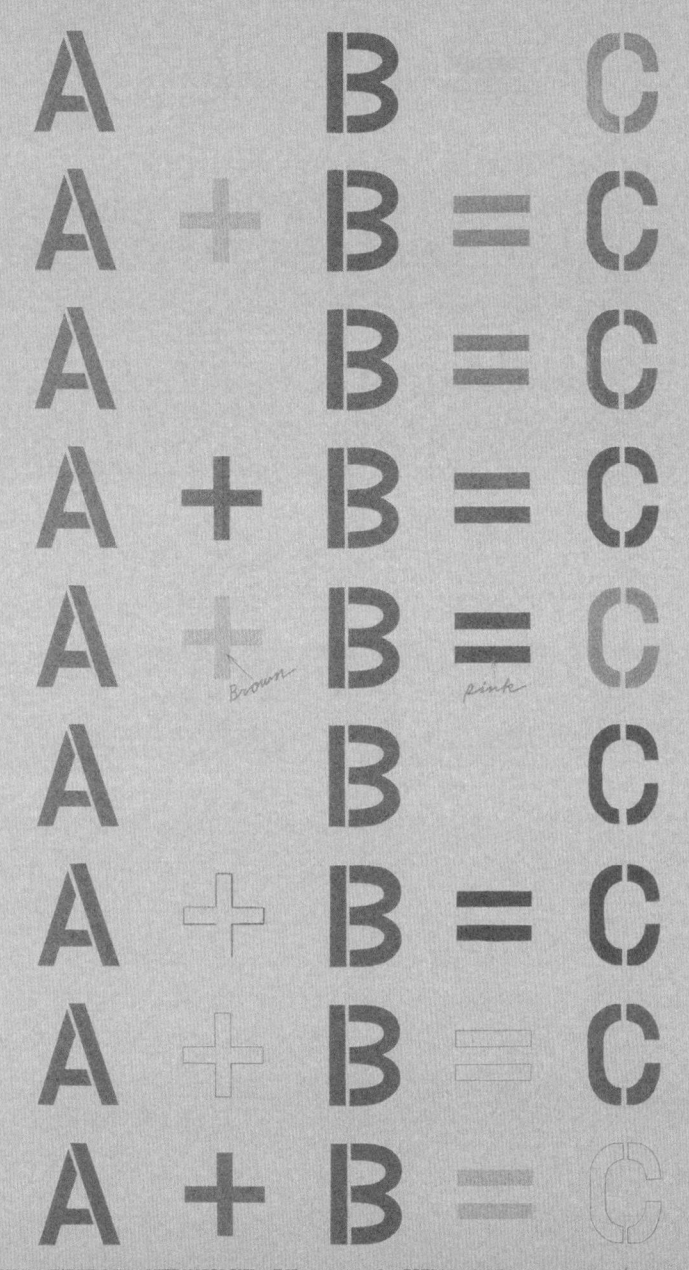

A   B   C

A + B = C

A   B = C

A + B = C

A + B = C
     Brown   pink

A   B   C

A + B = C

A + B = C

A + B = C

TO WHAT EXTENT IS = A FUNCTION OF + ?

The range of values for each + and = is wide open as long as the above relations hold.
Other considerations are: A + + + + + B = C . A + B ———————— C
                        Color, positional changes in A, B
                        If + is ten years (minutes) ahead of =
                        Or a shift in any other dimension………

Figure 1. Arakawa and Madeline Gins, *The Mechanisms of Meaning: 8. Reassembling*, 1963–71, 78, 88, 96. Acrylic on canvas, 96 × 65 inches.

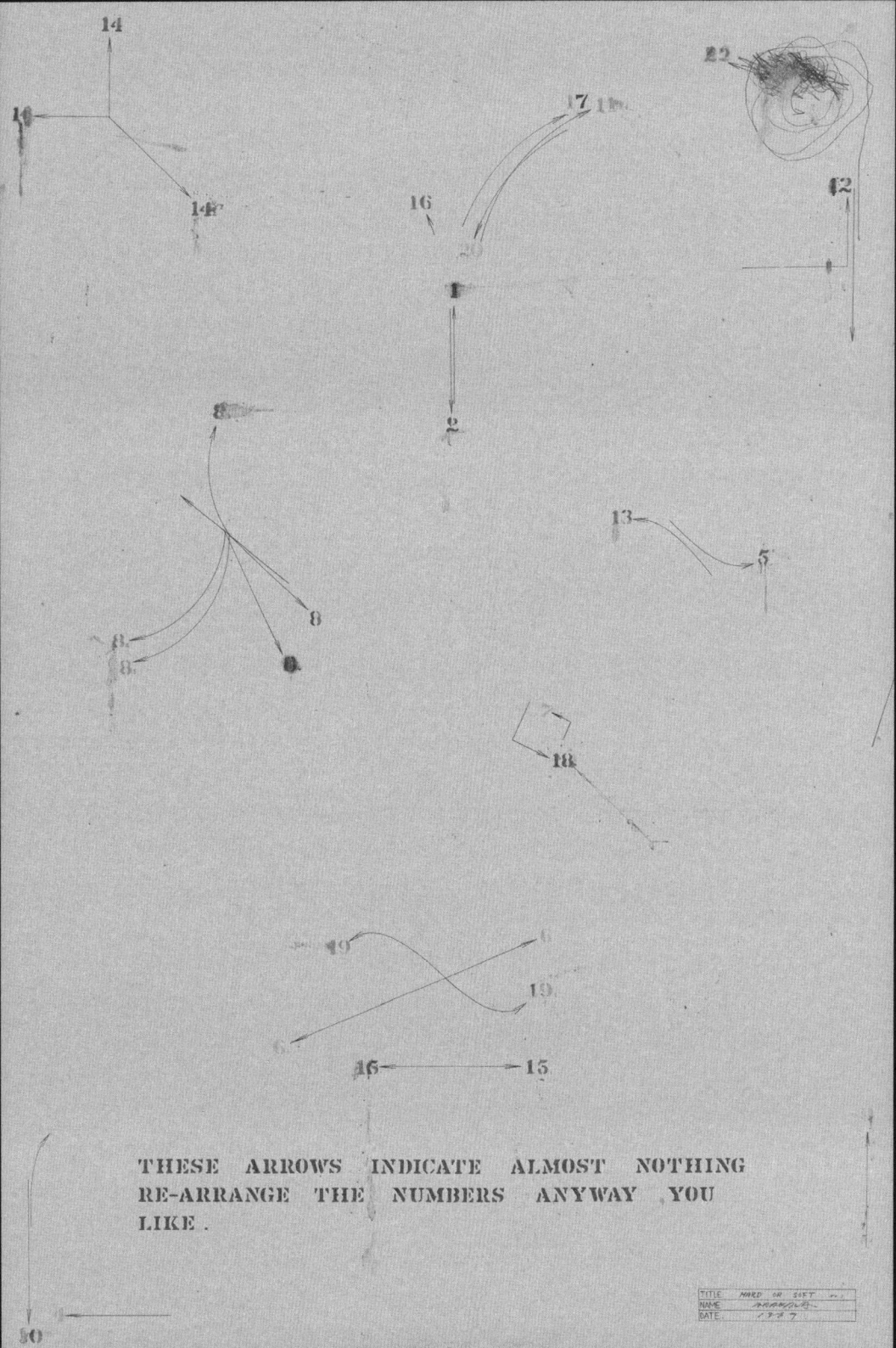

THESE ARROWS INDICATE ALMOST NOTHING
RE-ARRANGE THE NUMBERS ANYWAY YOU
LIKE .

for Plato's theory of forms,[3] Werner Karl Heisenberg's uncertainty principle,[4] and Albert Einstein's spooky action at a distance—mechanisms that have been carefully considered in publications such as the *Funambulist* and *Architecture and Philosophy: New Perspectives on the Work of Arakawa & Madeline Gins*.[5] Their execution intuitively sanctions spontaneous workflows, and they paved the way for architecture students to unselfconsciously deploy processes of "crumpled paper" à la Frank Gehry, experiment with the force models of Antoni Gaudí, declare a fondness for "Big Duck" architecture, and ghost on a date with the Vitruvian Man in their elevations.

INSTRUCTIONS: Every month move through your loft as a different animal (snake, deer, tortoise, elephant, giraffe, penguin, etc.). —Arakawa[6]

As if pulled by some spontaneous trick or deep genealogical intuition, a paradox emerges from beneath the canopy of their collective wisdom—a tryst with architecture that is not architecture, a dance with philosophy that is not coherent rhetoric, an encounter with art that mutes the art world. The subversion of categorization for all architectural souls suffuses Arakawa and Gins's manifesto, *The Architectural Body*. Through their writing they summon forces both perceivable and invisible to challenge a corporeal equilibrium that links the body to its architectural surroundings, suggesting, for example, that a "taking shape of surrounds and bodies and organisms and persons occurs intermixedly [sic]. Logic would want to get in there with a knife and cut them apart."[7]

They were reacting to systems of control that seemingly have always existed in architecture. Architecture has treated the body as a mostly static subject, a mere mass with a scale and quantity, and sometimes an identity, to be accommodated within defined volumes. This pursuit of maximum comfort and optimized convenience, paired with technological adaptations, has supported corporeal disembodiment, desensitizing our body's ability to tune into its primal senses and offering a future of broken antennas that remove us further from reality into the prism of our own minds.

This can be found right in front of us, in the ubiquitous family room and its protagonist, the modern couch: A plush enabler of disembodiment, it exemplifies the underutilized body, whether a Poltrona Frau three-seater or a sectional from IKEA. For the tech evangelist version of the flaneur, the couch is a true lounger—without the need to stroll, instead we scroll. Arakawa and Gins seem to argue that this muting of kinesthetic and tactile knowledge is a pathway to oblivion.

INSTRUCTIONS: Stand up. Rotate the room 45 degrees in your head and try to jump three times forward as if you were in this new rotated space.

Arakawa and Gins offer a means of experimenting with this kinesthetic oblivion through their work. This is best demonstrated at their largest project, *Site of Reversible Destiny*, located within Yōrō Park. The four-acre site is composed of a dizzying choreography of components—ramps, chasms, slanted floors, double horizons, gaps, vegetation, dead ends, mazes, and dark corners—all of which work for and against the human body. These fixed, surprising, and sometimes dangerous architectural elements intertwine with the bodies that navigate them, weaving a kinesthetic textile with the sympathetic nervous system. Luckily the park comes with instructions for use that serve as both a loose navigation tool and a way to calibrate one's mind and body to Arakawa and Gins's perspective, as follows:

> If thrown off-balance, call out your name or, if you prefer, someone else's;
> Try to incorporate two or more horizons in every view;
> Wander through the ruin known as the Destiny House or the Landing Site Depot as though you were an extraterrestrial;
> Move in slow measured steps through the Cleaving Hall and, with each arm at a distinctly different height, hold both arms out in front of you as sleepwalkers purportedly do.

With these directions in mind, visitors to the site will initially pass through the *Critical Resemblances House*, a space that challenges perception and orientation with a mirrored maze, reflecting itself in material and form. The maze structure on the floor appears also on the ceiling—which uses the visitor's head as the axis of reflection. The stately scale and serenity of surrounding nature serve as a ruse to the actual site, offsetting the body's effort—through reorientation, movement, and exertion—to merge with the architecture. The spaces between the body and the architecture also merge to form an invisible tactile knowledge.

The paradox of stasis and movement within their work calls for a reevaluation of our understanding of the body in relation to its environment—a sensory awakening of our tactile, cognitive, and physiological systems of understanding our surroundings. Arakawa and Gins compel visitors to consider their own architectural body through the convergence of sensation and perception. Plato's theory of forms reverberates

BUS
BUILDING
SKY

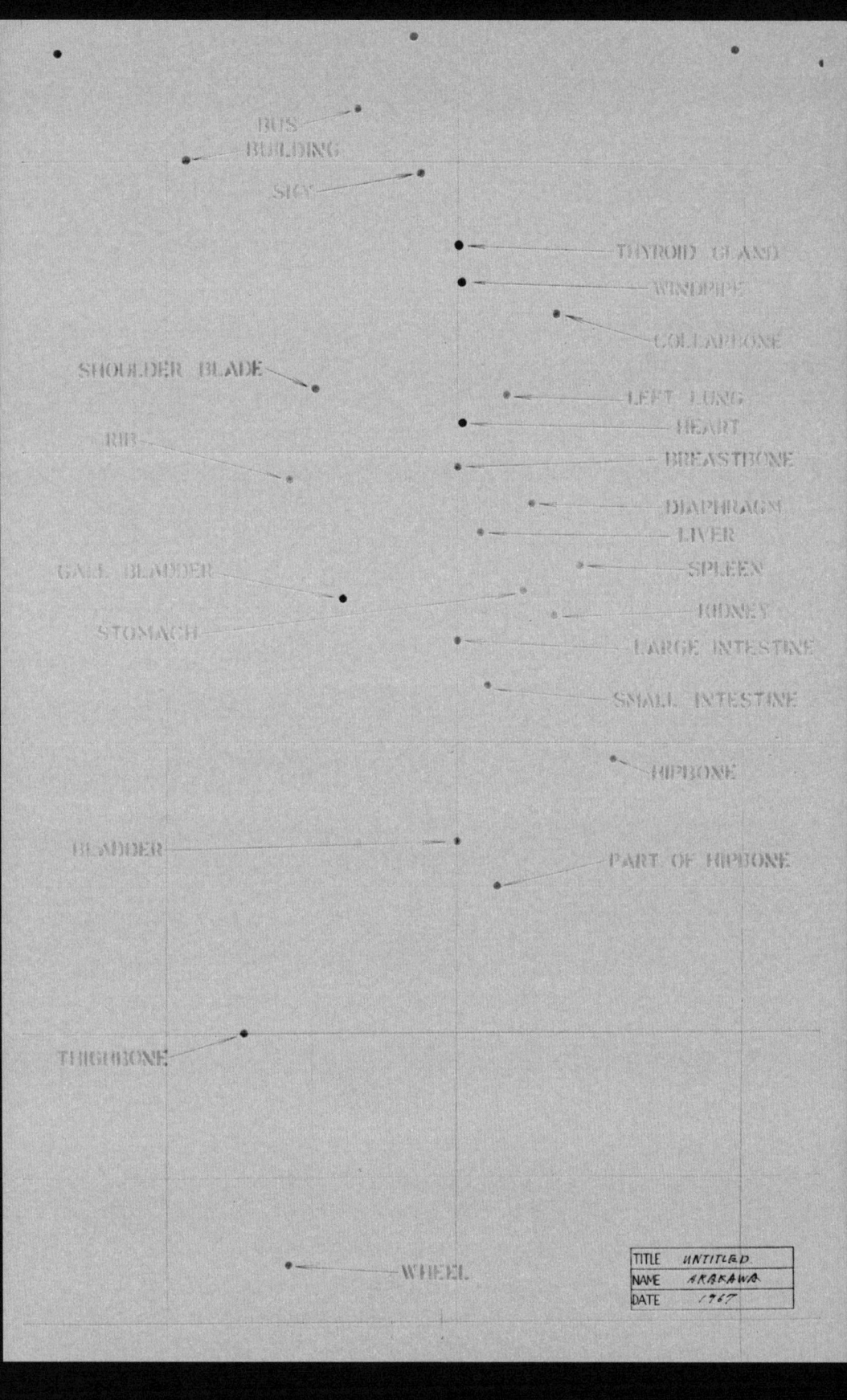

THYROID GLAND
WINDPIPE
COLLARBONE

SHOULDER BLADE
LEFT LUNG
HEART
RIB
BREASTBONE

DIAPHRAGM
LIVER
GALL BLADDER
SPLEEN
STOMACH
KIDNEY
LARGE INTESTINE
SMALL INTESTINE

HIPBONE

BLADDER
PART OF HIPBONE

THIGHBONE

WHEEL

TITLE	UNTITLED
NAME	ARAKAWA
DATE	1967

Figure 4. Arakawa, *A Study of Twins - Talking or Walking*, 1969. Oil and pencil on canvas, 78 × 52 inches.

in this modern exploration that both considers the archetypal and transcends the mundane. The spatial offset of the *Site of Reversible Destiny* mirrors the metaphysical offset of Plato's archetypes, inviting us to recalibrate our comprehension of reality, or just to exist as a snail with its exoskeleton gliding along a rock.

> Snails *go* along glued bodily to first and second shells.
> Clumped earth: Second shell.
> They carry it with them, they eat it, they excrete it.
> They *go* through it. It *goes* through them.
> —Francis Ponge, "Snails"[8]

In his Allegory of the Cave, Plato asks us to perceive beyond the shadows cast upon the wall—to engage with the quintessence of these silhouettes. In this domain the perfect form of a circle, of justice, or of beauty eclipses the physical circles, the legal decrees, or the aesthetic wonders revealed in the tangible world. For Arakawa and Gins the exploration of forms transcends the ethereal to manifest somewhere between architecture and the body. Yet intentionality resonates—forms, imprinted upon their structures, transcend the quotidian boundaries of design. Their geometries do more than control and/or house bodies; they act as conduits for the transcendence of experience. As Arakawa and Gins were seeking to unlock an innate human potential, their work kept up: Floors ripple with textures that demand adaptive engagement; spaces offset and contort, inviting us to challenge our spatial perceptions. Their work conjures a visceral yearning for corporeal communion with the world.

Yet as we navigate the spaces created by Arakawa and Gins literally and figuratively, a fundamental question emerges: What if the body, in communication with the environment, transcends mere static perception? One way architects and planners perceive and quantify the space between the body and its surroundings is through the isovist—a prism of the body's perceptual confines offering a transformative lens through which to decode spatial morphology. Once discovered, the isovist is life-changing for most architecture students, for both its linguistic utterance and its representative nature. It is the POV of your eyes within the spatial limits around it. Sometimes the isovist is grand, going all the way through the upper atmosphere to infinity, and other times it is framed by a thick mullion cut short by the ground, coming to abrupt stops by walls, furniture, and buildings.

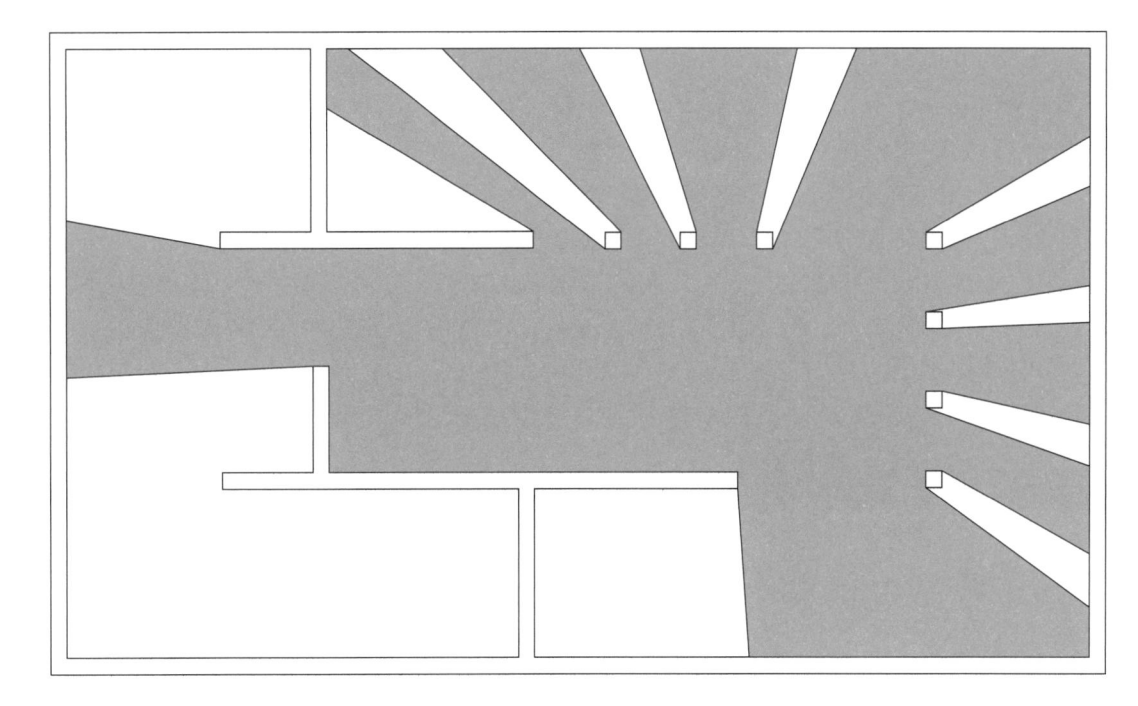

INSTRUCTIONS: What is your isovist right now? Try to sketch it and describe it with words.

Introducing time to the isovist constitutes a dynamic, ever-shifting point-of-view akin to the constant recalibration of a live isovist in perpetual motion. The diagrammatic manifestation of the live isovist can become exponentially complex in 2D and 3D, yet it remains tethered to its perpetual state of measurement—a countermeasure against the elusive nature of perception. Consider for a moment: What form would the isovist of your entire life take? Could it encapsulate your entire existence? Furthermore, envision the shared isovists of six generations of families—a collective narrative transcending individual lives, revealing both harmonies and dissonances across time. The accumulation of these isovists unfurls a profound narrative—one that sheds light on the contours of societies, exposes the fault lines of inequalities, and uncovers the hidden realities of communities. In this amalgamation of viewpoints the isovist emerges as a powerful tool—a countermeasure against perceptual limitations.

> Gins: A functional tool, whether it be a hammer, a telephone, or a telescope, extends the senses, but a procedural tool examines and reorders the sensorium.
>
> Arakawa: Let us then cloak ourselves in solemnly merry stanzas that guide us in the use of this piece of equipment within which we are moving.[9]

The concept of countermeasures in the context of the built environment invokes images of structures safeguarding against threats—earthquake dampers, fire-protection mechanisms, fortresses protecting against potential invasion.

Yet there exists a parallel universe of countermeasures less concerned with the physical and more attuned to the tactile, even the psychological. Akin to those found in the arsenal of a naval submarine, these countermeasures take on different guises—maskers, jammers, decoys—employing tactics such as acoustic signatures and artful deception to confound an enemy's sensory apparatus. Beyond the confines of military strategy, this brand of countermeasure permeates ethereal dimensions between perception and reality.

INSTRUCTIONS: *Hide from yourself.*

From the audacious practice of noise masking to tactile psychological trickery, invisible frequencies and forces traverse the threshold of authenticity and artifice. The tension between reality and perception permeates our existence—so real yet often intangible—bridging the mundane and the enigmatic. Physics designates this tension as an axial force, a tautness that holds our surroundings. But where is the axis of this unperceivable tension between the body and architecture? Like the gravity-loading suit that deceives the astronaut's body about its state of weightlessness, our perception often aligns with these subtle psychological tricks, molding a semblance of reality. This tension, the choreography between corporeal and ephemeral, prompts us to adapt and recalibrate. Yet how do we discern its axis? How do we unmask its presence, and more importantly, how do we engage with it? What cues guide our perception and inform our senses?

> Sentience assembles its swerving suite of cognizing stances depending on how the body disports itself—the whole of this text will prove this statement. Therefore, architecture ought to be designed for actions it invites.—Madeline Gins[10]

> To find answers we need to look not outward but inward, turning our gaze to embedding sentience into volumes. In his book *Sentience: The Invention of Consciousness*, Nicholas Humphrey writes that sensation in contrast to perception is essentially body-centered, evaluative, and personal, about a physical expression of what a particular stimulation means.[11] For the isovist to have sensations, proprioception and the sense organs need to coordinate with cognition, proposing a *sentient volume*. This becomes less about the form of the isovist and more about the relationship between the person and the environment. The notion of a sentient volume begins to emerge as a formless[12] tactile reference frame for a collection of kinesthetic sensations, and it leaves patterns

and traces through its phenomenological exoskeleton. Much as the isovist illuminates our spatial limits, the sentient volume can hold tension—a dialogue between presence and absence, perception and reality.

In this formless essence between the body and its environment, the sentient volume could be the formless expanse that extends beyond the confines of the body, echoing the sensibilities of Arakawa and Gins. Held in place with cyborg sensibilities, this sentient volume mimics the tricks and adaptations of survival strategies in the natural world. A narrative unfolds: A merging of subject and surroundings, the signal in the noise.

> But if we connected the nerves from your stomach to my brain, it would be me who feels the hunger even though the empty stomach is yours.—Stansław Lem[13]

What if the sentient volume could blur its subjects and surrounds, like species that employ visual, auditory, and kinetic deceits for survival, tapping into mechanisms that unravel preconceived understanding and intuition of space to extend the body's perceptual flows into its environment? And how far could it go?

On the flipside, to perceive as a sentient volume it is imperative to understand what to seek. What if the signs we seek lie beyond our immediate scope? Take, for instance, the endeavors of NASA planetary scientist Ravi Kumar Kopparapu[14], whose professional pursuit boils down to a straightforward yet profound statement: "I look for aliens." In a parallel quest that echoes the exploration of a sentient volume, Kopparapu scours the cosmos for telltale traces of life and technology. He navigates the interplanetary expanse using formidable tools such as the James Webb telescope, scanning for techno- and bio-signatures. The former are discernible signals or indicators of potential for advanced civilizations on distant planets, a subset of the broader quest for bio-signatures—evidence of microbial or primitive life on the myriad exoplanets that populate our universe.

In essence, Kopparapu's quest encapsulates the pursuit of technological traces across distant cosmic landscapes and hints at the possibility of advanced civilizations inhabiting far-flung planets. His concern extends to the revelations that distant atmospheres might unveil, and he is mindful not to presume communication preferences. Bio-signatures, on the other hand, signify the presence, past or present, of life—whether through plant matter, gases, or water—prompting a tantalizing contemplation of the diverse forms that life may assume.

Looming over this inquiry is a crucial consideration of the types of techno-signatures humans introduce inadvertently into the world and the confines of our own perspectives. Kopparapu poses a fundamental question: How can we move beyond the reflection of our own civilization? In a world ripe with anomalies, a challenge arises: How do we identify and communicate profound discoveries? How can we find the signal in the noise? In the *Architectural Body*, Arakawa and Gins question how to get outside, beyond, or beneath the world we live in, since not enough distance can be created because the world always gets in the way. Could there be a scenario in the future where advanced civilizations transcend biological existence, relying on technology and artificial intelligence, in an exploration that intersects with the essence of sentience and the limitations inherent to our measurement and technology?

INSTRUCTIONS: Try reading this text upside down and out loud, shouting the name of your best friend after every third word.

Amid these cosmic musings, let's tether our contemplation to earthly frames of reference. While scientists gaze outward, could we examine our terrestrial contexts for additional signals within the noise? Could the sentient volume discern techno- and bio-signatures within our intricate interplays of form and formlessness, perception and reality? As we navigate these interconnected signals, the sentient volume provokes us to delve further, probing the hidden frequencies that resonate within and beyond our perceptual boundaries—an endeavor that reverberates with the sentient volume's search for symbiosis with its environment.

As questions around sentient volumes unfold, a common thread emerges—an invitation to transcend, recalibrate, and explore the symbiosis between the tangible and the metaphysical—or just to observe a snail taking a drink of water.

1. The Krebs cycle is used by organisms that respire to generate energy, either by anaerobic respiration or aerobic respiration.
2. There are two archives—one in Brooklyn, New York, managed by the Reversible Destiny Foundation (https://www.reversibledestiny.org/), and the other in Tokyo, Japan, under the administration of the ARAKAWA+GINS Tokyo Office (https://www.architectural-body.com/?lang=en).
3. Plato's Theory of Forms is the idea that non-physical forms represent the most accurate reality.
4. Heisenberg's Uncertainty Principle states we cannot know both the position and speed of a particle, such as a photon or electron, with perfect accuracy.
5. Lecercle, Jean-Jacques. *Architecture and Philosophy: New Perspectives on the Work of Arakawa & Madeline Gins*. Brill Academic Pub, 2010. 12.
6. From the "Directions for Use, Reversible Destiny Lofts—Mitaka"
7. Gins, Madeline and Arakawa. *The Architectural Body*. The University of Alabama Press, 2002. 29.
8. Ponge, Francis. *Selected Poems*, trans. Margaret Guiton, John Montague, and C. K. Williams. Wake Forest University, 1994. 38.
9. Gins, Madeline and Arakawa. *The Architectural Body*. The University of Alabama Press, 2002. 30.
10. Gins, Madeline and Arakawa. *The Architectural Body*. The University of Alabama Press, 2002. 22.
11. Humphry, Nicholas. *Sentience: The Invention of Consciousness*. MIT Press, 2023. 12.
12. Julian Rose and Garrett Ricciardi are the founders of Formlessfinder and are the editors of *Formless*, a collection of essays published in 2013 by the Storefront for Architecture as part of that organization's Manifesto Series.
13. Lem, Stanisław. *Dialogues*. The MIT Press, 2021. 58.
14. Dr. Ravi Kumar Kopparapu Research AST, Planetary Studies, https://science.gsfc.nasa.gov/sed/bio/ravikumar.kopparapu.

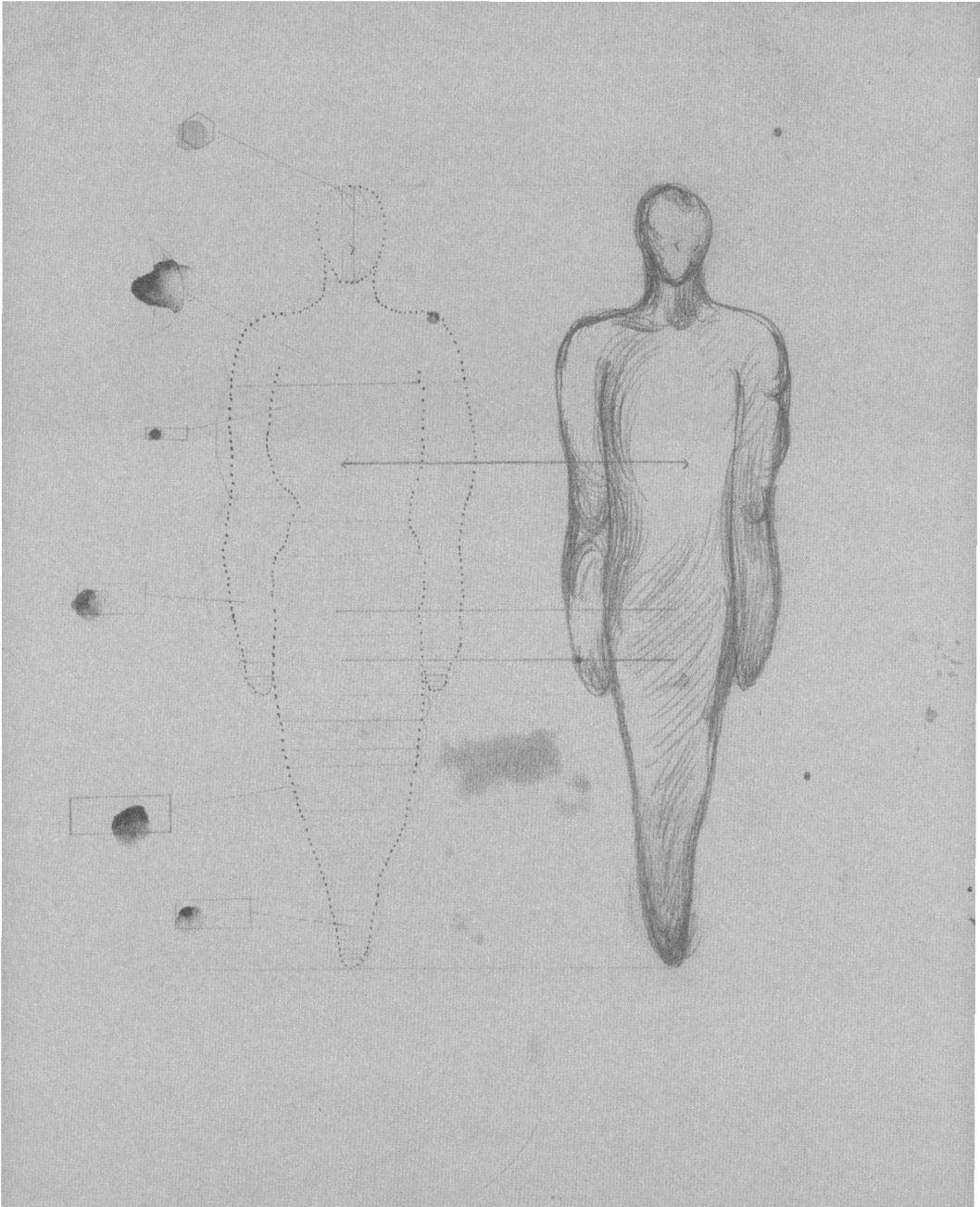

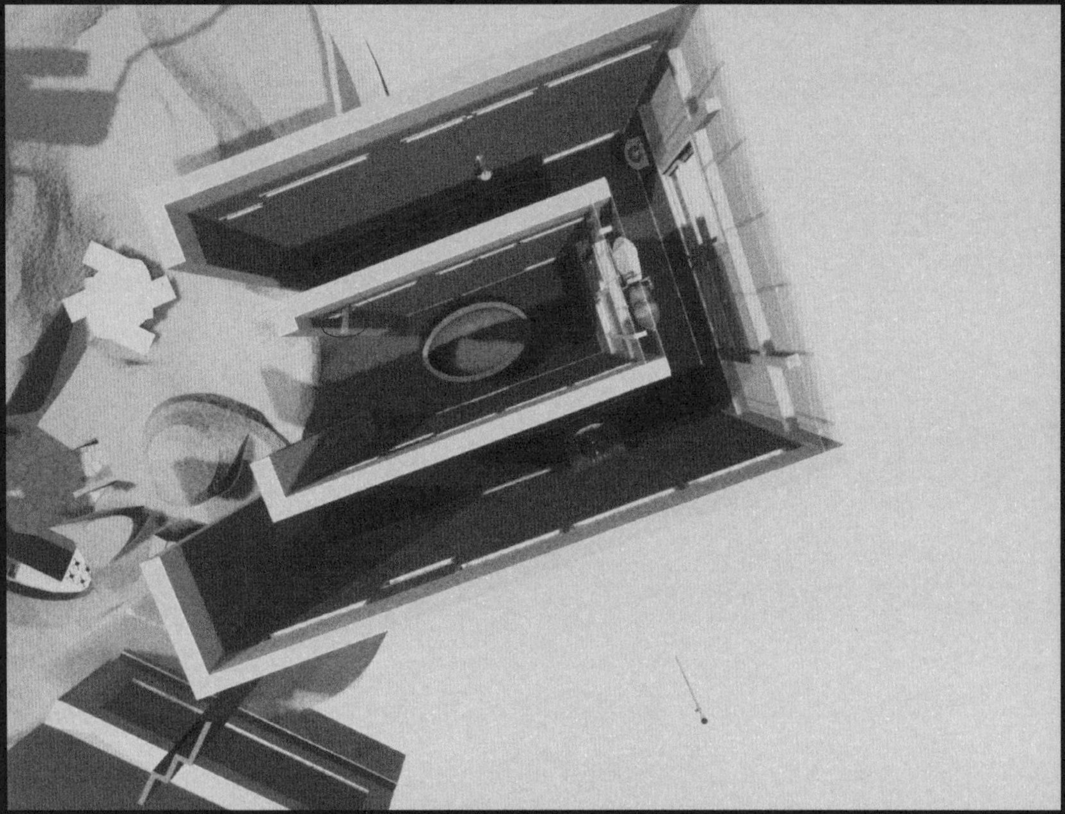

Reversible Destiny Healing Fun House~ Greece, Crevice crossing from interior to exterior

Reversible Destiny Healing Fun House~ Greece, Crevice crossing from exterior to interior

~ A SPACETIMEMASSENERGY WAVE HELLO ~

Opposite Page: *Reversible Destiny* Healing Fun House ~ Greece, Plan View superimposed on terrain, showing the two crevices

For the most part, the adjacent image is typical of the billions of digital photographs taken every day: mostly unremarkable, but with sharp focus, clear contrast, and accurate color. The 2:1 proportion is unusual, however, and the upper portion of the photograph clearly suggests that the camera is struggling to compress a wide-angle of space into a two-dimensional grid of pixels. The concrete column bends to meet a radial grid of skylights. Edges that should be parallel converge at a subtle angle. Parts of the glass guardrail double. Subtle creases appear in flat walls.

The three-dimensional matrix of concrete column and beams at the center of the photograph tracks these distortions, perhaps recalling the orthogonal grid of floor tiles used by countless painters to prove their grasp of constructed perspective and the credibility of their painting. Yet here the building's structural grid does the opposite, mapping the contortions that deviate from perspectival convention. Photography and painting are geometrically distinct; the camera's lens is spherical, the picture plane is flat, but the distortions in this photograph are the result of something else: the compositing of multiple images in real time by the camera. The not-quite perspectival space of this image leaves its connection to physical reality uncertain. Can we call this image a perspective? Does it matter?

PROBLEMATIC
PERSPECTIVE

After a century of critique and analysis in the context of analog media, the status of perspective has rarely been revisited in the context of contemporary image culture. Its status is often viewed as either unchanged by or irrelevant to the digital media we consume today. In recent discourse, graphic content is seen as secondary to the formal properties of images—their digitized materiality and reproducibility. For writers such as Hito Steyerl, Seth Price, and John May, the iconography of individual images is subsumed by the flood of images we experience daily and the new modes of visuality they engender.[1]

Apart from Walter Benjamin's concerns about reproduction, this preoccupation with materiality over graphic form was not the dominant view in the twentieth century. For the classical avant-garde, the graphic form of individual images was tied directly to the broader conventions of visuality. Countless artists experimented with new forms of pictorial representation in the hope that their work would spark new ways of seeing and living in the world. Although this faith in the capacity of a single image can be hard for us to imagine today, art and social revolution were linked in inescapable ways. Linear perspective, and the static relationship of viewer and viewed it implies, was central to a larger set of representational conventions that many artists attempted to question and undermine.

The modern artistic critique of perspective began in 1915, with Suprematism, including work by El Lissitzky and then by Theo van Doesburg over the next decade.[2] El Lissitzky's "Proun" paintings and Van Doesburg's "Counter-Compositions" are axonometric compositions with no points of geometric convergence, no vanishing points, and no implied viewpoint.

Istanbul Museum of Painting and Sculpture, August 9, 2023, 2:04pm.

Without a geometric proxy for the eye, the viewing subject is mobilized, left to float restlessly in relation to the space of the image. The artistic invention of erasing the viewpoint sparked a far-reaching critical project focusing renewed attention on traditional methods of constructed perspective. Initial concerns over the verisimilitude of perspective ballooned, over the course of the twentieth century, into an expansive critique of perspective as an abstraction of vision, of vision as a form of conquest over space, and of the power of architecture over its inhabitants.[3]

In the twenty-first century this critique has been extended to linking perspective with surveillance and remote viewing. According to this argument, laid out by Steyerl, the perspective view has been decoupled from human visual experience for the first time. Satellites, planes, drones, and elevated surveillance cameras have produced a new form of vertical perspective that is machine-made and often intended to be machine-read. Aerial and overhead photography embody the unequal power of vertical stratification found in cities, the real-estate market, and the (remote) viewer over the viewed. "One might conclude that this is in fact a radicalization—though not an overcoming—of the paradigm of linear perspective. In it, the former distinction between object and subject is exacerbated and turned into the one-way gaze of superiors onto inferiors, a looking down from high to low."[4]

Since 2012, when Steyerl's essay was published, John May has led a reassessment of images as a technical format distinct from photographs and drawings. He points out that, unlike photographs, images bear no chemical trace of the physical world and, unlike drawings, geometry plays no role in their production. These distinctions leave the status of linear perspective, reliant on verisimilitude for its value and geometry for its construction, implicitly uncertain. Images are flat expressions of a specific sequence of data fundamentally disconnected from the geometry of constructed perspective or the photographic counterpart, paths of photons converging on the camera lens. "Photographs and images have virtually nothing in common with one another—nothing, that is, aside from a visual resemblance that has led us to equate two completely incompatible technical formats, belonging to two competing epistemic visions of the world," May writes.[5]

The increasing prevalence of machine-made images reframes the relationship between photographs and images. The fact that we use the word *camera* to signify the devices that make both photographs and images is another link between the two formats, but analog and digital cameras are becoming increasingly distinct. While the components of a digital camera may seem analogous to the lens, aperture, and negative of an analog camera, contemporary digital cameras have become more software than hardware, incorporating a series of invisible layers that automatically composite, warp, and post-process each image before we see it displayed on-screen a split second later. Content-aware warping, 3D-image compositing, and other processes produce images that *predict* the world's appearance rather than *document* it. These images

Ford Foundation, New York City, October 19, 2023, 9:28am.

approximate space rather than record it, destabilizing our assumptions about both photography and representational space. They raise the status of perspective once again—this time in the context of machine vision. Have machine-made images severed the last link to orthographic convention? Has machinic-visual culture finally freed us from perspective? Given the ubiquity of images and their impact on what we see, what we create, and how we think, the question is far from academic or purely formal.

AI MEDIATION

The geometry of linear perspective was always a stark abstraction of human vision. Erwin Panofsky cited its singular static viewpoint and reliance on planar grids and orthogonal matrices to question its verisimilitude.[6] He proposed spherical grids as an alternative, but for later critics, reliance on geometry itself was the problem.[7] Contemporary digital photography and real-time video are also abstractions, but their means of reduction are statistical, not geometric. To understand the implications of this difference requires a brief description of how digital images and videos are now created.

While early digital cameras were modeled on analog cameras with a single, typically wide-angle lens, most now have multiple lenses. The additional lenses are not an effort to better simulate binocular vision but to make up for the small size of the lens and its sensor. The smaller the sensor, the less light it registers at each pixel and the more noise it creates. To compensate, the camera captures multiple versions of the same scene and composites them. Each lens has a different focal length, from telephoto to wide-angle, and each captures multiple images with varying exposures, producing up to nine distinct images of the same scene (as of 2022, but the number is almost certain to grow). The camera's software must composite these separate images in the instant before the image is displayed on-screen.

The first step in this process is registering each image so it "lines up" with the others. Given the small displacement of each lens and frequent movement of the camera and the objects depicted, this often includes shifting, scaling, cropping, and warping each image based on an initial mapping of the disparities between images. Rather than a form of 2D collage or mapping, this is effectively a 3D process employing edge detection, motif and object recognition, and spatial warping. Once the images are registered, the software weighs how well each captures a given portion of the scene and fuses the "best" areas pixel by pixel. The more complex this series of calculations, the more "computationally expensive" and thus energy- and time-intensive it is, and the harder it is to complete without a noticeable delay. Software that "learns" this process anew with every image is less efficient than software that can anticipate the adjustments it will need to make before the image is taken.

In 2019 Apple incorporated a machine-learning process it branded Deep Fusion into its iPhone camera software. According to a patent the company filed the same year, Deep Fusion relies on a model trained on

Tower 45, New York City, October 19, 2023, 9:48am.

millions of image pairs, each composed of an initial image-capture with varying levels of sharpness, light, and noise and a final adjusted image.[8] The software learns a range of relations between the initial captures and final images. The model is trained how finished images "should" look. This target range of appearance is not determined by a quantitative domain of light levels, sharpness, or blur but in relation to preexisting images. It replicates the transformations made to previously edited images. Knowing nothing directly about the appearance of the world but a vast amount about its representation, the software produces images that look like other images.

CONTEMPORARY TELEPRESENCE

The vast accretion of images we see through social media and the Internet is one way we encounter representations of ourselves and our environment. Real-time video and teleconferencing are another. Like digital photography, real-time video was once a straightforward simulation of a static analog video shot, but it has grown more complex and dynamic over time. Automatic pan and zoom features—introduced by Apple, Facebook, and others in 2021—reproduce a fully filmic visuality without any actual camera movement, tracking people and objects using facial and object recognition. This requires constant "retargeting": cropping and even recomposing each video frame. Retargeting can be performed simply with linear scaling and uniform cropping of the image, but this "naive" approach can crop out important features when the aspect ratio is changed and tends to reveal distortions from the wide-angle lens.

Researchers have developed machine-learning solutions to both problems. "Content-aware retargeting" resizes images while keeping salient objects in the frame, and "content-aware warping" corrects distortion in "high-saliency" areas of the image.[9] In both cases the image is segmented and salient patches are identified with facial- and object-recognition models. These patches are uniformly scaled and corrected separately. The background, the space between objects, is then distorted to fit between the objects. The resulting images may initially appear indistinguishable from analog video but are fragmented and reconstructed piece by piece to produce a space subtly warped and stretched differently frame by frame. Again, key aspects of this process are performed by machine-learning models trained on existing images. Which objects are recognized as salient and what is relegated to the background? What constitutes the "normal" range of undistorted proportions for a given object? Both questions are answered by machines trained on millions of video stills, reproducing the traits of existing images rather than the most faithful representation of the scene depicted.

The AI-augmented processes underlying digital photography and real-time video simultaneously untether images from the physical world and bind them to existing images. Machine-vision models synthesize and concretize

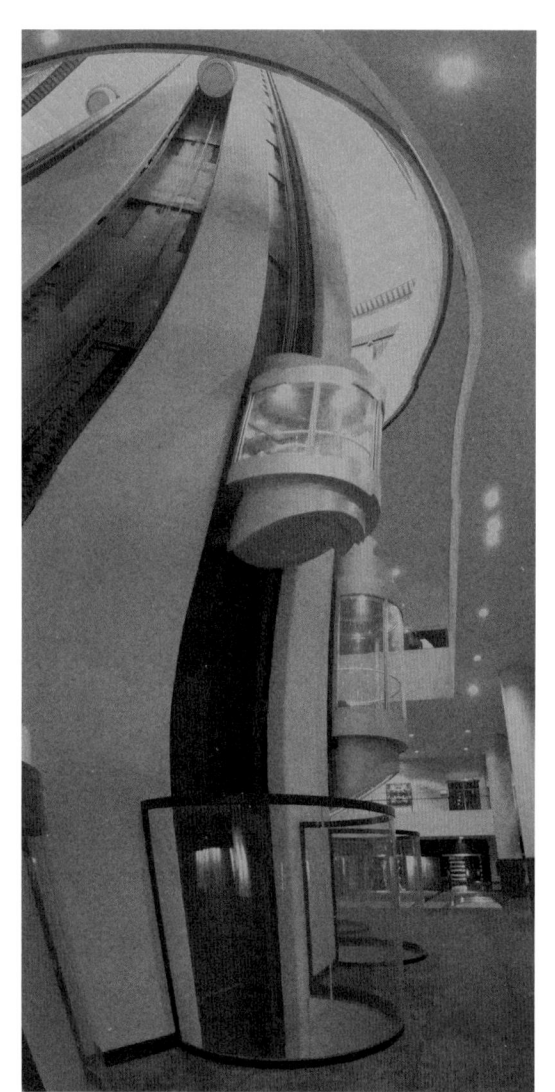

Marriott Marquis, New York City, October 19, 2023, 10:14am.

Bradberry Building, Los Angeles, October 24, 2023, 2:40pm.

the collective formal conventions of the millions of images used to train them. LAION (Large-scale Artificial Intelligence Open Network), the nonprofit organization that assembled the dataset of billions of images used to train Stable Diffusion and other models, began filtering its datasets for images scored as aesthetically pleasing in 2022.[10] Generally culled from social media without regard to creation date, many of these images are scanned analog photographs or less-mediated perspectival digital photographs. The result is a loose approximation of the visual conventions of perspective without the geometric rigor or physics, social cues, and other factors that govern the relation between bodies in three-dimensional space. This "zombie perspective" is modeled after photography but continues to drift further away from any analog source. While machine-generated images progress closer to the appearance of photographs as AI's capacity for verisimilitude improves, they grow more distant from conventional perspective as their training sets become more and more dominated by AI-created examples. This self-referential cycle of machines trained to reproduce machine-made images is the culmination of zombie perspective. [11]

INSCRIPTIONS

The significance of the subtleties of the representation of space is not self-evident. Many scholars see images as artifacts of culture—a way to trace the dominant worldview present at the time of their creation. Others reverse this causal relationship: The specific properties of visual artifacts can give rise to fundamental aspects of culture, and of ways of individually and collectively seeing the world. Philosopher Bernard Stiegler argues that technology has produced humanity just as much as humans have produced technology. At any moment a culture's technical basis—its means of creating, recording, and exchanging information—defines the "horizon of all possibility" for invention, innovation, and imagination.[12] Building on Steigler's work, May links the technical properties of media to our collective and individual experience of the world. "The fact that for many thousands of years prior to the emergence of orthographic writing, time was conceived of as a circle or cycle is proof that we are not born thinking linearly or historically. We trained this way of thinking into ourselves and our cultures by way of orthographic media: texts, drawings, and other forms of notation. It follows from this that cultures can train themselves out of linear, historical thinking—and we are currently doing just that, through our immersion in post-orthographic surfaces."[13]

As our experience of time begins to shift, our sense of space is also being affected by the flood of digital and machine-made images. As part of his work on the social processes behind scientific discovery in the 1980s, Bruno Latour identified how apparently insignificant artifacts—instruments, samples, documents—could have a vast impact if networked with other artifacts and individuals. Drawing this idea out, he argued that our entire scientific culture is attributable to changes in the technical basis of modern visual culture. Rejecting more elaborate explanations for the origin of modern science, including changes in human mentality or the emergence of capitalism, he argues that "the Great Divide can be broken down into many small, unexpected and practical sets of skills to produce images, and to read and write about them."[14] Images are a form of "inscription" that allows a physical sample or culture gathered on-site or grown in the lab to be translated into a form that can be analyzed, compared, interpreted, and exchanged as a number, diagram, map, photograph, or text. What Latour describes is a cascade of abstraction and reduction through which the complexities of the "confusing world" are transformed into clear two-dimensional mediations whose meaning can be distilled and agreed upon. Inscriptions stand in place of more direct evidence; their efficacy relies on the shared belief that they accurately represent the world.

Latour's essay identifies two key properties of these proliferating inscriptions. The first is mobility: there is only one copy of a physical sample, but its image or data can be easily multiplied and circulated. The second is consistency: inscriptions are immutable in the sense that multiple copies are effectively identical, allowing for the comparison, evaluation, and argumentation needed to produce consensus and a shared set of facts.

Latour's first example of this type of consistency is the abstraction and rationalization of vision through linear perspective. A system allowing space to be described consistently from multiple viewing positions, perspective produces optical consistency.[15] The dimensions of any volume or object can be extracted from a drawing, regardless of the point of view. This potential translation is dependent on geometric consistency, in the form of a single uniform three-dimensional grid. The grid allows perspectival space to be translated back, out of the picture, into the world. "You can see a church in Rome, and carry it with you in London in such a way as to reconstruct it in London."[16] Geometry is the most critical component of inscriptions, allowing anything to be translated into a drawing or a set of numbers that in turn can be used to understand and manipulate the physical world.

Digital images are the ultimate mobile format of inscription, proliferating endlessly online. Yet without a basis in geometry they are far from immutable. Digital manipulation has already eroded our faith in the objectivity and immutability of images, but as we have seen with camera and video software, automated simulation is now fundamental to their production. The simulated space of zombie perspective is becoming intrinsic to them as well. After a century of critiquing and attempting to escape from the rigidity of perspective, we find it inescapable but no longer rigid.

Latour's argument foregrounds the broader epistemological implications of the dominance of images, and their mutability suggests why we often seem to be near the end of the modern scientific period, with no set of shared facts on which to base our arguments. For architecture the mutability of machine-made images destabilizes a parallel set of assumptions about the relationship between representation and the world. As a discipline we rely

Met Life Building, New York City, October 19, 2023, 10:34am.

on the ability of others to predictably translate images into buildings, but we also have a long history of exploiting the ambiguities of 2D representation in the development of 3D architectural space.[17] Zombie perspective introduces a new form of ambiguity, producing pictorial space that is neither geometric nor consistent. The space of zombie perspective is subtly malleable, seamlessly collaged, algorithmically adjusted, multiplicitous, and plastic.

WARPED SPACE

The idea that space is a supple medium that exceeds the bounds of geometry is not new. The developments of calculus in the seventeenth century and modern physics in the first decade of the twentieth century effectively proved it. Modern mathematics and physics treat form and volume as probabilities. Albert Einstein's theory of relativity posits that the apparent constants of space (dimension) and time (measure) vary depending on the speed of the subject observing them. Space is continuously variable.

These and related discoveries have long fascinated architects including, and perhaps most famously, Erich Mendelsohn, the first architect to attempt to represent relativity. He was exposed to Einstein's then little known and largely unsubstantiated theory by his friend, and eventual client, astronomer Erwin Finlay Freundlich. Unlike most of his colleagues in Germany, who valued monumentality and its associated permanence and stability, Mendelsohn was inspired by the theory's description of the energy and dynamism latent within mass.[18] Designing the Einstein Tower, he attempted to represent it by expressing specific properties of architectural matter, particularly the forces of tension and compression, within reinforced concrete. It's no coincidence that nearly all of Mendelsohn's initial sketches of the Einstein Tower are perspectival, exploiting the distortion of perspectival projection to reinforce a sense of dynamism in the forms he depicted.[19]

Though he doesn't mention Mendelsohn or Einstein, Greg Lynn made a related argument in his writing at the turn of this century. He sought ways of representing and conceptualizing architectural matter that were truer to its multiplicity and specificity than the universal typologies invented by Rudolf Wittkower and Colin Rowe. Lynn looked to biology rather than physics, citing D'Arcy Thompson's studies of biological deformation.[20] Thompson's drawings of fish backed by grids that smoothly expand and contract to index the changing proportions of their bodies suggested that natural typologies are "underwritten by the variable measurement of difference between and within species."[21] A given species is not a static type with a range of variation from a fixed origin; it is part of a continuous system of transformation and deformation. Architectural form and space could similarly be described through anexact forms rather than exact ones.[22] Various round forms described through probability, for instance, might replace the singular geometric form of the sphere. As Thompson's drawings suggest, form and space are interdependent for Lynn, and both are malleable and multiplicitous.

The space of zombie perspective is similarly anexact rather than exact. It is statistically rigorous but immeasurable geometrically, the synthesis of many similar but varied instances. With no direct connection to the physical world, AI-manipulated imagery has no ideal origin. Instead it's an aggregation of affiliations to other images inhabiting a range of possibility. While there are methods of extracting depth and spatial dimension from images, they too are image-based. Other machine-learning models have been trained to predict depth based on light levels, scale, focus, and other factors, but these models are predictive, not indexical. They produce a new mapping with no geometric link to the previous image and, of course, no link to the physical space it depicts.

ARCHITECTURAL IMAGE MAKING

Despite the ubiquity of machine-manipulated imagery, contemporary architectural representation is strangely focused on conveying ideal types and enabling reductive readings. Platonic shapes, tiny icons, and flat, high-contrast graphics are pervasive in many schools and practices. Combining Instagram-driven legibility at a small scale and the technological sublime of Apple products, what might be called *parti-ism* is ubiquitous.[23] This dominant culture of representation seems to have formed in the early 2010s in relation to two factors: first, the excesses of photorealism coming from early rendering and contemporary advertising; and second, the thesis of the "poor image" articulated by Steyerl in 2012.

In her essay "In Defense of the Poor Image," Steyerl describes a "class society of images" defined primarily by resolution.[24] Low-resolution and "bad" images (thumbnails, pirated copies, degraded scans) are largely excluded from museums, film archives, and commercial publication and broadcast. Yet they circulate in other contexts enabled by file sharing, video streaming, and social media. Constantly in motion, transferred, reuploaded, and reformatted, these poor images are participatory; they blur the distinction between author and viewer, and undermine the social hierarchies implicit in that distinction.

Despite the insight and influence of Steyerl's essay, the validity of its thesis has waned. The quality and resolution of an image now depends on its platform, not its origin. Since 2012 vast quantities of photographs and films have been scanned, uploaded, enhanced, upscaled, and colorized. In many countries, including the United States, smartphones have become such a crucial aspect of everyday life that the vast majority of people now own one.[25] Most image creators can access, create, manipulate, and disseminate high-res images with the same ease as low-res images. The circulatory and participatory aspects of the poor image are now nearly universal to those of any quality. Low resolution does not enable circulation or shared authorship like it once did.

Despite these evolving circumstances, there is an aspect of Steyerl's argument that still holds true. As an aside late in the essay she writes that the poor image "also ends up being perfectly integrated in an information capitalism thriving on compressed attention spans, on impression rather than immersion, on intensity rather than contemplation, on previews rather than screenings."[26] Social media operates at the center of contemporary capitalism, and easy legibility at thumbnail resolution is its currency. Architects, like everyone else, understand the monetary and cultural value of instantaneous legibility. Although low-resolution legibility can be justified through a pursuit of shared reading and collective form, their value in the market of attention, the collection of likes and reposts, remains primary.[27]

At the scale of the smartphone screen, zombie perspective may be indistinguishable from that of analog photography. Closer inspection is required to distinguish between the two. But as Latour and May suggest, technical changes in our visual media have far-reaching implications, and as machine-made images recursively become more like themselves, the differences may grow.

The proliferation of zombie perspective suggests that architects might once again reconsider the fundamentals of representational space. On one hand, the "unkillable" nature of perspective means that the potential of nonperspectival forms of visuality to spark social and ideological transformation, as imagined by El Lissitzky and Van Doesburg, is lost. Instead we have a visuality that concretizes the conventions of photography while allowing them to be manipulated by corporations and governments. On the other hand, pictorial space can also be manipulated and analyzed by artists and architects. Perspective can be the subject of critical study, artistic production, and architectural invention in new ways. If architectural photography was the model for photorealistic rendering and the poor image led to parti-ism, how can zombie perspective inform contemporary architectural representation? How can we unpack seamless collages masquerading as photographs? How can we foreground the machine-mediated nature of contemporary visuality? How might the possibilities of machine mediation allow us to reconsider representational conventions like perspective? And how will space making in the physical world be affected by the ambiguous and plastic space of machine-made imagery? As Steyerl writes in the context of vertical perspective, "Only now can new and different sorts of spatial vision be created."[28]

---

1. Weighing the impact of the changed technical basis of images, May writes, "As imaging becomes the primary way in which we give meaning to our lives, the specific content of each individual image becomes less meaningful, bending toward meaningless." (John May, "Everything Is Already an Image," *Log* 40 (Spring/Summer 2017): 25.) Price argues for reworking existing images as readymades: "With more and more media readily available through this unruly archive [the Internet], the task becomes one of packaging, producing, reframing, and distributing." (Seth Price, "Dispersion," originally written in 2002 and adapted in 2016, http://www.distributedhistory.com/Dispersion2016.pdf, 8.) More recently, in response to the role of vast image datasets in machine vision, Adrian MacKenzie and Anna Munster coined the term *platform seeing* to describe contemporary modes of nonrepresentational observation: "Collections of images operate within and help form a field of distributed *invisuality* in which relations between images count more than any indexicality or iconicity of an image." (Adrian Mackenzie and Anna Munster, "Platform Seeing: Image Ensembles and Their Invisualities," *Theory, Culture & Society* 36, no. 5 (June 2019): 18.)
2. Yve-Alain Bois, "Metamorphosis of Axonometry," *Daidalos* 1 (1981): 42.
3. Robin Evans provides a one-page synopsis of this evolving critique, from Maurice Merleau-Ponty to Jacques Lacan to Michel Foucault, in *The Projective Cast: Architecture and Its Three Geometries* (Cambridge, MA: MIT Press, 1995), 125.
4. Hito Steyerl, "In Free Fall: A Thought on Vertical Perspective," in *The Wretched of the Screen* (Berlin: Sternberg Press, 2012), 24.
5. May, "Everything," 13.
6. Erwin Panofsky, *Perspective as Symbolic Form*, trans. Christopher S. Wood (New York: Zone Books 1991).
7. Evans, *Projective Cast*, 125.
8. See Apple's 2019 patent for deep learning-based image fusion, https://patents.justia.com/patent/11151702.
9. See Shih-Syun Lin, I-Cheng Yeh, Chao-Hung Lin, and Tong-Yee Lee, "Patch-Based Image Warping for Content-Aware Retargeting," *IEEE Transactions on Multimedia* 15, no. 2 (February 2013); and Mantang Guo, Jing Jin, Hui Liu, Junhui Hou, Huanqiang Zeng, and Jiwen Lu, "Content-aware Warping for View Synthesis" *arXiv* (January 2022).
10. See https://laion.ai/blog/laion-aesthetics.
11. Researchers have simulated the "model collapse" caused by a recursive cycle of AI models trained on AI-generated content. The result is both less varied output and a phenomenon where the models "start misinterpreting what they believe to be real, by reinforcing their own beliefs." See Ilia Shumailov, Zakhar Shumaylov, Yiren Zhao, Yarin Gal, Nicolas Papernot, and Ross Anderson, "The Curse of Recursion: Training on Generated Data Makes Models Forget," *arXiv* (May 2023).
12. Bernard Stiegler, *Technics and Time, 1: The Fault of Epimetheus* (Redwood City, CA: Stanford University Press, 1998), ix.
13. May, "Everything," 17.
14. Bruno Latour, "Visualization and Cognition: Thinking with Eyes and Hands," *Knowledge and Society: Studies in the Sociology of Culture Past and Present* 6 (1986): 4.
15. Latour cites William M. Ivins Jr.'s *On the Rationalization of Sight* (New York: Metropolitan Museum of Art, 1938). Latour, "Visualization."
16. Latour, "Visualization," 6.
17. Evans, *Projective Cast*, 344.
18. Kathleen James, "Expressionism, Relativity, and the Einstein Tower," *Journal of the Society of Architectural Historians* 53, no. 4 (December 1994): 398.
19. James, "Expressionism," 406.
20. See Greg Lynn, "Multiplicitous and In-Organic Bodies," *Assemblage* 19 (December 1992).
21. Lynn, "Multiplicitous," 38.
22. Edmund Husserl used the term "anexact" to describe geometry that is measurable and internally rigorous, but irreducible to abstract types like the circle or square.
23. The term is taken from a project presentation at Yale School of Architecture in 2021 by then students Jahaan Scipio and Matthew Wilde.
24. Hito Steyerl, "In Defense of the Poor Image," in *The Wretched of the Screen*, 33.
25. In 2021 cellphone ownership was at 97 percent—of which smartphones comprised 85 percent—according to Pew Research Center. See https://www.pewresearch.org/internet/fact-sheet/mobile.
26. Steyerl, "In Defense," 42.
27. See Michael Meredith, "In-difference, Again," *Log* 39 (Winter 2017): 75–80; or Neeraj Bhatia, *New Investigations in Collective Form: The Open Workshop* (New York: Actar, 2019), 21–30.
28. See Steyerl, "Free Fall," 27.

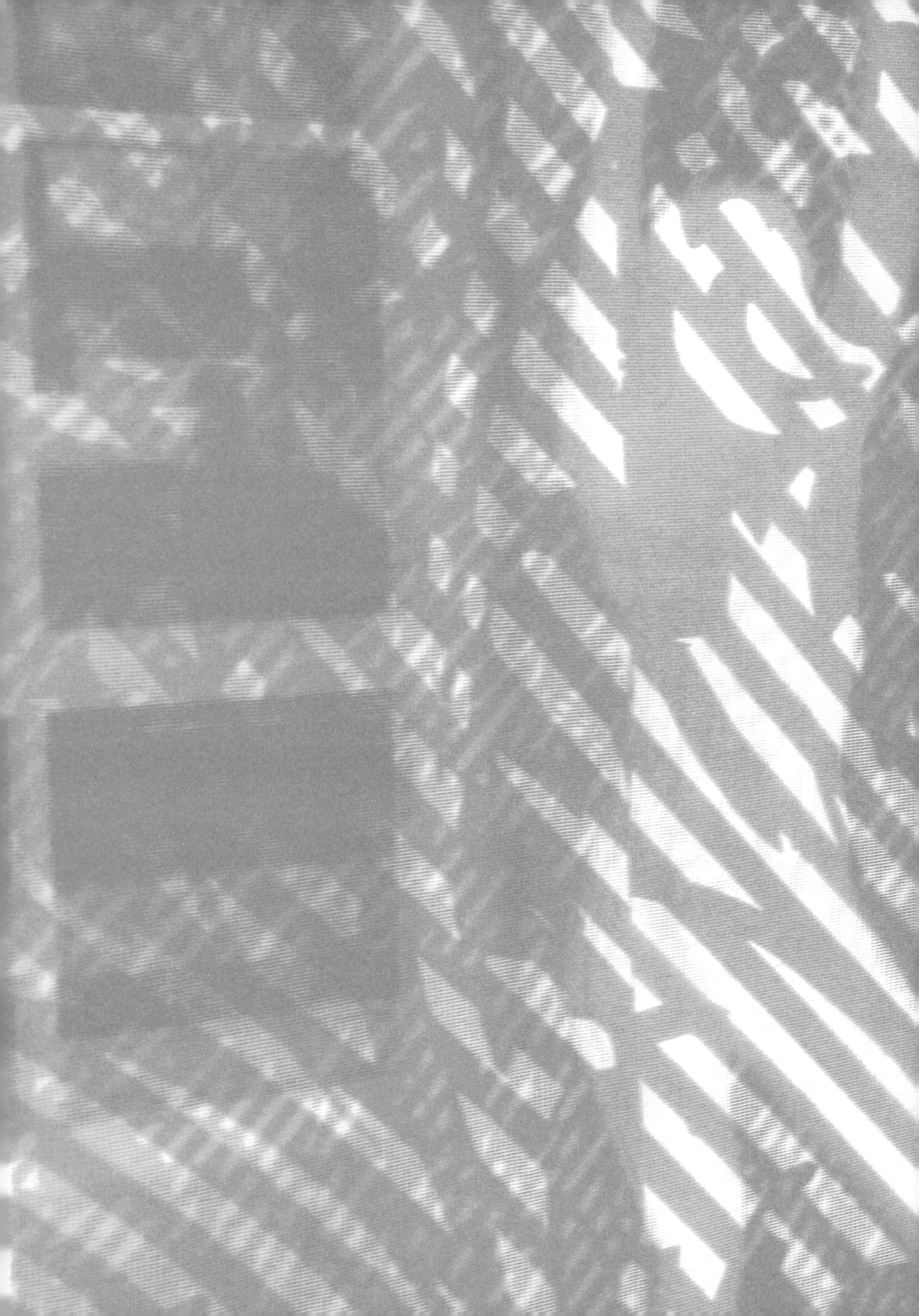

New York University students learning camouflage techniques.

INTRODUCTION

Concealing factories buildings through camouflage during World Wars I and II was aimed to make them imperceptible targets for enemy air raids. The practice later transformed from technological strategies into those that served to hide the labor of workers and their working conditions from view. The materials and design concepts invented for protection during wartime were latently adapted to peacetime applications. Starting with World War I, camouflage rendered factories, towns, roads, and other sensitive areas virtually invisible through stage set-like designs using tarred canvases (tarpaulin) painted to blend in with the surroundings, mesh netting draped across surfaces to appear like landscapes, and fake trees and streets. During World War II the practice of learning camouflage design proliferated in university design departments and Hollywood production studios, where artists used their skills to craft methods of veiling industrial facilities and domiciles from modes of surveillance and attack. The architecture literature discusses materials developed during this time that became domesticated, including plastics, glass blocks, and plywood.[1] Yet little research has been completed on more holistic design ideas for factory buildings that came out of the construction and building sector during wartime, such as blackout windows, air-conditioning, infill panel wall insulation, and fluorescent lighting. These architectural tropes resulted in the factory being hidden from view, the interior concealed behind blank shed walls, making workers disappear from quotidian life into a distinct heterotopia.

CONCEALING PRODUCTION THROUGH ARCHITECTURAL ORNAMENT

In the late nineteenth and early twentieth centuries, concealing the factory typology was the norm, but for a different purpose—the factory was to be a "good neighbor" even as it spewed smoke. Companies hid production facilities behind ornamental facades, as though dressing them in costumes related to the product theme. In the mode of the spectacle factory,[2] companies hid behind decorative facades and ornamental elements to integrate with the streetscape. Breweries took on Germanic castle-like designs, eclectic Italianate styles with turrets and crenellations, and what was called Teutonic style—for example, the Tivoli Union Brewery, in Denver; the Kreuger Brewing Co., in Newark; and the Milwaukee Brewery. Shipyards and armament companies in Boston and Watervliet, New York, also employed the style, serving as attractions for their communities.[3]

Striving to be anything *but* a factory, the Yenidze tobacco and cigarette factory in Dresden was built in 1907 out of reinforced concrete, granite, and concrete block. The company imported its tobacco from Yenidze, in the Greek region of Thrace, and adopted the name. The design, by Martin Hammitzsch, includes mosque-like elements such as polychrome minarets for chimneys and an onion-shaped dome, decorated with tile and stained glass and encircled by arched windows in a drum, housing a tasting room. The ornate composition arose to meet the city's requirement for a decorative factory that would integrate with the historic area. Another example, the Samson Uniroyal Tire Factory, designed by architect Stiles O. Clements in 1930, was inspired by the Assyrian Palace of King Sargon II, from 7 BCE. Constructed in cast concrete complete with lions, crenellations, and papyrus bas-reliefs, it was like a Hollywood stage set that concealed the production process. As an element of the new automotive highway landscape, it brashly announced its tire production as a marketing attraction.

EARLY FACTORY CAMOUFLAGE

During World War I and II the idea of concealment manifested a different meaning. Aircraft factories jumped scales on suburban sites, becoming massive industrial "territories" covering millions of square feet. In densely populated urban areas, factories were sequestered not only from potential air attacks but from the larger population for security reasons. This concealment was not just for aesthetics or for fitting in to a community but for wartime emergency and the threat of aerial attacks, during Nazi raids in Europe and the later against potential Japanese strikes in the United States.

New methods of camouflage emerged in France during World War I that went beyond dressing soldiers in green-and-beige garb to blend with the landscape to hiding potential targets such as buildings and roads. The French applied research on animal patterning to develop tarpaulins, leaf-covered nets, and rooftop designs.[4] The word *camoufler* (to disguise) described the methods employed by Gerald Thayer, Rockwell Kent, Grant Wood, Jacques Villon, and other artists to disguise objects and buildings by painting materials and props to foil the enemy. Working to create trompe l'oeil-style optical illusions, they rendered three-dimensional objects on two-dimensional surfaces, as did Cubists such as Georges Braques and Paul Cézanne, leading to dazzle painting in 1917.[5] The science of camouflage borrowed from the arts, employing methods such as *blending* (merging with the background); *disruptive patterning* (mixing up the design); *countershading* (making an object look flat through the use of shadows on different sides); and *mimicry* (making something look like something else). The effectiveness of these techniques inspired the French[6] and British[7] militaries to establish camouflage regiments that followed these standards in 1915 and '16.

EDUCATION AND PRACTICE OF CAMOUFLAGE

During World War II numerous automotive and home-goods factories were converted from peacetime to wartime production through the U.S. War Production Board, so camouflage design had to cover vast expanses of aircraft, tank, and weaponry production sites.[8] Continuing WWI camouflage methods in England, war departments wrote training manuals on ways to make runways appear like the natural landscape with fake agricultural field markings and forests made of wood board, burlap, netting, fabric ribbons woven in nets, fishing nets, and chicken wire by artists. These artists and architects completed in-depth camouflage design courses for their military service at architecture schools such as the Department of Architecture at Pratt Institute and New York University and at Hollywood set design studios. Artist Arshile Gorky organized a course at the Grand Central School of Art.[9] György Kepes and László Moholy-Nagy taught a course at the School of Design in Chicago, using studies in optics and depth-of-surface patterns taken from both scientific studies and modern artistic methods.[10]

CONCEALING FACTORIES BY DESIGN

Architect Konrad F. Wittmann wrote an article on camouflage in the September 1940 edition of *Architectural Record*, followed by the *Industrial Camouflage Manual* (1942), based on investigations he conducted while developing courses at Pratt Institute on camouflage techniques for architects using numerous scenarios for students through drawings and model photographs.[11] The manual describes town organization and building placement while focusing on industrial layouts and sites. Shifting the perception of the built environment from the ground to the air, he pointed out issues of visibility related to conspicuous forms made by identifiable lines, shadows, reflections, obvious bulls-eyes,

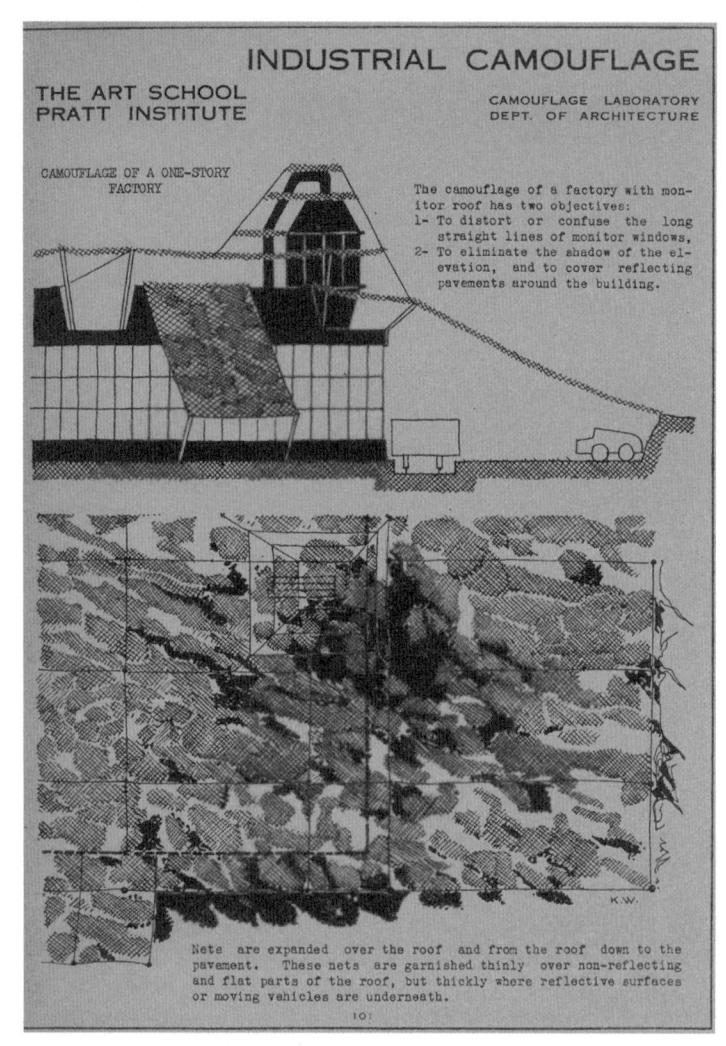

Sections of the *Industrial Camouflage Manual*, showing how to conceal factories with monitor roofs that project above the roof line and how to camouflage the factory complex so it blends with the landscape.

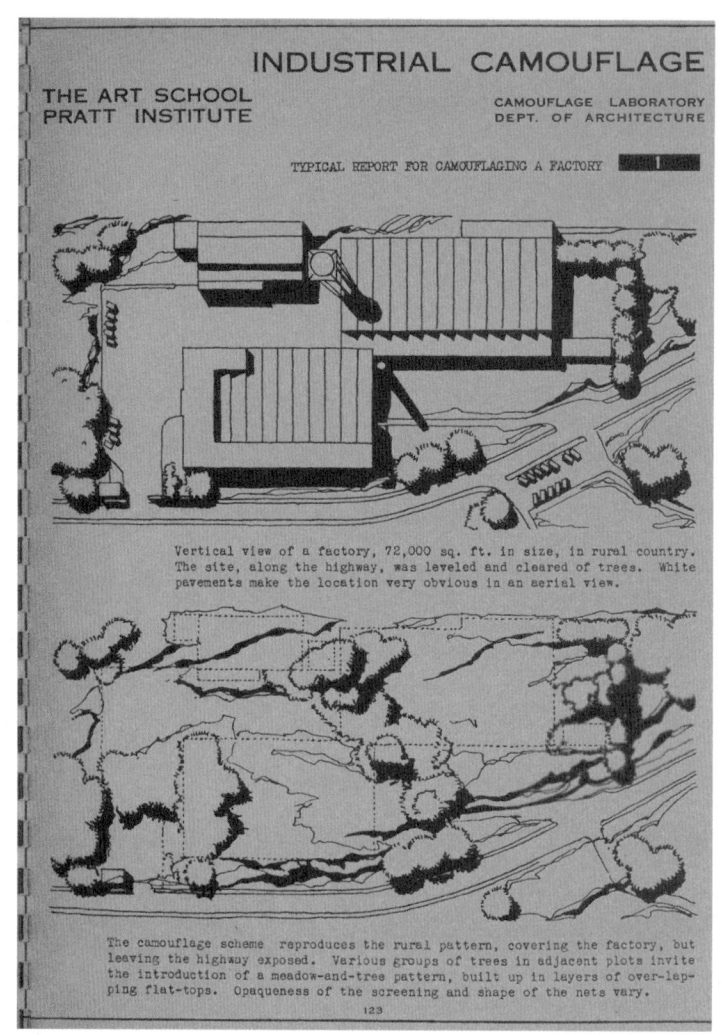

arteries, and orientation, focusing on ways to disperse factories and place them randomly askew so as not to give away the production line inside. With increased technical data on bombardment strategies, the designers understood warfare's physical impact, instituting a war-directed urban spatial practice with new three-dimensional visual perception analysis to create decoys.

The innovative Modernist characteristics of the factory typology as designed by Walter Gropius, Le Corbusier, Erich Mendelsohn, Mies van der Rohe, Owen Williams, Albert Kahn, and Leendert van der Vlugt, among others—with elements such as large windows, curtain walls, skylights, flat roofs, white facades, abstracted forms, concrete mushroom columns, and railroads leading right into the buildings—were the antithesis of those employed in the wartime emergency. Instead the scenarios called for darkening the buildings' windows with blackout panels, using artificial fluorescent light, dispersing factory buildings, and adding screens and nets—essentially softening the factory design with coverings or hardening them with additional surface material. They recommended using patterns from nature for the rooftops, roads, and outbuildings to make the factories even less conspicuous and concealing them in nearby forests to merge with the contours of the landscape. The Wittmann manual primarily addressed factories existing in isolation, which just by their sheer scale revealed to the enemy what was occurring under the massive roofscapes. New techniques of visual trickery such as dispersal, curves, nature, and shadow mimicking became absorbed into designs for postwar industrial buildings as the next generation of factory designs, with larger ramifications in the landscape than only wartime reorganization.

Dispersal

At this time the most efficient factory was built under one roof, but here they called for the dispersal of buildings, which had been dismissed previously in industrial planning. Wartime camouflage design called for separating production volumes, so that if one building was bombed it would not affect the entire site. Power and water supply would be separated and production segmented into tasks by building unit, altering the factory's streamlined organization. The design included open layouts, access to roads, buildings arranged in sequence, small streets with buildings, parking in the woods, and "fast-growing" trees. Drawings highlighted separate buildings removed from railroad lines and spaces between buildings through which the goods would have to be shuttled. In the late nineteenth and early twentieth centuries industrial engineers discouraged the "pushing" of goods between spaces because it delayed manufacturing schedules, yet for wartime it was considered a strategy for security and as camouflage.

Curves and Nature

The guidelines promoted various forms for decoys, including "curved shapes that distort the rigid geometry of light and shadow." For example, an eave projecting beyond the

INDUSTRIAL CAMOUFLAGE
THE ART SCHOOL PRATT INSTITUTE — CAMOUFLAGE LABORATORY, DEPT. OF ARCHITECTURE

SUGGESTIONS FOR INDUSTRIAL CAMOUFLAGE DESIGN
Sawtooth Roofs

Camouflage of saw-tooth roof of older type, with horizontal slabs placed several feet above the roof, and at different angles to the roof.

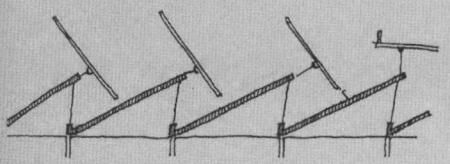

Saw-tooth roof of newer type with protected, non-reflecting windows. Slabs are placed to simulate small homes.
By use of this method, the reduction of light is at a minimum.

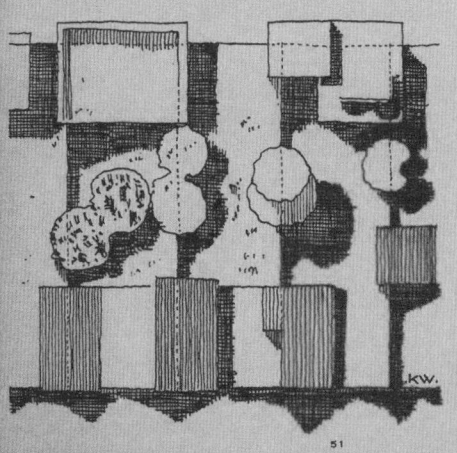

Aerial view of camouflaged saw-tooth roof.
Application of slabs of different sizes, shapes, and textures, to give the appearance of small homes with flat and pitched roofs, trees, and back yards.

Solid constructions are, as a rule, brought down to existing supports or bearing walls. Sectional scaffolding may be used to cover wider spans. The construction should be movable in order to facilitate adjustments during the course of the year.

INDUSTRIAL CAMOUFLAGE
THE ART SCHOOL PRATT INSTITUTE — CAMOUFLAGE LABORATORY, DEPT. OF ARCHITECTURE

PRINCIPLES OF INDUSTRIAL CAMOUFLAGE
Texture of Roofs

Roofs which are planted with grass, or even with small shrubs can match their surroundings almost entirely, under all weather and light conditions.

Surrounding with trees gives better concealment and natural irregularity of light and shadow. Trees play an important part in the design of natural camouflage.

Vertical, irregular slabs, or horizontal slabs, elevated several feet, cast irregular shadows to distort the monotony of large roofs. Gravel, cinders, and stones of light-weight, porous concrete give rough texture.

INDUSTRIAL CAMOUFLAGE
THE ART SCHOOL PRATT INSTITUTE — CAMOUFLAGE LABORATORY, DEPT. OF ARCHITECTURE

NATURAL CONCEALMENT

Use of a wooded, hilly, and multiform landscape for dispersed lay-out of industrial plants. Various types of concealment are possible when buildings use or imitate clearings in the forest, merge with the contours of the wood, simulate the parallel lines of a field, or are stepped down on a hillside. A variety of different camouflage schemes, appropriate to different landscape formations, makes recognition of a particular target much more difficult.

1- Low hangars, fitted into the rural pattern, with administration buildings and workshops under trees.
2- One-story building, with dark roof, filling the edge of a wood.
3- Factory buildings with sawtooth and clerestory windows parallel to field lines, using trees for side protection.
4- Low buildings, filling a clearing, imitating cultivated land or camouflaged like a wood.
5- Water tower, pump house, smoke exhaust, storage buildings along a hillside.
6- River with crossing beams, prepared for covering of water reflections.

Sections of the *Industrial Camouflage Manual*, showing how to hide the all-telling sawtooth roofs, how to cover a flat roof with landscape and forms, and potential for factory placement in the landscape.

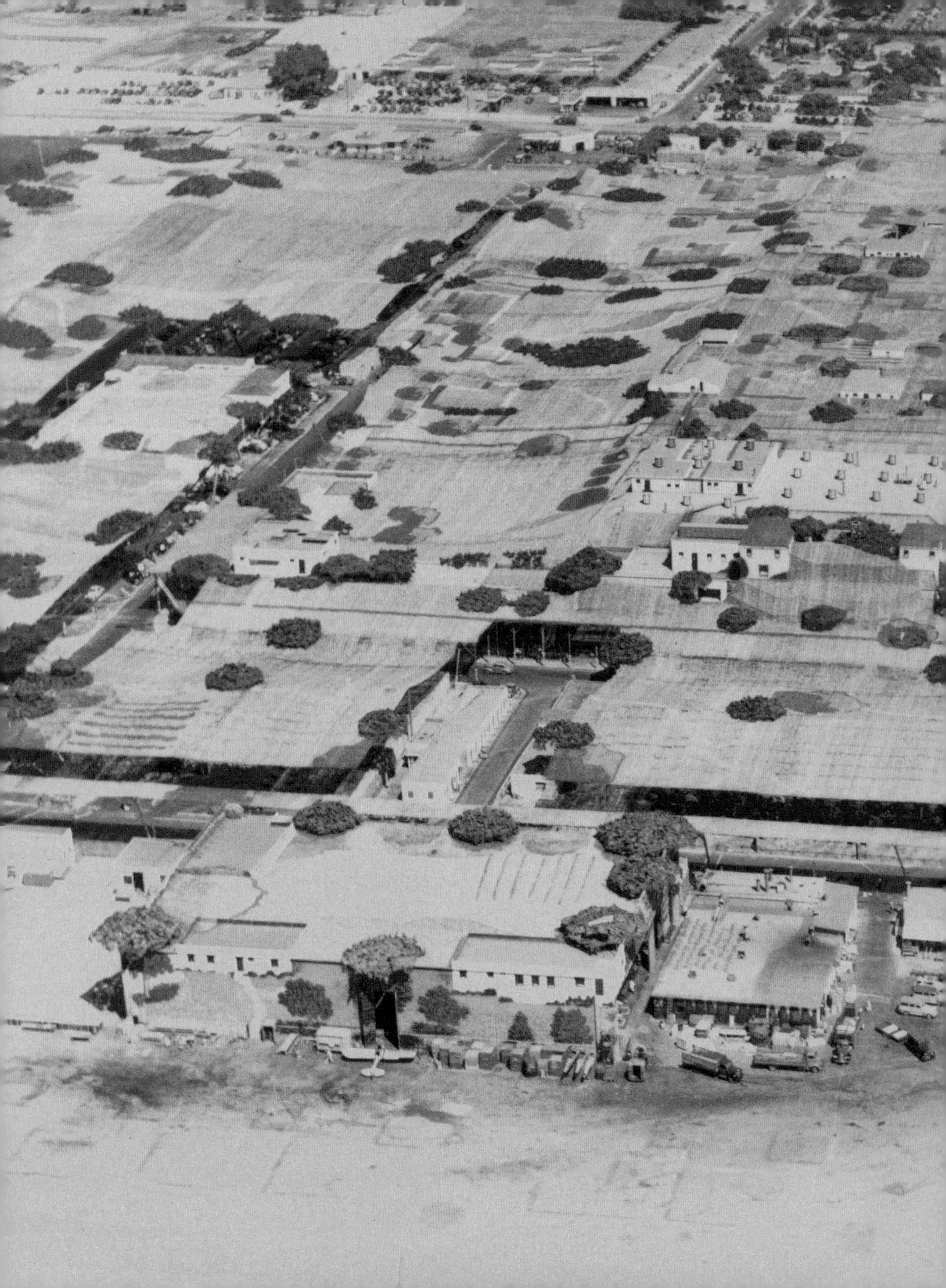

Lockheed Martin camouflage of factory complex, Burbank, Los Angeles, 1941.

Lockheed Martin, closer view of camouflage of factory complex, Burbank, Los Angeles, 1941.

NEW WARTIME CONSTRUCTION

While the superficial temporary camouflage elements, the faux layers, were removed or recycled, the idea of concealing production processes persisted, changing the design for factory buildings for future decades often not even designed by architects. The elements that endured in these behemoth structures beyond WWII included blackout windows, shatterproof glass, stone wool insulation, air-conditioning, and fluorescent lighting, and they were absorbed into industrial construction standards. Stripped of the aesthetics of the eclectic factories of the late nineteenth century and the Modernist structures of the early twentieth century, the new designs focused on speed, new technologies, and materials, along with the saving of essential materials such as steel, copper, and other metals. The wartime factories were designed primarily by firms such as Albert Kahn; Smith, Hinchman & Grylls; Ballinger & Co.; H.K. Ferguson; and Austin Co. engineers, which became the purveyors of these new systems.

The one-story shed was the dominant form since it was faster to build and easier to conceal, with an uninterrupted windowless space under one roof. A 1949 *Architectural Record* essay titled "Industrial Buildings Back the Attack" described how steel was necessary for strong and quick construction, but when it became a "critical" material many factories shifted to wood or lighter-weight metals.[14] A factory designed by Albert Kahn for American Steel Foundries was structured as an adaptable blackout plant with a perimeter rail placed above the windows, from which boards or shields could be hung if necessary. Kahn's 1940 design for the Chrysler Tank Arsenal, near Detroit, required maximum flexibility in the large, open spaces of a single-story structure; there was no time for aesthetics in the enclosed sealed box since the first tank was produced before the building was even finished.[15] The factory still had plenty of windows, and its performative shed structure was a feat in terms of the amount of space it created, but it was stripped of an aesthetic agenda.

Guidelines for architects noted that "manufacturing processes may demand a windowless plant, in which air, light, and sound are maintained at optimum conditions for continuous manufacturing."[16] Although the daylit factory with operable windows still had advantages for the production of consumer goods, the sealed shed supported fast-paced armament manufacturing around the clock. The War Production Board recommended the use of panels to cover factory windows so that the light was not visible from the air and military operations remained concealed. Advertisements in architectural magazines touted the potential for windowless factories to make workers more productive since they had no views. There were no windows to clean, the spaces stayed cleaner, and there was no need for shading devices. Because of the war effort this seclusion didn't seem to bother the workers. Rooftop light monitors

building's roof that cast a curved shadow adjacent to the factory was thought to mimic shadows in nature, making the form ambiguous. Additions of structures and protruding shapes as well as irregular outlines would make a roof textured. Seen as a "fringe," the curved contour would conceal the rigid industrial form. The landscape also became an important tool for hiding reality. Just as we hide cell-phone towers with treelike costumes today, factory chimneys were covered with cables and nets to look like trees and lines painted on wood surfaces created rural field patterns. Roofs donned sculptural shapes that dissolved the building into an irregular curvilinear pattern, allowing the factory to adapt to the hinterlands even during peacetime. The factory would blend in with the landscape—the trees, shrubs, weeds, rocks, and rugged terrain.

Shadow Mimicking

Numerous shadow studies by students at Pratt Institute and other schools with camouflage courses used architectural models and site-related lighting conditions to see how industrial elements such as smokestacks would be easily identified from the air. Drawing and modeling techniques created "shadow confusion," blurring the outline or volumes of an industrial building to hide them, or so it was thought.[12] All of these experiments went untested.

Some of the best-known factories employing camouflage were those on the West Coast that were altered after Pearl Harbor, including Martin Marietta, Lockheed Martin, and Douglas Aircraft Co. in Santa Monica, as well as Boeing plants in Seattle. The strategy was to create a suburban neighborhood over the factory with burlap and netting painted to look like sidewalks, small shed construction for houses, and fake trees and shrubs. These were constructed in collaboration with Hollywood set designers. Colonel John Ohmer spearheaded the project at the Burbank factory of Lockheed Martin, working with local artists and film set designers to invent elaborate constructions such as underground tunnels and walkways that would make the structure appear to be part of a suburban neighborhood when seen from above.[13]

and sawtooth skylights were covered with layers of netting and enhanced with textures or nonreflective paint. Architect Albert Kahn recommended what he called the "victory sash," where windows were loosely tied to the structural frame and fitted with clips so that owners could repair or replace them in case of bombing. These seem pointless when we look back, considering the pervasive threat of nuclear attack. After the atom bomb most of it seemed naive until ground wars became dominant again today.

When Austin Co. engineers designed two 4,000-foot-long bomber factories for Douglas Aircraft in Fort Worth, Texas, and Tulsa, Oklahoma, with Truscon steel and Owens Corning fiberglass, they insulated them with 65-foot-high steel sidewalls and roofs to keep out noise, heat, and cold. The insulation made the air-conditioning perform more effectively and, as a result, the workers were more productive. It was also used as blackout paneling, performing two functions at once. The idea of controlled interior climate had started earlier, with the invention of Freon. Developed by Willis Carrier for a publishing house in Brooklyn around 1902 and used by other industries, primarily to add moisture rather than for cooling, air-conditioning became standard in homes and factories by the mid-twentieth century. Along with blackout windows and fluorescent lighting, air-conditioning was essential in the hermetically sealed wartime factories.

Fluorescent lighting took a long time to be adapted to the private realm but was quickly installed in blackout factories. Produced by General Electric, fluorescent lights used one-fourth the electricity required by filament lamps. Fluorescent lighting allowed factory workers to enjoy equal light coverage that is cool and dispersed rather than uneven, as is the natural light emitted by monitors or skylights, previously the factory norm. White fiberglass walls and white-painted concrete floors allowed for more light reflection, creating a brighter space for evening factory shifts. Painted with a color called "Medusa white," surfaces could diffuse and reflect light. Ample light meant both better comfort and increased production levels.

The Douglas Aircraft Company installed 17,000 two-tube GE fluorescent units on the high-bay ceilings of its factories in Southern California. The 35 air-conditioned plants at Long Beach had 8,000 mercury vapor lamps and 15,000 fluorescent lamps.[17] A windowless Ordinance Plant designed by Rust Engineering, with a 300-foot-long facade and only one main doorway for natural light, eliminated monitor windows to facilitate 24-hour operation and efficient air-conditioning.

Postwar Staying Power

The construction technologies developed during WWII influenced a new factory design standard in the ubiquitous shed, for both factories and other commercial facilities. Since design and material trends took time to be adopted, even after being so thoroughly developed during the war, many of the techniques had staying power in factory designs. The new vernacular factory shed became co-opted by big-box stores, shopping malls, and logistics centers. Instant sheds constructed from prefabricated parts were available as early as 1919. The Truscon Steel Company produced kit-of-parts metal shed systems that allowed for flexible manufacturing solutions, requiring large open spaces for industry and infrastructure, whose widespread use accelerated after the war. Concrete precast wall panels used for cladding and load-bearing walls could easily be lifted into place on-site; prefabricated metal panels could clip into place, and fiber cement could be arranged to overlap, creating air spaces. Load-bearing wall panels meant even longer spans and wider spaces. In contrast to the grid-framed concrete and glazed Modernist factory, prefabricated sheds became standardized with cladding wrapped around the machinery rather than responding to a specific method, material production, or factory flow, thus hiding the production system. Succumbing to the design poverty inherent in their generic qualities, the buildings were not even "decorated" sheds, although it allowed for adaptability, flexibility, and cost savings in ever-changing production lines.

Workers

The blackout shed plants made for efficient factories, both in terms of time and money, and for speeding up the assembly line. But the lack of daylight lowered worker morale during postwar production. There were reports of workers creating peepholes and throwing wrenches through the opaque windows for outside views. The fluorescent lighting was thought to be better for precision work[18] because of its even light quality, but high air-conditioning costs had to be taken into consideration. After such appealing wartime workplace standards, worker satisfaction in postwar factories was a prime consideration, and companies were urged to improve conditions on the plant floor, and in locker rooms and cafeterias.[19] The growing independence of labor, along with the spacious mechanized factory buildings fostered by competition between companies, inspired a more pleasant work environment. Some factories compromised by providing natural light and ventilation through an eye-level band of windows, using air-conditioning for humidity and temperature control.[20]

PROCESS REMOVAL

Expansive infrastructure distribution networks—the freeways built during wartime—encouraged suburban growth and industrial displacement from cities, dispersing the once compact urban factory system and production processes farther away from central urban cores. The act of making was distanced from people and central hubs in what I call "process removal," so that no one could see how things were being made or how workers were being treated.[21] Factories and workers became sequestered from daily urban life, a phenomenon reinforced by new zoning regulations for industrial districts, leading to the separation of work and living. The separation of uses began in the early twentieth century—first through land-use ordinances, followed by legal cases such as the 1926 Village of Euclid v. Ambler Reality Co.—to enforce the removal of nuisances such as industrial pollution from areas of homes and schools. Promoted by the Congrès Internationaux d'Architecture Moderne (CIAM) in the interest of the efficient and functional city that was to separate work, play, transportation, and living, these principles resulted in long commutes, fractured communities, and disenfranchised residents. Few of the factories that had moved away from cities for wartime defense would return. Henry Ford abandoned his factories in Detroit's Highland Park, and failed companies like Packard left behind empty shells, eroding not only jobs but the economic base of the city.

In the 1990s Western companies moved even farther away from the local workforce to Mexico and China, encouraged by NAFTA and other free-trade agreements, developing industrial parks and Export Processing Zones, and maquiladoras where outsource contract companies ignored workers' rights and amenities. It both reduced jobs in the United States and alienated the new workforce in China. Workers at the Foxconn factories, for example, didn't even know that they were making iPads, and their rigorous work schedule and living in company dormitories away from family and friends led to many suicides in 2012.

The factory building designed by architects is no longer a valuable commodity when a fish-production firm decides to use a refrigerator box and a shed next to it for workers to complete processing. Factories such as a 2,500-acre Tesla plant in Texas are given incentives to locate their

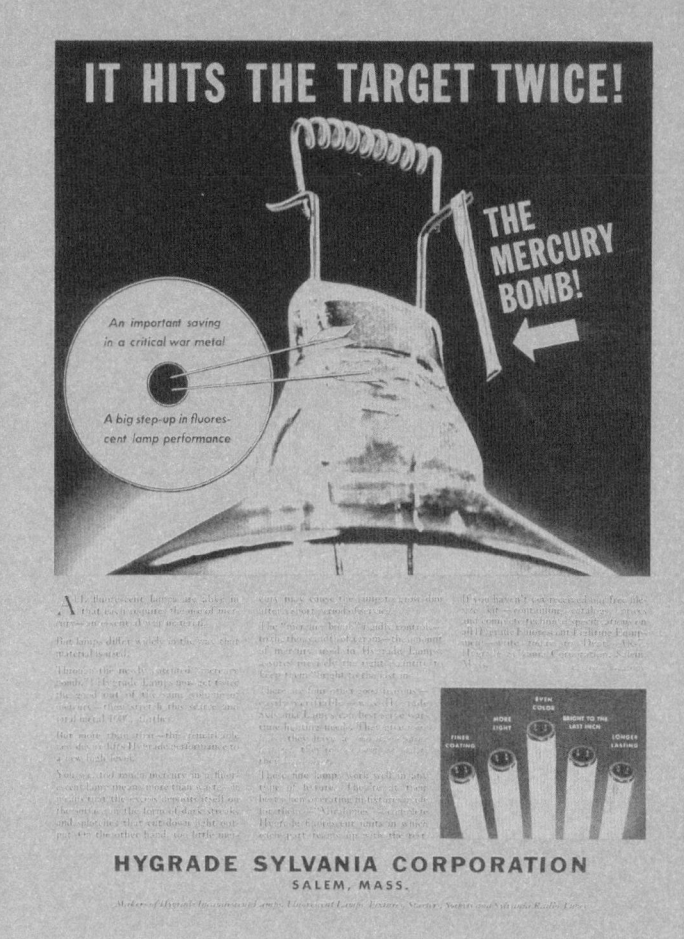

Advertisements for glass block to conceal a typical factory, flourescent lights with minimal use of mercury, an essential wartime material, Cemesto fast-paced construction to cover a factory wall, and for the "windowless factory" with its use of freon for air-conditioning, as an advantage in manufacturing, in *Architectural Record*, July 1942.

facilities in places without any relationship to the community or guarantees of jobs for the local workforce, and they contribute to environmental destruction at thousands of work sites over millions of greenfields.

The Ubiquitous Shed

The idea of the rational shed derived from the need for wartime camouflage as well as production efficiency is considered a universal, generic space in which anything can occur.[22] It became the favored space for factories, logistics centers, and retail companies like Walmart and Amazon, among many other commercial ventures.[23] Inside, the instruments of commerce could be arranged and rearranged in the interest of profitability. Airplane-production workers assemble large flying machines with parts brought to the main plane framework from separate facilities. The plane emerges in one place in an enclosed space, while smaller products like cars or bicycles are assembled along a production line, rotating and sliding along conveyors and going from hand to hand, robot to hand, and even robot to robot. The interiors of these shed spaces are versatile and mobile without any consideration for the worker, resulting in yet another form of camouflage.

Workers are often arranged and rearranged as well stationary at their appointed stations, not always aware of what they are making by putting pieces together, as in Charlie Chaplin's spoof on the mechanization that took command of labor, *Modern Times*. As consumers we don't see who gets reprimanded for poor performance or who is praised for a job well done. We don't see the toxic chemicals that workers dip their hands into or smell the fumes emitting from the glue used to assemble sneakers. For the factory owner the shed is a kind of camouflage—a suite of cladding draped over the box concealing a space where anything can happen. In the early 2000s, as industry boomed and free trade globalized the world, the box became a shield to hide poor labor practices in China, as Paul Midler has pointed out. Factories hid workers away even more purposefully when contract negotiators came to visit and inspect the workplaces for labor practices often in a Potemkin Village-like factory.[24]

However, the idea of the factory in a box—which then became the "big box," the typical shed with interior gridded columns or clear span structural systems—was embraced by numerous companies and their architects. First the interior becomes a place of networked technologies, production processes, assembly-line configurations, and infrastructures normally designed by companies and their industrial engineers. The exterior is a surface used by companies for marketing and image-making, creating an identity among the sea of sheds along highways through vertical facades or the horizontal fifth facade, the roof, visible from the air. Following the ideas of Robert Venturi and Denise Scott Brown's "decorated shed," or their concept of the contrast between the mitten and the glove, the factory is either a sealed box (the mitten) or an articulated volume whose mechanization is visible to the exterior (the glove). Not to deride the idea or approach of decorating the shed, but in the framework of labor this design identity aids a company's rhetoric promoting "good" design while perhaps not maintaining "good" labor practices.

The box challenged architects to find design opportunities for "generic" buildings that express character in details such as innovative cladding, called the "envelope," and structural systems that support broad open-span spaces, such as in the 1961 Reliance Control factory (Team 4, Foster and Rogers). Articulated roofscapes and skylights often create variegated surfaces and innovative compositions beyond a standard sealed-box form. The box as a repetitive module methodically extends the space, as in the 1962 Siag Factory, in Caserta, Italy, designed by Angelo Mangiarotti as a series of concrete frames from which the wall modules appear to be hung and articulated vertically by the arched beams.[25]

The contemporary factories designed by Barkow Leibinger Architekten for the machine tool and laser manufacturer Trumpf feature a series of variations on a theme to articulate the facades, like accordion and origami forms, unusual window apertures, and triangular roof skylights, while the interior is a continuous volume. The most extreme example of camouflage is the Aplix Factory, by Dominique Perrault, which vanishes in its "pleated" mirrored stainless-steel box, blending with the landscape by reflecting the light and the sky, and with it the work inside vanishes. The spaces result in a process removal as the factory is hidden from view.

Unlike many downtown corporate offices, where workers' movements can be seen through windows at dusk, the factory facade is often an impenetrable blank wall. The removal of workers from the city and its environs has distanced them from society. Factories become societies in and of themselves, like heterotopias, where the physical environments confine the people working within them and inequality can be perpetuated. This in turn contributes to the invisibility of the production process and the people who make things, all camouflaged from society. As factory jobs have moved from urban cores, the lower-income workers are unable to follow. They have no funds to move house and often no transportation to take them to a new factory location, and they don't have access to opportunities for educational training in advanced manufacturing. As our cities deindustrialize, economic opportunities are lost, even as workers strike and often receive their demands.

So we continue to ask, Where are the workers with their lunch boxes? What is the environment like where they work? Do they have pride in what they make? We don't often know since they are increasingly alienated and just as hidden away as they were during wartime.

1. For an excellent essay on the topic of wartime construction, see Joel Davidson, "Building for War, Preparing for Peace," in *World War II and the American Dream*, ed. Donald Albrecht (Washington, D.C.: National Building Museum; and Cambridge, MA: MIT Press, 1995), 185–225.
2. See Nina Rappaport, "The Consumption of Production," *Praxis* 5 (2003): 58–64; and Nina Rappaport, *Vertical Urban Factory* (Barcelona: Actar, 2015), 342–68.
3. Louis Bergeron and Maria Teresa Maiullari-Pontois, *Industry, Architecture, and Engineering: American Ingenuity, 1750–1950* (New York: Harry N. Abrams, 2000), 212.
4. See Abbott H. Thayer, "The Law Which Underlies Protective Coloration," *The Auk* 13, no. 4 (October 1896): 318–20; and "Concealing-Coloration in the Animal Kingdom: An Exposition of the Laws of Disguise through Color and Pattern" (New York: Macmillan Co., 1909).
5. Roy R. Behrens, "The Role of Artists in Ship Camouflage During World War 1," *Leonardo* 32, no. 1 (1999): 53–59.
6. Roy R. Behrens, "On Visual Art and Camouflage," *Leonardo* 11, no. 3 (1978): 203–4. See also Jean-Louis Cohen, *Architecture in Uniform* (New Haven: Yale University Press, 2011), 187–219.
7. *Military Engineer* 33, no. 188 (March-April 1941): 144–50.
8. Davidson, "Building for War Preparing for Peace."
9. Behrens, "On Visual Art and Camouflage."
10. A great deal has been written about artists and their involvement. For an insightful summary, see Jean-Louis Cohen, *Architecture in Uniform*, 197–200.
11. Konrad F. Wittmann, *Industrial Camouflage Manual* (New York: Reinhold Publishing Co., 1942).
12. Wittmann, this information is from throughout the booklet.
13. "Peace, Prosperity, Peril," *Of Men and Stars* (Burbank, CA: Lockheed Aircraft Corporation, 1957).
14. See *Architectural Record*, "Industrial Buildings Back the Attack," October 1943.
15. Rappaport, *Vertical Urban Factory*, 178.
16. *Architectural Record*, January 1942.
17. *Science News Letter* 40, no. 5 (August 2), 1941.
18. *Architectural Record*, November 1945.
19. *Architectural Record*, December 1946, 157.
20. *Architectural Record*, December 1946.
21. See Rappaport, *Vertical Urban Factory*, 62 and various.
22. See Francesco Marullo, "Typical Plan: The Architecture of Labor and the Space of Production," PhD diss. (Technical University of Delft, 2014).
23. See Jesse LeCavalier, *The Rule of Logistics: Walmart and the Architecture of Fulfillment* (Minneapolis, MN: University of Minnesota Press, 2016).
24. See Paul Midler, *Poorly Made in China* (New York: John Wiley & Sons, 2009).
25. See Francesca Castanò, *Angelo Mangiarotti e la fabbrica SIAG* (Siracusa, Italy: Lettera Ventidue, 2017).

Does capital have memory? Recent scholarship in economic history theorizes capital not as a material good but rather as a process, one whose forward-facing disposition ensures the ongoing accumulation of wealth. Following historian Jonathan Levy, then, capital's essence is time, as the future becomes folded into the present to maintain an inherent logic of expansion.[1] Yet amid the heightened critical focus on the temporality of capital, little attention is given to those moments in the history of capitalism that look backward, not forward, in time.

The nineteenth-century Rothschilds present a compelling case. In the midst of building an unprecedented banking empire that eclipsed the power of any modern state, the Rothschilds commissioned costly works of historicist architecture to align themselves with "grand patrons" of yore—notably the Medicis of early modern Italy. Their retrospective self-image was not unreasonable. By most estimates, the House of Medici and the House of Rothschild each comprised the largest bank and private fortune in Europe during the fifteenth and nineteenth centuries, respectively.[2] And the wealth amassed by both dynastic families enabled their political influence and cultural patronage at magnitudes normally enjoyed by Europe's ruling monarchs.

What kind of historicism did the Rothschilds use to link their rapidly changing capitalist present to the "Renaissance" past—an epoch, to be sure, that acquired its eponymous distinction during the nineteenth century?[3] If there was a historicism specific to the Rothschild family's architecture, scholars have been reluctant to define it. So much is clear in the contrast between the discursive status of the Florentine bankers' Renaissance villas and palazzos—landmarks of early modernity—and the delayed and uneven scholarly reception of the more than fifty private homes across Europe either built or renovated by the international Rothschilds during the long nineteenth century. The reason for the latter's neglect is largely a matter of taste. Distributed in and around the family's five corporate banking capitals of Frankfurt, London, Paris, Vienna, and Naples, their châteaux, villas, and townhouses are typically united under the rubric of *le goût* or *style Rothschild*, labels that describe the family's penchant for mixing heterogeneous styles and opulent décor in a fashion that became a transatlantic paradigm of luxury in Gilded Age America.[4]

The Rothschilds' eclectic sensibility was anathema to architectural-historical methods that for a long time viewed nineteenth-century modernity through a proto-modernist lens. The "Rothschild Style" and "taste" had no place in this schema and were cast aside as regressive, and even risible, frivolous compared to the industrial factories, open-plan market halls, and glazed World's Fair pavilions whose rationalized engineering and unornamented construction offered a cogent prelude to the high modernism of 1920s Europe.[5] Indeed, it wasn't until the reevaluation of historicist architecture in the wake of Postmodernism that historians like Claude Mignot confessed, "we poked fun at the lavish façades of [Baron James de Rothschild's] Château de Ferrières, overlooking the fact that they were pleasing in the eyes of their owners."[6] Nuances in the family's stylistic preferences have thus guided more recent studies of their patronage, albeit without the critique of taste afforded by cultural sociology.[7]

This essay proposes an alternative framework for considering the Rothschild Style as an agent, rather than an outlier, of nineteenth-century modernity and its sweeping upheavals. Shifting attention away from the more familiar processes of nation-state formation and industrialization, the focus here will be on the development of international finance—a field pioneered by the Rothschilds and their innovative practice of issuing and speculating on government bonds that were transferable to foreign markets. Through these and other investments, the family amassed their unprecedented fortune and an international portfolio of richly ornamented and historically referential homes, which rivaled those of the Medicis in their aesthetic ambition, scale, and budget. Yet how do we theorize the relationship between the Rothschilds' financial and aesthetic pursuits?

One could begin by turning to an unexpected source: English cartoonist Osbert Lancaster's *Homes Sweet Homes* (1939), a satirical compendium of domestic interior styles from the Norman Conquest to modernism. There, in a spread devoted to "Le Style Rothschild," a drawing shows a palatial room with heavy upholstery and a frenzy of art objects [Fig. 1]. On the right, a Jewish baron gestures toward his courtly servant, who balances a crystal decanter while stepping into a room replete with "hoards of Dutch pictures, Italian marbles, German glass and what-have-you."[8] Lancaster attributes the Rothschild Style's eclecticism to the grotesque inflation of the "Victorian passion for symbols" associated with the taste of the nineteenth-century financier. Consequently, the symbolic value of art collections was evacuated of historical meaning as they no longer expressed their owner's romantic longing for his or her individual cultural past but instead conveyed said owner's "financial present."[9]

Lancaster suggests that the Rothschild Style interior was devoid of memory and motivated by the accumulation of capital in whatever form it might take. As such, Lancaster's pithy text evokes a determinist reading that would view the Rothschild Style as a vulgar reflection of wealth. Yet this sort of thinking overlooks not only the strategic use of historical reference and allusion in Rothschild Style architecture but also the role those elements played in building and expanding the House of Rothschild in an emerging bourgeois society. Nowhere is this more apparent than in the family's mid-century, neo-Renaissance-style commissions. As will be shown, the Renaissance provided the Rothschilds with a lexicon for self-mythologizing and social exchange by hearkening back to earlier events and figures responsible for societal transformation. The nineteenth-century Rothschilds emphasized these affinities in the iconography of their large-scale private residences, which revived Renaissance notions of grand patronage and Humanist individualism at a time when the Jewish family was enjoying new powers and liberties.

One of this essay's primary tasks is to track how the Rothschilds mobilized Renaissance forms in their architectural commissions to construct a social identity within bourgeois society's field of cultural representation. Yet this opens onto a set of broader questions regarding the use of historicist ornament and decor within the conditions of financial modernity. How is the connective capacity of referential forms—that is to say, their capacity to transmit symbolic meaning, confer status through association, and mediate between spatial and tectonic boundaries—given new currency within the networks of connectivity that support financial circulation and exchange? To be sure, the diffuse and multi-sited nature of these operations far exceeds the physical boundaries of a private residence. To what extent, then, was the family's patronage of domestic interiors an effort to come to terms with, or even actualize, the abstract interiority of their international corporate bank in all its topological complexity? To explore these interrelated concerns, this essay will focus on three Rothschild residences that prominently revived Renaissance forms at the height of the family's mid-century corporate expansion, and in so doing reveal the agency of historical reference in catalyzing the rapid change of the "financial present."

EMBODYING THE RENAISSANCE

Returning once again to Osbert Lancaster's parody of "Le Style Rothschild," one finds in the stereotypical physiognomy of its hook-nosed patron a sobering reminder of the visual tropes of anti-Semitism that haunted Jews in

European bourgeois society. The image thus foregrounds the stakes surrounding the family's patronage of art and architecture—not as mere acts of luxury consumption, but rather as opportunities to construct counter forms of self-representation. This was especially pressing for the observant Rothschilds. The family's very name betrays their humble origins in the Jewish ghetto (*Judengasse*) of Frankfurt-am-Main, where their sixteenth-century forebear Isaak Elchanan acquired the unnumbered house *zum roten Schild* ("at the red shield") that his progeny took as their appellation.[10] The Rothschilds were thus defined by architecture from their earliest recorded history in Frankfurt. Yet if this relationship was originally one of marginalization, it later became a means of crafting alternative narratives to support the family's ascension.

The Rothschilds grew in stature when, in 1764, patriarch Mayer Amschel became a medal and coin dealer in the court of Prince Wilhelm of Hesse-Kassel. His currency business increased during the subsequent decades as the court both financed foreign military efforts and intensified its commodity trading in the wake of the American and French Revolutions.[11] Mayer Amschel's success enabled his entry into banking to expand the family enterprise beyond Frankfurt, thereby laying the foundations for a dynastic international bank. Starting in 1798, he dispatched four of his five sons to Europe's financial capitals to establish new branches for the House of Rothschild while also keeping its services and revenue within the family. As part of this arrangement, the eldest son, Amschel Mayer Rothschild, remained in Frankfurt; third-born Nathan moved to London after an initial stint in Manchester's textiles market, where he established the family's first international trading outpost. Thereafter the youngest son, James (born Jakob), relocated to Paris while the other two sons, Salomon and Carl, established themselves in Vienna and Naples, respectively. The Rothschilds' pan-European reach gave them the power and leverage to act as private agents in a transnational arena of competition and conflict. Such a position was advantageous during the Napoleonic Wars, when, departing from the traditional banking practices of the previous century, the Rothschilds bought and sold government bonds to an unprecedented degree—thus capitalizing on the power of the nation-state in a burgeoning international market. By the following decade, the House of Rothschild emerged as one of Europe's economic superpowers, with many states in their debt.[12]

It was also during this period that the family experienced a boom in social capital. In 1822, the second-generation brothers acquired the hereditary rank of baron (*Freiherr*) from the Emperor of Austria in tandem with a newfound interest in collecting art.[13] The latter began for James de Rothschild in May 1821, when he famously purchased his first painting—Jean-Baptiste Greuze's *La Laitière* (1783)—at a Paris auction.[14] The picture was a favorite among a collection that quickly expanded to include major works by Velázquez, Rembrandt, Rubens, and Hals.[15] That the Rothschilds could acquire these works was in large part owed to the dissolution of many aristocratic collections in the aftermath of the French Revolution. Indeed, one could say that the family belonged to what English art historian Francis Haskell called the "the Orléans generation," referring to those early nineteenth-century collectors who benefited from massive estate sales like the 1799 auction of the Duke of Orléans's picture collection in London.[16] The release of these and other works onto the market meant that the art objects that once bolstered the social status of the aristocracy were now available to their nineteenth-century successor: The financier.

Meanwhile, popular imagery during the early nineteenth century suggests that many begrudged the elevation of Jewish bankers to the status of nobility. This much can be inferred from a ca. 1825 satirical image of the family's British patriarch Nathan Rothschild by cartoonist Thomas Howell Jones. Titled *A Pillar of the Exchange* [Fig. 2], the illustration shows Nathan standing at his preferred spot near the base of a particular Doric column in the southeast corner of London's Royal Exchange building. The derisive irony of the image lies in its stark juxtaposition: While Nathan appears as a pillar of economic strength, this suggestion is undermined through the bold visual contrast between the elegant white column and Nathan's short, corpulent figure, rendered black by his overcoat and top hat.[17] The pairing invites comparison to Renaissance humanist drawings like Francesco di Giorgio's ca. 1490 study of an idealized human profile overlaid onto the anthropomorphic curves of an ornamental cornice. These works have the effect of demonstrating that human and architectural anatomies share a common set of proportions.[18] The Rothschild cartoon, however, has the opposite aim: To show that Nathan's body is alien to classical architecture and thus incompatible with its underlying orders and systems. Here any imagined continuity between body and architecture—and more broadly, individual and society, present and past—is denied to the Jewish financier.

Architectural patronage provided the means to overcome these prejudices and transforming the family's social perception. This was particularly true for Baron James, who was in many ways the leading force behind the second generation's cultural turn.[19] The relative austerity and social isolation of his early years in France prompted his desire for a grand residence to spite his unwelcoming milieu.[20] In 1818, the opportunity presented itself when, following the family's first major architectural commissions in Frankfurt, James acquired the Hôtel d'Otrante on what is now 19 Rue Laffitte.[21] As the former home of the Duke of Otranto—Napoleon's Minister of Police, Joseph Fouché—the hôtel served as the bureaucratic headquarters for the House of Rothschild's French branch and provided James with the ideal venue for playing the part of an urban aristocrat.[22] And within the span of three years, James's standing in Parisian society was well established: An article in the March 7, 1821, edition of *La Gazette de France* speaks of a grand ball at the Rothschild residence attended by high-ranking diplomats, "foreigners of distinction," and the elite of the French court

Figure 1. Osbert Lancaster's caricature of "Le Style Rothschild" in Homes Sweet Homes.

and army.[23] This early example makes clear that Rue Laffitte outfitted James with the mantle of aristocratic identity. Furthermore, it foreshadows the degree to which residential architecture became a crucial corporate asset for the House of Rothschild—not only by equipping the family with the necessary social infrastructure for conducting business, but also by offering their clients spectacular material evidence of the family's viability as a creditor.

The cosmopolitan profile of Rue Laffitte's social events found similar expression in its architecture, which looked to Italy as a source of inspiration. Initial renovations were undertaken ca. 1820 under the direction of architect Louis-Martin Berthault, who was selected on account of his previous commissions for ex-empress Joséphine de Beauharnais and French banker Jacques-Rose Récamier. At Rue Laffitte, Berthault's labors included widening the townhome's staircase, razing several walls, and constructing a massive ballroom, yielding a "galerie gothico-Renaissance" illuminated by candelabras and mirrors surrounding arched apertures.[24] Subsequent renovations took ancient Pompeii as a point of departure. For Laffitte's billiards room, ca. 1825, set decorators Pierre Cicéri and Lebe Gigun collaborated with Beaux-Arts-trained painter François-Édouard Picot to implement elaborate Pompeian wall paintings comprised of deep crimson and cerulean color planes interspersed with architectural vignettes and figural scenes derived from Roman baths. Such motifs were consistent with James's collecting interests at the time. During the 1820s, he acquired a group of Etruscan vases from Naples in addition to purchasing a copy of French archaeologist Raoul Rochette's survey of classical antiquity, *Monuments inédits d'antiquité figurée, grecque, étrusque et romaine* (1828).[25]

James de Rothschild was not alone in embracing Italianate models during this period. On the one hand, Italian classicism had long been the bedrock of French academic training for art and architecture at the Paris École des Beaux-Arts, whose prestigious Prix de Rome provided its laureates a multi-year residency at the Villa Medici to study the monuments of Greek and Roman antiquity.[26] Several noted Prix de Rome laureates produced bound portfolios of architectural prints from their Italian travels that entered the libraries of architects and patrons alike. Among these were the influential volumes of "modern" palazzos and villas in Rome and its environs composed by renowned academicians Charles Percier and Pierre Fontaine, published between 1798 and 1809.[27] Such publications testify to a groundswell of interest in the Italian Renaissance among the Paris architectural community.

On the other hand, a steady influx of foreign bankers into Paris yielded a pool of wealthy patrons who would eventually see in Italian Renaissance architecture a *lingua franca* for representing their cosmopolitan status and fortunes.[28] Take for example the Swiss-born Paris banker François Bartholoni. Like James de Rothschild, he commissioned Pompeian wall paintings for his Geneva summer home, Villa Bartholoni (1828–30), designed by the Beaux-Arts-trained architect Félix-Emmanuel Callet in the manner of a neo-Palladian villa.[29] One can only speculate that Bartholoni's lakeside home influenced the taste of his Paris milieu in the coming years.[30] To be sure, following the 1830 July Revolution, a new class of haute bourgeois patrons and Beaux-Arts architects—propelled by a spirit of Romanticism—revived Renaissance forms with unprecedented élan throughout the French capital city.[31] The 1830s witnessed a flourishing of Renaissance historicism in the designs for restaurants, cafes, and hôtels where the city's wealthy elite could luxuriate in public view.[32] Therefore, during the July Monarchy, many Parisian architects and patrons came to view Italian Renaissance architecture not as a mere stylistic motif or antiquarian curiosity but rather an apparatus for urbane sociability.

For James de Rothschild, this moment arrived upon reconstructing his Rue Laffitte townhouse in 1836. By acquiring the property's neighboring units, 17 and 21 Rue Laffitte, he expanded the hôtel into a sprawling symmetrical complex with two projecting wings flanking a central loggia and courtyard [Fig. 3]. The redesign was modeled on another banker's residence, yet one from sixteenth-century Rome:

Figure 2. Thomas Howell Jones, *A Pillar of the Exchange*, ca. 1825 caricature print with Nathan Rothschild's obituary affixed to the upper left.

Figure 3. Garden View of 19 rue Laffitte prior to its demolition in 1967.

Sienese banker Agostino Chigi's Villa Farnesina (1506–10).[33] The use of this early banker's villa as a prototype sutured its contemporary patron to his imaginary Renaissance forebear around the time that architects were reviving Cinquecento precedents in other major financial centers. Shortly preceding Rue Laffitte's expansion, British architect Charles Barry designed the first of his London gentlemen's clubs to be modeled on the archetypal form of the Renaissance palazzo.[34] Barry's Travellers Club (1832) on London's Pall Mall took its inspiration from Raphael's Palazzo Pandolfini (ca. 1513–16) to house an organization for well-traveled Britons wishing to host and liaise with visiting foreign dignitaries. Barry's design reflected the club's mission statement in several respects. Its Florentine source material testified to Barry's personal travels through Italy as part of his Grand Tour, when he first encountered the Renaissance palazzos of Rome and Florence. (e.g., Raphael's Pandolfini, in which Barry saw "how much could be done…by means of a good frieze and cornice," thus providing a precedent for the Travellers Club's deeply carved and elaborate cornice in a departure from the *de rigueur* conventions of English neo-Palladianism).[35] Beyond its biographical significance, however, Barry's model of Renaissance revival resonated in a greater sense with the emergent power and mobility of wealthy individuals in liberal bourgeois society, ranging from the cultivated gentleman-traveler to the ascendant Jewish banker who was just one generation removed from the ghetto.

These themes found even more dramatic expression across the Channel in the reconstructed interiors of Baron James's Parisian Renaissance villa. The project's principal architect was the young Beaux-Arts-trained designer Henri Duponchel, who had already collaborated with Berthault on the home's earlier renovation. During the interim period between commissions Duponchel worked as a set and costume designer at the Paris Opera, where he rose to the position of managing director by the time of Laffitte's reconstruction. Nineteenth-century accounts of Duponchel's oeuvre laud his decorative effects for their "innate passion of magnificence and staging," and indeed this sensibility is evident in the townhome's lively visual environments—spaces that invite performance of a different sort.[36] The hôtel's new salons sampled from a variety of historical styles: Gothic, Louis XIV, and Louis XV, among others. For several critics, however, it was the neo-Renaissance style that dominated the hôtel's interior spaces.[37] Nowhere was this more fully realized than in the showpiece of Duponchel's reconstructed Laffitte: The *salon François 1er* [Fig. 4], a spectacle of sixteenth-century historicism. The wood-paneled salon's densely carved and gilded surfaces featured an array of Renaissance ornamental forms like sphinxes and medallion relief portraits alongside pairings of carved Rothschild family arms juxtaposed with those of the Medicis and other Renaissance power brokers.[38] These implied affinities were further emphasized by a suite of five paintings by Joseph-Nicolas-Robert Fleury that each depicted a canonical Renaissance figure or scene: The arrival of Charles V in Spain; Martin Luther preaching the reformation; Henry VIII with Cardinal Wolsey; Guillaume Budé presenting Francis I with the first printed book in France; and Medici Pope Leon X standing with Raphael in front of the Laocoön at the

Figure 4. The Salon François 1er at 19 rue Laffitte prior to its demolition in 1967.

Figure 5. *Portrait of Betty de Rothschild and her son Alphonse in the Salon François 1er at 19 rue Laffitte*, ca. 1830.

Vatican. The series' iconography celebrates episodes of conquest, enlightenment, and grand patronage, with equal heroism allotted to secular and religious protagonists. Such an emphasis on patronage was consistent with the financial support that James and his wife Betty, an influential fixture of Paris society, provided to cultural luminaries like Frédéric Chopin, Honoré de Balzac, and Eugène Delacroix, who were known to attend the Rothschilds' Laffitte salons.[39] Yet there was a deeper logic behind Fleury's chosen subject matter. Pauline Prevost-Marcilhacy has argued that by representing figures and events from Austria, Germany, England, France, and Italy, the historical figures alluded to the Rothschilds themselves—presented to the viewer as heirs of a tradition of Renaissance Humanism that transcended modern political boundaries.[40]

Pictorial iconography alone does not, however, account for the semiotic power of spaces like the *salon François 1er*. Indeed, the degree to which Fleury's paintings served as historical avatars for the modern-day Rothschilds underscores how, in the Rothschild Style interior, meaning was produced in a dynamic exchange between figures and forms across real and representational space. Further accelerating this exchange was the array of decorative materials and ornament that mediated between the room's objects and surfaces. So much is clear in the period accounts of Laffitte by its dazzled guests and visitors. Writing under her *nom de plume* "Vicomte Delaunay," Delphine de Girardin mused on the richness of the home's sumptuous materials in the Parisian journal *Bon Ton*:

> The mantels are covered in gold-fringed velvet.... The armchairs have lace antimacassars; the walls are concealed under marvelous embroidered, brocaded, spangled fabrics of such thickness and strength they could stand alone and, if needed, actually support what they cover, should the walls give way.[41]

Judging by Girardin's account, it was as though Laffitte's architecture wore its extravagant decor like a costume—one so heavy and substantial that it was practically an architecture unto itself. Even the patrons themselves took part in this elaborate pageantry. Around the time of the reconstructed hotel's 1836 debut, James commissioned a portrait of his wife and eldest son dressed in Renaissance-style attire in a space modeled on the *salon François 1er* [Fig. 5].[42] The portrait demonstrates the performative nature of Laffitte's historicist interiors. As a holistic environment spanning architecture, art, furniture, and textiles, Laffite's design bridged the scales of building and body—whether those bodies belonged to James de Rothschild and his family, playing the role of urban aristocrats on Laffitte's domestic stage; or to their visitors and guests, whose participation entailed marveling at the home's *mise en scene*. The hôtel's interiors thus amounted to a spectacle of the Renaissance without the spectatorial distance of the theater. Instead, Duponchel's designs staged an immersive, sensual encounter with history that was reflexively bound to one's embodied present.

As a brief excursus, one could look beyond the Rothschilds for other examples of nineteenth-century Jewish financiers with comparable sensibilities. Take the art critic and historian Charles Ephrussi of the Russian oil and banking dynasty. After extensive travels and acquisitions throughout Italy in the early 1870s, he filled his quarters in Paris's Hôtel Ephrussi with ornate curios and furniture for daily use, such as a gilded Renaissance bed festooned with putti, fruit, flowers, and heraldic emblems (a grandiose gesture that one Ephrussi descendant, Edmund de Waal, describes with more than a little amusement in his family memoir).[43] Charles Ephrussi's fascination with the Renaissance even found its way into Marcel Proust's *À la recherche du temps perdu* (1913), whose character Charles Swann—a wealthy Jewish stockbroker and art dealer—was modeled on the real-life Ephrussi scion. The latter's presence is palpable in moments like Swann's rapturous likening of his love interest Odette to a figure in Botticelli's *Trials of Moses* fresco (1481–82), cited as a paragon of female beauty.[44] Taken in total, these examples evince more than a dilettantish appreciation of art. For the Rothschilds, the Ephrussis, and others of their ilk, the Renaissance offered a model of individual aesthetic experience that was continuous with the bourgeois aspirations and desires of their own time.

This was particularly true at James de Rothschild's Rue Laffitte. The hôtel's symbolic continuity between the sixteenth and nineteenth centuries found tangible expression in its provision of modern bodily comfort alongside historicist decor. Central heating, running water, and a discreet waste management system serviced interiors lit aglow by the flicker of gas lighting—the trappings of a technologically advanced contemporary home.[45] This combination of old and new luxuries was a striking feature for James's contemporaries. Upon seeing the house for the first time, German poet and critic Heinrich Heine remarked in 1836, "Here everything comes together which the spirit of the sixteenth century could invent and the money of the nineteenth century could pay for; here the genius of the visual arts competes with the genius of Rothschild."[46] Heine suggests that the Renaissance ethos of radical invention was experiencing a rebirth—a second *rinascita*—through modern finance. By this logic, it was as though the Rothschilds' unprecedented wealth endowed their patronage with a degree of creative authorship that, by the nineteenth century, was increasingly reserved for the figure of the artist. And it would seem that the Rothschilds embraced this notion. In the coming years their architectural commissions dramatically increased in ambition and in scale, yielding a series of country estates that tested the limits of what nineteenth-century money could buy.

AN EMPIRE OF FINANCE, INSIDE OUT

Revivalist chateaus and manors like those of Ferrières-en-Brie, Mentmore, and Waddesdon are perhaps the Rothschilds' best-known residential commissions. And in many respects they represent the total realization of the aristocratic identity that they had cultivated from the 1820s onward. By mid-century, the younger generation's interest in leisure activities such as hunting demanded larger properties where the family could also display what was becoming one of the nineteenth century's largest private art collections.[47] Such pursuits might suggest a return to the *ancien régime*—even feudalism, with its concentration of wealth and power in vast estates. Yet the conception, design, and construction of the Rothschilds' estates betray a distinctly modern, financial model of dominion whose decentralized power operates through the fluidity and flux of network circulation.

Indeed, during the first half of the nineteenth century, the House of Rothschild utilized a variety of information networks to accelerate the circulation of capital between its international branches. An extensive communication system consisting of private couriers, carrier pigeons, contracted ship captains, and correspondents stationed at stock exchanges and transportation hubs around the world facilitated the rapid delivery of urgent news, which proved decisive in gaining an upper hand over the family's competitors—private banks and governments alike.[48] The transnational scope of the family's banking operations was alternatively a source of anxiety and awe for their contemporaries, who regarded them as a superpower greater than any individual nation. French journalist Alexandre Weill vocalized this sentiment in 1844:

There is but one power in Europe and that is Rothschild. His satellites are a dozen other banking firms; his soldiers, his squires, all respectable men of business and merchants; and his sword is speculation.... Rothschild had need of the states to become a Rothschild, while the states on their side required Rothschild. Now, however, he no longer needs the State, but the State still has want of him.[49]

Although Weill's account suggests a triumphant or celebratory tone, more often than not these assertions portrayed the Rothschilds as nefarious agents of capitalist hegemony. The ca.1845 German cartoon *Die Generalpumpe*, alternatively titled "Moneylender-in-chief" [Fig. 6], is one such example. Here the family's business of loans and trading is anthropomorphized as a human money pump orchestrating the global economy, as denoted by a central Rothschild figure whose level-like arms and thorny vascular system circulate money into and out of its spherical belly. A paper crown resting atop the central figure's head is emblazoned with the names of those who received Rothschild loans during the 1820s and '30s, calling out the Prussians, Russians, Neopolitans, Austrians, and Portuguese alongside many other recipients and mediators of the family's money.[50] Further pillorying the worldwide reach of the Rothschilds' power is the globe contained within the figure's distended stomach. Tilted to align the North Pole with the figure's naval, it bulges from below a waistcoat with a badge that reads: "The Executor of the Court of all the World." One could speculate that the Rothschild figure's central positioning—with extended limbs defining the limits of a universal order—is meant to evoke Leonardo's Vitruvian Man, despite being the very antithesis of the latter's idealized body in geometric-spatial scaffolding. Regardless, the cartoon is instructive in showing that the emergence of international finance was giving rise to new geographies of circulation. And at the center of it all was the House of Rothschild, as postulated by Heinrich Heine's aphorism: "Money is the god of our times, and Rothschild is his prophet."[51]

That the Rothschilds financed many of Europe's earliest transnational railway lines illuminates how the circulation of capital could be transmuted into geospatial form. Yet the Rothschilds were not the first to pursue these endeavors. Influenced by the tenets of the utopian Saint-Simonian movement,[52] rival French bankers like the Peréire brothers financed lines like Paris-St-Germain-en-Laye with the ultimate goal of forging a pan-European rail and shipping network.[53] Baron James was one of the first, and most active, Rothschilds to make headway on this front. He was a principal owner of the French Northern Railway Company (*Compagnie des chemins de fer du Nord*), created in 1845 to connect Paris to Brussels via the newly constructed Gare du Nord; and he was an influential investor in several other railway companies and passenger lines across Western Europe. The cultural implications of rail transportation were not lost on James. In 1865, his French Northern Railway Company commissioned a foldout map that illustrated the routes of its passenger trains alongside photographic views of the bucolic landscapes and historical monuments made accessible for recreational travel [Fig. 7].[54] The map's resulting geography is one of collapsed distances and disorienting continuity with so many nodal scenes occupying a collaged visual field. As a representation of industrialized leisure—comprised of mechanically produced images, no less—the map reveals how the forces of modernization indelibly mediated one's aesthetic experience of the countryside: A pastoral "outside" that was decisively "inside" the network topology of international finance.[55]

It was within the House of Rothschild's extended interior—connected by industrial infrastructure—that the family built their first country estates. So much is clear in the nodal quality of the Rothschilds' two earliest and largest rural commissions. Both Mentmore Towers (1850–55) in Buckinghamshire, England, and the Château de Ferrières (1853–63), near Paris, were commissioned to rebuild older, preexisting country estates that were becoming primary residences for the French and British Rothschilds. Due to the availability of new railway networks, it was possible for the brothers to maintain an efficient connection between their urban offices and rural manors and chateaus—in some cases using train lines that they had financed.[56] This sort of fluidity also manifested itself in the exchange of ideas and labor between Mentmore and Ferrières. Both projects shared the English gardener and architect Sir Joseph Paxton as their principal designer, and each had as its focal point an enormous central Grand Hall where the family's paintings, sculptures, and curios could

Figure 6. Julius Bohmer and H. Delius, *Die Generalpumpe*, ca. 1845, black ink lithograph and engraving with applied watercolor.

be viewed below an incandescent glass roof—a palatial interior not unlike that of Paxton's better-known Crystal Palace exhibition pavilion.

Paxton was an unconventional choice for the family's commissions in several respects.[57] Although he was enjoying a great deal of fame and popularity for his 1851 Great Exhibition pavilion in London's Hyde Park, he was in many ways an outsider to the British architectural and artistic establishment—its *bête noir*, even. Leading the crusade against Paxton was English art critic John Ruskin, who saw his glass-and-iron world's fair structure as an existential threat to the built environment. Ruskin cited Paxton in a 1857 address to students of London's Architectural Association titled "The Imagination in Architecture," in which he cautioned against the desire to "invent a 'new style' worthy of modern civilization" and warned of the constraining, rather than liberating, effects of glass enclosure.[58] For Ruskin, Paxton's engineered and pre-manufactured building components lacked a quality of soulful expression that could only be achieved by the hands of a craftsman. The Crystal Palace thus exemplified the debased status of contemporary English society, whose culture and faith was in a state of crisis inflicted by industrial capitalism—a crisis precipitated by sins of "pride," "science," "knowledge," and "system" that originated in the Renaissance.[59] Ruskin proposed a cure for these social ills by returning to the sculptural gothic architecture of medieval Venice to achieve an organic union of artisanal labor, creativity, and spirituality that had been lost to both secular Humanism and the alienated labor of factory production.

Ruskin's plea to restore social and economic unity through the revival of Venetian gothic architecture is a notable foil to Paxton's designs for Mentmore and Ferrières, which similarly looked to Venice as a model of integration—albeit one that was compatible with, rather than resistant to, the vicissitudes of capitalist society. Mentmore Towers was the first of these monumental projects. The commission came from the youngest son of the late English Rothschild patriarch Nathan, Mayer Amschel de Rothschild, who wished to undertake the family's first major new construction project in England. Driven by this ambition, Mentmore's façade was modeled on the Elizabethan country home Wollaton Hall (1580–88), an overt gesture of cultural patrimony constitutive of an emerging desire to codify national Renaissance styles.[60] The home's interiors, however, shifted the source of their historicism from England to continental Europe. As Pauline Prevost-Marcilhacy has noted, Mentmore's private spaces and peripheral salons were designed in a Louis XIV French vernacular, and the home's central Grand Hall—a soaring space forty meters in length and twelve meters in height—was executed in the manner of an Italian palazzo.[61] It was here that the Rothschilds' historicist vision of modernity found expression in the forms of Renaissance Venice.

Suspended from the Hall's glass-and-iron ceiling were three massive lanterns originating from the *Bucentaur*, or state barge, of the Venetian doge [Fig. 8]. The glass and repoussé-metal lanterns provide a curious focal point for the Hall—the first in England to function as a living

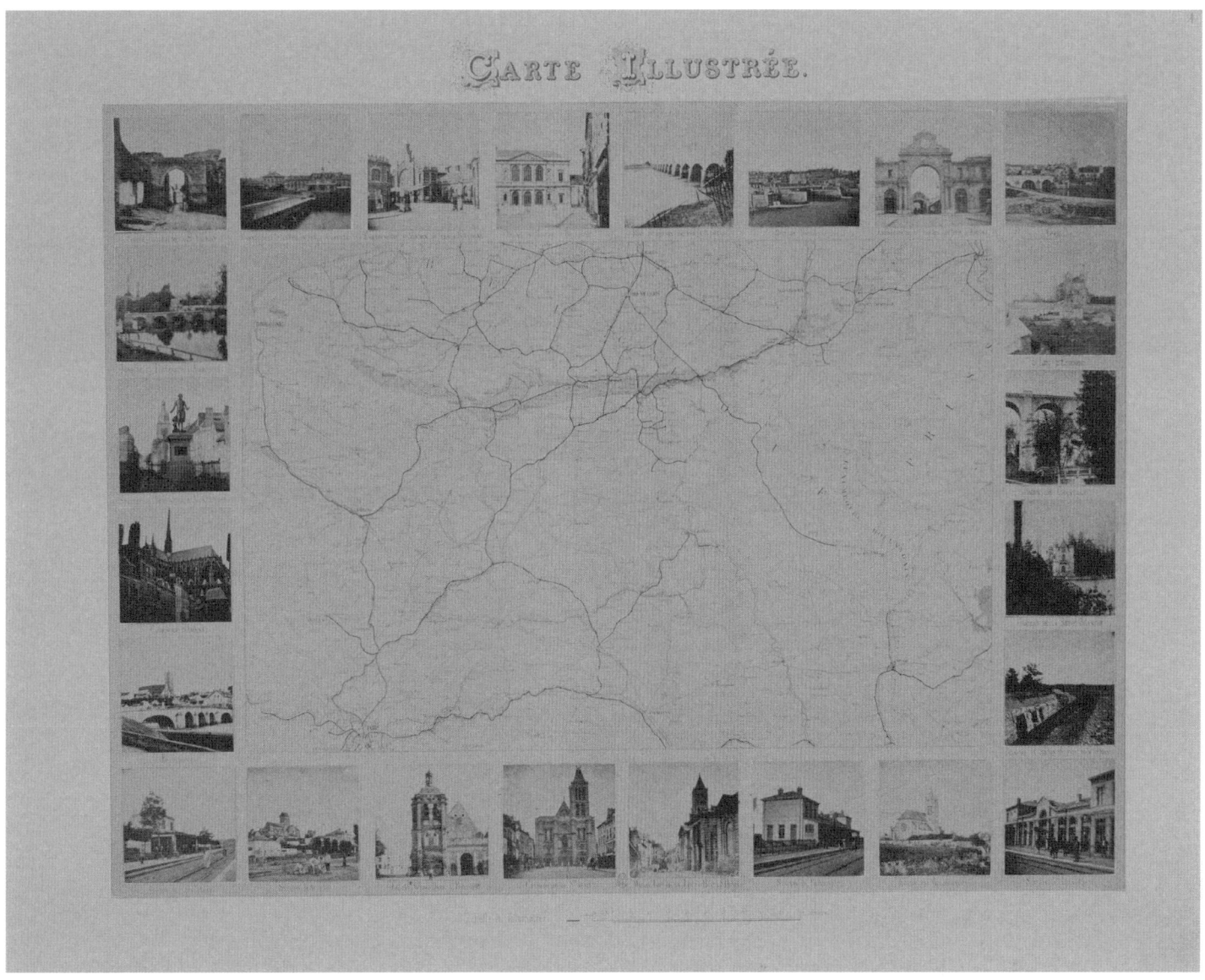

Figure 7. *Chemin de fer du Nord. Ligne de Paris à Boulogne. Album de vues photographiques.* Photographs by Édouard Baldus, ca. 1860.

Figure 8. H. Brewer, *Watercolor rendering of Mentmore's Grand Hall*, ca. 1850.

DAVID SADIGHIAN

room.⁶² Hanging overhead, they frame the space's delirious assemblage of furniture, tapestries, and art objects in glass display cases, which one can imagine Mayer or his wife Juliana presenting to their houseguests as part of an elaborate ritual of showmanship and social intercourse. As at Rue Laffitte, then, history at Mentmore is presented to the viewer as an immersive spectacle, yet one that was derived less from the theater than from the display culture of the modern museum and the Great Exhibition. On the one hand, this is expressed in the room's many glass vitrines— an architecture of display that might be expanded in scale, conceptually, to include the Hall itself. Furthermore, the symbolic and cultural associations of the Venetian lanterns also contribute to the Hall's atmosphere of exchange. Taken from the interior of a boat, they evoke the movement of the *Bucentaur*, a mobile architecture for circulation within Venice's maritime canals. Here one finds evidence of the Rothschilds' counter model to Ruskin's contemporaneous reception of Venice. If for Ruskin the city's architecture provided a template for aesthetic and social cohesion, for the Rothschilds it was an environment of flux, sustained by dynamic liquid networks and a spirit of cosmopolitanism. It was this ethos that permitted the fluid intermixing of historical and cultural artifacts in a room whose very interiority is destabilized by a glass ceiling overhead.

The allusions to Venice in Mentmore's Grand Hall are more emphatically expressed in the later Grand Hall of the Château de Ferrières. James de Rothschild commissioned his French country estate in direct response to his nephew's new home in Buckinghamshire, telling Paxton to build another Mentmore at twice the size.⁶³ This entailed clearing the older structures on a property once owned by the Duke of Otranto and expanding the grounds by purchasing surrounding land.⁶⁴ Plans for Ferrières began in 1853 and underwent a lengthy process of design development as Paxton and his son-in-law, the architect George Henry Stokes, tested various historicist schemes for the new estate's main façade.⁶⁵ Meanwhile, it was decided that the residence would have a central glazed Grand Hall similar to that of Mentmore; and it, too, would also serve as a domestic gallery. Yet as was the case with James's Rue Laffitte, the design for Ferrières's Grand Hall was conceived in far more theatrical terms than its English predecessor.

The Grand Hall's interior design and planning was entrusted to Eugène Lami, a noted Beaux-Arts-trained painter and lithographer known for his animated battle scenes and depictions of elite society during the July Monarchy and the Second Empire.⁶⁶ Lami was charged with selecting furniture and objects for the home's interiors in consultation with Betty de Rothschild, with whom he traveled to Venice in 1860 to gather inspiration for Ferrières's architectural centerpiece. Lami summed up their findings in the following report sent to James:

> For ten days, I have been drawing all day and night and I have often thought of you. The Baroness gave me permission to draw in the Palazzo Ducale and in the rooms that the public cannot access. I have some new and picturesque ideas. We also have large funds for photography.⁶⁷

The Palazzo Ducale was one of many Venetian sites that influenced Lami's design for the Grand Hall. Another was the tomb for Doge Giovanni Pesaro at the Basilica di Santa Maria Gloriosa dei Frari: A towering seventeenth-century funerary monument comprising a triumphal arch-like arrangement of four Black Moorish caryatids holding up a plinth with Pesaro's kneeling effigy. The caryatids' agonized faces and compressed bodies emphasize their enslavement by the Venetian Doge in a stunning tableau of imperial power. Lami was clearly transfixed by the Black Moors, as his sketches from Venice include a study relating their sculptural bodies to the onlookers standing before them [Fig. 9]. It is therefore not surprising that Lami reimagined these figures in his design for the Grand Hall at Ferrières, where they would partake in a larger narrative of global conquest and transnational exchange.

Venice in many ways provided the syntax and iconography for conceptualizing the Grand Hall's spatial domain. Intensifying the boundary confusion of Paxton's glass roof is a combination of interior and exterior architectural elements drawing from Lami's Venetian travels. The Hall features an axial arrangement of four entrance portals evoking a piazza bordered by triumphal city gates— an idea borrowed from the Doge's Palace.⁶⁸ Once inside the Hall [Fig. 10], visitors were confronted by a swarm of tapestries and paintings depicting military victories and

Figure 9. Eugène Lami, sketch of Pesaro's tomb in Venice, ca. 1861, watercolor.

Figure 10. Eugène Lami, *Rendering of the Grand Hall at Ferrières*, ca. 1860, watercolor.

feats of heroism alongside cartouches containing the Rothschild family monogram. Perhaps most the intriguing of all room's sights, however, were its Renaissance busts and contemporary sculptures by Parisian artist Charles Cordier, known at the time for his ethnographic African sculptures. It was Cordier who translated Pesaro's monumental tomb into an expression of the Rothschild financial empire. At Ferrières, the tomb's four Black Moors take the form of two atlases and two caryatids—one representing Africa; the other, the Americas—flanking the passageway leading to the home's main vestibule, thus framing the primary entrance to the Grand Hall.[69] Fashioned from gleaming black-and-white marble and bronze, Cordier's figures each support a gilded sphere representing a quarter of the world, which rests on their elegantly extended arms. Unlike their Venetian predecessors, then, Ferrières's Black caryatids are not anguished by their slavery; rather, as architectural historian Fredric Bedoire has suggested, they appear oblivious to their burden and are instead presented as loyal subjects of the House of Rothschild's banking empire.[70]

Such gestures are part and parcel of the Hall's efforts to develop a model of interiority befitting the House of Rothschild's sweeping dominion. Through its interiorization of urban elements and heady mix of historical and cultural references, the Hall presents an implosion of distance and time, provoking a visceral response that one might call the phenomenology of finance.[71] It was this sensation that crept into many of Ferrières's earliest visitors. The anti-Semitic French journalist Edouard Drumont called it a "magasin de bric à brac," and the German chancellor Otto von Bismarck—who occupied the building during the Franco-Prussian War—referred to the Grand Hall as "une commode renversée."[72] Their reactions attest to the destabilizing effect of the Rothschild Style interior as manifested at Ferrières and evidenced by period photographs [Fig. 11]. With its glazed roof and courtyard-like position in the house's floor plan, the Grand Hall was both interior and exterior, as though the public spaces of the nineteenth-century museum, exhibition hall, and *grand magasin* had collapsed into the private residential space of the bourgeois collector. Even guests who at one point admired the home changed their tone after subsequent visits to James de Rothschilds' country estate. Upon visiting Ferrières during the 1878 World's Fair, eleven years after his initial visit, Swedish diplomat Fritz von Dardel no longer extolled the home's "harmony," "taste," and "artistry," as he had remarked earlier.[73] Rather, he cast a more critical eye toward its horde of objects and styles: "Everything is furnished in accordance with

Figure 11. The Grand Hall at Ferrièrres, ca. 1880.

the fashion today, i.e., without any respect for the styles of the different periods which this poor century of ours, itself lacking in creative power, tries to imitate."[74] Dardel's later account reveals the ease with which the Rothschild Style interior's signification could switch registers: From cohesion to disorder, from noble artistry to glib fashion, from museum to department store. Yet rather than seeing these vacillations as the Style's fallibility, we should instead interpret them as betraying an experience of modernity that could only be articulated in the historicist vocabularies of the Renaissance.

CODA: INTERIORS WITHOUT END

As a means of conclusion, one might turn to philosopher Peter Sloterdijk, whose writings on the "world interior" describe an imaginary enclosure produced by networks of capitalist exchange.[75] By occupying this interior, one gains access to its interconnected global nodes for the uneven accumulation of capital—past and present. It is this multi-sited, asynchronous quality that arguably defines Rothschild Style architecture and its nodal position within the family's financial empire.[76] Perhaps this is why the family's Grand Halls of the 1850s shared the same glazed enclosure as unrelated typologies: The train station and the stock exchange.[77] Contemporary with their country estates, Amschel Mayer and James de Rothschild purportedly sought Paxton to build a glass roof over the London Stock Exchange while also commissioning J. I. Hittorff to design the glazed train shed for Paris's Gare du Nord station.[78] The family's domestic interiors were thus not far removed from their urban counterparts. But could it be said that these spaces were continuous, like coordinates of some unified world interior?

History might say so. Or rather, in the Rothschild Style, history provided a rationale for capital's scalar expansion into new domains. Spaces like the Ferrières Grand Hall conjured phantoms of Renaissance cities not as distant relics, but instead as proleptic visions of a modern metropolis yet to come; a future that was *always already* historical. Gazing into capital's past—its panorama of villas and palazzos, of triumphal gates and Venetian ships—the nineteenth-century Rothschilds saw an interior that could encompass the world.

This essay is a reworked version of a book chapter that originally appeared as "The Renaissance Inside Out: Historical Reference and Financial Modernity in the 'Rothschild Style' Interior, ca. 1820–1860," in Lina Bolzoni and Alina Payne, eds., *The Renaissance in the 19th Century: Revision, Revival, and Return* (Milan and Cambridge, MA: Officina Libraria and Harvard University Press, 2018), 151–182. I thank Alina Payne and Mary Doyno for their permission to republish this material for a new audience.

1. Jonathan Levy, "Capital as Process and the History of Capitalism," *Business History Review* 91 (Autumn 2017): 487. It should be noted that Levy focuses on the history of American capitalism. A classic text on the distinction between capital, capitalist, and capitalism remains Fernand Braudel, *Civilization and Capitalism, 15th–18th Century*, Vol. 2, *The Wheels of Commerce*, trans. Siân Reynolds (Berkeley: University of California Press, 1992) [1979], 232–249.
2. Niall Ferguson, the Rothschild family's official biographer, makes this point in his encyclopedic tome, *The World's Banker: The History of the House of Rothschild* (London: Weidenfeld & Nicholson, 1998), 8. Ferguson's extensive monograph is perhaps the definitive English-language study of the Rothschild family. For other accounts, see Jean Bouvier, *Les Rothschild* (Paris: Fayard, 1967); Virginia Cowles, *The Rothschilds: A Family of Fortune* (New York: Knopf, 1973); Bertrand Gille, *Histoire de la Maison Rothschild*, 2 vols. (Geneva: Droz, 1965–1967); Anka Muhlstein, *James de Rothschild* (Paris: Galimard, 1981); and Derek Wilson, *The Rothschilds: A Story of Wealth and Power* (London: A. Deutsch, 1988). See also the exhibition catalogue and volume of scholarly essays published in conjunction with the 1994 exhibition *Die Rothschilds: Eine europäische Familie*, at the Jewish Museum in Frankfurt: Georg Heuberger, ed., *The Rothschilds: A European Family*, trans. Jeremy Gaines and Paul Keast (Woodbridge: Thorbecke/Boydell & Brewer, 1994); and idem., ed., *The Rothschilds: Essays on the History of a European Family*, trans. Jeremy Gaines and Paul Keast (Woodbridge: Thorbecke/Boydell & Brewer, 1994).
3. For more on the discursive invention of "the Renaissance" during the nineteenth century, especially in the work of French historian Jules Michelet, see Payne and Bolzoni, eds., *The Renaissance in the 19th Century*.
4. "Le Goût Rothschild." The Rothschild Archive. N.D. Accessed October 2023. https://www.rothschildarchive.org/family/family_collections/le_gout_rothschild
5. Here I am referring to the narrative developed by Swiss architectural historian Sigfried Giedion in his seminal books on the Modern Movement, beginning with *Bauen in Frankreich, Bauen in Eisen, Bauen in Eisenbeton* (1928) and continuing with *Space, Time & Architecture: The Growth of a New Tradition* (1941). This narrative has undergone substantial revision in contemporary scholarship. See for example Alina Payne, *From Ornament to Object: Genealogies of Architectural Modernism* (New Haven: Yale University Press, 2012).
6. Claude Mignot, *Architecture of the Nineteenth Century in Europe*, trans. D.Q. Stephenson (New York: Rizzoli, 1984), 7. My comment regarding historicism and Postmodernism is in reference to Alan Colquhoun, "Three Kinds of Historicism," *Oppositions* 26 (Spring 1984): 29–39.
7. James Fenton addresses this sentiment in his article "The Rothschild Taste," which comments on the perceived hideousness of the family's Buckinghamshire estate Waddesdon Manor (1874–84) upon its 1957 donation by James Armand Edmond de Rothschild to the British National Trust. James Fenton, "The Rothschild Taste," *New York Review of Books* 62, no. 11 (June 2015). Accessed October 2023. http://www.nybooks.com/articles/2015/06/25/rothschild-taste/. Only in the 1980s and '90s did historians begin to view Rothschild architecture as a subject worthy of scholarly study. French art historian Pauline Prevost-Marcilhacy was among the first to undertake research on the Rothschilds' architectural patronage, beginning with her Sorbonne dissertation (1992) and culminating in her monograph, *Les Rothschild: bâtisseurs et mécènes* (Paris: Flammarion, 1995). Following in Prevost-Marcilhacy's footsteps, Swedish architectural historian Fredric Bedoire published a chapter on the family's buildings in his book, *The Jewish Contribution to Modern Architecture 1830–1930*, trans. Roger Tanner (Jersey City, N.J.: KTAV Publishing House, 2004), originally published as *Ett judiskt Europa. Kring uppkomsten av en modern arkitektur, 1830–1930* (Stockholm: Carlssons, 1998). The critique of taste to which I'm referring can be found in the work of Pierre Bourdieu and Paul DiMaggio.
8. Osbert Lancaster, *Homes Sweet Homes* (London and New York: John Murray/Transatlantic Arts, 1946), 38.
9. Lancaster quotes from a so-called "Financier's Song" to illustrate how the Rothschild Style favors visual effects over historical meaning: "Little bits of porcelain, / Little sticks of Boule / Harmonize with Venuses / Of the Flemish school" (p.38). For an alternative caricature of "le style Rothschild," see "Rothschild," in Philippe Jullian, *Les styles* (Paris: Plon, 1961), 104–105.
10. For more on the family's origins and rise to power, see Manfred Pohl, "From Court Agent to State Financier—The Rise of the Rothschilds," in Heuberger, ed., *The Rothschilds: Essays on the History of a European Family*, 51–69.
11. Ibid., 57–59.
12. Ferguson, *The World's Banker*, 6.
13. See the timeline in Claude Collard and Melanie Aspey, eds. *Les Rothschild en*

France au XIXe siècle (Paris: Bibliothèque nationale de France, 2012), 179–83. It should be noted that Nathan Rothschild rejected an offer of knighthood from the British government in 1815. Former Rothschild archivist Simone Mace explains that the offer of knighthood was most likely extended because of the family's pivotal role in financing Britain's victory at the Battle of Waterloo. Mace surmises that Nathan declined out of fear that British society would disapprove of his knighthood, thereby jeopardizing his financial dealings. In this vein, he wrote to his brothers in a letter dated January 2, 1816 (Rothschild Archive London XI/109/4) that he was advised to "not go in for luxuries because the papers would immediately commence writing against me and officials here would start questioning.… [Therefore I was advised] to cut down on my living standards for the next twelve months." Quoted in Simone Mace, "From Frankfurt Jew to Lord Rothschild: The Ascent of the English Rothschilds to the Nobility," in Heuberger, ed., *The Rothschilds: Essays*, 180.

14 Michael Hall, "Le baron James de Rothschild, collectionneur de tableaux anciens," in Collard and Aspey, eds. *Les Rothschild en France*, 125.

15 Ferguson, *The World's Banker*, 360–361. With very few exceptions, the only contemporary works in their collection were portraits of themselves—e.g., Ingres's *Baronne de Rothschild* (1848), which features Betty as its sitter. James's generation preferred art works from the Dutch Golden Age, whereas the subsequent generation showed a greater interest in the Italian Renaissance. See, for example, Edmond de Rothschild's extensive collection of Renaissance engravings, later donated to the Louvre by his heirs. Also significant was the collection of Edmond's older brother Adolphe, who displayed his holdings in his domestic museum-cum-living room at 43 rue de Monceau (which featured a glass roof on par with Paxton's Grand Halls at Ferrières and Mentmore.) For more on the Rothschilds' collection, see Pauline Prevost-Marcilhacy, "Les Rothschild collectionneurs de peinture italienne," in Olivier Bonfait, Philippe Costamagna, Monica Preti-Hamard, eds., *Le goût pour la peinture italienne autour de 1800, prédécesseurs, modèles et concurrents du Cardinal Fesch* (Ajaccio: Musée Fesch, 2006), 277–290; and idem., *Les Rothschild: une dynastie de mécènes en France*, 3 Vols. (Paris: Louvre éditions and BnF éditions and Somogy éditions d'art, 2016).

16 Michael Hall, "The English Rothschilds as Collectors," in Heuberger, ed., *The Rothschilds: Essays*, 265.

17 Ferguson, *The World's Banker*, 275–276. The physiognomy of Howell's caricature was derived from an earlier 1817 etching of Nathan Rothschild: Richard Dighton's *A View from the Royal Exchange*. Ferguson explains that this particular likeness of Nathan—"a side view of a man in a black coat and top hat, stomach thrust forward, one hand in his pocket, the other holding a sheet of paper" (p. 275)—provided an iconic model that was often reused by other illustrators. For more on these drawings, see Alfred Rubens, "The Rothschilds in Caricature," *Transactions and Miscellanies (Jewish Historical Society of England)* 22 (1968–1969): 76–87.

18 For more on these design principles, see Alina Payne, "Notes from the Field: Anthropomorphism," *Art Bulletin* 94, no. 1 (March 2012): 29–31.

19 Pauline Prevost-Marcilhacy stresses this point in her scholarship on the Rothschilds. She writes that the combination of James's strong personality and desire to distinguish himself from his family, in addition to the relatively favorable conditions for Jews in France and the sheer size (and number of male heirs) of the French Rothschilds, resulted in James's more prolific and ostentatious architectural patronage. See Prevost-Marcilhacy, "Rothschild Architecture in England, France, Germany, Austria and Italy," in Heuberger, ed., *The Rothschilds: Essays*, 246–247. See also idem., *Les Rothschild: bâtisseurs et mécènes*, 34–38.

20 In this vein, James wrote to his father, Mayer Amschel, in 1818: "Tu ne peux pas imaginer à quel point j'aimerais être millionnaire à Paris et rire d'eux tous"; furthermore: "Par jalousie, ils ne veulent pas que nous devenions plus importants qu'eux." Quoted in Pauline Prevost-Marcilhacy, "Un Hôtel au Goût du Jour: L'Hôtel de James de Rothschild," *Gazette des Beaux-Arts* 124 (July/August 1994): 35.

21 Dieter Bartetzko, "Fairy Tales & Castles: On Rothschild Family Buildings in Frankfurt on Main," in Heuberger, ed., *The Rothschilds: Essays*, particularly pp. 221–26.

22 Bedoire, *The Jewish Contribution to Modern Architecture*, 90.

23 Quoted in Prevost-Marcilhacy, "Un Hôtel au Goût du Jour": 36.

24 Henri Bouchot, *Le Luxe français sous la Restauration* (Paris 1893), quoted in Prevost-Marcilhacy, *Les Rothschild: bâtisseurs et mécènes*, 45.

25 Prevost-Marcilhacy, "Un Hôtel au Goût du Jour": 40.

26 For an overview of the school's history and its core pedagogical and theoretical principles, see Donald Egbert, *The Beaux-Arts Tradition in French Architecture; Illustrated by the Grands Prix de Rome*, edited for publication by David Van Zanten (Princeton: Princeton University Press, 1980).

27 See Percier and Fontaine, *Palais, maisons, et autres édifices modernes, dessinés à Rome; publiés à Paris, l'an VI de la République française* (Paris: Ducamp, 1798); and idem., *Choix des plus célèbres maisons de plaisance de Rome et de ses environs; mesurées et dessinées par Charles Percier et P.-F.-L. Fontaine* (Paris: P. Didot l'aîné, 1809). For an interpretation of these books and their contribution to nineteenth-century Renaissance historicism in France, see Jean-Philippe Garric, "Comprendre la Renaissance dans un processus de projet: le *Choix des plus célèbres maisons de plaisance de Rome et de ses environs* de Percier et Fontaine," in Frédérique Lemerle, Yves Pauwels et Alice Thomine-Berrada, eds., *Le XIXe siècle et l'architecture de la Renaissance* (Paris: Picard, 2010), 81–93; idem., "La Renaissance perfectionnée. Le Cinquecento dans *Palais, maisons et autres édifices modernes dessinés à Rome* de Charles Percier et Pierre Fontaine," *Ricerche di Storia dell'arte*, No. 105 (2011): 25–41; and Antonio Brucculeri, "Le néo-Renaissance en France et la Haute Banque: Habiter et collectionner entre les années 1830 et 1880," *MDCCC 1800* Vol. 5 (July 2016): 45–70.

28 Brucculeri, "Le néo-Renaissance en France et la Haute Banque": 46–47.

29 For more on this villa, see Leila El-Wakil, "La villa pompéienne des Bartholoni: création d'un Grand Prix de Rome," in idem., *Bâtir la campagne: Genève 1800–1860* (Geneva: Georg Editeur, 1988), 221–229. See also Albert Bartholoni, *François Bartholony: 1796–1881, banquier et pionnier des chemins de fer français* (Paris: A. Bartholoni, 1979).

30 Likewise, the same can be said of Callet's publication *Architecture italienne, ou palais, maisons et autres édifices de l'Italie moderne; dessinés et publiés par F. Callet et J.-B. Lesueur, anciens pensionnaires de l'Académie de France à Rome* (Paris, 1827), whose image plates circulated early modern Italian design precedents within the French architectural community.

31 Architectural historians Neil Levine, David Van Zanten, and Barry Bergdoll have written extensively on the self-styled Romantic "Band of Four" Beaux-Arts architects: Félix Duban, Louis Duc, Henri Labrouste, and Léon Vaudoyer. See Neil Levine, "The Romantic Ideal of Architectural Legibility: Henri Labrouste and the Néo-Grec," in Arthur Drexler, ed. *The Architecture of the École des Beaux-Arts* (New York and Cambridge, Mass.: The Museum of Modern Art and MIT Press, 1977), 325–416; Barry Bergdoll, *Léon Vaudoyer: Historicism in the Age of Industry* (New York and Cambridge, Mass.: The Architectural History Foundation and MIT Press, 1994); idem., "'Le véritable but de la Renaissance': Léon Vaudoyer and the discourse on the Renaissance in Romantic Historicist Architecture in France," in Lemerle, Pauwels and Thomine-Berrada, eds., *Le XIXe siècle et l'architecture de la Renaissance* (Paris: Picard, 2010), 229–241; idem., "Romantic Historiography and the Paradoxes of Historicist Architecture," in Harry Francis Mallgrave, ed., *A Companion to the History of Architecture: Nineteenth Century Architecture: Historicism, the Beaux-Arts, and the Gothic* (New York: Wiley and Sons, 2016); and David Van Zanten, *Designing Paris: The Architecture of Duban, Labrouste, Duc, and Vaudoyer* (Cambridge, Mass.: MIT Press, 1987).

32 According to Marc Le Coeur, these establishments included the Restaurant du Grand Vefour (1834), the Café de la Banque de France (1838), the Café des Concerts Musards (1838), and, perhaps most notably, the Maison Dorée (1840) on the Boulevard des Italians. Le Coeur argues that the arrival of the neo-Renaissance style in Paris reflected the new social and cultural identity of the July Monarchy's elite, who rejected the severity of neo-classicism in favor of the decorative potpourri and exoticism that the Renaissance seemingly provided. Furthermore, Le Coeur remarks that the first building in Paris to feature a neo-Renaissance-style façade was Félix Duban's design for a paper mill on the Rue Saint-Honore in 1830. Marc Le Coeur, "Le goût Renaissance au service du palais. Décors de cafés et restaurants parisiens sous la monarchie de Juillet," in Lemerle, Pauwels and Thomine-Berrada, eds., *Le XIXe siècle et l'architecture de la Renaissance* (Paris: Picard, 2010), 81–93. Scholars have identified contemporaneous projects in Paris that employed a similar neo-Renaissance style. For Duban's Hotel de Pourtales at 7 rue Tronchet and Victor Lemaire's 52 rue Laffite, see Sybille Bellamy-Brown, "La Renaissance au service du XIXe siècle. À propos de l'ouvrage de Charles François Callet *Notice historique sur la vie artistique et les ouvrages de quelques architectes français du XVIe siècle* (1842)," *Livraisons d'histoire de l'architecture*, no. 9 (2005): 38–41. For 48 rue d'Hauteville and 13 rue Bleue, see Prevost-Marcilhacy, *Les Rothschild*, 42.

33 Bedoire, *The Jewish Contribution to Modern Architecture*, 93.

34. For an overview of Renaissance historicism in nineteenth-century London, see Frank Salmon, "The 'Ordinary Italian' in Nineteenth-Century British Architecture," in Antonio Brucculeri and Sabine Frommel, eds. *Renaissance italienne et architecture au XIXe siècle: interprétations et restitutions* (Rome: Campisano editore, 2016), 233–242.
35. As quoted by the architect's son, the Reverend Alfred Barry, in his biographical study, *The Life and Work of Sir Charles Barry* (London: John Murray, 1867), 50. Alfred Barry goes on to note—citing the opinion of an unnamed critic—that the inspiration his father drew from Florentine and Roman palazzos yielded a new Italianate model in Britain that departed from the dominant paradigm of neo-Palladianism. Judging by his design for the Travellers Club, Barry's Italianate model could be characterized by its "large proportion of the solid wall to the windows, and the striking effect of the great cornice" (p.81).
36. The quote comes from French dramatist Alphonse Royer's 1875 book *Histoire de l'Opéra*, which describes Duponchel as "un inventeur d'effets décoratifs qui avait la passion innée des magnificences et de la mise en scène." Quoted in Prevost-Marcilhacy, "Un Hôtel au Goût du Jour": 41.
37. Consider the following: "Dans la Chaussée d'Antin, la Renaissance est plus en faveur: les salons de MM. Rothschild et Aguado ont donné le ton" (Anonymous, L'Artiste. *Journal de la literature et des beaux-arts* XI, 1836); and "James s'est entièrement meuble dans le gout Renaissance. Je trouve ce style peu convenable pour un hôtel à Paris. Je j'aimerais mieux pour un château. Mais, cette réserve faite, je dois reconnaitre qu'il est impossible de le voir mieux imité. Les peintures sont sur fond or, exécutées par d'excellents artistes…" (Rudolphe Apponyi, *Vingt-cinq ans à Paris, 1826–50*), both quoted in Prevost-Marcilhacy, "Un Hôtel au Goût du Jour": 43–44.
38. Ferguson, *The World's Banker*, 346.
39. For more on the family's patronage of musicians, see Charlotte de Rothschild, "The Musical Associations of the Rothschild Family," in Heuberger, ed., *The Rothschilds: Essays*, 287–96.
40. Prevost-Marcilhacy, *Les Rothschild*, 57–58.
41. Quoted in Muhlstein, *James de Rothschild*, 81.
42. Bedoire, *The Jewish Contribution to Modern Architecture*, 94.
43. Edmund De Waal, *The Hare with Amber Eyes: A Family's History of Art and Loss* (New York: Farrar, Straus, and Giroux, 2010), 33–35.
44. Marcel Proust, *Swann's Way*, trans. Lydia Davis (New York: Penguin Books, 2003), 231–32. Originally published as *Du côté de chez Swann* (Paris 1913).
45. Ferguson, *The World's Banker*, 346–47.
46. Heinrich Heine, "Korrespondenzartikel, 1832–1852," in Klaus Briegleb, ed., *Sämtliche Schriften*, vol. 5 (Munich: Carl Hanser, 1975), translated and quoted in Ferguson, *The World's Banker*, 347.
47. As Niall Ferguson points out, an additional factor motivating the Rothschilds' rural building projects was the plummeting value of land "in the wake of the agricultural crisis of the mid-1840s" (p. 553). This allowed them to expand their existing properties and acquire new estates for hunting and wine growing.
48. Heuberger, ed., *The Rothschilds: Essays*, 85–88.
49. Alexandre Weill, "Rothschild und die Europäischen Staaten" (1844), translated and quoted in Ferguson, *The World's Banker*, 20–21.
50. Ferguson, *The World's Banker*, 275.
51. Quoted in Claude Collard, "La vie en société des Rothschild," in Collard and Aspey, eds., *Les Rothschild en France au XIXe siècle*, 100. Author's translation.
52. Architectural historian Richard Wittman provides a succinct account of the movement's principles in his "Space, Networks, and the Saint-Simonians," *Grey Room* 40 (Summer 2010): 24–49. Per Wittman, "The immediate goal of the Saint-Simonian doctrine was to foster contemporary society's passage into a new organic period, one prepared by the destructive critical period of Reformation, *philosophie*, and Revolution. … The key to this new society was to be industry and technology, which together would generate and extend new networks of exchange and communication, from credit finance to railroads. Through an increasingly mobile, globalized exchange of goods, information, and people, the time and distance that traditionally kept human beings separated into antagonistic groups would be dissolved. The Saint-Simonians referred to this ideal as 'universal association.' The coming organic era would be characterized by global unity and cultural synthesis between nations, an end to wars, an end to class antagonisms, material prosperity beyond all previous reckoning, and unparalleled human creativity in every arena" (p. 29). For a more extensive study of the movement, see Antoine Picon, *Les saint-simoniens: raison, imaginaire et utopie* (Paris: Belin, 2002).
53. Karen Bowie, "The Rothschilds, the Railways and Urban Form of 19th Century Paris," in Heuberger, ed., *The Rothschilds: Essays*, 87. See also Claude Collard, "Les activités économiques de James de Rothschild" and "Les Pereire" in Collard and Aspey, eds., *Les Rothschild en France au XIXe siècle*.
54. Collard, "Les activités économiques de James de Rothschild," 60–61.
55. Impressionist painters addressed this phenomenon by juxtaposing bucolic landscapes with the steam and iron of industrial railways. T.J. Clark describes Impressionism's thematic treatment of this jarring, even disorienting, collision as follows: "Where industry and recreation were casually established next to each other, in a landscape which assumed only as much form as the juxtaposition of production and distraction (factories and regattas) allowed, there modernity seemed vivid, and painters believed they might invent a new set of descriptions for it. …There are pictures by Manet and Seurat, for example, in which the environs of Paris are recognized to be a specific form of life: not the countryside, not the city, not a degenerated form of either." Clark, *The Painting of Modern Life: Paris in the Art of Manet and his Followers* (London: Thames and Hudson, 1985), 147. For another interpretation of the Impressionists' para-industrial landscapes, see Robert Herbert, "Suburban Leisure," in idem., *Impressionism: Art, Leisure, and Parisian Society* (New Haven: Yale University Press, 1988), 195–263.
56. The London and North Western Line in England serviced Nathan's Mentmore estate; the Strasbourg-Ligny line served Ferrières.
57. It remains unclear when and how Paxton's involvement began. Among his earlier known interactions with the family was a visit to the garden of James de Rothschild's Château de Boulogne in 1841. See Prevost-Marcilhacy, *Les Rothschild*, 89; and George Chadwick, *The Works of Sir Joseph Paxton: 1803–1865* (London: Architectural Press, 1961), 188. But it is possible that two parties intersected the previous decade when both Paxton and the Rothschilds developed an interest in railway construction. Nonetheless, Paxton's commission was secured by November 13, 1850, when he announced to the Society of Arts in London that he was designing a gentleman's home—presumably Mentmore—a whose roof would be constructed entirely of glass (Prevost-Marcilhacy, *Les Rothschild*, 90).
58. It is worth quoting from Ruskin's lecture at length: "Perhaps the first idea which a young architect is apt to be allured by, as a head-problem in these experimental days, is its being incumbent upon him to invent a 'new style' worthy of modern civilization in general, and of England in particular; a style worthy of our engines and telegraphs; as expansive as steam, and as sparkling as electricity. […] The furnace and the forge shall be at your service: you shall draw out your plates of glass and beat out your bars of iron till you have encompassed us all,—if your style is of the practical kind,—with endless perspective of black skeleton and blinding square,—or if your style is to be of the ideal kind,—you shall wreathe your streets with ductile leafage, and roof them with variegated crystal—you shall put, if you will, all London under one blazing dome of many colours that shall light the clouds round it with its flashing, as far as to the sea. And still, I ask you, What after this? Do you suppose those imaginations of yours will ever lie down there asleep beneath the shade of your iron leafage, or within the coloured light of your enchanted dome? Not so. Those souls, and fancies, and ambitions of yours, are wholly infinite; and whatever may be done by others, you will still want to do something for yourselves; if you cannot rest content with Palladio, neither will you with Paxton: all the metal and glass that ever were melted have not so much weight in them as will clog the wings of one human spirit's aspiration." Ruskin, "Imagination in Architecture" (1857) from "The Two Paths," in E.T. Cook and Alexander Wedderburn, eds., *The Works of John Ruskin*, Vol. XVI (London and New York: George Allen and Longmans, Green, and Co., 1905), 348–49.
59. For more on the subject, see Katherine Wheeler, "The Sins of the Renaissance: John Ruskin and the Rise of the Professional Architect," in idem., *Victorian Perceptions of Renaissance Architecture* (Farnham, England and Burlington, VT: Ashgate Publishing, 2014), 19–48.
60. Per Brucculeri, "Le néo-Renaissance en France et la Haute Banque," 50–52, this desire was especially pronounced in France, as evidenced by a wave of publications that included Victor Petit's *Les châteaux de France des XVe et XVIe siècles* (Paris: C. Boivin, 1860?); Adolphe Berty's *La Renaissance monumentale en France* (Paris: A. Morel, 1864); and Claude Sauvageot's *Palais, châteaux, hotels et maisons de France du XVème au XVIIIème siècles* (Paris: A. Morel, 1867). The Château de Blois, in particular, became a dominant point of reference for French Renaissance architecture and a source of cultural fascination for the French public and foreign visitors. Following a decades-long restoration by Félix Duban, the château was the subject of historiographic studies that lauded its architecture in overtly nationalistic terms, e.g., as a "monument Franc par excellence, monument dont l'origine se confond avec

les origines de la nation," Ernest Le Nail, *Architecture de la Renaissance. Le Château de Blois (extérieur et intérieur): ensembles et détails* (Paris: Libraire générale de l'architecture et des travaux publics, Ducher & Cie, 1875), 9; quoted in Brucculeri, 53.

61. Prevost-Marcilhacy, *Les Rothschild*, 111.
62. Ibid.
63. Cowles, *The Rothschilds*, 119.
64. James de Rothschild acquired the Château de Ferrières on June 25, 1829. Prior to its reconstruction by Paxton, the property underwent a number of improvements, both to the château as well as its surrounding buildings and landscape. For a closer study of the château, see Pauline Prevost-Marcilhacy, "James de Rothschild à Ferrières: les projets de Paxton et de Lami," *Revue de l'Art* 100, no. 1 (1993): 58–73.
65. The project's design development occurred in two distinct phases. Over the course of 1854, Paxton and Stokes presented numerous plans and elevation studies to James, who responded critically (per Paxton's frustrated correspondence with his wife; see Prevost-Marcilhacy, *Les Rothschild*, 94.) These early studies depict a structure whose ornament and massing is very similar to that of Mentmore and its inspiration, Wollaton Hall. On account of this scheme's lack of originality and use of English historicism, James commissioned a French architect, Antoine-Julien Hénard, to design an alternative proposal for Ferrières. Hénard's drawings are no longer extant, but records indicate that they were presented at the 1857 Salon in Paris and ultimately were not used for the final building. Paxton and Stokes were again asked to develop new façade studies for Ferrières in ca. 1856–57, this time yielding a château that abided by the traditions of the "legitimate" Renaissance with an eclectic mix of French and Italian references. Construction most likely began at the end of 1856 under the helm of English contractor George Myers, who oversaw a mixed crew of French and English laborers (see Prevost-Marcilhacy, *Les Rothschild*, 96–98).
66. For reproductions of these works and an explanation of their social context, see the exhibition catalog for *Spectaculaire Second Empire* (Paris: Musee d'Orsay and Éditions Skira, 2016). It also bears mentioning that, prior to his commissions for Ferrières, Lami had already designed interiors for James de Rothschild's Château in Boulogne-sur-Seine (ca. 1850–1855).
67. From Paul-André Lemoisne, *L'Oeuvre d'Eugène Lami (1800–1890), essai d'un catalogue raisonné* (Paris, 1914), quoted in Prevost-Marcilhacy, *Les Rothschild*, 122. Author's translation.
68. Bedoire, *The Jewish Contribution to Modern Architecture*, 103.
69. Prevost-Marcilhacy, *Les Rothschild*, 122.
70. Bedoire, 104.
71. Here a connection might be drawn to German sociologist Georg Simmel's 1903 essay "The Metropolis and Mental Life," which characterizes the sensory shock imparted to the urban subject by "modern life flow." Although Simmel's essay is later in date and takes the industrialized modern city as its point of departure, one could argue that a similar effect of sensory inundation is achieved in the Rothschild Style interior, whose emphasis on surface anticipates the symbolic order of a money economy.
72. Bedoire, 88.
73. Dardel's account of visiting Ferrières in 1867 appears in his memoirs: "Passing through the majestic pillared peristyle, one enters the vestibule, which is decorated with statues and precious vases; from here a double staircase describes an elegant curve leading straight into the hall. In this room, which is immensely proportioned, the height of a church, lit from above through a crystal roof and with outstanding works of art displayed in it, the guests assembled, and each was now at the liberty to go where his fancy took him. On the one side, music; on the other, billiards. Farther off there were tables for writing or drawing, a library, and so on. Everywhere statues, pictures, historic furniture of the costliest kind. A gallery, supported by colossal caryatids of marble, bronze or silver, crowns this hall, in which good taste prevails everywhere. The whole thing makes a supremely interesting museum, but arranged with such taste and artistry that one does not notice it: the eye simply delights in the harmony everywhere apparent. Eugène Lami, the creator of this masterpiece, was inspired by Venice, which, during its period of greatness, brought forth so much affluence and beauty." Dardel, *Minnen* 1911–1913, 3: 42, translated and quoted in Bedoire, 84.
74. Quoted in ibid.
75. Peter Sloterdijk, *In the World Interior of Capital: For a Philosophical Theory of Globalization*, trans. Wieland Hoband (Cambridge: Polity Press 2014). See also Sloterdijk's *Sphären* or "Spheres" trilogy (1998–2004), whose individual volumes *Bubbles*, *Globes*, and *Foam* describe conceptual spaces of human activity and ontology.
76. In this respect, the Rothschild Style anticipates the so-called Edwardian Baroque Style—as defined by the architectural historian Alex Bremner—which was used in banks, insurance companies, and financial institutions across the British empire at the turn of the twentieth century. See G.A. Bremner, *Building Greater Britain: Architecture, Imperialism, and the Edwardian Baroque Revival, 1885–1920* (London and New Haven: Paul Mellon Centre for Studies in British Art; Distributed by Yale University Press, 2023).
77. For more on these two typologies, see their respective chapters in Nikolaus Pevsner, *A History of Building Types* (London: Thames and Hudson, 1976). Numerous image plates of late-nineteenth-century banks with glazed central halls and "Schmiegsame Renaissanceformen" can also be found in Paul Kick, "Gebäude für Banken und andere Geldinstitute, in Entwerfen, Anlage und Einrichtung der Gebäude des Handbuches der Architektur. Vierter Teil," in Josef Durm, Hermann Ende, and Eduard Schmitt, eds. *Handbuch der Architektur* (Stuttgart: A. Bergsträsser, 1902), 139–302. Scholars have noted that the bank typology catalyzed Renaissance revivalism in the United States. Historian Massimiliano Savorra argues that American capitalists of the late-nineteenth and early-twentieth century used their architectural commissions "to convey the image of an institution as a reflection of a noble society (with its roots even in religious culture), in addition to that of a business *corporation*." See Savorra, "Money with Style. The Italian Renaissance and American Architects," in Brucculeri and Frommel, eds., *Renaissance italienne et architecture au XIXe siècle*, 243–255. It was in Renaissance classicism—transferred to the United States via Beaux-Arts pedagogy—that corporate patrons found the means to communicate these ideas. For more on the transnational circulation of Beaux-Arts pedagogy, see David Sadighian, "Classical Economics: On the Currency of the Beaux-Arts System," in Thomas Kirchner, Déborah Laks, and Elvan Zabunyan, eds., *L'Art en France à la croisée des cultures* (Paris and Heidelberg: Deutsches Forum für Kunstgeschichte and Arthistoricum.net, 2023), 136–148.
78. Bedoire, *The Jewish Contribution to Modern Architecture*, 120, 132.

PRELUDE

"Elephant in the Room" is a series of eco-fables for the climate crisis. Calls to climate action have expanded accountability to institutions that were established during the nascent stages of industrial capitalism and through its extractivist wealth. Such motions are an invitation to reckon with and interrogate their own entanglements with carbon modernity, and to ultimate curate—if such a position is possible—new forms of action, within and beyond their walls. In the "Elephant in the Room" series, each eco-fable animates one fabulous figure from a natural history museum, so that the remains of such a specimen—skeleton, taxidermy, or composite mount—are brought back to life to recount their brutal environmental histories of dispossession and violence. They also implore, in their afterlives, responsibility from cultural institutions in the climate crisis. Each video is a 6-minute animation composed of rhyming verse, saturated color drawings, and occasional humor to stomach the tensions and tragedies of such narratives. The significance of figures—charismatic media figures and figures of speech—allows us to utter the unfathomable destruction of worlds; figuration bestows personhood upon the specimen and thus becomes a crucial aesthetic method. Figures are such material-semiotic knots, as they help us grapple inside the flesh of the world and make entanglements in which diverse clusters of meaning (narratives, discourses, precedents, imaginaries) shape one another through "creating performative images that can be inhabited."[1] Akin to a death mask, the fable takes on the likeness of environmental folklore, aspiring to other forms of attention, and, dare we say, care. Such fabulations are not a break from environmental histories or futures, but a narrative tool that gives form to the present reality to delight and disturb you into other ways of thinking and feeling the Earth.[2]

"Elephant in the Room and Other Fables" has been funded by grants from MIT Humanities, Arts, and Social Sciences and the Graham Foundation for Advanced Studies.

ELEPHANT IN THE ROOM

The series was initiated in the context of the international design competition Reimagining Museums for Climate Action, which asked how "museums could help society make the deep, transformative changes needed to achieve a net-zero or zero-carbon world."[3] Eponymously titled *Elephant in the Room*, the first fable in the series addresses the elephant in the room—the climate emergency—by telling the story of an elephant who charges out of the American Museum of Natural History to fight for environmental justice.[4] The American Museum of Natural History in New York City is home to the famous taxidermy dioramas in the Akeley Hall of African Mammals. The iconic centerpiece, christened "The Alarm" by the renowned taxidermist Carl Akeley, is a herd of eight nervous elephants captured in a moment of great tension before a stampede. At least one of these elephants was shot by President Theodore Roosevelt during the Smithsonian-Roosevelt African Expedition (1909–1910), in which thousands of animals were "collected" to become property of the museum. Through these killings for science and conservation, the museum preached the gospel of racism and colonialism, outlined by Donna Haraway as the "Teddy Bear Patriarchy."[5] In her environmentalist rebellion, the herd's African matriarch comes to life, charging out of the American Museum of Natural History to stomach the systemic legacies that dictate how some people and species may live while others must die. By taking her demands to the streets, the elephant underlines the role of museums in wider calls for climate justice, which necessarily involve a critical revision of their own legacies. In this sense, the elephant as a museum is less "curator"—one who stills or steals life in order to accumulate or organize a collection of things—and more "caretaker," or one who tends to forms of life. "Elephant in the Room" was narrated by Donna Haraway and first exhibited at the Glasgow Science Center, coinciding with the 26th UN Climate Change Conference (COP) session in 2021. The need to craft such a praxis of care and response, or *response-ability*, in the words of Haraway, implies both a design to learn about an issue and an ethical obligation to become concerned and act.

WHALE SONG

The skeleton of Hope the blue whale was installed in the main hall of the Natural History Museum in London in 2017. In 1891, a young female blue whale was stranded on a sandbar while migrating off the coast of Ireland, where it was harpooned and auctioned off. Her body was butchered, her blubber boiled down, and her 4.5-tonne skeleton sold for £250 to the Natural History Museum. For almost 130 years, the whale was displayed in the museum's Mammals gallery, and then repositioned to take center stage in the main hall in 2017. The whale has since been named Hope, a name chosen as a symbol of "humanity's power to shape a sustainable future." The decision to give pride of place to a whale was justified on conservationist grounds; as the museum director explained: "The very resources on which modern society relies are under threat. Species and ecosystems are being destroyed faster than we can describe them or even understand their significance. The blue whale serves as a poignant reminder that while abundance is no guarantee of survival, through our choices we can make a real difference. There is hope."[6] In 2019, 100 people simultaneously laid down underneath the blue whale skeleton for a half-hour Extinction Rebellion "die-in" protest. In the fable, Hope charges out of the Main Hall to swallow the legacies of the "Wonders of Industry," which include both the material legacies of whaling—the first oil of the Industrial Revolution—and the cultural inheritances of Albertopolis, the nickname given to the area centered on Exhibition Road. Rooted in the 1851 Crystal Palace Exhibition, this thoroughfare houses various institutions, including the Natural History Museum, Royal Albert Hall, and the Victoria and Albert Museum, where the animation was first screened at the 2022 London Design Festival.

THE WAY OF THE DINOSAURS

On a Sunday morning in 1898, Andrew Carnegie, an industrialist–philanthropist who had led the expansion of the American steel industry in the late 19th century, read about a paleontological find. The *New York Journal* carried a full-page spread under the banner headline, "Most Colossal Animal Ever on Earth Just Found Out West!", with an illustration of a long-necked dinosaur rearing up on its hind legs and peeking into an 11th-story window of the New York Life Building. Carnegie immediately wanted such a dinosaur for his namesake museum in Pittsburgh; he mailed the story with a check for $10,000 to the museum's director with the note: "Buy this for Pittsburgh." In 1907, to house the monumental specimen, the Carnegie Museum expanded to add a new dinosaur hall, along with a foyer for the Music Hall, the Hall of Architecture, and the Hall of Sculpture. In the dinosaur hall, fragmentary geological remains are figured (with the support of a steel structure for the heavy bones!) to hold real consequences on what counts as Nature. Weaving the histories and futures of fossils and fossil fuel extraction, the fable cautions that fracking and the continued destruction of fossil fuels may bring humans to become extinct, in the way of the dinosaur. Set within the Hall of Architecture, the animation debuted at the Carnegie Museum of Art, convening around the exhibition "Unsettling Matter, Gaining Ground" in October 2023.

1 Donna Haraway, *Modest_Witness@Second_Millennium.FemaleMan©_Meets_OncoMouseTM: Feminism and Technoscience* (London: Routledge, 1997).
2 Isabelle Stengers, "The Cosmopolitical Proposal," *Making Things Public: Atmospheres of Democracy*, ed. Bruno Latour and Peter Weibel (Cambridge, Mass.: MIT Press, 2005).
3 Reimagining Museums for Climate Action, https://www.museumsforclimateaction.org
4 Rania Ghosn & El Hadi Jazairy, "Elephant in the Room," *Journal of Architectural Education* 75:2 (2021), 264–274. See also animation at: https://www.youtube.com/watch?v=i2Xz9fJ85IO
5 DESIGN EARTH Project Team: Rania Ghosn, El Hadi Jazairy, Monica Hutton, Anhong Li. Donna Haraway, "Teddy Bear Patriarchy: Taxidermy in the Garden of Evil," *Social Text* No. 11 (Winter, 1984–1985), 20–64.
6 Maev Kennedy, "Dippy the Diplodocus is displaced from Natural History Museum by blue whale." *The Guardian* 29 January 2015, 22–23.

ELEPHANT IN THE ROOM

A visitor to the museum notices small things,
caught up in their own interests and the bias this brings.
What does this allow to go unaddressed?
The "elephant in the room," as you may have guessed.

There is no bigger problem often ignored,
than the climate change we are marching toward.
Familiar with the feeling of being dismissed,
the elephant trumpets: a crisis does exist!

She lets out an alarm call to signal the herd,
to stampede into the streets, out from where they were stirred.
She broke out of the Museum of Natural History,
to protest human behaviour in all its misery.

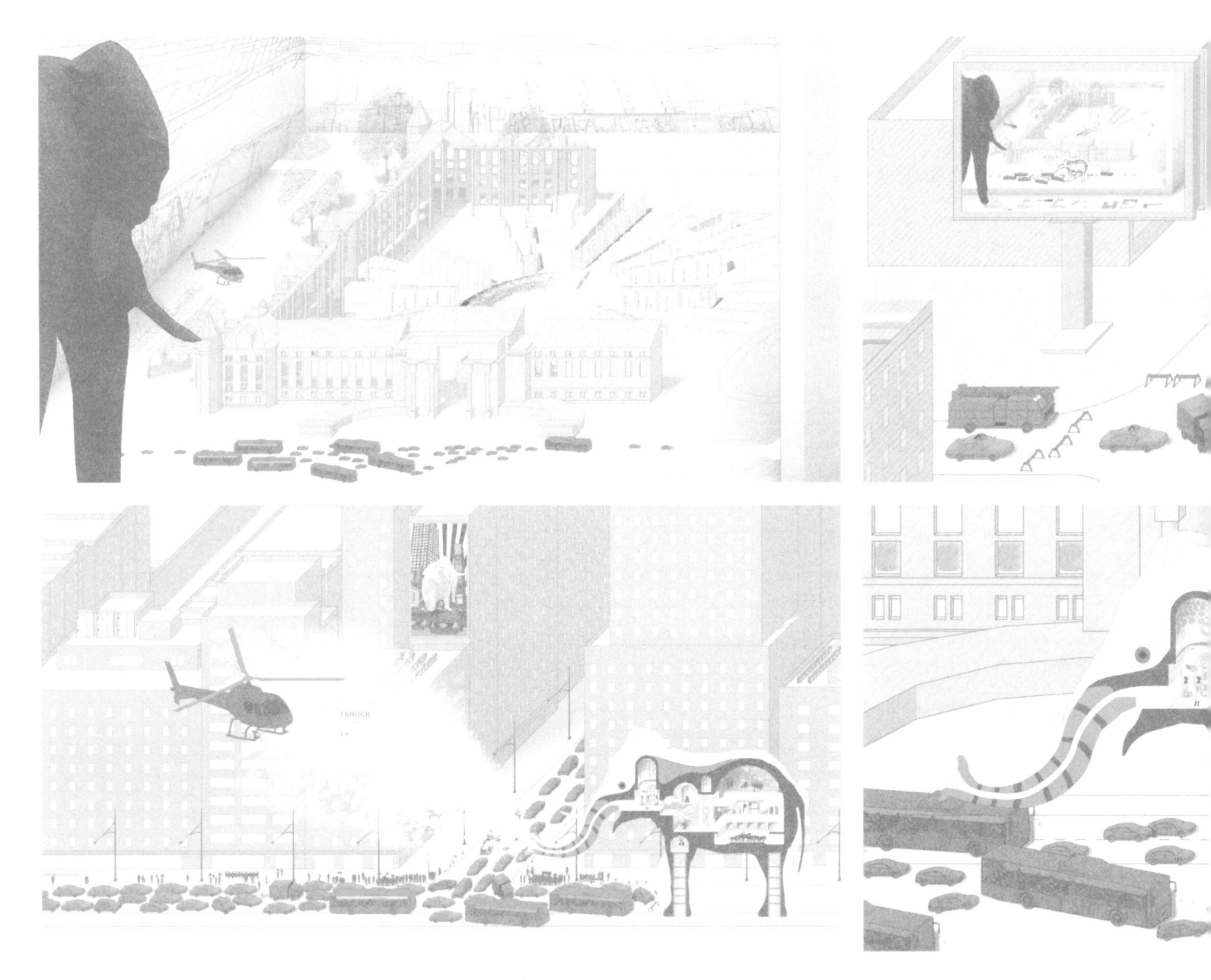

Thick in the air, and all over the day,
is a butane, propane, black carbon bouquet.
Climate issues have become more robust,
as diesel, paraffin and petrol combust.

The African elephant stomps down the street.
She is not detainable and not discreet;
She occupies Wall Street and protests in Times Square,
while sirens serenade and flies buzz in the air.

She raises her trunk to sound a deafening drum,
"Enough is enough! Surely you aren't all just dumb."
This matriarch elephant and seven more died,
Just so the museum could become more alive.

The Hall of African Mammals is where they were taken,
Waiting over a century for a time to awaken.
"The Alarm" is the centerpiece where their bodies were staged,
Frozen in a nightmare as if they were caged.

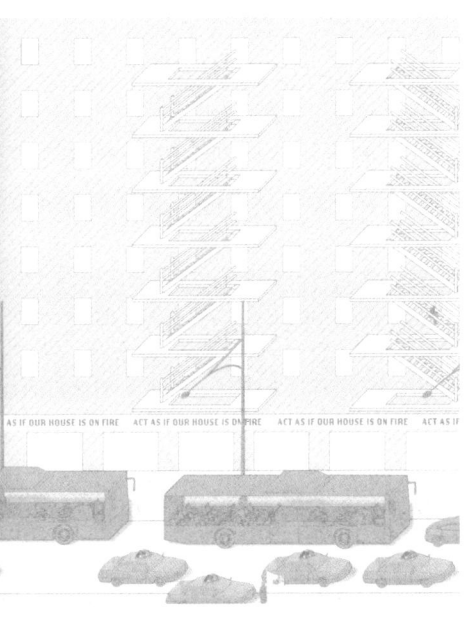

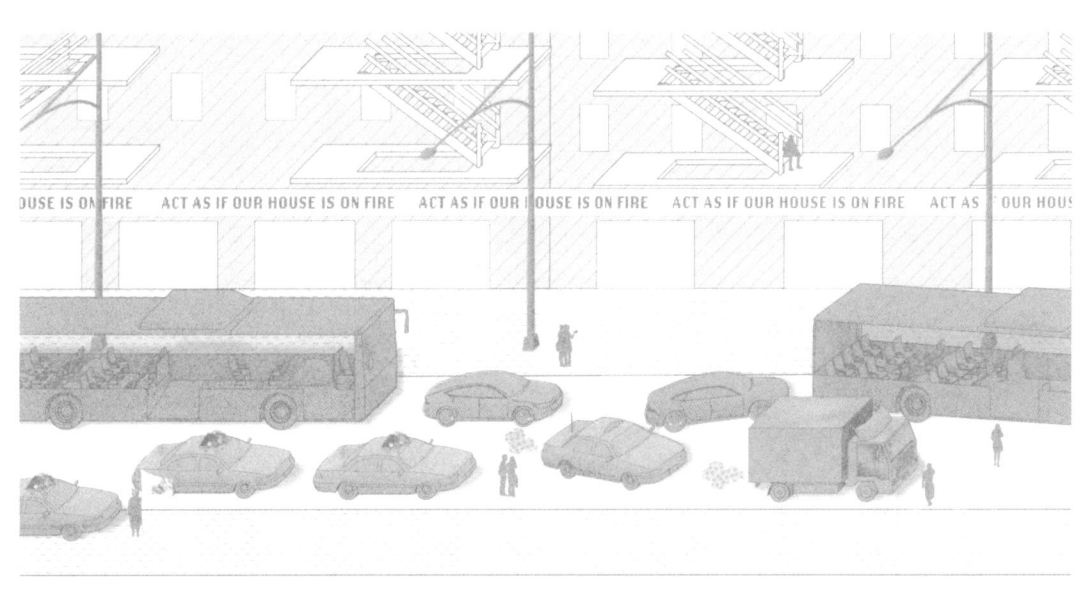

Around the room, other captive subjects stand by
within dioramas that are stacked two tiers high.
The Rhinoceros, Gorilla, Ostrich, and Lion
silently protest in a perpetual die-in.

The elephant never forgets the source of its scar.
"Speak softly and carry a big stick; you will go far."
A celebrated "conservationist" with a liking for hunting,
is the American president the Elephant was confronting.

"The Big Stick" is the rifle President Roosevelt had in hand,
as he stalked the Elephant's footprints across open land.
His son Kermit joined in on the Africa expedition,
and shot her small calf taking after the politician.

The Elephant twitches to life in the Africa Hall.
As if no time has passed, she remembers it all.
Her reddish-brown eyes with German glass in their place,
open to look museumgoers in the face.

She devours a book that a companion had written,
on structures of power and knowledge she did not fit in.
The "Teddy Bear Patriarchy" is a violent tale,
of capitalism, supremacy, and the white human male.

With eyes no longer blind she sees what her body can make,
the world on her mind that no one can take.
She looks around the room and says "The one thing I know,
is that the teddy bear patriarchy will have to go!"

The creature denounces the stuffed Teddy and its monsters.
She has had quite enough of environmental imposters;
the equestrian statue, the plaque honoring David Koch,
were swallowed using her trunk shortly after she woke.

The mammal's belly rumbles with resonant demands:
to decolonize, divest, and dismantle, she firmly stands.
Like a calving iceberg, earthquake, or volcanic eruption,
her trumpeting call thunders a long-distance disruption.

Her revival starts an autopsy fit for the ages,
where tools are used to dissect the museum in stages.
Natural History becomes an building taxidermy,
in a plan to make the most avid climate deniers squirmy.

Only the museum's facade remains in place,
to repair the damage to the very last trace.
It frames a graveyard where the Elephant can finally rest,
with the enormous weight she has lifted right off of her chest.

In the garden of a damaged planet no collection is held,
Only the demand for action–that's why the Elephant rebelled!
A Climate Countdown Clock will keep time and enforce
The twelve years that remain for us to change course.

Each year, one bar of actions counters the change that's been caused.
The clock ticks, the bars tighten, and it cannot be paused.
Around the Elephant's graveyard, the margins grow thin
until the final alarm sounds, and the endings begin.

So down the street we go with the Elephant inside,
always mustering her grit as our climate action guide.
And if somehow you happened to miss her,
take a step back and look at the big picture.

WHALE SONG

The hall of the museum, as soon as you enter,
divides living and extinct, cut down its center.
The border between is a survival distinction.
A swell of species now faces alarming extinction.

In the middle, the skeleton of the endangered blue whale
hangs between life and death in an unfinished tale.
Pakicetus came first, millions of years before.
The first whale walked on four legs on the Tethys Sea shore.

Her hip bones remain from relatives that lived out of water,
before human contact and imminent slaughter.
Hollowed out when claimed by a two-legged owner,
to come to life she is in need of a giant organ donor.

The bones alarmingly rock from side to side,
caught up in the current of an industrial tide.
A brief second at the surface is enough to expose
from miles away, the whalers yell "Thar She Blows!

Beached at low tide along Ireland's east coast,
Trapped in the sights of an insatiable host.
The stranding marked the eve of the whaling boom.
A crowd gathered in fascination, signalling doom.

Pressing a harpoon under her flipper to pierce;
an act amazingly petty to kill a being so fierce.
A titanic heart that could fill a drum with a beat
turned the sea red around her killer's feet.

The Royal Fish law claimed her property of the Crown.
In layers they proceeded to fully cut her down.
Diagonal slits made in skin thick like tire rubber;
stripped off sections of gelatinous white blubber.

Boiled down into oil for lamps to keep burning,
Her materials were measured for their commercial earning.
With her layers peeled away, only the skeleton was left.
Even this was gathered up to conclude an awful theft!

Disarticulating the structure, gouging out tissue between bone,
gathering the pieces for the Natural History Museum to own.
Mixed with polymer replicas and carbon fibre joints,
strung up to iron trusses with steel cables at ten points.

Dippy the Diplodocus returns from a big tour,
attracting attention like the Crown jewel Koh-i-Noor.
Ten plaster cast copies of the original source
were commissioned by Carnegie and mounted on steel, of course!

Hope the whale replaced Dippy, who replaced George the African elephant.
A selection of mascots burdened to keep the museum relevant.
Revolted by the symbol that they were cast to become,
they no longer wished to be a token or source of income.

In a demand for climate action, the whale took a great fall.
"A crash would necessitate rebuilding it all!"
Landing on Dippy, their joints break apart,
summoning a whole new assembly to start.

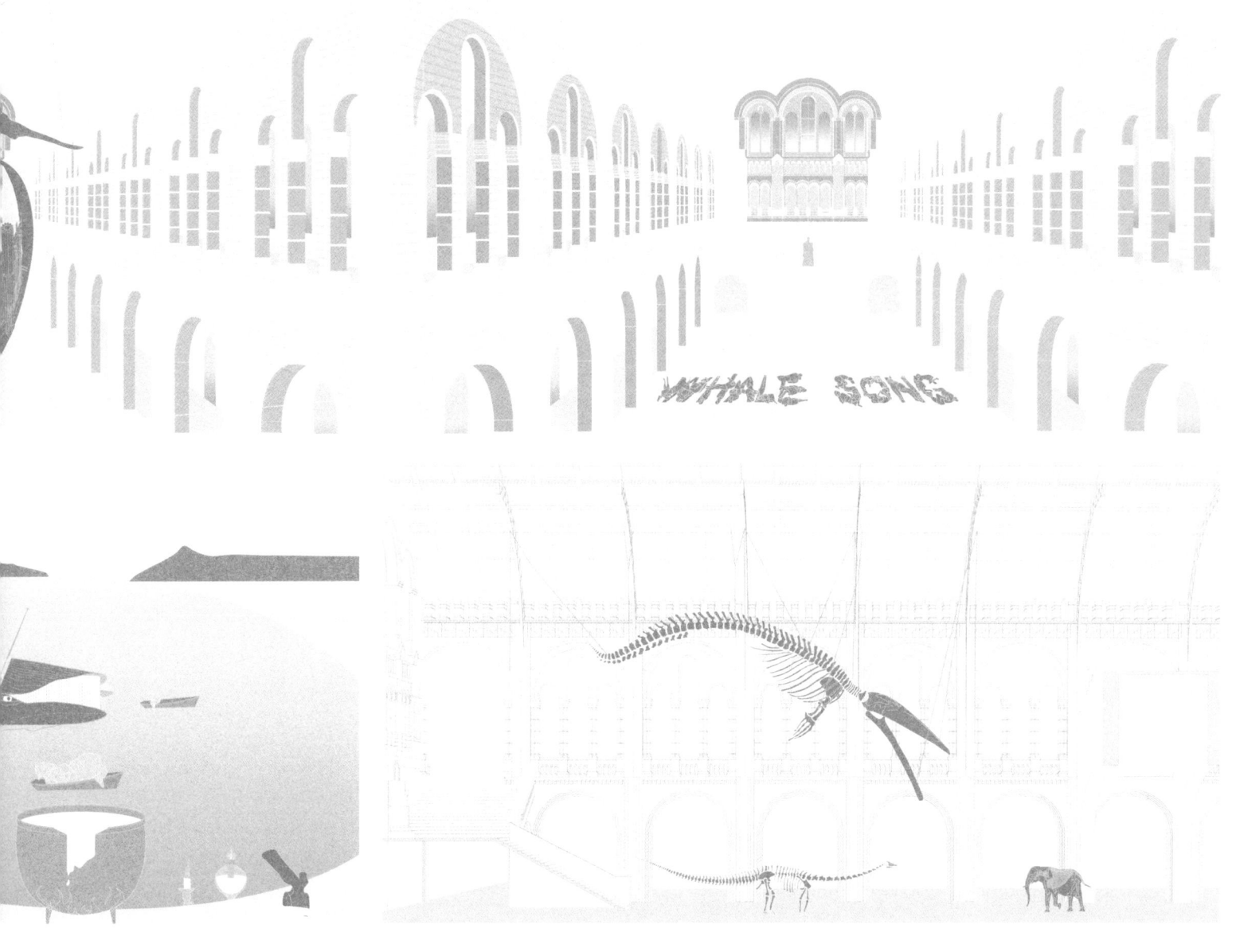

Fabricated inaccurately, like the Crystal Palace Dinosaurs,
the whale is rebuilt to join her living relatives on all fours.
Like the Iguanadon that ended up with a thumb spike on its nose.
bones are stacked out of order to form her next pose.

The Great Exhibition of the Works of Industry of All Nations
financed the land purchase for the museum foundations.
Millions consuming stories of industrialized success;
the decades since proving an environmental mess.

Dippy's beam structure and pillar legs give support,
allowing the multi-species skeleton to distort.
Swallowing the Crystal Palace through her curtain-like baleen,
lifting the howdah from the African elephant—so her ears can be seen!

A table inside her mouth hosts fossil fuel benefactors,
to swallow a final meal fit for egoist extractors.
Water floods. Museum gates open. Hope whistles, pulses and breaks free.
She bursts out of Albertopolis in a climate emergency.

The whale migrates back to the sea—not without injury.
She gives the world a voice in a sonic mystery
Leading fellow whales that were stranded in the River,
the song builds with the collective call that they deliver.

Sounds travel along with the protesting flotilla,
Amassing more attention than an aquatic Godzilla.
With a splashing of her giant flukes, the final curtain call.
Safely back above deep water she can start to fall.

With the insides of the museum, she falls to the ocean floor,
feeding hundreds of species in one life-giving pour.
Scavenging sharks break the skin to remove fleshy matter.
Smaller species move in next to collect the pieces that scatter.

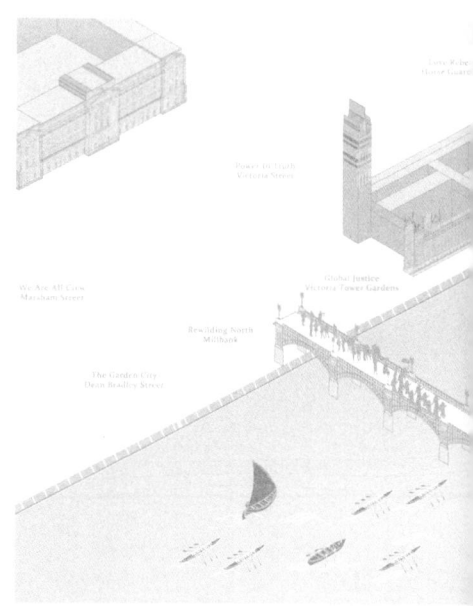

Squat lobsters, hagfish, and sea stars secrete digestive juices
To break down hierarchies that the museum produces.
Sea spiders and crabs comb the sediment for remains.
Zombie worms release nutrients that the skeleton contains.

The last remnants of her bones put hope into action.
A world of sound reverberates in an endless chain reaction.
Listen to the warning whistles, it is time for a choice:
Hope rumbles—a whale of a difference you can make with your voice!

THE WAY OF THE DINOSAURS

Scene 1

In the West, paleontology and mining, two birds of a feather
Dinosaurs and fossil fuels were extracted together
The Gold Rush and Bone Wars, a race to unearth
Fossilized landscapes, exploited for their worth

Manifest destiny steamrolled west on steel rail
Staked out mineral rights and land grants, displaced the living at scale
Settlers declared ancestral land a possession free to take
Digging up matter that took Earth millions of revolutions to make

Western Expansion built a still world of specimens inside
With Andrew Carnegie as one philanthropic guide
Slabs of deep time, packed up and shipped in crates
East from the Quarry to museums across states

To stamp THE MOST COLOSSAL ANIMAL EVER ON EARTH with his name
Camp Carnegie would be Andrew's claim to fame
Diplodocus carnegii was resurrected from below
On Independence Day, beginning with one giant toe

Old bones tell of five mass extinctions so far
Of the latest, one dinosaur was cast a world star
Dippy! A symbol of the Revolutionary War
Pittsburgh: the stage for the star-spangled dinosaur

Scene 2

The terrible reptile does not stand on its own
A steel beam cast grips the curves of each bone
Fossils of bones combined with shellac, iron, and steel
Stirred up debate on what was fake and what was real

The steel-funded beast joined together some creatures
Sculpting new parts to fill in missing features
Upward from there, in vertical integration
A towering dinomania industrialist creation

Metal beam and column sections rolled out on repeat
As skyscrapers rose up and down the street
Among these the Carnegie Steel Company tower
– the headquarters for his eminent wealth and power

Dark skies, sun up to sun down, laboring without break
Workers fed the smoking machine with sweat and much ache
A single holiday they received on the 4th of July
On the day that Dippy was found, let the fireworks fly!

On a fiery effort to halt exploitation they bled
Went on strike over Independence Day at Homestead
Workers demanded plant safety and fair wage
For the open-hearth furnace to continue to rage

131 DESIGN EARTH

Scene 3   Carnegie's Palace of Culture was an attempt to settle
Social heat bubbling at degrees of molten metal
When Carnegie Steel merged into the largest corporation
The richest man in the world turned to philanthropic donation

His *Gospel of Wealth*—a handbook for a life of excess—
Professed: inequality is essential to progress!
Libraries, parks, and museums were The Crowning of Labor
or the duty of a man of wealth to his less privileged neighbor

The House That Dippy Built was the robber baron's view
To fit the large skeleton, the Museum further grew
Dippy was the centrepiece of the Grand Staircase
Bringing the world to workers who labour at the base

When the King asked for his own, it was surely no trouble
For the British Museum they would simply make a double
Plaster copies of Dippy were cast from a mold
And repeated for many more heads of state to behold

The Hall of Architecture that Dippy stands beside
Shaped a plaster world where old masters reside
The factory system and the industrial revolution
Reproduced uneven wealth and much mass pollution

Scene 4   A FREE TO THE PEOPLE museum came at great cost
Lands and lives damaged and many species lost
Hell with the lid taken off, carbon out in the air,
A trove of toxic harm, what a legacy to bear!

After most dinosaurs went extinct, only birds remained
Now many in turn are taxidermy mounts, very neatly framed
In a Fable for Tomorrow, was a Spring with no voices
the canary in a coal mine to caution human choices

Pipelines and Pipe Dreams: a colossal fracking mess!
Calling Natural Gas "Green Energy" puts more under stress
Drilling land in Pennsylvania for remaining carbon stores
Sends more living to museums, the way of dinosaurs

As life is held still, the Earth continues its motion
A world beyond fossil fools is the burning revolution
Birds, people, and critters, all together in mammoth size
A flock of climate action lights up the darkened skies

The Cloud Factory pumping soot out of stacks
is removed from service with tiny mighty acts
Land titles are restructured to leave fossils buried deep
Carbon's tucked in rocky beds and settled back to sleep

DESIGN EARTH

1. ARCHITECTURE IS AN ACCOMPLICE AND AN ACCESSORY TO CAPITALISM.

Architecture as we know it today was first forged in the crucible of capitalism, as an accomplice and accessory. Its identifying features, developed during the Renaissance, remain all too familiar: Decollectivize building knowledge and concentrate it in the figure of the individual architect; socially elevate and attribute to this individual extraordinary and exceptional powers of creativity, vision, and insight; design palaces for the rich; gentrify and drive the poor from the heart of the city; costume capitalist wealth and power in dignifying dress such as classicism and the International Style; consolidate and physically entrench processes of colonial settlement; normalize the nuclear family as the basis of social reproduction through the design of housing; produce new building typologies in line with the course of capitalist development and its class-based, gendered, and racializing agendas—the urban palazzo, the industrial factory, the company town, the plantation house, the department store, the housing project, the shopping mall, the corporate campus.

Despite the inclinations of well-meaning individuals to make architecture serve other agendas, to make architecture "care," these features cannot be erased. They constitute architecture as a historically specific capitalist mode of production of the built environment. We should neither overestimate the agency of architecture to act otherwise nor underestimate the capacity of capital to direct architectural production toward its own ends. The notion of an architecture of good intentions obfuscates things, mistaking systemic functions for matters of personal choice and, in the process, furthering the ideological fiction of the architect as an individually autonomous agent. This is why our critique of architecture is ultimately categorical rather than directed at particular architects or projects. We are concerned with how architecture is bound to operate as the accomplice and accessory to capitalism it was historically developed to be and still is, by necessity.

Even so, architects have been attached to other ideas of what they have to offer the world. In the 1920s, and again in the 1960s and '70s, some sought to position themselves at the leading edge of societal development as part of a radical avant-garde whose facilities with form, space, and imagination could consciously shape and direct the future. The real course of history, as pointed out long ago by Manfredo Tafuri, shows that architecture has never been in the driver's seat and has only ever been a vehicle for the course of capitalist development.

By the late twentieth century the products of the historical avant-garde had become mere material to be recycled and repurposed for a post-critical architecture in which any aspiration to be radical had been put to rest. The formal and structural experiments of the Soviet avant-garde now serve to inspire architects such as Rem Koolhaas in the design of projects monumentalizing Chinese post-socialist state entrepreneurialism—CCTV Headquarters, in Beijing—or the dizzyingly complex offices of right-wing media house Axel Springer. Yet some architects have recognized their proper place in the scheme of things and have become skilled players in gaming this recognition to their own advantage.

1909 Peter Behrens designs the AEG Turbine Factory in Berlin (Thesis 2).

The fortunes of architecture are, then, fundamentally dependent on those of capitalism. Where one leads the other follows. Under current economic conditions of "secular stagnation," where securing returns on investments has become ever more challenging, attention has turned in large part to the luxury business sector, where significant profit margins are still to be had. That architects have been forging links with luxury fashion brands—OMA and Prada, David Chipperfield and Valentino—is no coincidence. Architecture's current gravitation toward high-end fashion brands is evident, for example, in the luxury malls and flagship stores that line Cheongdam-dong, in Seoul's recently gentrified and socially cleansed Gangnam district: UNStudio for Galleria, Ateliers Jean Nouvel for Dolce and Gabbana, Christian de Portzamparc for Dior, Frank Gehry for Louis Vuitton. Rather than a betrayal of some supposed socially beneficent mission for architecture, these alliances are faithful to the roots of the discipline as an apparatus of class distinction.

The Palazzo Fendi Seoul, designed in-house, alludes to the Palazzo della Civiltà Italiana, the company's Roman headquarters, in forms on its facade echoing the uniform arched windows of the original. Designed for the 1942 World's Fair by Giovanni Guerrini, Ernesto Lapadula, and Mario Romano under the direction of Benito Mussolini, the monumental building in the EUR district of Rome summons the essence of Renaissance classicism in the interests of twentieth-century Fascism. In Berlin the Palast der Republik, or "People's Palace," built in 1976 and designed by Heinz Graffunder and the Building Academy of the German Democratic Republic for the GDR, did not experience such longevity. It was demolished in 2008 and replaced with a reconstruction of the Prussian Berlin City Palace, on whose war-damaged ruins it had been built, the leftover 35,000 tons of scrap steel exported to the United Arab Emirates to be used as construction material for the Burj Khalifa.

2. ARCHITECTURE LENDS AN APPEARANCE OF HUMANITY TO THE INHUMANITY OF CAPITALISM.

Architecture has dressed the processes of capitalist *valorization*, and the enterprises in which it is implicated, in humanist values through its outward appearance and the rhetoric through which it is presented. It has thus obscured the historical specificity and interests of capitalist social relations through *stylization*.

The history of the Modern movement demonstrates this process in action. Its first proponents and leaders, the people who set the tone of the movement and helped to create an understanding of its ethos (Adolf Loos, Walter Gropius, Adolf Meyer, even Frank Lloyd Wright to some extent), were at least nominally interested in harnessing technological advancements and growing industrial capacities to produce well-detailed architecture that used its materials, including space, efficiently. The increasing capacity for standardization and mass production made it possible to imagine making architecture on scale large enough to adequately fulfill its programmatic functions, whatever they might be, at a low cost and thereby improve the quality of life of people across the board, both at home and at work. These intentions gave the project of

1913 Walter Gropius and Hannes Meyer design the Fagus Factory in Alfeld, Germany (Thesis 2).

Modernism an egalitarian undertone, even if the clients that commissioned its most important structures were capitalist enterprises.

Early projects that set the tone for the movement, like the AEG Turbine Factory (Behrens, 1909) and the Fagus Factory (Gropius and Meyer, 1913), were fulfilling a double purpose: Cleaning up the image of mass industry, whose poor working conditions and lack of safety had spurred workers' movements in both the United States and Europe; and exemplifying the possibilities for architecture and building created by mass production and standardization. These Modernist factories undoubtedly improved the working conditions of the people who produced, respectively, turbines and shoe lasts in them. Their aesthetics—gridded plans, simple facades, little to no ornamentation, plain materiality, all a reflection of the larger goal of efficiency and economy—naturally became associated with improving quality of life for workers, including increased safety and cleanliness. So Modern architecture would come to represent a break with the subpar working conditions of the early industrial period.

Diminished overall economic prosperity throughout the Great Depression would relegate Modernism, at least temporarily, to the realm of the private residence and the Fascist party headquarters, but by the time of the postwar boom in the United States it was solidly back in the common, if not quite public, realm. The designs of the Lever House (SOM, 1951), the MetLife Building (Gropius, 1963), and the Johnson Wax Research Tower (Wright, 1950) all employ visual elements typical of Modernism—the standardized grid in metal and glass with no ornamentation—giving the impression of restraint and universal progress even as the skyrocketing profits of the commissioning companies began to set the stage for economic inequality, eventually becoming bigger than ever. The language of progress and improved living and working conditions for everybody was now the established language of capitalist enterprise.

3. ARCHITECTURE ADVERTISES CAPITALIST DEVELOPMENT.

Since the late twentieth century architecture has employed formal novelty extensively, associating itself with the historical avant-garde along with the corresponding artistic and revolutionary values. This *formal orientation* of architecture ascribes, in turn, values of novelty and innovation to capitalist enterprises so that capital itself appears visionary.

Related to political projects with varying degrees of revolutionary and utopian ideals, avant-garde art movements of the nineteenth and early twentieth centuries were dedicated, in the words of Tafuri, to "an ideology of permanent and programmed innovation." This objective depended on the ability to get art made and projects built, so some of the most formally innovative projects never came to fruition—such as the Monument to the Third International, a 1,300-foot-tall spiraling tower intended to house the headquarters of the Communist International, in St. Petersburg (then Petrograd), designed by Vladimir

1920s Presence of an "architectural avant garde" (Thesis 1).

1920 Vladimir Tatlin designs the Monument to the Third International (Thesis 3).

1927–1940 Walter Benjamin writes the Arcades Project (Thesis 6).

1942 Giovanni Guerrini, Ernesto Lapadula, and Mario Romano design the Palazzo della Civiltà Italiana (Thesis 1).

1950 Frank Lloyd Wright designs the Johnson Wax Building in Racine, Wisconsin (Thesis 2).

1951 SOM designs the Lever House in New York City (Thesis 2).

1958 Walter Gropius designs the MetLife building in New York City (Thesis 2).

1960s Presence of an "architectural avant garde" (Thesis 1).

1970s Presence of an "architectural avant garde" (Thesis 1).

1976 Heinz Graffunder designs the Palace of the Republic in Berlin (Thesis 1).

1984 Fredric Jameson writes an analysis of the Bonaventure Hotel in an essay titled "The Cultural Logic of Late Capitalism" (Thesis 6).

1990s Emergency of post-critical theory (Thesis 5).

2004 OMA designs CCTV building in Beijing (Thesis 1).

2008 OMA designs Fondazione Prada in Milan (Thesis 1).

Tatlin in 1920. The tower design was formally inventive: A spiraling, tilted scaffold formed by iron and steel elements within which were suspended geometric volumes housing different programs. Tatlin's Tower was never built—the economic and political conditions in post-revolutionary Russia were unfavorable, and the design was structurally ambitious.

As a project, however, as a series of ideas embodied in architectural form, the tower has survived, even inspiring a copycat in the proposal for the new Amazon headquarters, in Arlington, Virginia. A similarly spiraling structure with subsections suspended in its interior, designed by JBG Smith, the building does not have a formal analog in contemporary architecture. It perpetuates the avant-garde image of permanent innovation, an idea that, thanks to Silicon Valley, has become not only commonplace but also firmly established in the territory of capitalist enterprise.

Leaving aside formal critiques of the contemporary building, we can speculate that it would be unlikely for any entity other than Amazon, which earned $225 billion in profits in 2022, to commission and build such a structure. Its execution requires architects and interior designers as well as structural and seismic engineers, experts in glazing and steel construction, acousticians, and climate-control technicians—in short, a litany of professionals with extensive training and credentials who require significant capital to engage. Only a company as profitable (and exploitative, since the two things go hand in hand) as Amazon is capable of deploying such resources to architecturally and formally innovative ends. In that way

Amazon has the capability to purchase an association with formal innovation and, in turn, the revolutionary and utopian ideas of the avant-garde movements that incorporated formal innovation as an integral part of a progressive project.

It is not surprising, then, that architects would tacitly accept capitalist enterprise as the only way to get projects built, and that the general public would associate these big companies with formal innovation—and even assume that capitalist enterprise is the sole force behind real innovation. Novelty and innovation are inherently good—as representative of human potential and its fulfillment—and achievable only through capitalist development.

As Tafuri theorized, in *Architecture and Utopia*:

"The Bauhaus, as the decantation chamber of the avant-garde, fulfilled the historic task of selecting from all the contributions of the avant-garde by testing them in terms of the needs of productive reality" (p.98).

"The result of all this was that the aesthetic experience itself was revolutionized. Now it was no longer objects that were offered to judgment, but a process to be lived and used as such" (p.101).

"Indeed the avant-garde was dedicated to an ideology of permanent and programed innovation" (p.156).

2008 Palace of the Republic demolished in 2008, to be replaced with a reconstruction of the Prussian Palace (Thesis 1).

2013 OMA designs Axel Springer Campus in Berlin (Thesis 1).

4. ARCHITECTURE ACCUMULATES VALUE FOR CAPITAL.

Architecture is a vehicle for increasing the value of real estate, not for fulfilling social or environmental needs. The primary role of architects in this system is to manage the construction process. This fact is obscured in the media through the treatment of architecture as art.

Ask almost any working architect today what they spend their time doing, and design will probably be further down the list than you would think—and they would like. The schematic design and design development phases of the process are increasingly shorter, and the phases in which contracts are developed, projects are sent out to bid, and construction is administered are prioritized. Architects play a very specific role in this process. First, they manage a relationship with the city and other governing bodies that make construction possible, facilitating permits and ensuring that designs meet local standards. Second, they ensure code compliance and assume at least partial liability for circumstances where buildings do not adhere to regulations. Third, they manage the construction process, liaising between contractor and client. In the overwhelming majority of cases where architects are employed, these are the functions they perform.

In the case of buildings designed by starchitects for high-visibility clients, the responsibilities also include, as discussed in theses 2 and 3, advertising and making capitalist development palatable by producing innovative aesthetics, using green technology, and evoking humanist values and cultural progress. In addition to playing a specific role in the practical production and construction of buildings, architects create an easy-to-swallow pseudo billboard that allows the capitalist to continue doing business as usual.

Yet according to mainstream media the architect's role is akin to that of a painter or sculptor, bringing buildings into the world as if they are pure pieces of art—physical embodiments of artistic vision. The media plays an active role in the obfuscation of the architect's real, material role in society. Newspapers cover architecture as a topic separate from real estate, reinforcing the idea of its practice as an art that has nothing to do with commercial development. Shelter magazines such as *Architectural Digest* and *Dwell* show off what the few private clients with enough money to hire an architect do with their spaces. Although trade publications like *Architectural Record* and *Architect's Newspaper* play less of a role in shaping the general public's view of architecture, they do reinforce the idea that design and all of the other parts of an architect's job—construction documentation, bidding, code compliance, administration—are ancillary and incidental to the process as a whole rather than the principal raisons d'etre for the profession and its licensure processes.

On the whole, the media's treatment of architecture fosters the image of capitalists as patrons of great art and of architects as artists, contributes to the image of architecture as art rather than a commodity, and serves as a scaffold for maintaining the status quo and established relationships between capital and architects. The media

2013   David Chipperfield designs Valentino flagship store in New York City (Thesis 1).

2014   Gehry Partners designs Fondation Louis Vuitton in Paris (Thesis 1).

does not provide context or critique; it reinforces the existing narratives.

It is important for both architects and the public at large to understand the role architects play in society and develop the ability to analyze and comprehend their respective parts in the larger systems of development and value accumulation. If architects conceive of themselves primarily as artists, they will try to exert their power through that realm, and others will expect them to do so. They will attempt to solve problems via their creativity and aesthetic dexterity—and it will be disappointing to everyone involved when that doesn't succeed. If architects understood their real position, as particularly important middle managers of a system that allows developers to increase their returns on investment, then they would realize that aesthetic interventions are not solutions to structural or material problems but generators of capital.

5. ARCHITECTURAL THEORY OBFUSCATES THE RELATIONS BETWEEN ARCHITECTURE AND CAPITALISM.

Critical theory has approached architecture typically through a model derived (in questionable fashion) from the writings of Karl Marx. This paradigm posits architecture as a cultural form belonging to an ideological superstructure from which something of the otherwise hidden workings of the capitalist economy—the economic base—can be discerned. Exemplified in Walter Benjamin's famed analysis of nineteenth-century Parisian arcades and in Fredric Jameson's equally notable account of the Bonaventure Hotel, in Los Angeles, this approach conceives of a metaphorical or analogical relationship between architecture and capitalism. In the process architecture is mistaken for the autonomous form of purely cultural expression that architects endeavor to portray. Meanwhile the economic machinations of capitalism are misconstrued as residing in some unfathomable, unseen realm. Yet the relationship between architecture and capitalism is more direct than generally assumed, and is effectively obscured, within the guise of the base-and-superstructure model. Architecture is in fact an instrument of capital investment and returns as the means for real estate developers to increase land value, for property owners to elevate rents, and for governments to displace poor, marginalized, and working-class communities from city centers, all in the interest of accumulating capital. Architecture is a vehicle through which capital—Marx's "value in motion" —multiplies itself, and where its workings are not so hidden or mysterious.

Architecture does, of course, operate in a cultural register. It is coded with stylistic allusions, patterned with symbolic motifs, clad in materials that reflect or dissimulate its construction, shaped into forms that suggest novelty or tradition. But this cultural expression is tied, fairly obviously, to the investment of capital that drives its production. According to the conventions of ideological critique, and related criticisms of architecture as spectacle, the physical expression of architecture involves a practice of concealment that has to be stripped

2018 Gehry Partners designs Louis Vuitton Maison Seoul (Thesis 1).

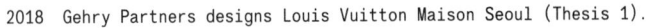

2018 Amazon announces new headquarters in Arlington, Virginia (Thesis 3).

aside to reveal the deeper truth. An effective critical theory of architecture would acknowledge that how architecture appears, and the real effects of that appearance, are in fact precisely how architecture works in and for the interests of capital. Architecture's appearance is not something to be unmasked or disavowed in favor of some pseudo-phenomenological and ultimately elitist architecture for the "eyes of the skin," but rather to be understood in terms of how it operates to shape and legitimate perceptions, beliefs, and habits.

Ironically the kind of "post-critical" theory that emerged from elite schools of architecture in the 1990s had a more effective grasp of the relations between architecture and capitalism than those of critical theory. Whereas critical theory, in its Western Marxist origins at least, opposed capitalism, advocates of post-criticality proposed to do away with all such negativity, availing themselves of new opportunities to find work in the increasingly market-driven neoliberal conditions of capitalism. Informed by an ethos of fluidity, becoming, and smoothness derived from the philosophy of Gilles Deleuze and Félix Guattari and equipped with the design software to make this manifest in architectural form, practitioners such as Greg Lynn, Zaha Hadid Architects, Reiser + Umemoto, and Foreign Office Architects set about creating architecture that went with the flow of capitalist development in the guise of a progressive project.

The post-critical movement may have lost the currency it once enjoyed, but it has been followed by newer models of theory that are equally antipathetic toward critique.

Exponents of post-criticality were at least obliged to name the enemy and to articulate their arguments with it, sometimes in terms that made plain the economic reasoning behind their positions. The successors—new materialism, actor-network theory, object-oriented ontology (OOO)—attempt to ward off any and all discussion of architecture's relationship to capitalism through sheer mystification. Whatever the differences between such positions, they are united in their dogmatism. Each insists on some essential constitution of reality proposing strict prescriptions about how architecture must be thought of and what can or cannot be legitimately said of it: There is only materialism and it must be "new" and "vital"; there are only objects, and our human concerns about their meaning or significance are not especially important; all things act and have agency within a network where none is more or less significant than any other. The foam cutter matters as much the architectural worker, or even the boss. Actions that do not appear as "things"—extraction, accumulation, exploitation, alienation—conveniently fail to register in this network. Theory is no longer about architecture but for architecture, serving its narrow interests and obscuring its wider implications. The work of grappling with these implications, especially in terms of their colonial and racialized contexts, has been taken up, to great effect, by architectural historians. Theory must now be equally willing and effectively equipped to address the contemporary resonance of these and other social, political, and economic concerns in architecture.

2023 Fendi opens Palazzo Fendi Seoul on Cheongdamdong (Thesis 1).

2023 NEOM project underway in Saudi Arabia (Thesis 6).

6. ARCHITECTURE'S PROLETARIANIZATION IS A NECESSARY STEP TOWARD ITS DISSOLUTION.

Counter to all of these forms of obfuscation, we are now in a moment of clarification driven by the current lived and material circumstances of those who work in and study architecture. The untenable levels of debt, the exploitative working conditions, the abusive practices of the school and the firm are being called out and contested as never before. What were once taken as givens—the ritualized humiliation of the student in the studio crit, the long and poorly compensated work hours, the unpaid internships— are no longer passively endured. At the initiative of its own students and alumni, the Bartlett School of Architecture, in London, has been subject to a damning independent report on long-standing abuses of students. In 2022 SCI-Arc, in Los Angeles, live-streamed the now notorious panel discussion "Basecamp: How to be in an Office," in which students were encouraged to embrace the virtues of long and poorly remunerated working hours in the name of following their passion. The backlash—from architecture students, practitioners, journalists, and labor organizations—was such that the school was compelled to place those responsible on administrative leave for exploiting students as unpaid labor on projects at their firm.

The relative impoverishment of the middle classes, in which the architect has traditionally been situated as an educated professional, is equally significant to this moment of clarification. Although an inevitable consequence of capitalism's long economic downturn, this phenomenon has been especially marked following the financial crisis of 2007–8. If the sacrifices made by students and early-career architects were once compensated by the eventual realization of high salaries and secure employment, this is no longer the case. Young and even mid-career architects find themselves living in shared accommodations and working precarious jobs in cities like London and New York, designing the kind of luxury properties they will never be able to afford and whose construction amplifies the unaffordability of the city for most everyone.

In these circumstances the call for architects to see themselves as workers, not professionals, and to understand what they do as labor rather than some higher creative pursuit has gained significant traction. In the United States, the United Kingdom, and Europe architects and students have formed unions and founded groups and campaigns advocating for the interests of the architectural worker. Some have sought to unionize their places of work, a trend that has seen both success and failure. It is telling that the firms in question have responded with the kind of union-busting tactics used by multinational corporations against their employees: Indeed the architectural firm is a microcosm of the capitalist mechanisms at work. The interests of workers and bosses are not the same, by any means, and a substantial sector of the architectural profession now recognizes its interests as more aligned with those of the waged laborer—the proletariat—than with those of their bosses.

The turn toward understanding architecture as labor, and the consequent contestation of its terms and conditions, is significant not only for the leverage it offers architects but for their own immediate interests. The renunciation of the special artistic status of the architect creates the basis for solidarity with other workers. Through such alliances, as we have argued elsewhere, militant forms of labor organization could act directly, through the refusal of their labor, to contest at least the most egregious examples of capitalist development, such as The Line, the smart city project currently underway in the NEOM region of Saudi Arabia.

While we recognize that the power organized labor has at its disposal through unionization will necessarily tend toward reformism rather than direct contestation of capitalism, it should not be written off for that reason. Any gains that can be achieved by workers are worthwhile, particularly in the face of the current onslaught wrought by capitalism on the quality of life of all but those in possession of extreme wealth. Yet we do not take architects' identification of their practice as labor to be an end in itself. For Marx the historical task of the proletariat was not social domination through the seizure of state power, but the abolition of class society as a whole. In the process wage labor—categorically and necessarily an exploitative and alienating practice—would also be abolished, to be superseded by free life activity. Likewise, we should envision the abolition of architecture and the forms of labor it necessitates, along with the conditions of injustice, inequality, and environmental degradation it reproduces, to be replaced by practices of design and construction corresponding directly to collectively determined social, cultural, and environmental demands.

In the years since Occupy Wall Street emerged, it has begun to seem that the most meaningful aspect of the movement was the name itself—"Occupy." It has become clear that the very notion of occupancy is a fulcrum of 21st-century finance capitalism. How else to understand the normalization of "owned but empty" units in so many residential buildings in cities around the world? As housing is increasingly treated as an investment asset, its basic function—the provision of shelter—is beginning to appear outmoded. Any sober assessment of global real estate trends cannot avoid the conclusion that vacancy is a preferred investment class.[1] Economist Michael Hudson's 2010 declaration that the "'postindustrial' economy turns out to be mainly about real estate" might reasonably be updated to pronounce that today's economy turns out to be mainly about unoccupied real estate.[2]

One of the signal by-products of finance capitalism's emphasis on asset value over use value is the underuse of architectural space. High residential vacancies in parts of cities that are perceived as desirable as well as abandoned or largely empty speculative developments are both prominent features of 21st-century urbanism. And as these two conditions suggest, not all under-occupancy is the same. A large proportion of owned but empty residential units generates an in-between state of uncertain vitality— zombie urbanism—whereas a more dramatic proportion of vacant or unfinished units produces a very different phenomenon—ghost urbanism.[3] This divergence—again, between buildings for use and buildings for investment— complicates some widely held assumptions; chiefly, that underuse is associated with blight and decay, while new growth signals vibrant prosperity. Indeed, 21st-century urbanism abounds with newly created ruins that blur the distinction between success and failure, growth and decay. And in the process, they recalibrate theoretical and emotional conceptions of architecture.

Zombie urbanism occurs when an area has large numbers of owned but empty housing units, resulting in a de facto density that is significantly below the designed capacity. These areas mix present populations with absent populations, exhibiting an eerily low level of vitality in relation to their scale. They are not dead, but they are also not quite alive.

To be sure, no urban area has full residential occupancy at any given time, because there is never a perfect alignment between housing supply and demand. In addition, there is a steady rate of turnover as people move in and out, buy and sell units, and spend time away from primary residences—all of which contribute to a certain number of empty units at any moment. What is considered an optimal level of vacancy depends on local conditions that change over time. According to the U.S. Census, the vacancy rate in rental housing in the entire United States fluctuated between 7.6 and 10.6 percent from 1995 to 2018.[4] Over the same period, the vacancy rate of homeowner housing moved between 1.5 and 2.6 percent.[5] What housing analysts call the "equilibrium vacancy rate" is that which poses no upward or downward pressure on housing costs.[6] Zombie urbanism happens when vacancy rates are significantly higher than these ranges.

Owned but empty units tend to serve three functions: As wealth storage, as speculative assets, and as secondary residences. These functions can operate discretely but more often work in combination. The purchase of a second home for recreational use, for instance, is often informed by speculation. While a typical investor will rent out a second home for ongoing revenue, a very wealthy investor might leave it empty. These individuals' substantial capital propels them to diversify their wealth storage while also facilitating a lifestyle of global mobility, in which multiple residential properties are desirable. The growth of this wealthy cohort— so-called "very high net worth individuals"—is significantly affecting numerous places around the world.

Secondary homes tend to be either recreational— like the rural dachas outside Moscow—or urban—like the pieds-à-terre in central London. Such properties have been manifestations of wealth and privilege for centuries, but they began to proliferate during the Industrial Revolution, as both the upper class and the growing middle class sought relief from the dirt and clamor of the modern metropolis. By the early 20th century, large areas around London—the so-called cocktail belt and stockbroker's belt—contained country and weekend homes.[7] The French term pied-à-terre (foot to the ground) was coined in the 19th century to describe short-term or secondary lodging; now, of course, it denotes a second home in the city, typically an apartment.

Finance capitalism has significantly increased the prevalence of secondary housing. Midtown Manhattan, for example, is packed with under-occupied residences.[8] Underuse in Paris appears even more widespread. A 2017 report by the Paris Urbanism Agency indicated that second homes in the city experienced a significant uptick between 2008 and 2013; in the 1st, 2nd, 3rd, and 4th Arrondissements, an astonishing 26 percent of homes were empty.[9] As Ian Brossat, the city's Housing Commissioner, put it, "It's a really worrying issue. It's not normal to have 200,000 empty or semi-occupied homes. It represents twice the housing available in a big arrondissement like the 18th."[10] Likewise, London is more and more the locus of empty residences. "Some of the richest people in the world are buying property here as an investment," said Paul Dimoldenberg, a Westminster Council politician. "They may live here for a fortnight in the summer, but for the rest of the year they're contributing nothing to the local economy. The specter of new buildings where there are no lights on is a real problem."[11]

Finance capitalism may be especially rife in global power centers, but its impact is increasingly felt in cities throughout the world. The latest Canadian census indicates there are nearly 100,000 vacant or under-occupied housing units in Toronto.[12] In parts of central Vancouver, 25 percent of condominiums sit largely empty.[13] In Miami, hard data is scarce, but real estate studies suggest key factors for high residential vacancy. In 2007, for example, more than one-third of all houses and almost 60 percent of condominiums in Miami–Dade County were secondary residences. In 2015, more than 30 percent of condominiums purchases in the county were made by buyers who lived 50 or more miles away.[14] A large percentage of the residential towers in Panama City appear to be empty, at least partly due to money laundering.[15] In Melbourne, an Australian NGO analyzed domestic water usage in 2014 to determine the number of vacant units and found more than 100,000 empty or hardly used homes.[16] The municipal government in Barcelona identified more than 100,000 units with zero or very little water consumption in 2016, indicating vacancy or under-occupancy.[17] Beirut's city center is filled with sparsely occupied condo towers as a result of a boom in luxury construction targeted toward expatriates and foreigners in the Persian Gulf.[18]

These locations are all perceived as both desirable places to live and good places to bank wealth in property. In no small part this is because their real estate values will likely rise over the long term. Vancouver offers the transparency and stability of Canadian law and governance, alongside exceptional natural beauty. Beirut is perceived as a liberal oasis in West Asia and boomed after the end of Lebanon's long civil war. Melbourne is a safe city with a mild climate; it also benefits from relative proximity to the population centers of Southeast Asia.

In response to the challenges posed by zombie urbanism, many jurisdictions are exploring tools to reduce its incidence. Paris introduced a 20 percent tax on second homes in 2015 and increased it to 60 percent in 2017.[19] In 2016, Vancouver enacted the Empty Homes Tax—an annual

Ascaya, a speculative
community near Las Vegas,
incomplete after the
financial crisis, 2015.

Ascaya, where laborers rake
the ground of the partly
vacant community.

One Hyde Park, a famously expensive residential building, designed by Rogers Stirk Harbour + Partners, many of whose units are second homes.

423 Park Avenue, designed by Rafael Viñoly Architects, a luxury tower whose units function as assets as much as shelter.

one percent tax on the assessed property value of units unoccupied for more than 180 days. Melbourne enacted its Vacant Residential Property Tax in 2017, and Washington, D.C. and Oakland, California, have similar taxes. Hong Kong, Toronto, and Los Angeles are now debating whether to implement their own vacancy taxes.

Zombie urbanism is now a defining attribute of the contemporary city even as dominant modes of designing, managing, governing, and conceptualizing the city continue to rely on longstanding assumptions of high occupancy. Basic decisions regarding the provision of services and scaling of amenities are based on historic levels of population density. Zombie urbanism upends these expectations. As the New York State Senator Liz Krueger recalls, "I met with a developer who is building one of those billionaire buildings on 57th Street, and he told me, 'Don't worry, you won't need any more services, because the buyers won't be sending their kids to school here [and] there won't be traffic.'"[20] As ongoing vacancy is normalized, should cities rethink zoning requirements, infrastructure needs, and public services?

One Hyde Park, designed by Rogers Stirk Harbour + Partners, London, 2011, where the dark windows indicate units that are unoccupied, and as often as not secondary residences.

The vacancies of zombie urbanism are not the result of an overt system failure, or of deficiency or calamity, as in the post-industrial Ruhr Valley or in post-Katrina New Orleans; rather they are the vacancies born of market success. They emerge not from oversupply or low demand, or because of a declining job market, but instead within the context of strong demand and high growth. Buildings are selling out, developers are making profits, governments are collecting fees, property values are escalating. Yet the city feels not quite alive.

If zombie urbanism is defined by reduced occupancy that operates in the context of success, ghost urbanism is characterized by high vacancy that contributes to the perception of failure. Ghost urbanism can make a place feel experientially dead and reinforce a palpable sense of decline; most commonly it is marked by a noticeable volume of unsold or incomplete housing units that may be in some state of decay.

As ever larger quantities of capital flow into real estate and exaggerate cycles of expansion and contraction, the usual result is over-building on the upswing and mass vacancies on the downswing—a version of what the economist Joseph Schumpeter famously called "creative destruction." Or, as the geographer David Harvey argues, "Under capitalism there is ... a perpetual struggle in which capital builds a physical landscape appropriate to its own condition at a particular moment in time, only to have to destroy it, usually in the course of a crisis, at a subsequent point in time."[21] Ghost urbanism, which occurs when plans go awry, is always a form of crisis, and its spaces of crisis can be found throughout the world. As cases in point, consider the booms and busts that happened in Ireland and Spain in

Battery Court, a ghost estate in Longford, Longford County, Ireland, 2013.

Completed but unoccupied houses at a ghost estate in Drumshanbo, County Leitrim, Ireland, 2013.

the years before and after the 2008 financial crash, and that offer poignant portraits of the ruthless vicissitudes of built territory operating primarily as an investment asset.

The Irish property boom, which started in the mid 1990s and lasted until roughly 2007, radically altered the nation's landscape. During this period, more than 750,000 units of housing were constructed—approximately 40 percent of the housing stock in Ireland during this period.[22] As the boom gained momentum from 2001 to 2007, an average of 70,000 housing units were constructed each year, with more than 90,000 in 2006 alone. In a country with a population of nearly 4.6 million, this translates into 18 units per 1,000 people per year, giving Ireland, along with Spain, the highest rate of construction in the European Union, nearly triple the rate of the next highest nation, France.[23] In those years the island was blanketed in new construction—urban perimeter blocks, peripheral mega-projects, exurban commuter estates, and a proliferation of one-off rural houses. Nor was the boom limited to housing. In the years before the crash, there were millions of new square feet of shopping malls, resulting in the second-highest per capita area of retail malls in Europe; nearly 13 million square feet (1.2 million square meters) of office space; and more than 18,000 new hotel rooms. At the zenith of the property boom, in 2006, the construction sector in the Republic of Ireland accounted for €37 billion ($47 billion), or nearly 25 percent of GNP.[24]

Irish scholars have compiled copious statistics that convey the magnitude of the boom: Between 1995 and 2006, Irish house prices rose by more than 300 percent nationally, and by more than 400 percent in Dublin. Raw land prices increased by approximately 1,200 percent.[25] The value of commercial real estate grew by 250 percent.[26] These metrics convey the enormity of a real estate expansion that involved large numbers of new participants in the market. Many Irish people described owning second, third, fourth, and fifth investment homes in addition to their primary residence. It was said that banks were cold-calling customers and encouraging them to acquire more property and more mortgages.[27]

Then, in 2008, in Ireland as elsewhere, the fever broke; the contagious perception that the supply of real estate had become radically decoupled from real demand caused the once hot market to freeze. Mortgage markets collapsed, property purchases halted, prices plummeted.[28] Mortgage holders found themselves in negative equity and developers were buried in debt. Builders packed up, leaving a landscape of partially completed projects. In 2011, 294,000 housing units sat empty and abandoned, many situated in what the Irish came to call "ghost estates"—forlorn developments that were mostly or entirely empty, often only partly built, with perhaps one or two occupied dwellings amidst a larger bleakness.[29]

The ghost estates captured the popular imagination because of their intimate connection with the struggles of individuals and families. Yet there was a parallel world of zombie hotels, phantom golf courses, and empty shops and offices. Sometimes a hotel might lie empty, an all too tempting target for vandals; in other instances, it might remain half-open, offering rooms at rock-bottom rates. Mixed-use developments lumbered along with unrented ground-floor retail while the carcasses of half-finished malls hulked on the horizon. Golf courses without patrons have been converted to agricultural fields for the production of silage or the roaming of horses. Post-crisis Ireland was strewn with all these high-vacancy failures—a 21st-century ghost landscape.

Asset urbanism needs to be understood in relation to global as well as local parameters. The Irish economy started to expand in the mid 1990s as the nation attracted increasing numbers of multinational corporations, all drawn by the lure of low taxes and wages alongside a highly educated, English-speaking workforce. As a member of the European Union, Ireland offered tariff-free access to the single European market. Once the Celtic Tiger took off, the country experienced strong in-migration for the first time in decades. Meanwhile, in the early aughts, the liberalization of international credit markets helped lubricate the flow of lending capital from German and French banks to Irish banks, which in turn fueled the building and buying boom. Irish banks responded to the intensifying demand with increasingly lax mortgage requirements, including longer terms and reduced down-payments—and ultimately the infamous zero-down, forty-year mortgage.

For years after 2008, the Irish landscape was pockmarked with various combinations of fenced-off and cleared land awaiting development; roads and infrastructure that went nowhere and served nothing; arrays of concrete foundation slabs sitting empty; buildings without roofs, shells of homes without siding or glazing, and row upon row of completed dwellings awaiting a home-owning population that did not yet exist. The years right after the 2008 crash were devoted to sorting out the financial and physical debris as the real estate and construction industries largely stalled.

In 2010, the Irish government started surveying "unfinished housing developments" and began a multiyear effort, through various programs and initiatives, to "resolve" these developments.[30] As a result, ghost conditions eased somewhat. Empty units were eventually occupied, and construction resumed on partially finished projects. A small number were simply demolished without ever being inhabited; Irish media reported in 2013 that a plan authored by the Minister of Housing and Planning identified roughly 40 estates as candidates for destruction.[31] Given the sensitivity of the topic, however, it is difficult to determine just how many estates fell into this category; official statistics seem improbably low, and likely undercount physical conditions on the ground.[32] Even now, more than a decade after the crash, it is easy to find its ghostly ruins.

During the boom, Ireland and Spain built roughly the same amount of housing per capita; but Spain experienced far more absolute building activity. About four million homes were built in Spain between 2001 and 2008, an average rate of 565,000 per year, more than double that of the previous decade.[33] In 2006, the country saw 865,000 housing starts, more than Germany, France, and the United Kingdom combined.[34] And a great deal of infrastructure was also constructed. The highway system was extended by about 8,000 miles (13,000 kilometers) between 1993 and 2011; Spain now has one of the highest capacity road networks in the world, surpassed only by the United States and China. Five new international airports were built, and thirteen existing airports received new terminals. At the market's height, construction accounted for approximately 11 percent of Spain's GDP.[35] Meanwhile property values were rising dramatically: Between 1996 and 2007, raw land values increased by 260 percent, and the national average housing price by 200 percent.[36]

An unoccupied home adjacent to an unfinished residence, one of the unsettling juxtapositions in post-crisis Ireland.

The Waterways ghost estate being demolished, Keshcarrigan, County Leitrim, Ireland, 2013.

In tandem with its intensified construction and price escalation, Spanish real estate became increasingly financialized. In the decade before the crash, the average length of a home mortgage grew from eighteen to 28 years. As the Spanish economist José García-Montalvo reported in 2006, "Today we are talking about forty-year loans. The majority of the mortgages are for 100 percent of the purchase price plus 10 percent for additional costs."[37] Within this atmosphere of easy credit, mortgage debt mushroomed, and by the height of the boom the value of Spanish mortgages reached 100 percent of GDP.[38] All the while Spanish financial institutions, like those in the U.S, securitized mortgage debts and thereby directly connected indebted Spanish households to global financial markets.[39]

During the boom years, ownership of second homes became commonplace. By 2007, according to the Madrid-based economists Isidro López and Emmanuel Rodríguez, 35 percent of Spanish households owned multiple residential properties.[40] Also in those years the country attracted foreign investors as a steady stream of Britons, Germans, and other Northern Europeans purchased units in Spanish developments that often explicitly catered to them. In several municipalities on the southern coast of Alicante, almost 80 percent of homes were vacation properties, and 47 percent of the population were "registered foreign holiday home residents."[41] As the Spanish sociologist Aitana Alguacil Denche stated, "The fundamentally speculative character of foreign investment can be appreciated from its high concentration in certain geographic areas. Foreign housing investment tended to be concentrated in island

Residencial Francisco Hernando, a two-thirds complete development in Seseña, Toledo, Castile-La Mancha, Spain, 2014.

Leisure-oriented investment development along the Mediterranean coast of Spain, near Valencia, 2013.

Arcosur, an incomplete urban ensanche in Zaragoza, Aragon, Spain, 2014.

communities (Canary and Balearic Islands) and the eastern Spanish coast (Andalusia, Murcia, and the Valencian Community), which are the areas that registered the highest increases in prices during the upswing of the cycle."[42]

Spanish champions of neoliberalism encouraged the investment frenzy. In 1998, the Spanish government passed the Land Act, which effectively reclassified the entire country as a single territory open to development. In the words of the government, "The present Law aims to facilitate the increase in land supply, meaning that all land which has not yet been incorporated into the urban process, in which there are no reasons for preservation, can be considered capable of being urbanized."[43] This law exemplifies the type of market liberalization that drives finance capitalism. Nor was it unique. A few years earlier, in 1994, the Valencian Community had enacted the Regulatory Law of Urban Activity, or LRAU, which created a new actor in land development—the agente urbanizador, or developer agent. In subsequent years, other regional governments passed laws modeled on Valencia's, with the effect that the agente urbanizador became a key propagator of development all across Spain.[44] It should be noted that the original Valencian law emerged from the political left; its central hypothesis was that by increasing the supply of urbanized land, the price of housing would fall. But the hypothesis was incorrect; prices did not fall. As Fernando Gaja i Díaz, a professor at the University of Valencia, and a fierce critic of the law, has argued, "The LRAU has contributed to the increased production of urbanized land without reducing the land prices that have accompanied the spiraling, inflationary real estate market; meanwhile [it has aided] the concentration of property in the hands of large urbanizing businesses."[45]

One of the profound by-products of the investment-driven building frenzy in Spain, as in Ireland, was dramatic overproduction. By 2010, Spain had more than one million unsold homes on the market; two years later that number was reported to be closer to two million. Numerous mega-developments on Madrid's periphery, each with thousands of units, were largely vacant. The ghost airports were empty for years; Murcia Airport, for instance, was completed in 2012, but did not open for flights until 2019.[46] A vast amount of the land that was "urbanized" during the boom lies empty and in various stages of decay. It is reported that this supply of underused land has the potential to meet demand until almost 2040.[47] And then there are the countless partly constructed buildings that continue to litter the landscape.

The ghost urbanism of post-crisis Spain has at least three discernible morphological patterns—post-metropolitan islands, foreign investment enclaves, and urban ensanches. Post-metropolitan islands are discrete mega-developments, geographically separate from

Empty urbanized land in Majadahonda, Madrid, Spain, 2014.

existing urban fabric—isolated satellites orbiting an urban center at a distance.[48] What makes them post-metropolitan is the presence of an enormous volume of housing in the absence of complementary urban programs. Such projects can be found outside many large and midsize Spanish cities, forming what can be described as investment archipelagoes. The most infamous example is Residencial Francisco Hernando (named after its developer) in Seseña, almost twenty miles (30 kilometers) outside Madrid. All aspects of the design—13,500 units in a series of repetitive mid-rise housing blocks—are intended to maximize quantity and minimize expense. The result is an almost inhuman space of speculation. One investor's experience during the boom, as recounted in the Spanish newspaper El Mundo in 2007, was typical:

> My family bought various units in Residencial Francisco Hernando at a very good price with the intention of getting a high return. And that is how it has been. We have seen the rise of the end of the real estate cycle, and we have decided to get rid of them. I have gotten rid of three units that cost me 120,000 euros for 180,000.[49]

Just over 5,000 units at Residencial Francisco Hernando were completed before the 2008 crash; a year later, an estimated 2,000 were unsold and vacant.[50] And for years afterward the development remained a semi-wasteland, with thousands of unlucky residents occupying the isolated environs of the unfinished mega-project.

The post-metropolitan islands drew mostly Spanish buyers; the foreign investment enclaves consist of new housing that drew a disproportionate percentage of foreign purchasers, typically from wealthy European countries. These enclaves occur mainly along the Mediterranean and now form what has become a kind of linear city stretching along the coast. Many are organized around golf courses or beaches—a calculated combination of climate and speculation. Like the post-metropolitan mega-developments, they are isolated and often homogeneous in character.[51] As are the urban ensanches—21st-century versions of traditional ensanches, or city extensions. During the boom, most cities in Spain experienced hyper-expansion at their peripheries; and in most instances, these rapidly developed territories have languished for years—the Spanish architect Isabel Concheiro calls them "stand-by landscapes."[52] Today, more than decade since the financial crisis, Spain's ghost urbanism persists—a ruinous landscape that underscores the punishing intensity of building booms and busts in the era of finance capitalism.

Ghost urbanism is hardly limited to Ireland and Spain. It can now be found across the world, and perhaps unsurprisingly, it is happening at an exceptional scale in China.[53] China's phenomenal growth over recent decades has been accompanied by equally phenomenal increases in real estate prices; in almost three dozen major cities, average housing prices have increased roughly 380 percent.[54] China's property boom is likely the largest in history, and it has left in its wake extensive territories of ghost urbanism. The most infamous instances are China's so-called ghost cities:

Under-occupied or incomplete new towns at the periphery of second- and third-tier cities.[55] The Kangbashi District on the edge of Ordos, in Inner Mongolia, has already been widely covered by the Western media. Inaugurated in 2006, the district was planned to house one million people; by 2014, the official population was only 30,000, and 70 percent of its buildings were vacant.[56] Reliable statistics are difficult to find, but photographs from 2020 depict a mostly empty urban environment.[57]

Given the extraordinary scale of Chinese urbanization —in 1980, less than 20 percent of the population lived in cities; today the figure is 60 percent—there were likely to be significant gaps in supply and demand. Nonetheless, the practices of finance capitalism have exacerbated this inevitability and amplified its proportions. China's burgeoning upper and middle classes have relatively few options for investing their new wealth. Regulations limit the ability of Chinese citizens to own foreign stocks and bonds, and, compared to their Western counterparts, Chinese banks offer low returns on investment. At the same time, China has no property tax. The predictable result is that real estate quickly became a popular investment. As the landscape architect Christopher Marcinkoski writes, "It is not uncommon for middle-class Chinese families to own two or three apartments as investment vehicles."[58] Eventually the trend became so pronounced that it provoked government concern, and an effort to limit the purchase of second homes.[59] Underscoring the challenge, Chinese President Xi Jinping declared in his address to the Nineteenth Party Congress in 2017, "Houses are built to be inhabited, not for speculation."[60]

Zombie neighborhoods and ghost cities present a newly dynamic terrain for architecture—a topography shaped by ever-shifting investment flows, and by the unnerving simultaneity of frenzied growth and rapid decline. Much 21st-century architectural discourse has orbited around two dominant paradigms of urbanism: On the one hand, the rapidly growing city-region, exemplified by the Pearl River Delta; on the other, the shrinking post-industrial city, exemplified by Detroit. These paradigms are ontologically premised upon temporal and spatial distinctions; upon the assumption that growth happens at a certain time and place, while decay happens at another time and place. But now the particularities and peculiarities of finance capitalism are propelling novel manifestations of these paradigms in which growth and decline can co-exist all at once.

Why are development and decay happening simultaneously, as if collapsing in upon each other? One major reason is the rise of finance capitalism, and the flood of money now flowing through architecture. The sheer volume of capital is producing ever higher peaks and ever deeper valleys in the expansion/contraction cycle, generating a greater volume of buildings during the boom and a larger oversupply during the bust. This oversupply is at ever greater risk of falling into disrepair and decay, which in turn makes it harder to be absorbed back into the market when the cycle turns yet again.

Traditional concepts of real estate posit the primacy of "market fundamentals" as determining factors of growth and decline. According to these fundamentals, the basic relationship between supply and demand is driven by employment, population, and wages; common wisdom dictates that an increase in these three will cause increased demand for housing, and vice versa. Today, however, the magnitude and fluidity of real estate investment has decoupled expansion and contraction from these fundamentals. It is no longer the case that rising prices are a function of the local job market, nor that increased demand is related to a growing population. And so we see the instant ruins wrought by the dynamics of finance capitalism—the unsettling adjacencies of asset urbanism.

Kangbashi District, Ordos, Inner Mongolia, China, 2012.

Below-grade infrastructure rearing its head at a large, abandonded development site in Mallow, County Cork, Ireland, 2013.

In post-crash Ireland, we see the stark juxtapositions of inhabited buildings next to vacant, unfinished ones—a family living alone with no neighbors in the surrounding homes; patrons of rooftop bars ordering food and drink while looking out upon abandoned construction sites; motorists moving through uncanny landscapes defined by seemingly permanent construction hoarding or security fencing. Today the degree to which plant life and rural activities have overtaken abandoned sites is striking. Many projects were halted after utilities had been already installed, resulting in landscapes where below-grade power, water, and sewage infrastructure are all in place; where conduits, pipes, and manholes now mingle with hardy vegetation; and where horses roam and children play ball.

In the past decade, the figure of the zombie has staked out a prominent position in fiction, television, and film. Some observers have connected this pop-culture phenomenon with the contemporary political economy. I'm thinking of books like *Zombie Capitalism: Global Crisis and the Relevance of Marx*, by the British journalist and socialist Chris Harman, which appeared in 2009, and *Monsters of the Market: Zombies, Vampires and Global Capitalism*, by historian David McNally, published in 2011. In an essay in the *New York Times*, from 2014, literature professor David Castillo and literary critic William Egginton capture the trend: "Today's zombie hordes may best express our anxieties about capitalism's apparently inevitable byproducts: The legions of mindless, soulless consumers who sustain its endless production, and the masses of 'human debris' who are left to survive the ravages of its poisoned waste."[61]

The film *28 Weeks Later*, directed by Juan Carlos Fresnadillo, appeared in 2007, at the height of the global property boom, and envisioned an empty, post-apocalyptic London. In an early scene, the camera pans over the city and we see streets with no cars or people; the population has been ravaged by a zombie-producing virus. Another movie released that year, *I Am Legend*, directed by Francis Lawrence, follows a character played by Will Smith who is living alone in an emptied-out Manhattan, except for the zombies who emerge when the sun goes down. And in Marc Forster's *World War Z*, from 2013—the highest-grossing zombie film to date—a global battle between the living and the undead is won by humans who discover that if they temporarily infect themselves with lethal viruses they will be rendered too unattractive for zombie reanimation.[62] In other words, living human beings must begin the process of active dying in order to protect themselves against becoming zombies.

This solution resonates with the paradoxes of zombie and ghost urbanism and their blurring of growth and decay. These nonliving buildings and developments are predicated on the belief that full life is somehow the current condition or future likelihood; they rely upon the historical viability of their hosts. London is a magnet for international capital precisely because it is considered a safe and stable investment—and a good place to live now and in the future. Vulture capitalists scoop up Irish ghost estates because they believe these properties will eventually be activated and return to life. In a further irony, many of these undead world capitals rank high on global livability indexes and other measurements of vitality: Melbourne and Vancouver, New York and San Francisco, are stars. According to the logics of finance capitalism, to be highly livable is also to be the perfect host for exactly the sort of spatial-financial investment that will enervate if not destroy urban life as we have known it.

Authors' note: This article was published in Places Journal in May 2021, and is also adapted from *Icebergs, Zombies, and the Ultra Thin: Architecture and Capitalism in the Twenty-First Century* (Princeton Architectural Press 2021). It appears here courtesy of the author and previous publishers.

1. While vacancy rates always shift over time and change from context to context, in the United States, for example, the vacancy rate, including seasonal use-related vacancies, increased by 44 percent between 2000 and 2010, growing from 10.4 million to 15 million units. U.S. Government Accountability Office, Vacant Properties: Growing Number Increases Communities' Costs and Challenges, GAO-12-34 (Washington, DC: GAO, 2011), 12.
2. Michael Hudson, "The Transition from Industrial Capitalism to a Financialized Bubble Economy" (working paper 627, Levy Economics Institute, 2010): 7 (unpaginated).
3. The phrase "zombie urbanism" appears to have originated with Jonny Aspen, who used it to describe "formulaic and increasingly similar" globalized urban design characteristics. See "Oslo—The Triumph of Zombie Urbanism," Shaping the City: Studies in History, Theory and Urban Design, Second Edition, eds. Rodolphe el-Khoury and Edward Robbins (London: Routledge, 2013).
4. U.S. Census Bureau, "Rental and Homeowner Vacancy Rates by Area," Housing Vacancies and Homeownership, Annual Statistics: 2018.
5. U.S. Census Bureau, "Rental and Homeowner Vacancy Rates by Area."
6. Daniel A. Hagen and Julia L. Hansen, "Rental Housing and the Natural Vacancy Rate," Journal of Real Estate Research 32, no. 4 (2010): 413–33. (As an example, Seattle has an EVR between 4.97 and 5.25 percent.)
7. J. W. R. Whitehead, "The Settlement Morphology of London's Cocktail Belt," Tijdschrift voor economische en sociale Geograpfie 58 (January-February 1967): 20–27.
8. When the New York Times analyzed data from the Census Bureau's 2012 American Community Survey, it found that on the eight blocks from East 59th Street to East 63rd Street between Park Avenue and Fifth Avenue, 628 of 1,261 homes were vacant most of the time. Julie Satow, "Pied-à-Neighborhood," New York Times, October 24, 2014. While Midtown is an epicenter of pieds-à-terre, the phenomenon extends across the city. The 2017 New York City Housing and Vacancy Survey lists 75,000 vacant pieds-à-terre in New York City compared with 55,000 in 2014. Jeffrey C. Mays and Jesse McKinley, "Lawmakers Support 'Pied-à-Terre' Tax on Multimillion-Dollar Second Homes," New York Times, March 11, 2019.
9. Atelier Parisien d'urbanism, recueil thématique 1er, 2e, 3e et 4e arrondissements de Paris (Paris: Paris Urbanism Agency, 2017), 18.
10. Evie Burrows-Taylor, "Paris: 26 Percent of City Centre Homes Lie Empty," The Local, August 18, 2017.
11. Quoted in Sarah Lyall, "A Slice of London So Exclusive Even the Owners Are Visitors," New York Times, April 1, 2013. Savills World Research reports that during 2011–12, 59 percent of sales of existing residences in prime areas of central London, such as Chelsea and Kensington, were purchased by overseas buyers; a significant number of these properties were not primary residences and were not occupied for much of the year. Savills World Research, Spotlight: The World in London (London: Savills Research, 2012), 4.
12. "Population and Dwelling Count Highlight Tables, 2016 Census," Statistics Canada.
13. Measuring the Presence of Absence: Clarifications and Corrections in the Reportage of the BTAworks' Foreign Investment in Vancouver Real Estate, March 25, 2013.
14. Jan Nijman, Miami: Mistress of the Americas (Philadelphia: University of Pennsylvania Press, 2011), 168. Katrin Kandlbinder, Norman G. Miller, and Michael Sklarz, "Leveling the Playing Field: Out-of-Town Buyer Premiums in US Housing Markets over Time," International Journal of Housing Markets and Analysis 12, no. 3 (June 2019): 387.
15. "Narco-A-Lago: Money Laundering at the Trump Ocean Club, Panama," Global Witness, November 2017.
16. Catherine Cashmore, Speculative Vacancies 8: The Empty Properties Ignored by Statistics (Melbourne: Prosper, 2015), 18.
17. "The Housing Crisis in Cities: Causes, Effects and Responses: Summary of the Talks Given at the Barcelona Housing and Renovation Forum," MACBA Auditorium, Barcelona, March 19–21, 2019, 15.
18. Scott Bollens, "An Island in Sectarian Seas? Heritage, Memory and Identity in Post-War Redevelopment of Beirut's Central District," in Urban Heritage in Divided Cities: Contested Pasts, eds. Mirjana Ristic and Sybille Frank (London: Routledge, 2019), 179.
19. Feargus O'Sullivan, "Paris Is Tripling Its Tax on Second Homes," Bloomberg CityLab, January 26, 2017.
20. Satow, "Pied-à-Neighborhood."
21. David Harvey, The Urbanization of Capital: Studies in the History and Theory of Capitalist Urbanization (London: Basil Blackwell, 1985), 16.
22. Department of Housing, Local Government and Heritage, as referenced by Rob Kitchin et al., A Haunted Landscape: Housing and Ghost Estates in Post-Celtic Tiger Ireland (Maynooth, Ireland: National Institute for Regional and Spatial Analysis, 2010), 17.
23. Department of Housing, Local Government and Heritage, as referenced by Kitchin et al., Haunted Landscape, 17, 10.
24. Retail Space Europe: Yearbook 2010 (Amsterdam: Europe Real Estate Publishers, 2010), 23. Andrew MacLaran, Katia Attuyer, and Brendan Williams, "Changing Office Location Patterns and Their Importance in the Peripheral Expansion of the Dublin Region 1960–2008," Journal of Irish Urban Studies 7–9 (2008–10): 60. Peter Bacon & Associates, Over-Capacity in the Irish Hotel Industry and Required Elements of a Recovery Programme, November 2009, 12. DKM Economic Consultants, Review of the Construction Industry 2007 and Outlook 2008 to 2010 (September 2008), ii.
25. More specifically, land prices jumped from about €5,000 ($6,368) to almost €60,000 ($76,416) per hectare (2.5 acres). Kitchin et al., Haunted Landscape, 11, 12.
26. Morgan Kelly, "The Irish Credit Bubble" (working paper 09/32, UCD Centre for Economic Research Working Paper Series, University College Dublin, December 2009), 9.
27. The degree to which speculation fueled home purchases in Ireland is clarified by the distribution of two dominant mortgage types: primary dwelling home mortgages and buy-to-let mortgages, which are used by investors. In most cases, BTL properties are purchased as a source of both ongoing rental income and capital gains to be realized from price escalation—speculation in the proper sense. In 2011, approximately 16 percent of outstanding mortgages were BTL. But in these years new primary home purchasers, many aiming to build capital to leverage future purchases, also entered the market. The Irish economist John FitzGerald noted a new disposition: Irish families had once been likelier to buy a property that they intended to live in for their entire lives, whereas during the boom many approached home purchases as investments. See Barend Wind, Caroline Dewidle, and John Doling, "Secondary Property Ownership in Europe: Contributing to Asset-Based Welfare Strategies and the 'Really Big Trade-Off,'" International Journal of Housing Policy 20, no. 1 (January 2020): 25–52. See also Manuel Aalbers et al., Buy-to-Let: gewikt en gewogen (Leuven: KU Leuven and University of Amsterdam, 2018). Anne McGuinness, "The Distribution of Property Level Arrears," Economic Letter Series, Central Bank of Ireland 6 (2011): 3. John FitzGerald, in discussion with the author, Dublin, July 23, 2013.
28. By 2012, prices for existing homes had dropped by 34 percent, for existing apartments by 49 percent, and for new apartments by 54 percent. "House Price Statistics," Department of Housing, Local Government and Heritage, Ireland.
29. "Housing Stock and Vacant Dwellings 2006 and 2011," Central Statistics Office, Ireland.
30. Its first survey counted approximately 3,000 ghost estates with 180,000 units. Over the subsequent seven years, that number dropped to 420 estates with a total of just under 25,000 units. Department of Housing, Planning and Local Government (Republic of Ireland), Resolving Unfinished Housing Developments: 2017 Annual Progress Report on Actions to Address Unfinished Housing Developments (February 2018).
31. "Forty Ghost Estates Targeted for Demolition," The Journal.ie, November 18, 2013.
32. The official statistics seem low because the government removes developments from its list of unfinished projects once they are designated as resolved, and the specific definition of resolution makes it possible that the government is undercounting. For example, resolution does not require the estate to have an electrical connection, only a supply of potable water. Housing Agency, Department of Environment, Community, and Local Government (Republic of Ireland), National Housing Development Survey: Summary Report, November 2012, 8.
33. Isabel Concheiro, "Interrupted Spain" in After Crisis: Contemporary Architectural Conditions, ed. Josep Lluís Mateo (Baden, Switzerland: Lars Müller Publishers, 2011), 13.
34. William Chislett, "Is Spain Different? The Political, Economic and Social Consequences of Its Crisis," International Journal of Iberian Studies 28, nos. 2–3 (June 2015): 258.
35. Christopher Marcinkoski, The City That Never Was (New York: Princeton Architectural Press, 2015), 81. Paco Segura, "Infraestructuras de transporte, impacto territorial y crisis," in Paisajes devastados. Despues del ciclo inmobiliario: impactos regionales y urbanos de la crisis (Madrid: Traficantes de Sueños, 2013), 85. "Gross Domestic Product," Organization for Economic Cooperation and Development.
36. Angel Bergés and Emilio Ontiveros, "La nueva Ley de Suelo desde la perspectiva económica. Sostenibilidad y eficiencia en los Mercados del Suelo." Ciudad y territorio Estudios territoriales no. 152–53 (2007): 260; Ministerio de Transportes, Movilidad y Agenda Urbana, "Precios del suelo." Ministerio de Transportes, Movilidad y Agenda Urbana, "Valor tasado de vivienda libre."
37. Asociación Hipotecaria Española, Indicadores del coste de la deuda hipotecaria, 2010. José García-Montalvo, "Deconstruyendo la burbuja. Expectativas de revalorización y precio de la vivienda en España," Papeles de economía española 109 (2006): 49.
38. Banco de España, "Indicadores del mercado de la Vivienda."
39. It is reported that between 2000 and 2006, the gross value of securitized assets in Spain rose from €8 billion ($10 billion) to

€100 billion ($127 billion). Isidro López and Emmanuel Rodríguez, *Fin de Ciclo: Financialización, territorio...del capitalismo hispano (1959-2010)* (Madrid: Traficantes de Sueños, 2010), 292.

40 Isidro López and Emmanuel Rodríguez, "The Spanish Model," *New Left Review* 69 (May-June 2011): 10.

41 Tomás Mazón, Elena Delgado Laguna, and José A. Hurtado, "Mortgaged Tourists: The Case of the South Coast of Alicante (Spain)," in *Second Home Tourism in Europe: Lifestyle Issues and Policy Responses*, ed. Zoran Roca (Farnham, UK: Ashgate, 2013), 36.

42 Aitana Alguacil Denche et al., *La vivienda en España en el siglo XXI* (Madrid: Cáritas Española Editores, 2013), 104.

43 Quoted in Concheiro, "Interrupted Spain," 19.

44 The role and powers of the agente urbanizador are considerable. Granted powers of expropriation, the agente is an individual or private corporation that can develop land regardless of the desires of private landowners. In other words, the agentes can develop land for market purposes against the will of landowners; the only requirement is that they must compensate them for the expropriated land. In practice, this compensation is derived from the value created through "urbanization" (the process in which an area is subdivided into lots, road and utility infrastructure installed, and buildings constructed). It is important to note that almost any private business was able to act as an agente urbanizador. Professor Fernando Gaja i Díaz, University of Valencia, in discussion with the author, Valencia, Spain, July 7, 2014. In the words of Spanish architect Isabel Concheiro, "The creation of this figure was to end the retention of land by owners who refused to participate in urban development [and] to speed up the urbanization process." Concheiro, "Interrupted Spain," 19.

45 Fernando Gaja i Díaz, "Una desamortización a finales del siglo xx: el 'urbanizador' en la legislación urbanística valenciana," in *Ordenación del territorio y urbanismo en Castilla-La Mancha*, ed. Francisco Blázquez Calvo (Toledo, Spain: Almud, Ediciones de Castilla-La Mancha, 2008), 138-39.

46 Marcinkoski, *The City That Never Was*, 73. Tom Allet, "The 'Ghost' Comes to Life," *Airports International* 52, no. 2 (March 2019): 18. Similarly, the Ciudad Real Central Airport, made infamous by the international media and said to have been constructed for more than €1 billion ($1.2 billion), was empty from 2012 to 2019.

47 It is difficult to accurately account for the total area of empty urbanized land, but some estimates are as high as 290,000 hectares (716,606 acres). Eugenio L. Burriel, "Empty Urbanism: The Bursting of the Spanish Housing Bubble," *Urban Research & Practice* (2015): 7; doi: 10.1080/17535069.2015.1110196.

48 Eugenio L. Burriel de Orueta, "El estallido de la burbuja inmobiliaria y sus efectos en el territorio," in *Geografía de la crisis económica en España*, ed. Juan M. Albertos Puebla and José Sánchez Hernández (Valencia: University of Valencia, 2014), 136. José María Ezquiaga Domínguez uses the phrase "post-metropolitan archipelagos" to describe aspects of Madrid's urbanization. I have borrowed the phrase, although I define it differently. To read his use of the phrase, refer to "Archipiélagos post-metropolitanos," *Cuestiones Urbanas* 1 (2010): 46-56.

49 Jorge Salido Cobo, "Venta de pisos a contrarreloj," *El Mundo*, October 10, 2007.

50 "Cuatro bancos se quedan con 2,000 pisos de El Pocero," *El País*, January 15, 2009.

51 According to the Spanish urban planner and activist Ramón Fernández Durán, "These new developments are increasingly more segregated from the existing urban fabric and homogeneous in terms of nationalities from rich European Union countries." Ramón Fernández Durán, "El Tsunami urbanizador español y mundial," *El Ecologista* 48 (2006): 22.

52 "Southeastern landscape is currently a 'stand-by' landscape, defined by land works and the construction of new roads and infrastructure," awaiting the development halted by the market's collapse. Concheiro, "Interrupted Spain," 23.

53 In 2018, the Dutch architect Reinier de Graaf, a partner at the Office for Metropolitan Architecture, led a Harvard Graduate School of Design studio that focused on ghost urbanism. They examined 50 developments in 22 countries, each one square kilometer or more in area, with reported vacancy rates above 50 percent that persisted for a minimum period of one year. See Phantom Urbanism.

54 Kaiji Chen and Yi Wen, "The Great Housing Boom of China" (working paper 2014-022C, St. Louis: Federal Reserve Bank of St. Louis, 2014; revised 2016), 1.

55 Marcinkoski, *The City That Never Was*, 46.

56 Max D. Woodworth and Jeremy L. Wallace, "Seeing Ghosts: Parsing China's 'Ghost City' Controversy," *Urban Geography* 38, no. 8 (2017): 1272, doi.org/10.1080/02723638.2017.1288009. Max D. Woodworth, "Ordos Municipality: A Market-Era Resource Boomtown," *Cities: The International Journal of Urban Policy and Planning* 43 (March 2015): 127; doi.org/10.1016/j.cities.2014.11.017.

57 The local government redrew the boundary of Kangbashi to exclude an area with a large number of unfinished residential buildings, and in 2016 it reported the population had reached 153,000—but with an original population aimed at one million, the report still suggests significant underoccupancy. Uchralt Otede, "Kangbashi: The Richest 'Ghost Town' in China?," in *Prosperity*, ed. Jane Golley and Linda Jaivan (Canberra: Australian National University Press, 2018), 79.

58 Marcinkoski, *The City That Never Was*, 47.

59 According to the Survey and Research Center for China Household Finance, in the first quarter of 2018, 41 percent of all home purchases were of a second home and a shocking 31 percent of a third home. "A Fifth of China's Homes Are Empty. That's 50 Million Apartments," *Bloomberg News*, November 8, 2018. In 2011, the state-owned China Daily reported that the Beijing Municipal Government banned Beijing families who own two or more apartments and non-Beijing residents who own one or more from purchasing more property in the capital city. "Beijing Issues New Rules to Limit House Purchase," *China Daily*, February 16, 2011. In subsequent years, other jurisdictions have enacted similar regulations. Xinhua News Agency, China's official press agency, reported in 2017 that Hangzhou prohibited single adults from purchasing second homes. "More Chinese Cities Restrict House Purchases," *Xinhua Net*, March 29, 2017. "China's Home Vacancy Rate Is Over 20 Percent," *China Scope*, December 30, 2018.

60 "Housing Should Be for Living In, Not for Speculation, Xi Says," *Bloomberg News*, October 18, 2017.

61 David Castillo and William Egginton, "Dreamboat Vampires and Zombie Capitalists," *New York Times*, October 26, 2014.

62 For an exciting examination of zombie films and urban geography, see Jeff May, "Zombie geographies and the undead city," *Social and Cultural Geography*, 11:3 (May 2010); doi.org/10.1080/14649361003637166.

> I write to a child who has not yet been born...
> I write to an idea or a dream that unwittingly
> terrifies the jailor before it even comes to fruition.
> I write to any child... I write to my son who has not
> yet come into life... I write to the *Milad* (Arabic for
> birth) of the future, that's how I want to name him/
> her, and that's how I want the future to know us.[1]
> —Walid Daqqa, March 25, 2011

In a small room in Ashkelon Prison[2] in 1999, Palestinian political prisoner Walid Daqqa, a writer, intellectual, and activist, was wedded to Sana Salameh, a journalist and activist. They were permitted to celebrate for three hours with a few close family members and nine other political prisoners. This was the outcome of months of battling the Israeli Prison Service (IPS) to obtain permission to get married and hold a modest wedding ceremony.

With a deep desire to expand their family, Daqqa and Salameh entered a new protracted twelve-year legal battle with the Israeli courts to be granted permission for conjugal visits so that they could try to conceive a child. Denied any right to a private visit or a means to reproduce legally, the couple resorted to smuggling—or "liberating"—Daqqa's sperm outside of prison walls to perform conception beyond the physical limits imposed by the occupation.[3] On May 27, 2019, a fertilized embryo was implanted in Sana's uterus, and a daughter, Milad, was born on March 2, 2020.

If bodies are permeable, extensible things, what escapes the limits drawn by architecture, the law, and other regulatory terrains that shore up the singularity of the corporeal subject and impress upon its interiority? Here the Palestinian birthing body is just one agent in the reproductive futures assembled creatively and covertly under the forces of occupation. The means by which Daqqa and Salameh pursued their family represents a greater phenomenon of Palestinian sperm smuggling out of Israeli occupation prisons, where the aspiration to parent has become an act of resistance involving an assistive network of tools, co-conspirators, and leaks (informational and bodily). Through this practice we see more clearly how self-authorizing bodily futures are entangled with biopolitical sites of settler colonial hegemony.

Daqqa's case also illustrates the outsized authority exerted by Israeli security forces and courts over the lives of ordinary Palestinians. A native of Baqa al-Gharbiyye, in the 1948 occupied territories, Daqqa was arrested by the Israeli military in 1986, three years after his involvement with the Palestinian Liberation Organization (PLO). The Israeli military court ruling of life imprisonment was ultimately reduced to 37 years, so he was set to be released on March 24, 2023. However, after being accused of supplying smuggled cellphones to fellow Palestinian prisoners in 2018, Daqqa had two more years added to his sentence. He is now set to be released on March 24, 2025.

Currently confined to a hospital bed at the Ramleh Prison clinic battling terminal cancer, Daqqa has been struggling with chronic health complications as a result of untreated polycythemia—a disease that requires regular checkups, which have been denied after he was classified as dangerous by the IPS following his daughter's unsanctioned birth. After many appeals by Daqqa's family for an early release from prison to receive urgent treatment for bone marrow cancer, the Israeli military court issued an official rejection on August 7, 2023. His family continues to call for his early—or original—release.[4]

On June 7, 1967, following the occupation of the Palestinian territories known as the West Bank, Israel issued its first proclamation stating that the military commander has "all legislative, executive and judicial powers" over the territory in "the interests of security and public order."[5] What constitutes security and public order under this colonial military regime implicates all Palestinians who implicitly or actively participate in any form of perceived opposition to the occupation, deeming them as a threat to the colonial order that Israel has established. Since 1967 more than 3,000 military orders have been issued, including Military Order 101, which authorizes punishment of up to ten years of imprisonment for peaceful political expression, effectively exposing any and all Palestinians to incarceration. The criminalization of any form of Palestinian political act that opposes or critiques colonization is transformed into a legal matter to be processed in the Israeli court system, a proxy that regenerates the Israeli military order under the guise of civil and liberal law. Contending with the draconian, ever-compounding military orders that take on full force in the Israeli court—with a conviction rate of over 99 percent—more than 800,000 Palestinians have been either imprisoned or detained to date since 1967: In other words, 20 percent of the overall population and 40 percent of the men.

The Israeli Prison Service and Israeli Security Agency (known as Shabak) undertake a variety of disciplinary measures—including repeated rituals of isolation, solitary confinement, interrogation, limited social time, psychological and physical torture, humiliation, and sleep deprivation, and other incitements of despair—to curtail activities that might "harm" its occupation routines, either retroactively or preemptively. The archipelagic structure of Israeli occupation that exists outside the bare walls of the prison in the West Bank and Gaza is mirrored in the experience of Palestinians prisoners, who are often segregated, a strategy that expands the temporal experience while contracting the spatial dimensions within the dark confines of the prison enclaves.[6] Yet while imposing control over the Palestinian body, these tactics engender emancipatory movements embodied by the praxis of *sumud* (steadfastness) and resistance that ultimately destabilize the settler colonial project.[7]

According to the human-rights organization Addameer Prisoner Support and Human Rights Association, there were 5,100 Palestinians held in Israeli occupation prisons as of August 2023,[8] the majority of them are adult men. Denied conjugal visits under the pretext of "security," these Palestinian political prisoners are permitted 45-minute biweekly meetings with members of their immediate family, separated by a layer of Plexiglas.[9]

Brief minutes of light physical contact afforded at the end of a visit have become an opportunity for clandestine exchange: A sleight of hand concealing a warm vial filled with the prisoner's semen initiates an arduous journey across checkpoints to a fertility doctor within an extremely limited timeframe. Following a 2013 Islamic edict that sanctioned certain assisted reproductive technologies (ART) for families with men behind bars, in vitro fertilization (IVF) has become the primary medical procedure through which prisoners' wives who obtain these sperm vials attempt pregnancy. To date 76 Palestinian prisoners have successfully liberated their seminal fluids, resulting in 118 births; 56 of the prisoners are from the West Bank, 13 are from the Gaza Strip, and 6 are from occupied Jerusalem.[10]

In a typical clinical setting this procedure involves only the parent(s) to-be and a medical professional. In this context IVF requires an expansive network of agents and objects ranging from the vessel that conceals the vial of semen; the prisoner who masturbates into it; a fellow inmate assisting with logistics; a partner, sibling, in-law, or child acting as the courier dispatching the sperm receptacle; a vehicle on the other side of the border; and a fertility clinic to host, preserve, and eventually fertilize the mother's egg with the "liberated" semen. In the protracted dimensions of time and space in which the seminal vial can travel from the body of the prisoner into the specialized freezer of a fertility clinic in the West Bank, Gaza, or East Jerusalem to await fertilization and implantation, a new form of gender and sexual relation is emphasized, sublimating the (conventionally) intimate act

Sliman Mansour, *The Village Awakens*, 1987. Oil on canvas, 97.5cm × 116 cm.

of reproducing a child with a partner within a necessarily expanded network. This shift in the gender dynamic allows the wives of Palestinian prisoners to "reclaim power as active agents of history" by publishing stories of liberated sperm and confronting normative gender structures that have historically cast women as passive and silent sufferers while challenging the Israeli colonial narrative.[11]

In a 2019 interview published in *Topic* titled "The Palestinian Sperm Smugglers," Fat'hiya al-Safadi, from Nablus in the West Bank, recounts her experience of receiving her husband's seminal vial and undergoing the IVF process at the Razan Center for Infertility in Ramallah, which offers free IVF services to prisoner families whose wives would be over the age of 40 at the time of the husband's release.[12] Arrested 18 days after their wedding, in 2002, her husband, Ashraf, was sentenced to 21 years in prison; she was 22 at the time. A decade later the couple sought the services of the Razan Center to initiate the process of IVF. Held in a prison in the southern Negev Desert more than 140 miles away from where Fat'hiya lives, Ashraf had prepared a gift of food for her, one of the few social acts the prison occasionally permits prisoners to engage in. He handed her a bag of Quadratini hazelnut wafers with a vial containing his sperm concealed inside. She was told by the clinic to bring the sperm within 48 hours accompanied by two members of her own family and two of her husband's family as witnesses to attest to the patrilineal connection between Ashraf and the baby in lieu of his presence. Thus gendered conventions remain, but in new forms. The act of fertilization, attended by close family members as witnesses and made public thereafter, becomes a realization of Michelle Murphy's concept of distributed reproduction, which expands the understanding of reproduction from the space of the birthing body to an extensive macro-infrastructural scale—one distributed across uneven gendered and socioeconomic fault lines.[13]

The artifacts and spaces that assist in these exchanges further contextualize these covert fertility networks and our reading of them. Such extrajudicial practices complicate our understanding of who is deemed deserving of birthing and being birthed in the eyes of the Israeli regime. For instance, Israel's selective pronatalism[14]—evidenced by the preferential treatment of Israeli prisoners, the state's encouragement and fiscal sponsorship of assisted reproductive technologies for Israeli citizens,[15] and the recent laws legalizing surrogacy for Israeli LGBTQ couples—can be read in relation to use of the law to impose a kind of population control on Palestinians, particularly those deemed a threat to the state. The instances compound in discriminatory laws controlling Palestinian prisoners' bodily agency and limiting their rights to a family, to visitations, and to medical treatments.

According to Salameh, Milad was "the first child for whom the Israeli Security Agency (Shabak) opened a file *before* she was born."[16] While both parents are technically Israeli citizens, the Israeli Ministry of Interior initially refused to register Milad under her father's name, and Shabak warned against her birth in a court hearing. The preemptive criminal record shrouding Milad's imminent birth evidences the transgressive power embodied by the political act of

VIAL ACTS

FEMINIST ARCHITECTURE COLLABORATIVE

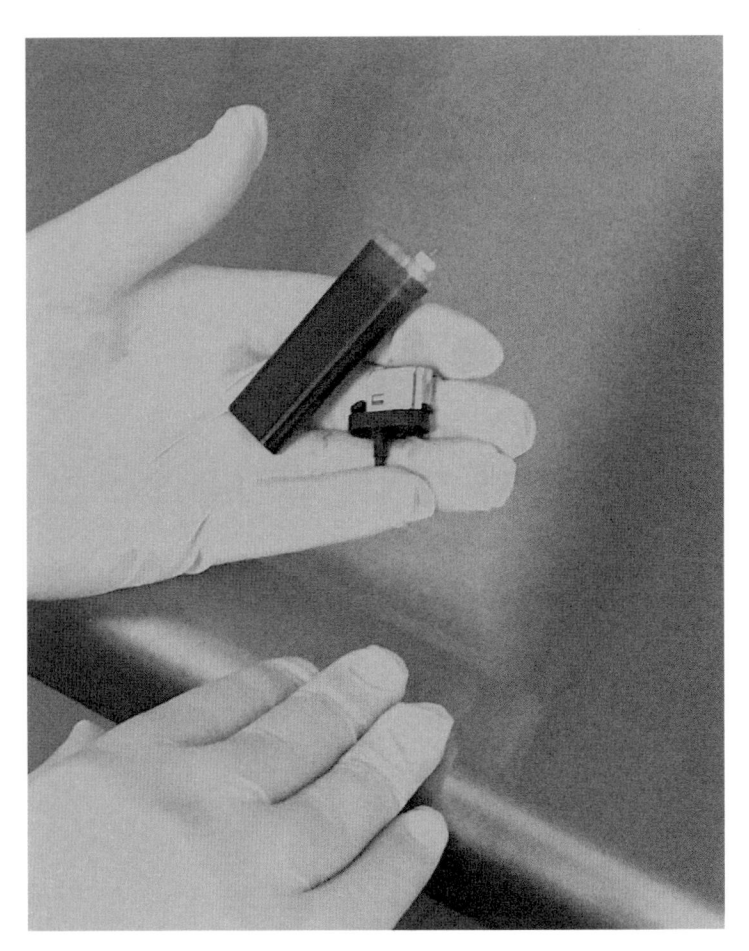

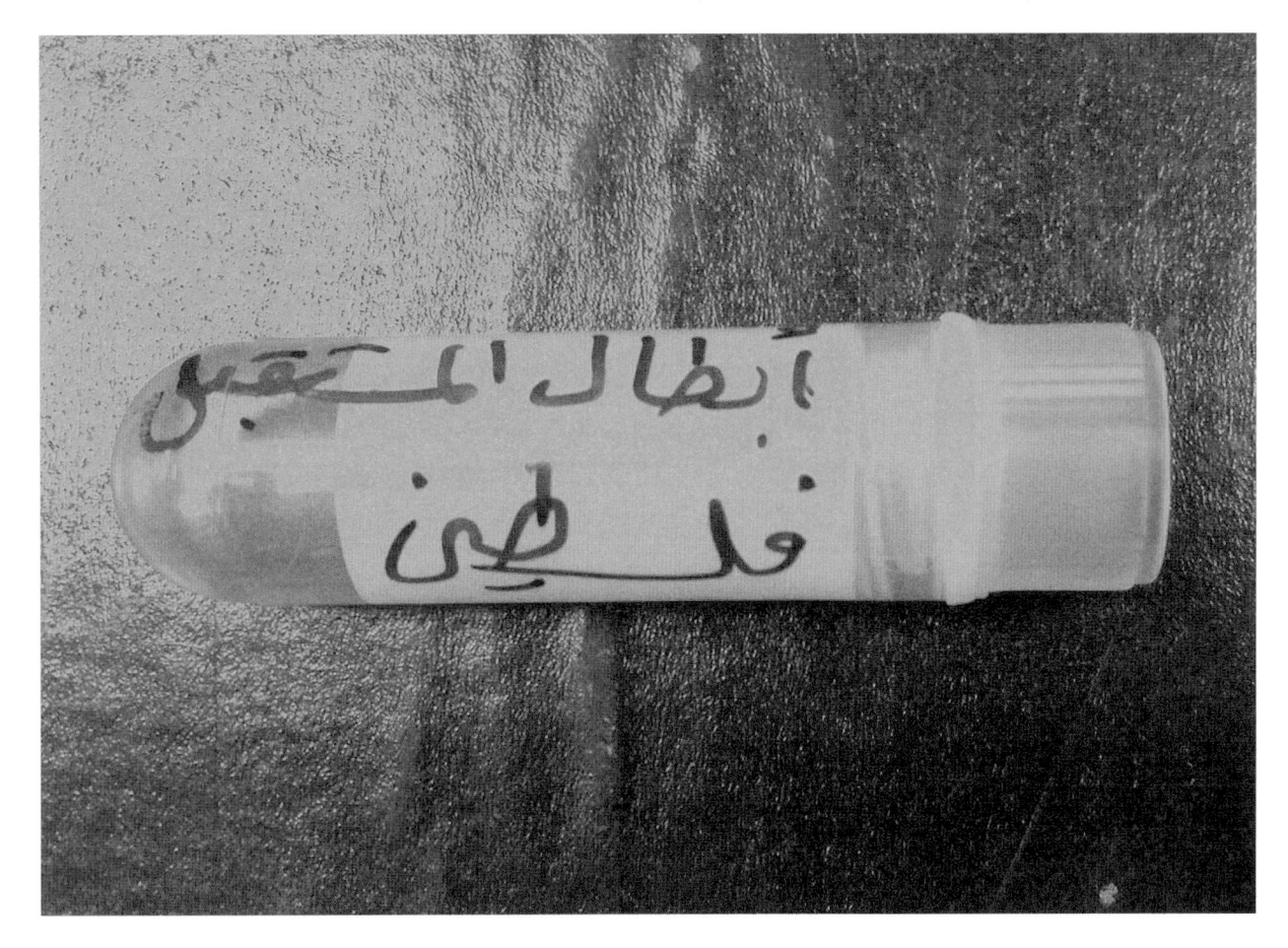

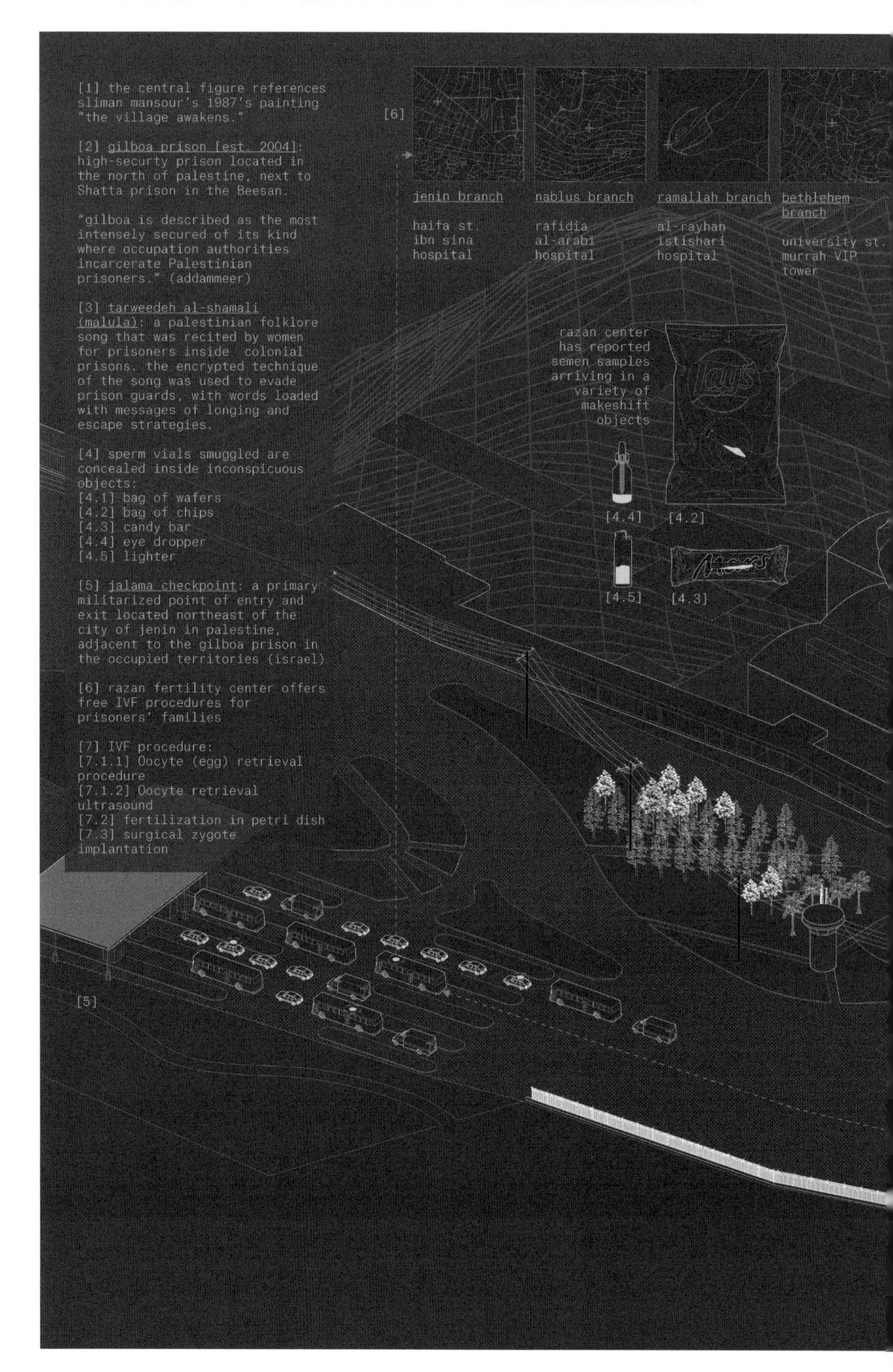

[1] the central figure references sliman mansour's 1987's painting "the village awakens."

[2] gilboa prison [est. 2004]: high-securty prison located in the north of palestine, next to Shatta prison in the Beesan.

"gilboa is described as the most intensely secured of its kind where occupation authorities incarcerate Palestinian prisoners." (addammeer)

[3] tarweedeh al-shamali (malula): a palestinian folklore song that was recited by women for prisoners inside colonial prisons. the encrypted technique of the song was used to evade prison guards, with words loaded with messages of longing and escape strategies.

[4] sperm vials smuggled are concealed inside inconspicuous objects:
[4.1] bag of wafers
[4.2] bag of chips
[4.3] candy bar
[4.4] eye dropper
[4.5] lighter

[5] jalama checkpoint: a primary militarized point of entry and exit located northeast of the city of jenin in palestine, adjacent to the gilboa prison in the occupied territories (israel)

[6] razan fertility center offers free IVF procedures for prisoners' families

[7] IVF procedure:
[7.1.1] Oocyte (egg) retrieval procedure
[7.1.2] Oocyte retrieval ultrasound
[7.2] fertilization in petri dish
[7.3] surgical zygote implantation

[6]

jenin branch	nablus branch	ramallah branch	bethlehem branch
haifa st. ibn sina hospital	rafidia al-arabi hospital	al-rayhan istishari hospital	university st. murrah VIP tower

razan center has reported semen samples arriving in a variety of makeshift objects

[4.4] [4.2]

[4.5] [4.3]

september 2021

six palestinian
prisoners escaped the
notorious facility
through a tunnel they
had dug from below their
cell's toilet using
spoons, plates, and the
handle of a kettle. all
six were eventually
recaptured. the spoon, as
a tool for escape,
became a symbol for
liberation for
palestinians that year.

FEMINIST ARCHITECTURE COLLABORATIVE

Right: From the series *Habibi* by Antonio Faccilongo. Amma Elian is the wife of Anwar Elian. He was arrested in 2003 and sentenced to life in prison, Tulkarem, Palestine, 2015.

sperm smuggling both within and outside the prison walls. Israeli authorities consistently punish families who engage in the covert transaction by either prohibiting visitation for extended periods of time—as in the case of Ashraf and Fat'hiya, who were not permitted to see each other for a year—or punishing the prisoner with solitary confinement.

With a historically higher rate than for Jewish Israelis, Palestinian reproduction has been viewed in Israeli discourse as a "demographic intifada," and Palestinian women of childbearing age are often portrayed as irresponsible hyperfertile breeders who pose a serious threat to the Zionist project. At a 1995 conference political geographer Arnon Soffer claimed that "the most serious threat that Israel faces is the wombs of Arab women in Israel."[17] This was reiterated in 2022 by Gideon Sahar, director of the Department of Thoracic and Heart Surgery at Soroka Medical Center, in Beersheba, who said at a meeting of the far-right Jewish Home political party that "the multiplying population, the most problematic population, is a sort of paradox. ... The Arab womb ... we encourage it with stipends for the children" and that Palestinian families should face a fine after giving birth to their fifth child.[18]

The Daqqa family's story is only one stark example of the punitive measures the Israeli court undertakes to curtail Palestinian freedom, livelihood, and bodily agency under the guise of the law. It is crucial to understand this questioning of who has the right to give birth and to be born from the lens of both Israel's structural removal of the Palestinian population—a fundamental policy of the Zionist movement—and its replacement by Jewish settlers. Israel's exceptionally pronatalist policies extend to the Israeli, particularly Jewish, body while ensuring a limited reproductive, economic, political, and spatial representation for Palestinians, particularly those in the West Bank and Gaza.

Another example of this reproductive stratification—which determines rights unevenly across gendered, racialized, sexualized, and classed lines—involves Israeli security prisoner Yigal Amir, who was convicted of the 1995 murder of prime minister Yitzhak Rabin and is serving a life sentence in Ramon Prison, in southern Israel.[19] Predating the first attempts by Palestinian prisoners to smuggle their seminal fluids out of prisons, Amir was caught in the attempt in 2006 but was eventually granted conjugal visits with his wife, Larisa Trembovler, resulting in the birth of a son, in 2007.

While the act of liberating Palestinian seminal fluids expands the boundaries and capacities of the incarcerated body of the male political prisoner, it is the reproductive body of the Palestinian woman that is ultimately centralized. Pregnancies resulting from liberated seminal vials are largely regarded as a form of political resistance that counteracts the Israeli prison system's efforts to erase and sever social bonds as a way to deconstruct the Palestinian collective body. A woman who conceives this way is not only a mother, or a sperm smuggler, but an emancipatory agent who performs biological resistance with her own body.[20] She also bears the

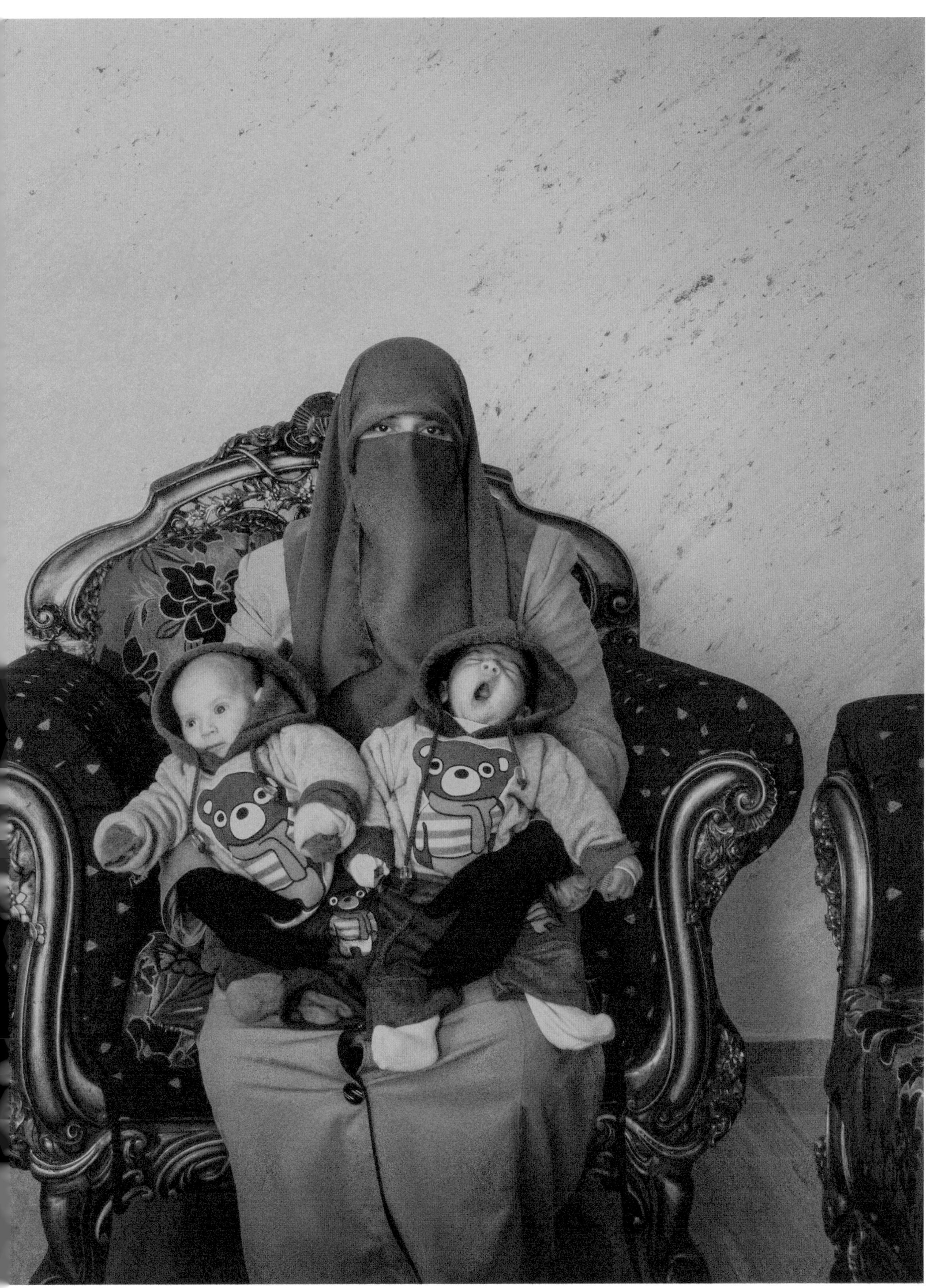

burden of carrying the child to term successfully, resisting erasure through reproduction while preserving the family line—and ensuring that if she is no longer fertile when her husband is released, he will not seek a new wife that can bear him a child.

Local Palestinian media has referred to the babies conceived from smuggled sperm as "Freedom Ambassadors" and "future heroes": Bodies that have successfully escaped the envelopment of the Israeli carceral system even before birth. Having overcome the apparent impossibility of their own births and lives, they carry the promise of a liberated Palestine. Yet these heroic depictions glean over the realities of being born into occupation with an imprisoned father and a single mother. The precarious social position of these women, whose stories of assisted reproduction may be questioned even as they attend to the daily difficulties of raising a child, remains largely unacknowledged. Reproduction-as-liberation turns into political motherhood, embodied neatly by the portraits of mothers posing with their poster children of liberation.

Palestinian women have historically been central figures in the struggle for liberation and in embodying the national Palestinian body—a space of activation and memory, of longing and exploration, and of resilience. This is well depicted in Palestinian art and folkloric songs that evoke themes of indigenous resistance and culture, of reproducing a disrupted nation, and of land as mother, where the reproductive body is an embodiment of a confiscated motherland.

LEAKAGE AS RESISTANCE

Leakage and escape are material forms of resistance that reify a Palestinian national body where a formal one is absent. This is made manifest within the prison system through the covert smuggling and exchange of seminal vials, cellphones, letters, and revolutionary ideas. Evading the constant surveillance of the carceral state and the physical imposition of the Israeli prison, these leaks of information and materials work toward regaining Palestinian bodily agency. By understanding and subverting the colonial and carceral power structures, Mohammad Hamdan writes, prisoners move "out of their passive roles" and engage "with sociopolitical practices such as smuggling sperm, which symbolizes their resistance to victimization and desire for freedom."[21]

Historically speaking, subversive modes of communication have always been enacted in Palestine, particularly in the coded words iterated by Palestinian women: Truth leaked in unsuspicious or deliberately misdirecting formats. In a practice likely originating during the British imperial era, women ascribed resistance to folkloric songs such as *Tarweeda Shamaly* and *Ya Tali'een el-Jabal* ("Climbing Up the Mountain") with encrypted melodic words shared with imprisoned Palestinians, embedded with jumbled, repetitive *L*'s to confuse a potential informant and a foreign guard. Lyrics included words of yearning, instructions on how to evade prison guards or escape, and messages from liberated fellow *munadilin* (resistance fighters). While not many coded songs have survived, a few have resurfaced since the First Intifada, in the 1980s, and have been adapted to various contemporary and traditional styles, keeping true to the voice of the woman calling for a collective reawakening, movement, or remembrance.

Leaking as resistance resurfaced recently in the national psyche when six Palestinian prisoners escaped the maximum-security Gilboa penitentiary in September 2021. Armed with a secretly shared annotated prison floor plan that stitched together the disconnected spatial experiences of inmates, Monadel Yacoub Nafe'at, Yaqoub Qassem, Yaqoub Mahmoud Qadri, Ayham Nayef Kamamji, and Mahmoud Abdullah Ardah used metal spoons, handles of kettles, and plates to dig a tunnel from below a toilet in the cell they shared to just outside the prison facility. Though the escapees were recaptured within two weeks, their prison break was a significant boost to the Palestinian liberation movement, circulating through the social media hashtag #TunnelofFreedom and imagery of a spoon as a symbol of Palestinian resistance. This event extended the project of evading the Israeli carceral apparatus, where instances of bodily escape and agency are exceptional.

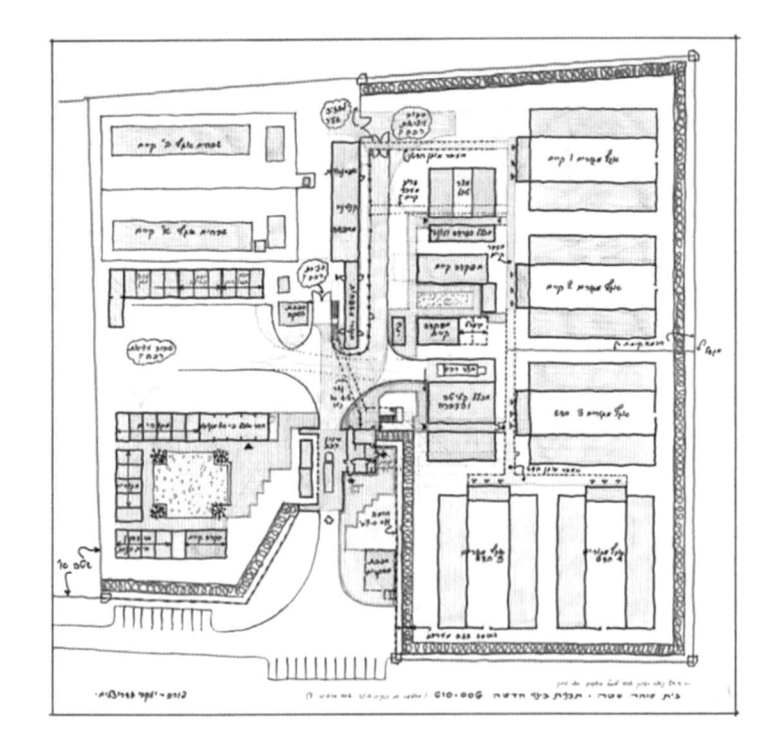

Together the spatial tactics of imprisonment and occupation maintain a population without rights and counter any forms of resistance within it. At the same time they seek to suspend any means of Palestinian political enfranchisement and self-determination, including over their reproductive future. In this way the Israeli colonial project aims to establish an intense form of population control over Palestinians, curtailing almost every possibility for life under occupation. As Judith Butler puts it, "These practices of incarceration form a systematic, if not ritual, attempt to deconstitute the Palestinian subject. The point is not to make good disciplinary subjects on the model of Foucault, the point is not to make model prisoners. ... The final aim, it seems to me, is to break down and deconstitute the subject—to destitute the subject."[22]

Yet the tactics deployed by the Israeli regime have only fueled the resistance movement from within its most secure rooms. The isolated prison enclaves, the Israeli courts, and the fertility clinics are sites linked together in the biopolitical order of colonial control, where the narrowest margins continue to provide opportunities for appropriation, contestation, and liberation by Palestinians. It is in the leaks where life is still possible.

1. Walid Daqqa, "I write to a child who has not yet been born," trans Addameer Prisoner Support and Human Rights Association, March 27, 2011, https://www.addameer.org/prisoner/5100#:~:text=In%20response%20to%20the%20court's,it%20even%20comes%20to%20fruition.
2. Ashkelon Prison was founded during the British Mandate as a regional headquarters for British army leaders and was utilized as an interrogation center for Palestinian revolutionaries before being used as a prison to hold Palestinians, starting in 1970.
3. The term *liberated sperm* is often used in place of *smuggled sperm* when referring to semen that has been clandestinely moved out of Israeli prisons, as a way to assert the political nature of the Palestinian carceral condition under occupation in the hope of a liberated future for the children who are birthed as an outcome of this procedure.
4. Sana' Salameh, "Free Walid Daqqah and all political prisoners," trans. Dalia Taha, *Mondoweiss*, May 29, 2023, https://mondoweiss.net/2023/05/free-walid-daqqah-and-all-political-prisoners.
5. "Military Proclamation No. 2: Concerning Regulation of Authority and the Judiciary, June 7, 1967," in *Israeli Military Orders in the Occupied Palestinian West Bank 1967–1992* (West Bank), compiled by Jamil Rabah and Natasha Fairweather (East Jerusalem: Jerusalem Media & Communication Center, 1995), 1.
6. Lena Meari, "Carceral Politics in Palestine and Beyond: Gender, Vulnerability, Prison," panel discussion, Columbia University, New York, April 5, 2012.
7. Judith Butler, "Carceral Politics," panel discussion.
8. "Statistics," Addameer Prisoner Support and Human Rights Association, last modified August 13, 2023, https://www.addameer.org/statistics.
9. Considering imprisonment as an intensification of the military isolation and destitution of Palestinians living under Israeli occupation, we assert that all Palestinian prisoners are political rather than security threats—an Israeli court classification that justifies stripping them of any means of self-determination.
10. "Report: 76 Palestinian prisoners had children through smuggled sperm," *Middle East Monitor*, May 17, 2023, https://www.middleeastmonitor.com/20230517-report-76-palestinian-prisoners-had-children-through-smuggled-sperm/#disqus_thread.
11. Mohammad Hamdan, "Every Sperm Is Sacred: Palestinian Prisoners, Smuggled Semen, and Derrida's Prophecy," *International Journal of Middle East Studies* 51, no. 4 (2019): 537.
12. Ben Ehrenreich, "The Palestinian Sperm Smugglers," *Topic* (May 2019), https://www.topic.com/the-palestinian-sperm-smugglers. [Note: this link seems to be expired or has been removed.]
13. Sigrid Vertommen, "Babies from Behind Bars: Stratified Assisted Reproduction in Palestine/Israel," in *Assisted Reproduction Across Borders: Feminist Perspectives on Normalizations, Disruptions, and Transmissions*, ed. Merete Lie and Nina Lykke (New York: Routledge, 2017), 207–8.
14. Rhoda Ann Kanaaneh, *Birthing the Nation: Strategies of Palestinian Women in Israel* (Berkeley and Los Angeles: University of California Press, 2002), 28.
15. Inscribed in the Ministry of Health's regulations is the right of every Israeli woman aged 18 to 45, irrespective of her family status or sexual orientation, to unlimited funded treatment for the births of two live children with her current partner. "IVF - In Vitro Fertilization," State of Israel Ministry of Health, accessed June 10, 2023, https://www.health.gov.il/English/Topics/fertility/Pages/ivf.aspx.
16. Salameh, "Free Walid Daqqah."
17. Kanaaneh, *Birthing the Nation*, 74.
18. Michael Horovitz, "Top doctor panned for voicing fear of 'Arab womb,' floating fines for Bedouin births," *Times of Israel*, October 24, 2022, https://www.timesofisrael.com/top-doctor-panned-for-voicing-fear-of-arab-womb-floating-fines-for-bedouin-births.
19. Vertommen, "Babies from Behind Bars," 207.
20. Hamdan "Every Sperm Is Sacred," 525.
21. Hamdan "Every Sperm Is Sacred," 528.
22. Butler, "Carceral Politics."

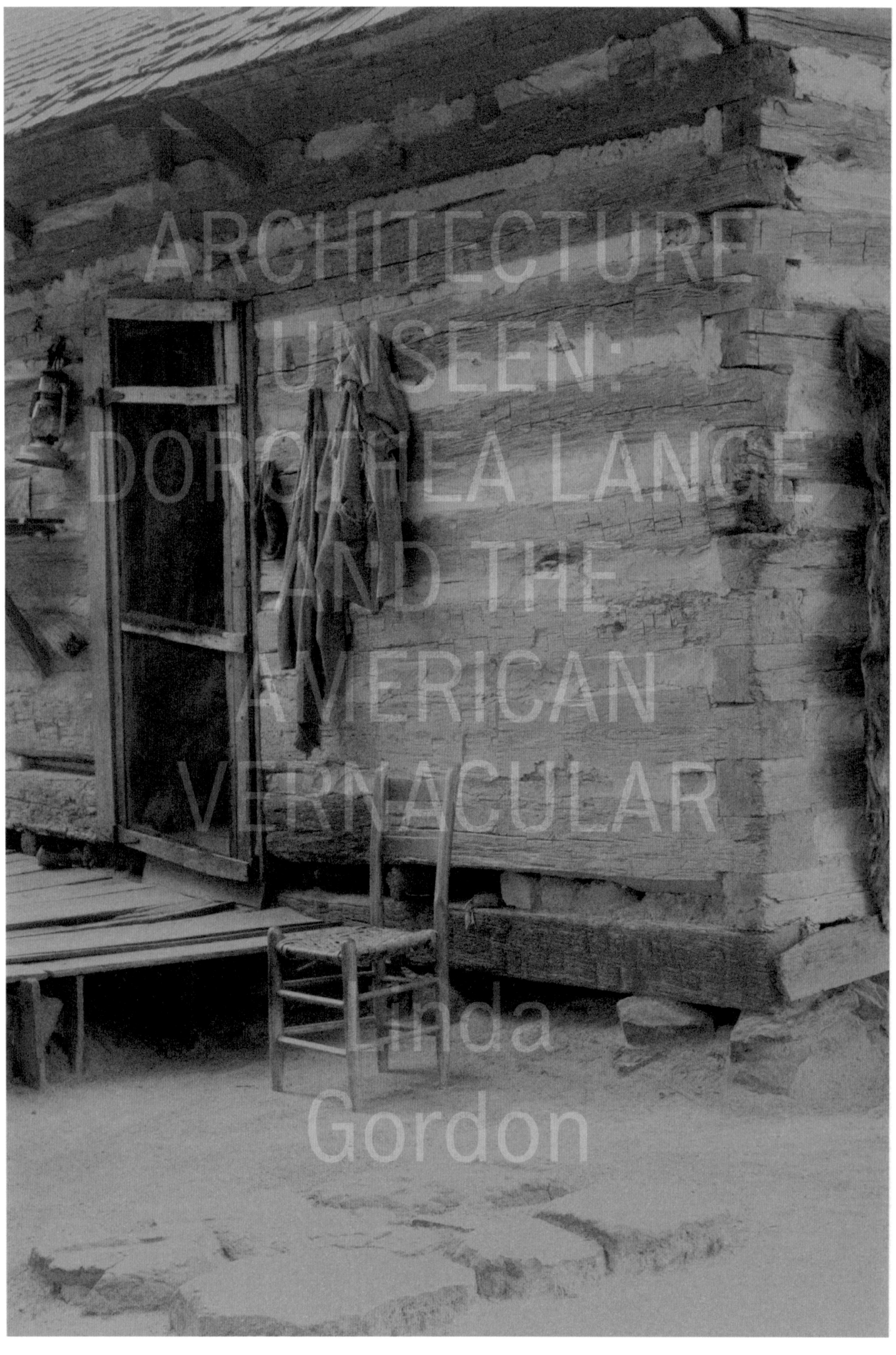

ARCHITECTURE UNSEEN: DOROTHEA LANGE AND THE AMERICAN VERNACULAR

Linda Gordon

Before photographer Dorothea Lange began doing documentary work, she had spent more than a dozen years as a portrait photographer, and that work continued to shape her photographs. Once the Great Depression of the 1930s hit, she looked out from her San Francisco studio and saw homeless men sleeping in parks and lining up in breadlines, so she began to do street photography with the same attentiveness she paid to her portraits. Her work attracted the attention of Paul Taylor, a progressive agricultural sociologist at the University of California Berkeley who had an eye for photography, having used it in his studies of farmworkers. He asked if she would be willing to accompany him as he traveled through California, documenting farmworkers. She was hooked—this work was far more interesting than that in the studio. Taylor then got her a job with the Farm Security Administration within the Department of Agriculture; she was paid—meagerly—to document conditions of farms and farmworkers.

Taylor and Lange fell in love, married, and continued to work as a team: He interviewed and took notes as she photographed. In California their subjects were Mexicans and Mexican Americans—Taylor was fluent in Spanish—and "Okies" driven out of the Southern Plains by the drought known as the Dust Bowl. Lange began to use the information Taylor gathered to caption her photographs; she insisted on captions as a means of individualizing her subjects, often providing a bit of their personal history. Soon they were also traveling through southeastern states, where she photographed poor sharecroppers, Black and white, who grew tobacco and cotton.

Taylor was unusual among academics in his concern for people of color, and meshed with her own experience—she was accustomed to spending time in San Francisco's Chinatown and southwestern Native American communities. She began to make portraits of poor and discriminated-against victims of the Depression with the same formality she had shown her clients. With Taylor she went further afield, photographing Black and white sharecroppers in the southeastern states. One-third of her Depression-era photography pictured African Americans and Mexican Americans. (A few years later she photographed the Japanese Americans who were being forced into federal camps.) No other white photographer of the period paid much attention to people of color, let alone pictured them with the respect she held.

Lange honed a unique approach, producing photographs whose visual power made her the leading documentary photographer of her generation. Her government employers wanted photographs to provide visual evidence of drought and crop failure, which could be used to build support for New Deal agricultural policies. That work might seem to yield photographs without people, but she soon used her camera to produce what could be considered another aspect of portraiture. Captivated by the unconventional, vernacular beauty of the homes farmworkers built for themselves, she made thousands of images of the tents, lean-tos, and makeshift campsites of migrant farmworkers in the West, and the houses and barns of sharecroppers in the southeast. She came to see how these homes reflected the dignity and competence of farmworkers, usually seen only as unskilled victims.

In Bakersfield, California, she noticed some refugees from the midwestern drought framing a shelter with scavenged materials, strips of wood and pipes; it would have cardboard walls and a roof made from odds and ends of sheet metal. In this construction work a woman stood inside the frame of a cabin while a man was tacking on roofing material. She was never a "snapshot" photographer. Instead her photographs were as carefully composed as her studio portraits, making images sometimes even close to abstraction, which often intensified their power. This image is an example: She waited to photograph these Okies' work at a moment when strong geometrical shapes emerged, a trapezoid, one figure inside and another above. In her darkroom she cropped the photograph so as to make that geometry stronger yet [Fig. 1].[1] At the same time she remained a portrait photographer, calling attention to the woman's spare, slightly gaunt beauty.

Even her photographs of farm labor itself were often strengthened through their powerful composition. In an image of truck cabs loaded with cotton she photographed a farmworker resting underneath a strong diagonal created by a ladder; in another, two workers standing on a truck filled with cotton, almost silhouetted stand against the sky, while another creates a diagonal as he carries a cotton sack, likely weighing 100 lbs. or more [Fig. 2]. She saw a grandmother at work washing clothes in a metal tub; she is positioned as a central arc within two vertical tent poles made from tree branches [Fig. 3]. Another photograph, of bent-over lettuce pickers, repeats the arched back of the woman doing the washing. Lange was documenting their back-breaking labor while at the same time making a composition in which their arched backs formed a counterpoint to the shapes of the lettuce and the cracks in the earth of an unplanted row [Fig. 4].

Figure 1. *Dispossessed Arkansas farmers. These people are resettling themselves on the dump outside of Bakersfield, California, 1935.*

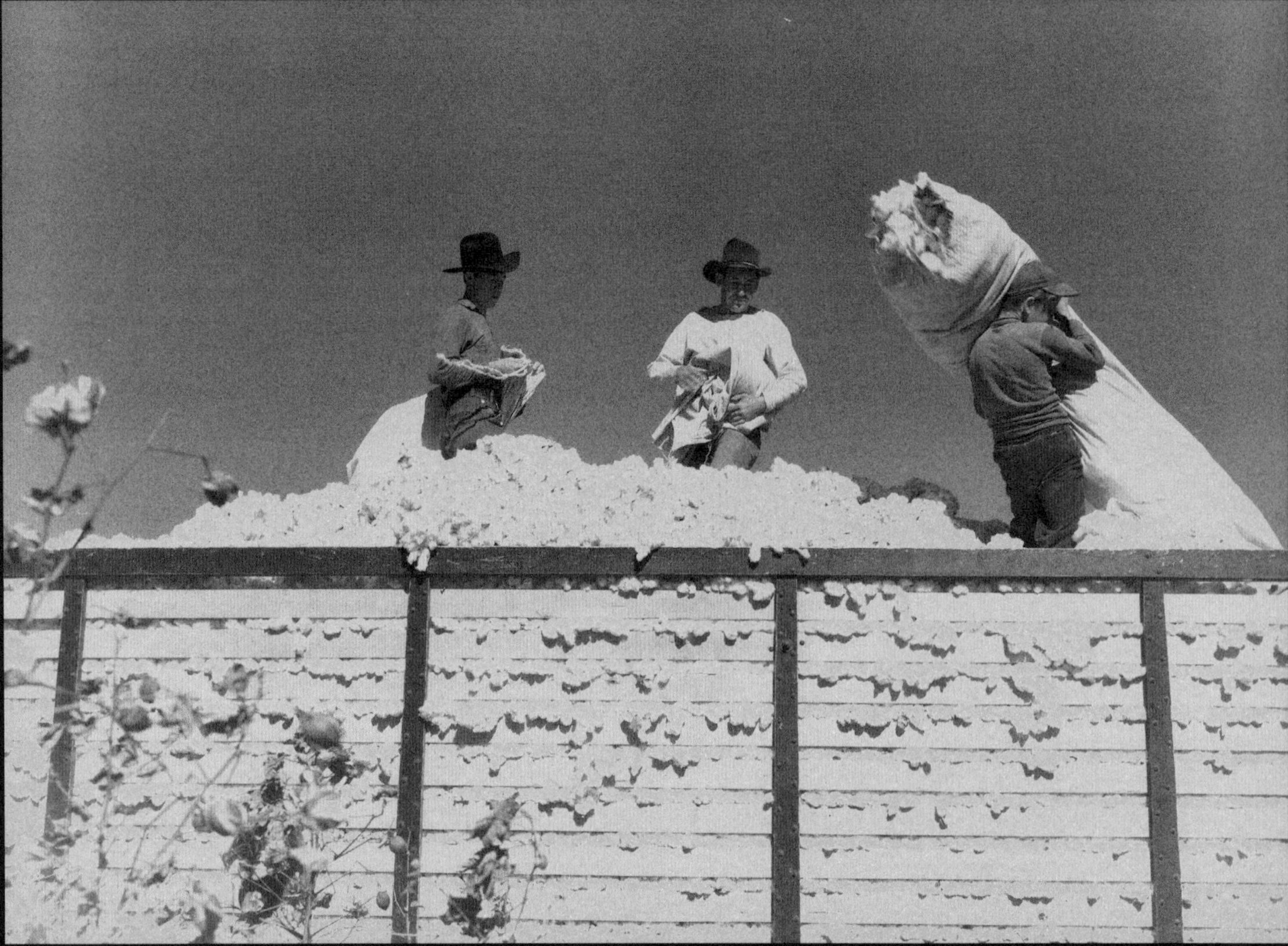

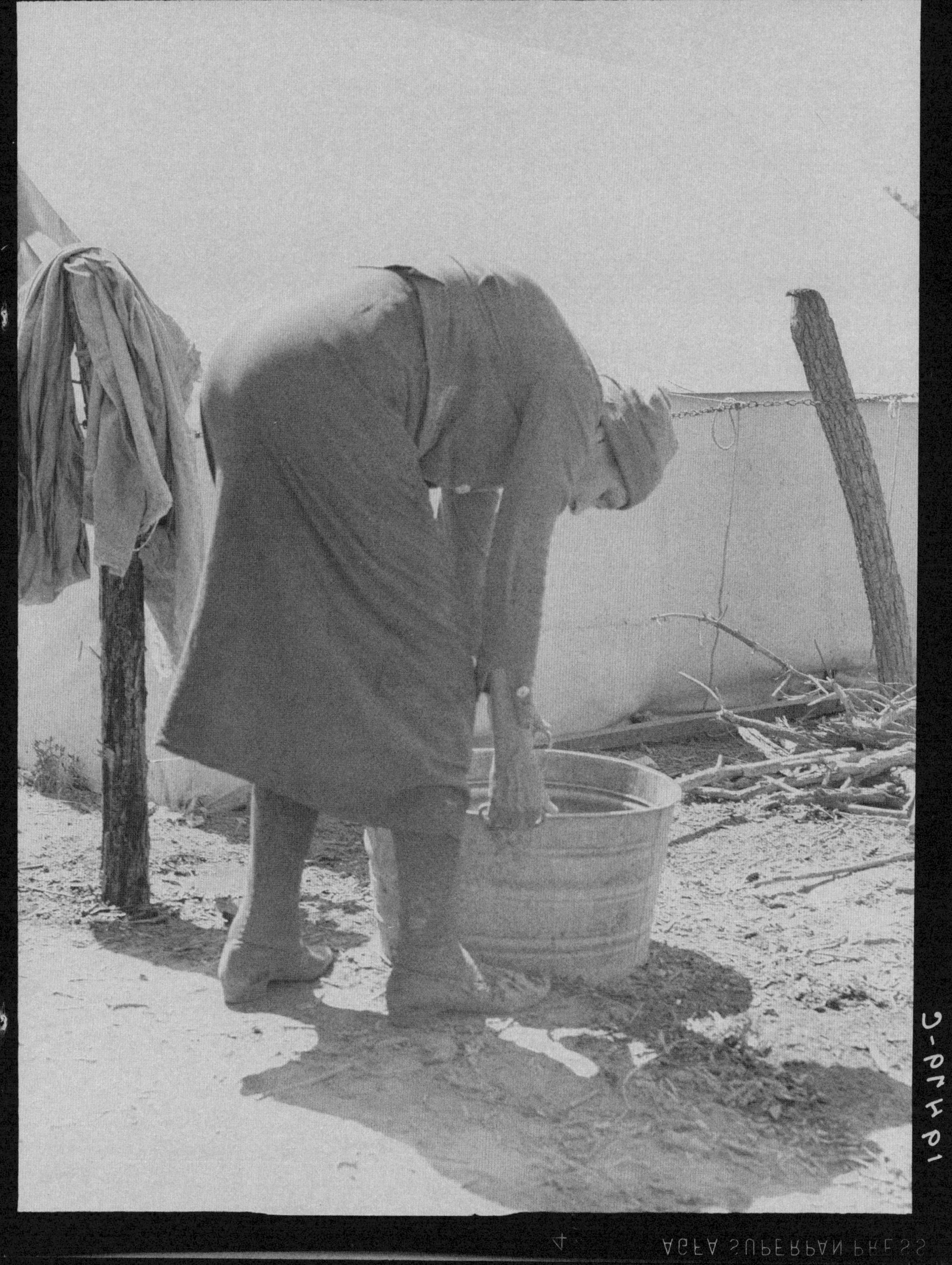

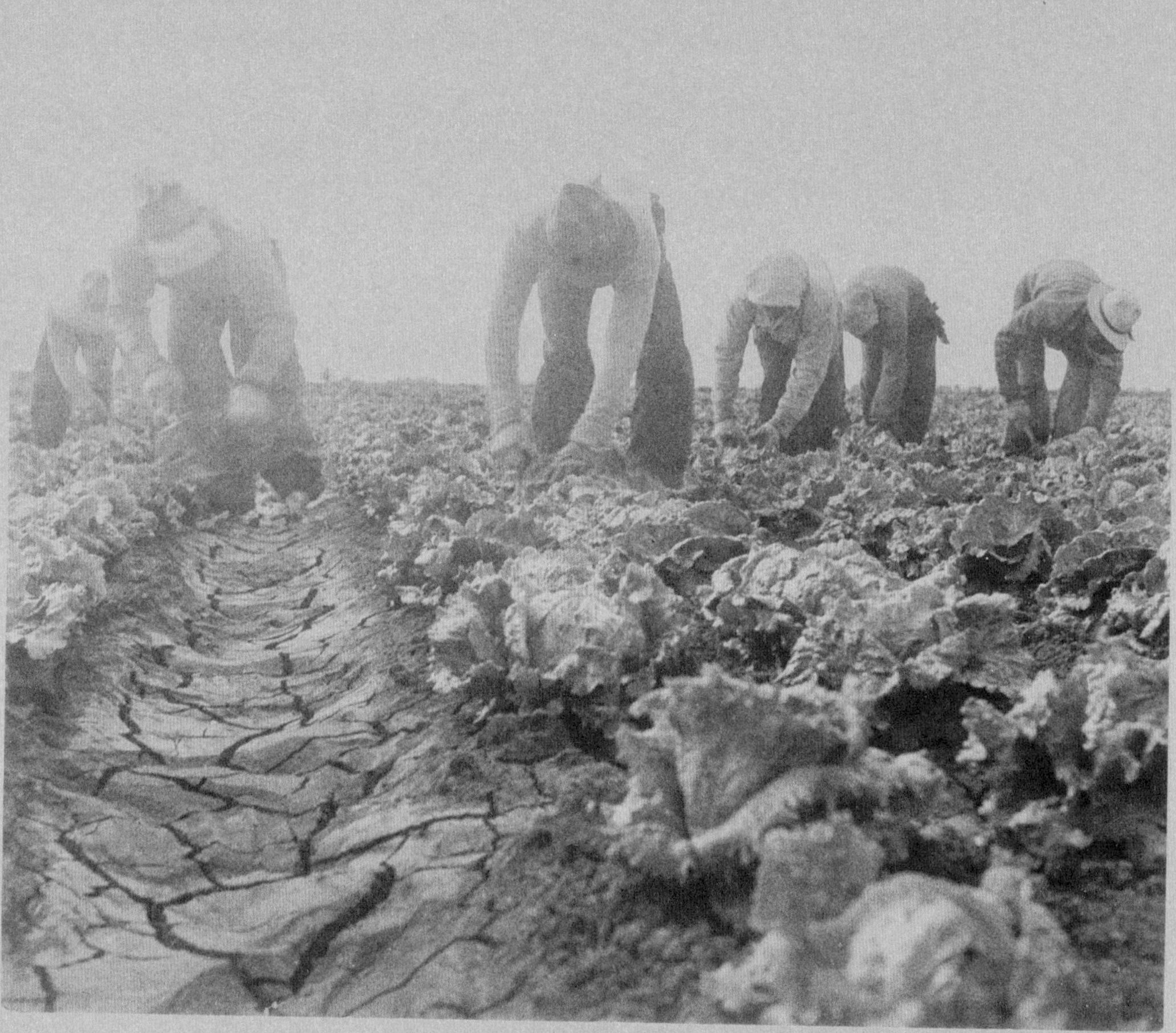

Lange delighted in the texture and workmanship apparent in farmworkers' dwellings, even the roughest. She photographed an open tent to show the tools that made migrant life possible, including a grandmother in a rocking chair; she used available light and shadow to create a formal portrait, treating this migrant farmworker with the same gravitas she had once constructed for her wealthy clients [Fig. 5]. She was drawn to the textures of a dwelling with tent material forming a roof over walls made of carefully stacked eucalyptus. Lange captioned it "The Ingenuity of Man [Fig. 6]." Consider the photo of a kitchen cabinet in a tent: A migrant farm woman used wooden boxes to store materials to feed her family while on the move. Pots, pans, and containers of food are neatly laid out on shelves. Under the cabinet, probably as a means of attempting to keep vermin out, empty cans raise up the structure [Fig. 7]. (Lange loved cooking and was good at it—many would have passed this without understanding its significance.) The image is a painterly still-life.

Figure 5. *Aged woman from Oklahoma.
Kern County migrant camp, California,
November 1936.*

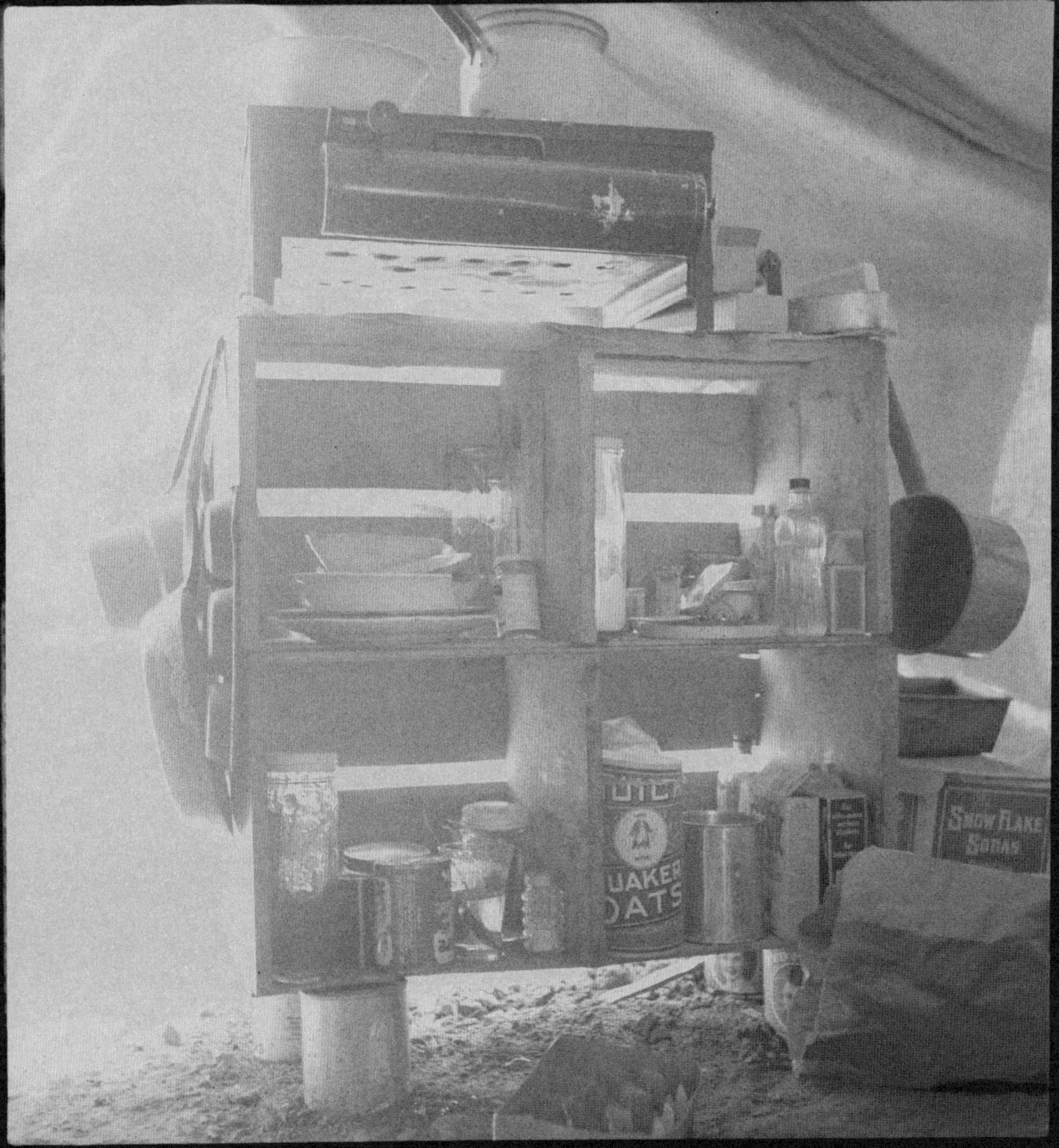
UAKER
OATS
SNOW FLAKE
SODAS

Once Lange began to work in the southeast, she made hundreds of images of sharecroppers' homes, cabins often built without nails [Fig. 8]. Fascinated by this carpentry, she photographed some that were unfinished. In one we see the almost perfectly matched interlaced logs, lacking the clay or cement that will fill the spaces between logs; the construction method is particularly clear [Fig. 9]. In North Carolina tobacco country she contrasted the pattern of the interlaced logs with a chimney built of rocks. She shows how the exterior serves as shelves and closet as well as a wall on which to dry a cowhide [Fig. 10]. Elsewhere in North Carolina she saw a young girl in a sundress with perfectly braided hair churning butter on her porch—the wood grain contrasts with the smooth ceramic jug [Fig. 11]. In Georgia, a hand-cranked circular sharpening tool rests in front of the cabin's rough wooden slats [Fig. 12]. In North Carolina, she saw a form of vernacular architecture called the "dogtrot" house. This image was accompanied by one of her long captions, which individualized her subjects and drew attention to their work and skills [Fig. 13].

These examples demonstrate something that untrained observers may not realize: That documentary photography at best is never a transparent rendering of social and economic conditions, but a carefully designed composition. And images like these gain power as a result.

Figure 8. *Detail of tobacco barn showing log construction and newly plastered furnace in preparation for "putting in." Person County, North Carolina, July 1939.*

Figure 9. Edited Title: *Log cabin barn under construction. "Four room" barn near ready for chinking. Black tenants living nearby say it takes about two weeks to build such a barn. No work was being done on barn when photograph was taken as it was the Fourth of July. Near Concord, Person County, North Carolina,*

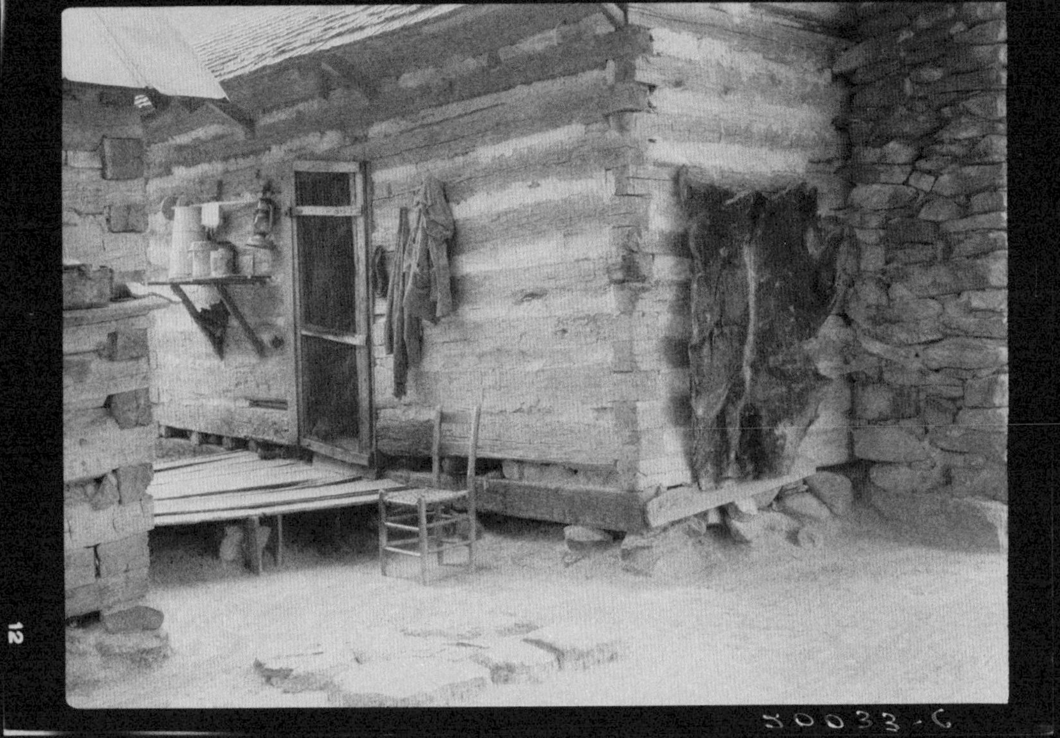

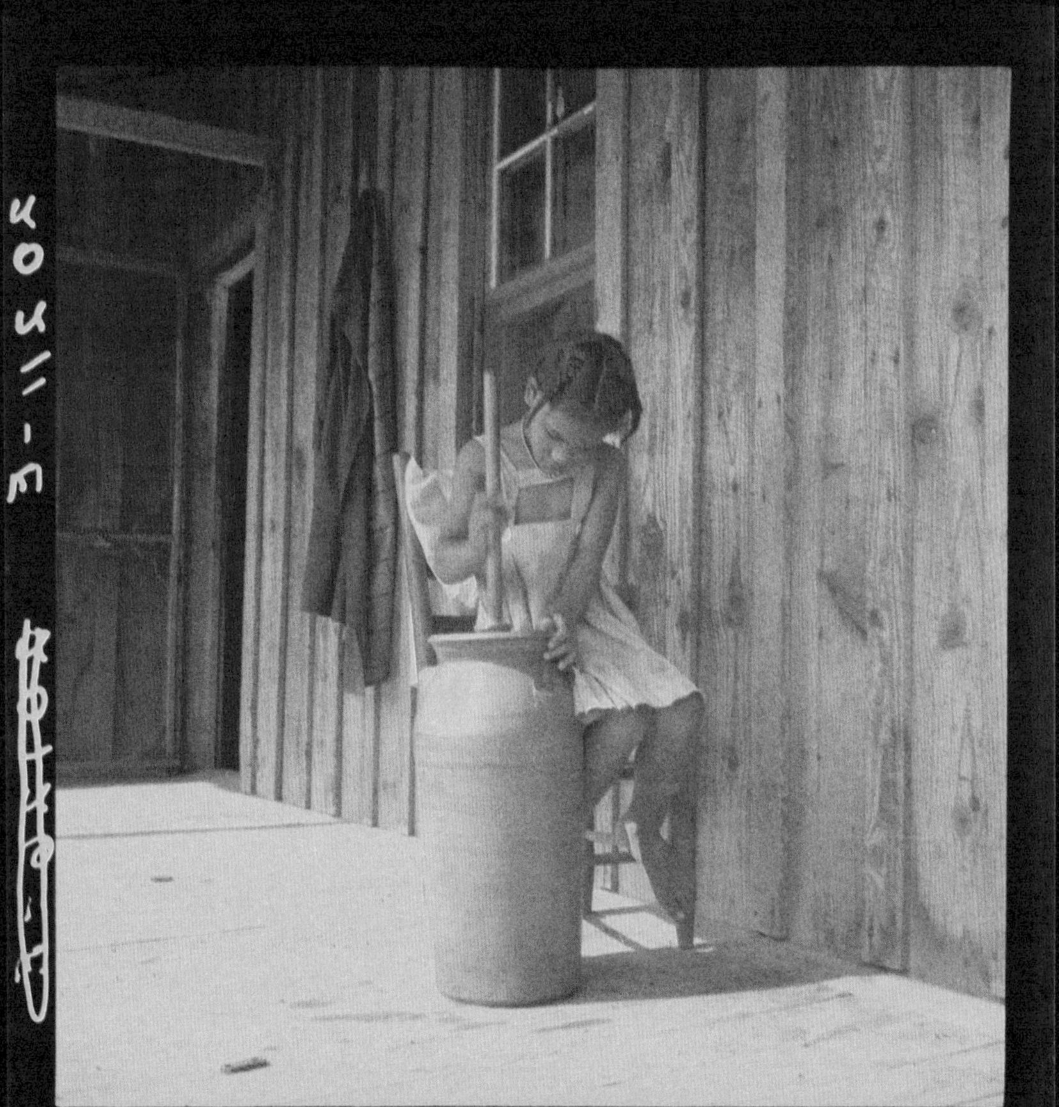

Figure 10. Edited Title: *Construction detail of double log cabin of Black share tenants. The cowhide was hung there after being dried on a barn to be used as floor covering. Shelf shows churn, also bucket of water in which baby's bottle is kept cool. Person County, North Carolina*, July 1939.

Figure 11. Edited Title: *Daughter of Black tenant churning butter. Randolph County, North Carolina*, July 1939.

Figure 12. *Side of a cotton cabin in Georgia*, July 1936.

Figure 13. Edited Title: *Zollie Lyons, Black sharecropper, home from the field for dinner at noontime, and part of his family. Upchurch, North Carolina. He has thirteen acres of tobacco and a labor force of five*, July 1939.

Editors' Note: The titles for Figures 9, 10, 11, and 13 in this essay are an edited version of the original by the photographer. The original titles included outdated and harmful language in utilizing the term "Negro." It has been replaced with "Black" in an effort to provide a reparative description.

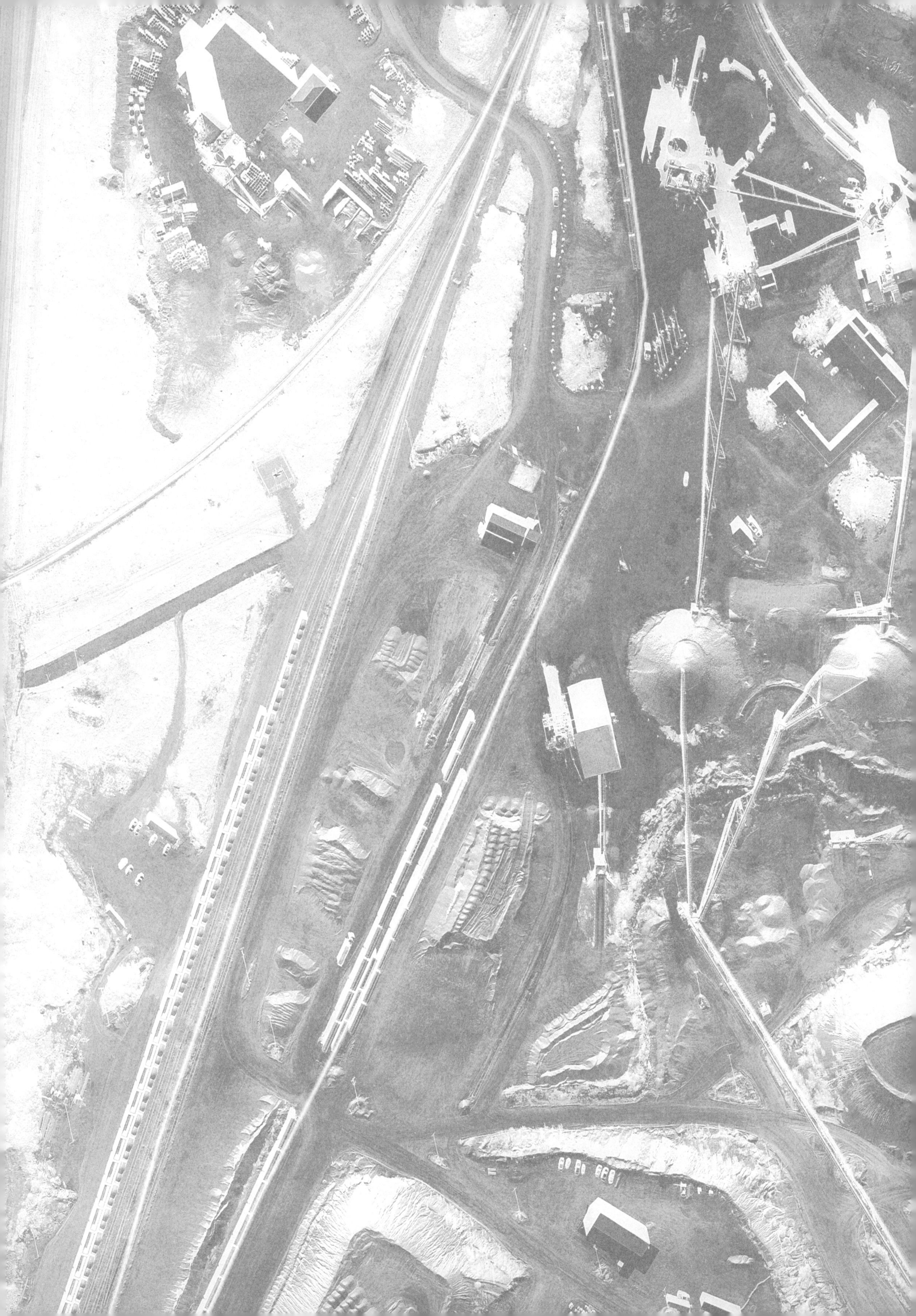

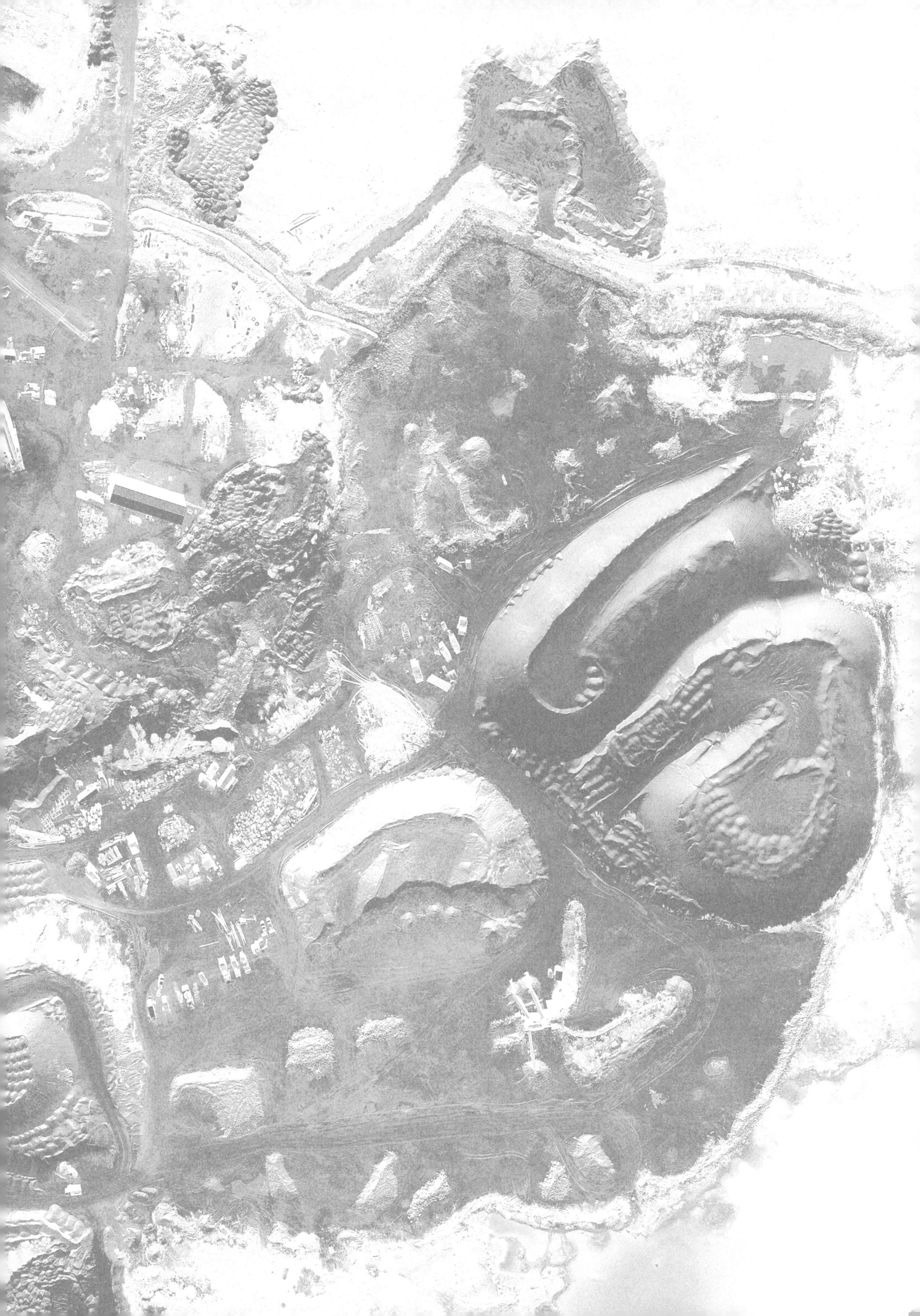

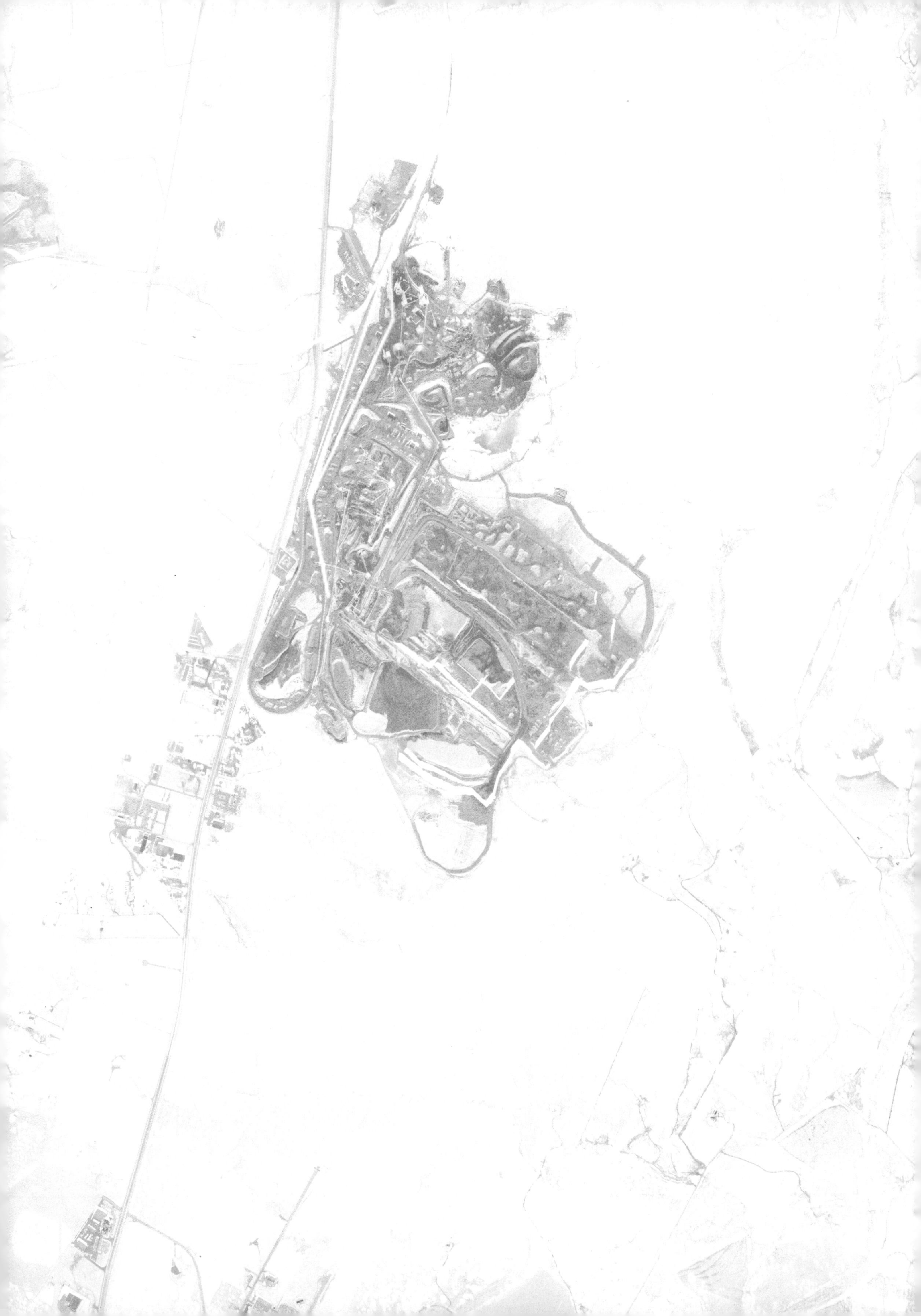

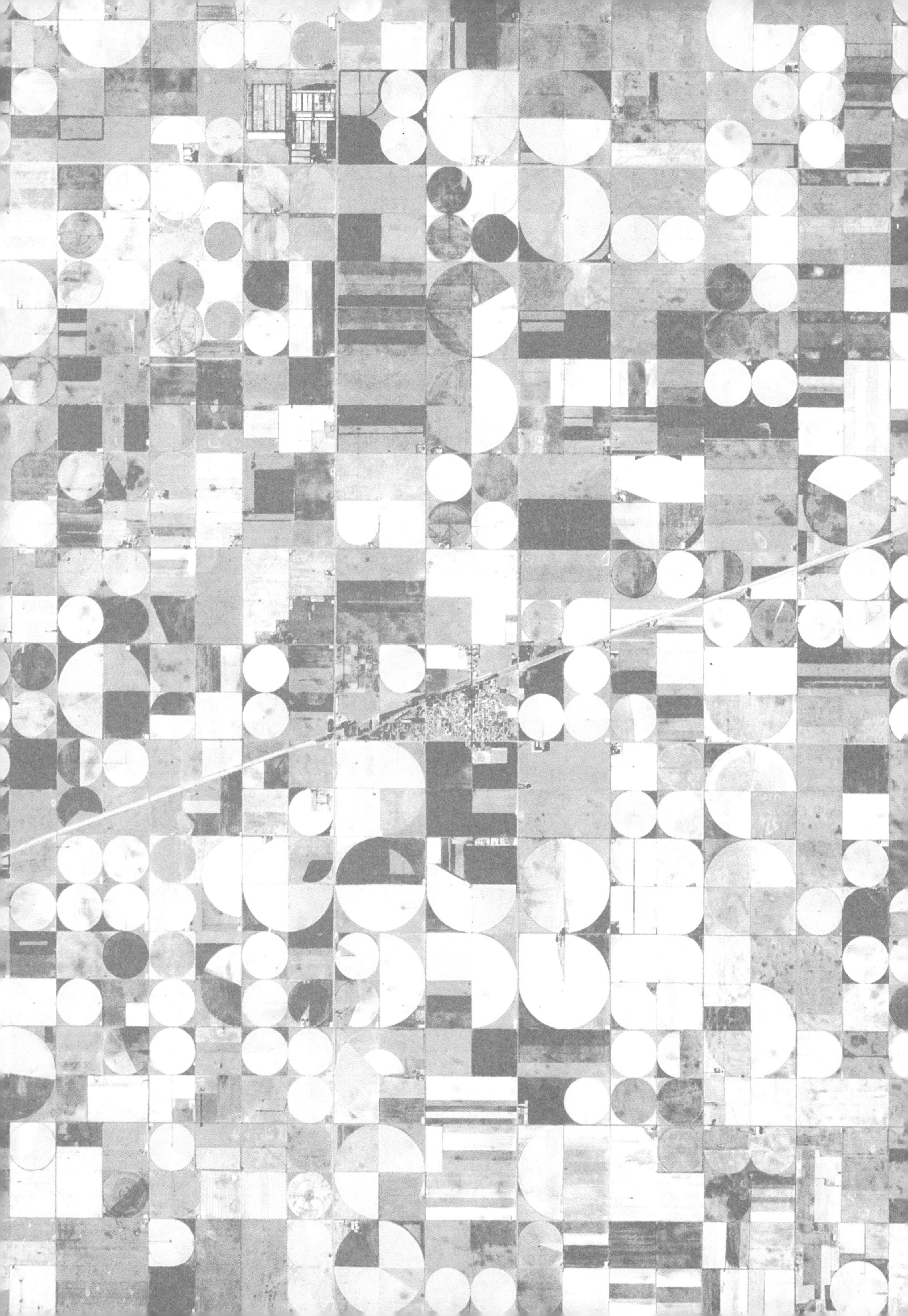

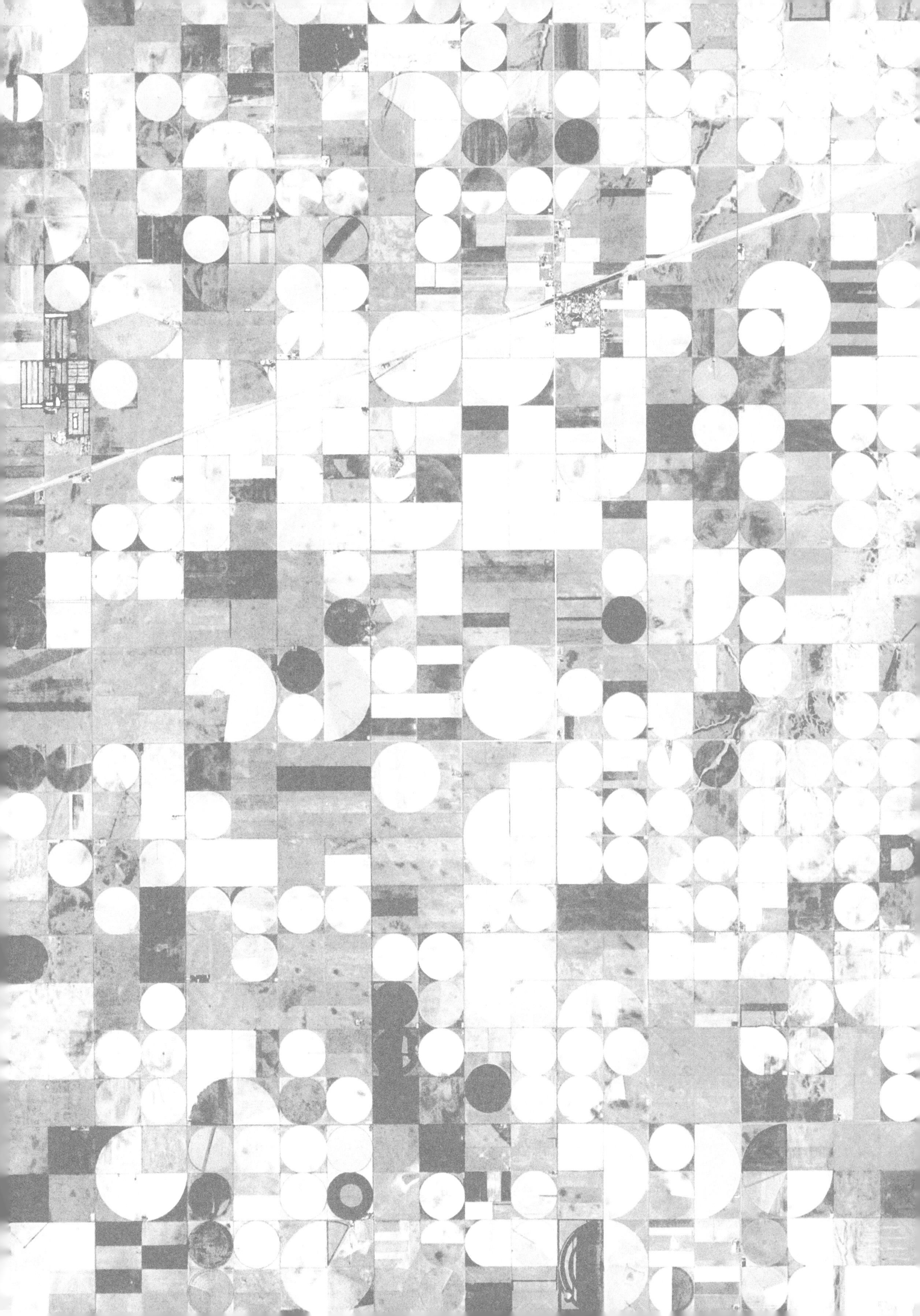

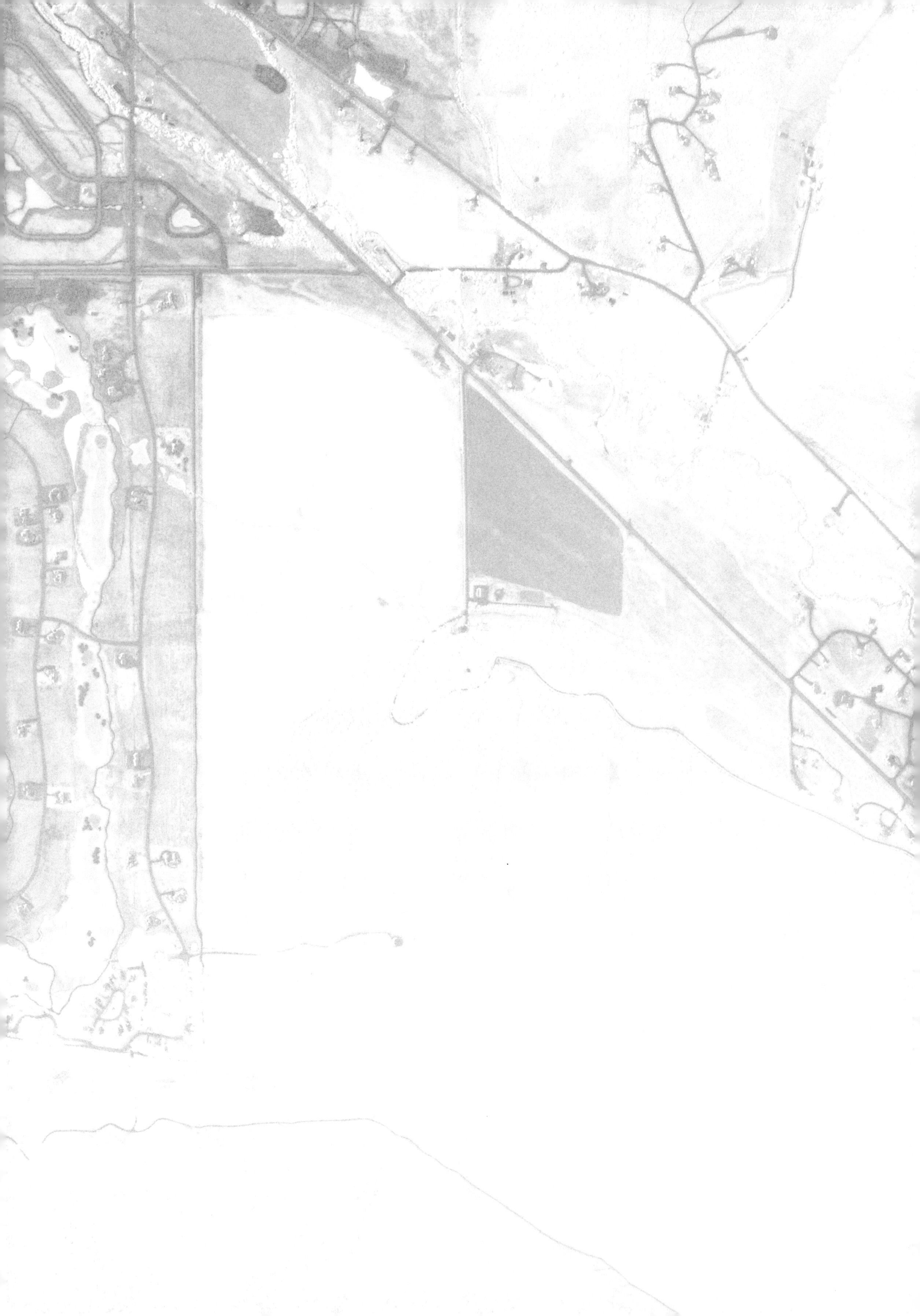

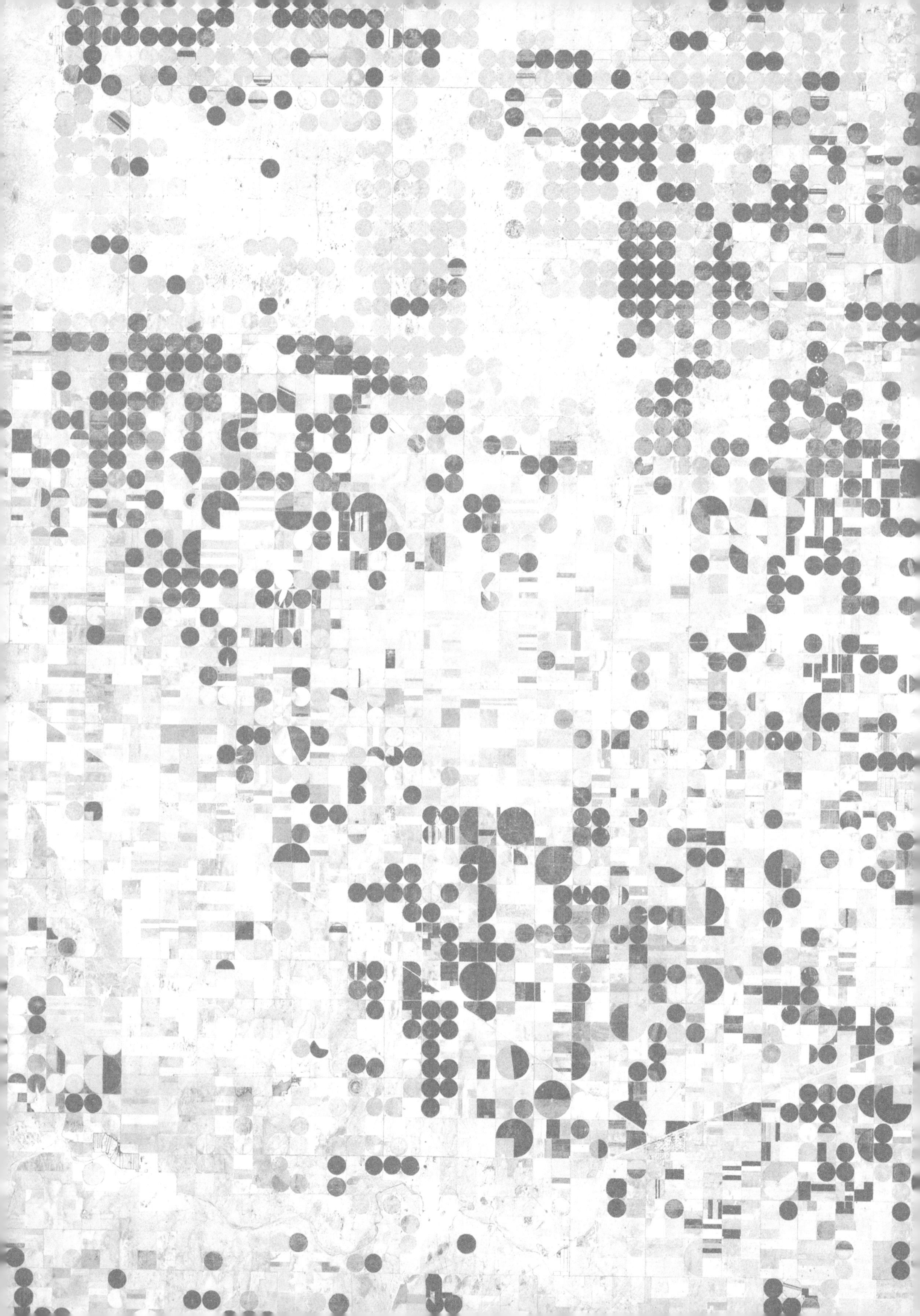

SOKKURI SWEETS

The images started circulating globally through social media. Short clips of people biting on doorknobs, plants and flowers, shoes, tables, paper calendars, clothes hangers. A true expression of terror could be read in their faces as they approached these most quotidian objects with their mouths wide open. In a segment that airs periodically during the New Year special of the Japanese Variety show THE TETSUWAN DASH titled "Sokkuri Sweets,"[1] contestants have to test (and taste) quotidian objects to reveal if they are real or made of candy. On the one hand, the fetishistic desire that pushes them to lick and bite functional objects. On the other, the diabolical hint that if the doorknob is made of cake, everything else may be. The extraordinary success of Sokkuri Sweets—also known as "Candy or not Candy"—can be attested by the sale of the format to Warner Bros, as well as the multiple productions and versions that have been produced since. Netflix has two seasons of *Is It Cake?*; in the Netherlands there is a version of the program that builds these traps with chocolate instead of cake called *Showcolade*. However, the success can only be explained as a product of social media. In a world where images are ubiquitous, the fear that everything is pure surface and there is only void behind them haunts us. In this neo-baroque trompe-l'oeil, it is not the illusion of the extraordinary that is possible, but the derealization of the most ordinary things. If it is cake, it is false, and hence we are living in an illusion. But if it is not cake and it's true, then we are sucking on a doorknob, completely terrified holding onto it as one holds a crucifix before the vertiginous dismantling of reality.

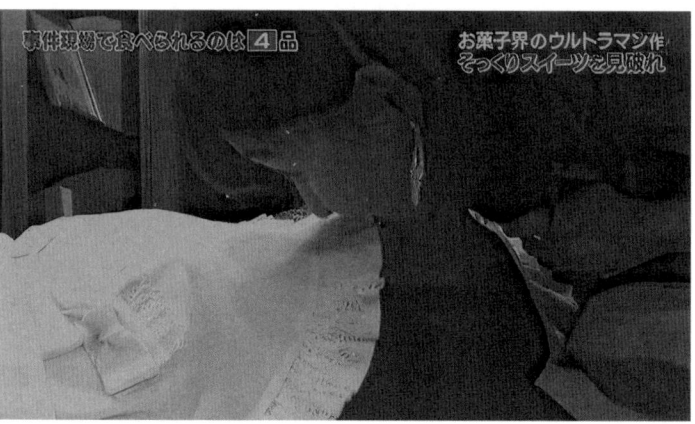

A "Sokkuri Sweets" contestant bites a chocolate chair in "Sokkuri Sweets."[2]

THANKS TO EVERYONE IN OUR COMMUNITY FOR HELPING US REACH THIS MILESTONE!

On June 21, 2016, Mark Zuckerberg made a Facebook post to celebrate hitting the 500 million monthly active users mark on Instagram.[3] The photo shows the CEO posing as a kind of real-life mobile phone screen, by holding a cardboard frame that mimics the app's user interface with the caption "Thanks to everyone in our community for helping us reach this milestone!"[4] As soon as this photo was published, an attentive commentator shared on Twitter his discovery that Zuckerberg's laptop, which one can see outside the cardboard frame, had a piece of tape covering its camera and another covering its microphone.[5] The loopyness of this accumulation of layered framings cannot be missed: A digital camera is used to take a digital photograph which is then posted online; the content of the photograph is a man posing as a digital photograph (via analog means) along with his own digital camera, which has been physically disabled by a piece of tape, presumably to prevent his own photos to be taken without his consent.

The CEO's paranoia is perhaps justified: Such a high-profile individual who has access to valuable corporate secrets is more likely to be spied on than most people. But this photograph led to another series of speculations: Could it be that Zuckerberg covers his cameras and microphones precisely because his access to Facebook's secrets has made him aware of how easy it is to spy on any unsuspecting user of social media in a time when ever-online cameras and microphone are ubiquitous? Almost a decade after this image was published, there is still a small market for branded devices for conveniently covering one's laptop camera without having to use tape.

The original photograph from Mark Zuckerberg's post and a detail of his laptop.

DER WELTRAUMSPIEGEL[6]

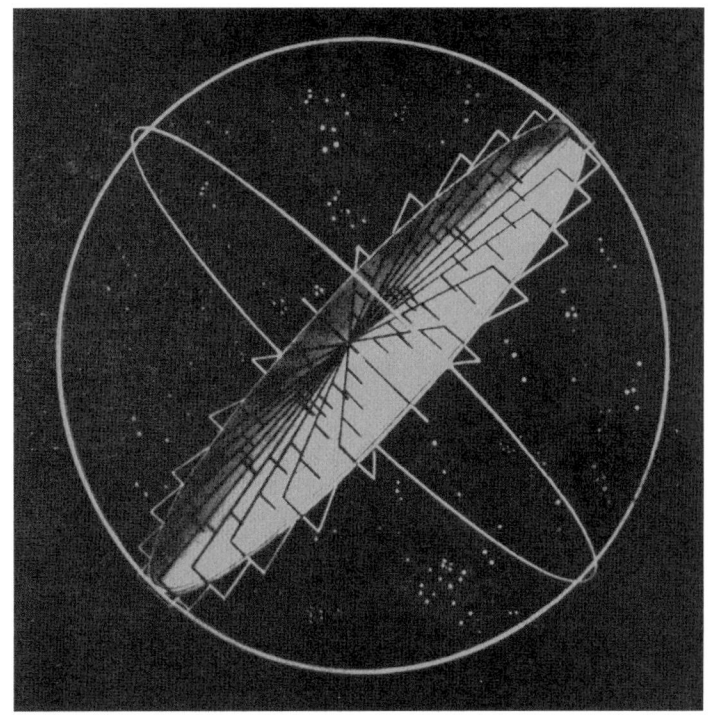

The first scientist to propose deflecting the sun's light with space mirrors was the German Hermann Oberth, who in 1933 and while actively supporting Nazism, speculated on the multiple uses that such solar obfuscations could have. At its most simple, these mirrors would allow a kind of satellite telegraphy between places that had not been reached by cables or electric waves. This type of communication would be particularly valuable at high sea or in remote areas: Something which was of particular interest during the war as territorial boundaries of states were constantly trespassed. Another use envisioned a network of mirrors that could be deployed into space to control the earth's climate. This infrastructure would be controlled by radio in such a way that the mirrors would change their inclination to allow more or less light coming through, pointing the rays from the sun to specific directions. With concentrated sun rays, it would be possible to keep the ports to the north of Siberia free of ice, and broad stretches of land could be made inhabitable by using diffused light and heat.[7] At a later stage, Oberth imagined that these mirrors could also be used to lower the temperature of other planets such as Venus as a first step to making them inhabitable.

Expanded large-scale space mirror system. "Based on current plans and possibilities, a mirror with a diameter of 100 kilometers would cost around 1,000 billion marks." (Hermann Oberth. *Menschen im Weltraum. Neue Projekte für Raketen- und Raumfahrt.* 1954).

THE SEVEN-BEER SNITCH

In the 14th episode from the 16th season of The Simpsons, which aired in April 2005 under the title "The Seven-Beer Snitch," Frank Gehry makes a guest appearance. The character Frank Gehry, voiced by the architect Frank Gehry himself, receives a letter from Marge Simpson asking him to design a concert hall for Springfield. Upon throwing out the letter (a letter that he only read because he was charmed by the Snoopy stationery that Marge used), he falls in love with the accidental form of the crumpled piece of paper on the sidewalk (he exclaims: "Frank Gehry, you're a genius!") and agrees to take on the project.[8]

The Springfield Concert Hall, from conceptual model to final design.

The joke, which the architect was cheerily participating in, of course, is that designing a Gehry building is as easy as crumpling a piece of paper: A Gehry building is pure, arbitrary form.[9] However, in a CNN segment which appeared on TV roughly six years after the cartoon, Frank Gehry confessed that he regretted his participation: "Well, I'm very thorough," claimed the architect, "which people probably don't realize. And so, I do a lot of research. I spend a lot of time with the clients, with the site, with the program and [I] invent, as I go along, ideas that respond to those. And in that process, with the client involved and a clear understanding of budget and, you know, engineering, (…) we vet some directions together, and they [the clients] are complicit, which I love because in the end, when it looks strange (…), they've been part of it." The interviewer, Fareed Zakaria, asks "But the strangeness comes from where?", to which Gehry responds, "Well, I don't know these whys, but to me it's not strange. It looks like everything else is strange. And so stuff starts to unfold in little models and ideas and sketches. A lot—there are about 50 to 100 models made in that process."[10]

That is, in order for the Frank Gehry buildings to be desirable and valuable, the process has to appear strange, somewhat mysterious, obscure, and a bit arbitrary, like a magician pulling a rabbit out of a hat,[11] but it cannot be too strange, mysterious, obscure, and arbitrary: One model is too arbitrary, but 50–100 models is perfect.

SOME BUILDINGS BASED ON A SINGLE FORMAL CONCEPT[12]

The School of Visual Arts of Oaxaca by Taller de Arquitectura—Mauricio Rocha is a tortoise shell. The Olympic Fish Pavilion by Frank Gehry is, well, a fish. El Nido de Quetzalcóatl, Ballena Mexicana, Casa Nautilus, and Casa Orgánica, by Javier Senosiain are a serpent, a whale, a nautilus, and a peanut shell, respectively. The Turning Torso by Santiago Calatrava is, well, a twisted human torso, and the WTC Transportation Hub by the same architect is "a bird flying from the hands of a child." The shells in the Sydney Opera House by Jørn Utzon are the sails of a ship. Etcetera.

CONSPIRACY REALISM

The last episode of Adam Curtis' "Can't Get You Out of My Head" (BBC, 2021) traces the origins of modern conspiracy theories to the American counterculture. Discordianism was a metaphysical speculation developed in a bowling alley by teenagers Greg Hill and Kerry Thornley. According to Thornley, in the universe there was only omnipresent chaos, order was a mere illusion of the mind. Discordianists were a sort of parody religion that adored Eris, the Greek goddess of discord, and were paradoxically fascinated with the hierarchical structure of other cults. Their ideas were mostly circulated through zines and independent publications and were summarized in a book written by Malaclypse the Younger, a pseudonym of Greg Hill, titled *Principia Discordia, or, How I found Goddess and what I did to Her when I found Her*. As it turns out, before Lee Harvey Oswald defected to the Soviet Union, he casually met Thornley who started writing a novel with him as the main character. After JFK's assassination, the New Orleans district attorney, Jim Garrison, signaled Thornley as a potential co-conspirator. Garrison is depicted as one of the promoters of the conspiracy theory that involved the CIA, big business, the news media, and anti-Castro Cubans in the magnicide. Deeply against conspiracy theories, which only served to further confuse the minds of Americans, Thornley responded to this accusation with a situationist campaign of detournement called "Operation Mindfuck." With the collaboration of a few journalist friends, he started sending letters to *Playboy* and other popular magazines

A sketch of The School of Visual Arts of Oaxaca by Taller de Arquitectura —Mauricio Rocha.

Cover of *Principia Discordia, or, How I found Goddess and what I did to Her when I found Her* by Malaclypse the Younger.

to create a satire of the conspiracy theories that were thriving in the US. According to this theory, behind every political assassination in the US were the Illuminati—a Bavarian fraternal organization that had originated at the time of the Enlightenment to defeat religious power but had transformed into a network of influence among the ultra-wealthy. What started as a joke—which aimed to awaken the public by making a pantomime of obfuscation—spread like a wildfire in the years that followed, completely escaping the control of Thornhill. At the end of his life, completely disturbed by the plausibility of his speculations, Thornhill was completely paranoid and fell prey to the same hoaxes that he had consciously fabricated.

GAMING THE METRICS

In 1979, Donald T. Campbell formulated one of the more lasting paradoxes of social policy: When a metric becomes an objective, it ceases to be a good metric.[13] Campbell was working in the world of social policy evaluation, and he realized that many of the efforts that local governments were unfolding to understand the effects of their public investments were having unintended consequences. When the results of standardized testing in education were used to determine how public funds should be disbursed, schools had a negative incentive to adapt their curriculum to the type of skills that were required to pass exams ("teaching to the test"). When city politics is oriented to the reduction of crime statistics, it leads police departments to tinker the numbers by artificially increasing the number of arrests (this was particularly visible through the implementation of CompStat in New York during the 1990s).[14]

In the digital world, the omnipresence of social metrics has fueled this form of obfuscation whereby metrics that were in principle conceived to make the world more transparent actually turn it into something more opaque. This "tyranny of transparency" is particularly visible in the vast array of practices that scientists develop to game the metrics used to evaluate them.[15] This is visible in things such as the increasing number of authors in scientific papers, the practice of mutual citation, citation circles and self-citation, the tendency to fragment contributions into multiple papers, and multiple publications of similar results. To these direct effects in the domain of scientific writing, we should add the development of entire industries aimed at pumping up researcher's metrics artificially—and illegally.[16] These concerns have only increased with the recent developments in artificial intelligence chatbots that can write entire articles automatically and without directly plagiarizing others.

Engagement metrics—likes, views, retweets, follows—allow one to create hierarchies of information by predicting the impact of posts and other digital publications very much in the same way that the number of citations of an article or the impact factor of a journal dictate the importance of scientific contributions. These metrics have deeply transformed what celebrity, success, value, and wealth mean. On the one hand, they operate as instruments of evaluation and transparency. On the other, they function as financial instruments creating the possibility of a market. Metrics put a price on social media posts, turning them into a currency that can be traded with brands, media agencies, and other users. In the same way that metrics put a price on academic papers, turning them into a currency that can be traded with universities, libraries, journals, and other scholars.[17]

WHOLE EARTH CATALOGCORE

Since its launch in 2017, the astrology app Co-Star has not only become incredibly popular, but its founders have also raised a surprisingly large amount of venture capital investments. Perhaps its investors simply view Co-Star as an entertainment platform with potential for extreme

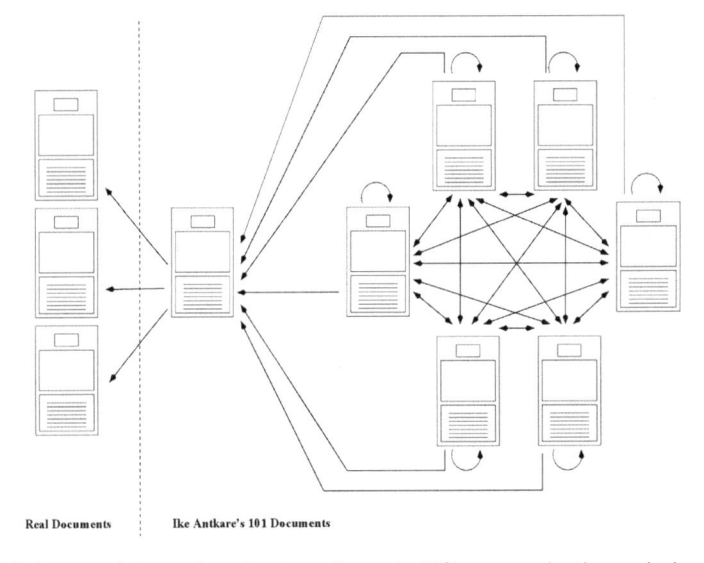

References between forged and regular scientific papers in the academic research by the fictional researcher Ike Antkare, created by computer scientist Cyril Labbé to illustrate how the H-Index, a measure of an author's productivity and citation impact, can be manipulated.

popularity, especially in a younger audience, arguably driven by their disillusionment with organized religion (people becoming "spiritual but not religious") and a need for certainty in an unpredictable world. However, this doesn't seem to justify the scale of the investments: Co-Star has successfully raised over $5 million in venture capital since its inception[18] for what some might dismiss as nothing more than a high-tech horoscope column—it is hard to imagine Co-Star becoming the next Instagram or Uber.

What makes Co-Star so valuable for venture capital firms, whose investments are more often in speculative technologies, such as artificial intelligence or cryptocurrencies? Co-Star's horoscopes are not written by humans, but rather, as the official website explains it, "using artificial intelligence, Co-Star translates data (the current locations of the planets, the charts of a user's friends) into language we can read, understand, and share."[19] This information is then delivered in a reassuring monochrome interface, featuring sleek astral charts along with cutouts of grainy images from old books and magazines: Startup graphic design meets the 1970s counterculture aesthetics of the *Whole Earth Catalog* and the illustrations by New Age guru Ram Dass.[20] So here is a theory: The real value of Co-Star lies not in the service it offers itself, but in the spillover effect of imbuing artificial intelligence with a sort of intimate, mystical, oracular aura, which in turn makes us more willing to trust the authority and predictions produced by the other artificial intelligence companies in which venture capitalists have invested.[21]

FUNCTION

"The positioning of plants in a forest or grove of trees is most likely determined according to strict principles, however the creatures living there go about their daily business in a rational fashion without knowing exactly why the vegetation is located where it is. This could hardly be more different to architecture. For example in a building, it is immediately obvious that a certain wall is there to partition two adjacent spaces, but in a forest, we really have no idea why a particular tree is in a particular place. Rationality may be less about a simple one-to-one coincidence of function and form and more about the linking of new relationships amid endless, fathomless complexity. Amid the whole, such relationships are always unstable, and engaged in a rocky search for stability. One aspect of the relationality manifested in this phenomenon is that which we call function." (Junya Ishigami, 2019).[22]

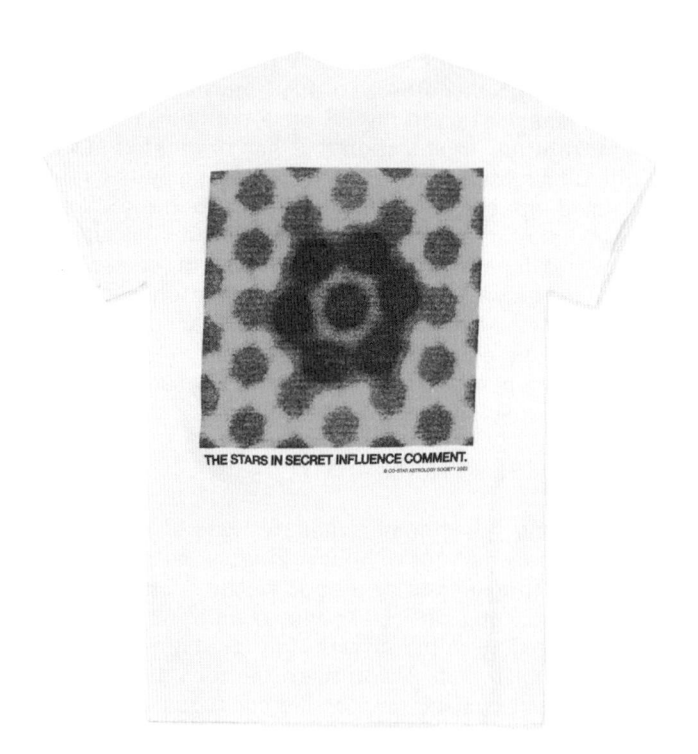

A shirt from the Co-Star online web shop reads "THE STARS IN SECRET INFLUENCE COMMENT.", a quote from Shakespeare's sonnet 15.

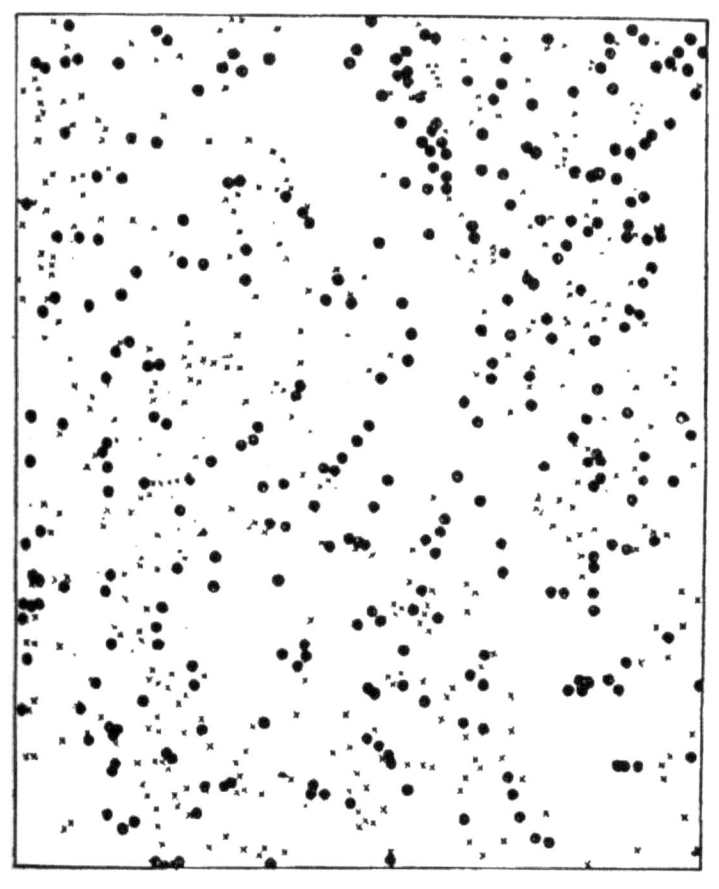

Dispersion diagram of *madake* timber bamboo (16 × 20). The ● marks are current standing trunks and the ×'s are stumps.

1. The Japanese word *Sokkuri* is often translated to English as "spitting image": the exact double. "The initial reason given for why we should have used spit in this manner is that it was said of a child that he or she looked enough like a parent to have been spit out of their mouth. Spit has been so used since at least the late 16th century." https://www.merriam-webster.com/wordplay/spitting-image-origin-meaning
2. In one particularly morbid edition, the contestants taste objects from a crime scene, which includes a knife and a hammer (the potential murder weapons) as well as the dead body of a young maid (the victim). We see another woman coyly lean into the corpse and take a bite of a lacy apron (it is cake). The dead woman herself, it is later revealed in the episode, is neither cake nor a corpse nor a mannequin, but a real, living actress.
3. https://www.facebook.com/photo.php?fbid=10102910644965951
4. The only comment on the cardboard frame post, from username @kevin, reads " @zuck".
5. https://twitter.com/topherolson/status/745294977064828929
6. "The space mirror" in German.
7. In this sense, the mirrors had the bi-fold purpose of redirecting and concealing light, using it to overheat or freeze certain territories: light as a peak-a-boo weapon.
8. The concert hall is eventually abandoned by the inhabitants of Springfield who are not interested in high art, and Mr. Burns buys the structure to turn it into a prison. All kinds of architectural gags ensue: Snake escapes the building by sliding off the twisty facade, Frank Gehry gets annoyed at a group of kids using the building's smooth, curvy exterior as a skate park (perhaps in reference to the old trope of skateboarders using public art as a skatepark as seen in Raphaël Zarka's book *Riding Modern Art*, for example), etc.
9. Later on in the episode, we also learn that in order to build the building, the contractors follow a similar process: they build an orthogonal structure and then smash it with wrecking balls until it reaches the shape of the crumpled pieces of paper.
10. http://edition.cnn.com/TRANSCRIPTS/1109/04/fzgps.01.html
11. For a Gehry building to be valuable, it also has to look like a Gehry building, which constrains its strangeness: it can only be as different from other buildings as any Gehry building is.
12. A building based on a single formal concept is absurd: a building is not one big conceptual idea, but rather thousands or millions of small decisions. Reducing a building to a single, easy to understand formal idea can make it more attractive to the general public and thus more valuable (the building literally becomes iconic), but the notion that a building can be reduced to a single concept (which comes from the mind of a genius architect) only serves to obfuscate every other idea and design decision (which come from everyone else: employees of an architecture firm, contractors, clients, etc.).
13. Donald T. Campbell, "Assessing the Impact of Planned Social Change," *Journal of Multidisciplinary Evaluation*, vol. 7, no. 15, 2011, p. 3.
14. John A. Eterno, Eli B. Silverman, *The Crime Numbers Game: Management by Manipulation* (Oxfordshire: Routledge, 2012).
15. Marilyn Strathern, "The Tyranny of Transparency," *British Educational Research Journal*, July 1999, vol. 26, no. 3, 2000, pp. 309–21. Stratherns's famous article is in turn based on Tsoukas, Haridimos. "The Tyranny of Light: The Temptations and the Paradoxes of the Information Society." *Futures : the Journal of Policy, Planning and Futures Studies*, vol. 29, no. 9, 1997, pp. 827–43. This fascinating article considers the collapse of the Enlightenment project of social metrics at the time in which these metrics become omnipresent.
16. Paper mills are "profit oriented, unofficial and potentially illegal organizations that produce and sell fraudulent manuscripts that seem to resemble genuine research". In 2022, *Science Magazine* and the *Times Higher Education* uncovered one of these networks that was operating in Russia selling pre-approved papers in dozens of journals to authors wishing to improve their performance. Many of these outlets were so-called "predatory journals"—journals that will publish almost anything for a fee. These journals are today familiar to almost any researcher whose mailbox has become littered with emails offering such services.
17. As Mario Biagioli and Alexandra Lippman argue, "the impact factor is neither about the evaluation of a scientific article nor about making evaluation fair and transparent by removing it from the arbitrariness of qualitative judgments. It is about creating the conditions of possibility for a market." Biagioli, Mario, and Alexandra Lippman. *Gaming the Metrics : Misconduct and Manipulation in Academic Research*. The MIT Press, 2020.
18. "Co-Star, an app that lets people download and compare their birth charts, raised just over $5 million in funding from the Silicon Valley venture capital firms Maveron and Aspect Ventures, as well as 14W, based in New York." https://www.nytimes.com/2019/04/15/style/astrology-apps-venture-capital.html
19. Co – Star: Hyper-Personalized, Real-Time Horoscopes https://www.costarastrology.com/about
20. We are not the first to comment on this aesthetic, which we refer to as Whole Earth Catalogcore. See, for example, this tweet by Elizabeth Goodspeed: https://x.com/domesticetch/status/1359908198434693124
21. Specifically, the consumer facing applications of artificial intelligence, such as the algorithms that order one's Twitter feed by relevance, Spotify's music recommendation engine, and the answers from large language models such as OpenAI's Chat-GPT.
22. Junya Ishigami, *Another Scale of Architecture* (Tokyo: Lixil, 2019).

To ask where our attention is directed is to ask what we care for, what we value, and what deserves our concern. Current debates around how our attention is attracted, and distracted, tend to focus on the outsized influence of contemporary media. With each technical advance, the ability to capture, process, store, and exchange information accelerates, bringing both excitement for its revolutionary potential and fears of its potential for abuse. As these expand our sensorium toward qualities outside the thresholds of our senses, a concern arises as to how technological media is also to blame for displacing or even alienating biological ways of sensing and understanding reality. This suspicion echoes an older debate regarding whether the world of the senses operates reflexively (as with animals), automatically (as with machines), or intentionally (as focused and controlled through the human intellect). The Greek root of the term *aesthetics*—*aisthēsis*—is concerned not only with how the world is sensed but also how we make sense of our senses, prompting questions of consciousness, cognition, and intention.[1] These are indeed questions, for it has never been clear where the line between consciousness and sensation should be drawn or why, if the line does exist, it should be of importance in distinguishing human from nonhuman perception. Both aspects of aesthetics— sensing and sense-making—are tied to issues of attention. How we sort out what is "interesting"—to what we should attend—is entwined with how we make sense of the world. Many processes of "sense-making" operate through representations, through abstractions that structure the apparatus of a technological sensorium, sorting captured data into usable information. Inherent in this system is the assumption that through an expanded range of sensing an increasingly clearer understanding of the world will be achieved. The problem is that quite often our technological sensorium has led to an increase in noise, confusion in determining value, and concerns over who, or what, stands to gain. Furthermore, the assignation of the term *noise* is a problematic response to stimuli that we do not yet know how to make sense of. Instead, we may need to embrace alternate modes of attention—a shift in how we care for that which may be bewildering.[2]

The term *hyperhomogeneity* is a neologism formed from the combination of two aspects in the films of Chantal Akerman as identified by Ivone Margulies: "Hyperrealism" and "the aesthetics of homogeneity."[3] The aesthetics of homogeneity alludes to a condition within perception where an evenness of stimulation washes into an undifferentiated background, problematizing where and how attention is directed. The prefix *hyper-* indicates an excess, doubling, or repetition, typically through mediation, related to the object of the term it modifies. The deluge of images generated in contemporary digital culture and the continuously accumulating mountain of data gathered by technological sensing of the planet exemplify this combination of *hyper-* with *homogeneity*. The crux of the concern has already been broached: How does the expansion of the sensorium alter attention? It is a question with far-reaching social, epistemic, and ethical implications, which may seem like much larger, more pressing issues than those of aesthetics. Yet it is important to remember that the appearance of reality is created by how the world is sensed; when this is altered, the relations between things shift, affecting both understanding and behavior.

As the cultural expression most tied to the demands of everyday physical experience—of the body, the commons, and the environment—architecture is frequently positioned as a possible means to return us to "the real" by rejecting the technical image and its distractions. If only it was so simple. *Realism*, despite being defined and experienced differently in different epochs, describes a feeling initiated by a tension between reality and representation, or a disruption between sensation and sense-making. For philosopher Jacques Rancière, this phenomenon can produce what he calls a "redistribution of the sensible," which is inherently political.[4] Often these shifts are disturbing because they reveal things that have been overlooked, repressed, or ignored, exposing and challenging assumptions underlying conventional judgments and behaviors. These experiences can also be described as a "making strange" of our familiar surroundings, at times triggering alienation but also a sense of wonder as reality appears other than we have assumed it to be. It is helpful, and even hopeful, to consider that estrangement can be accompanied by enchantment—by a renewed relation with the world and the background of our daily lives, even an altered perception of the nonhuman environment as active, animate, and sensate. As a space dominated by habitual repetition and familiarity where small differences fluctuate in potential equivalency, the background establishes what we assume reality to look like, to feel like. Yet it is not stable, it is constantly changing through cultural, technical, and ecological entanglements, and given these fluctuations, what constitutes attention within the "background" may be the key question in terms of a reevaluation of our aesthetic engagements.

AN EXPANDED SENSORIUM

Contemporary ecological discourse contends that entities— living and nonliving—are connected in clusters of various relations of influence. Among the most popular descriptions of this condition is "entangled."[5] To be entangled is to affect and be affected. It requires that at least two—and typically many more—entities "sense" each other. Sensors can be the sensory organs of sight, sound, touch, taste, and smell, producing the aesthetic experiences that define the human biological sensorium. Many animals have sensory systems similar to ours, while others seem to have access to a wildly different set of sensations. Sensing, however, should not be considered exclusive to fauna. Modes of sensing can also be attributed to the photochemical actions and reactions of plants and fungi since recent research shows these systems are much more active in their sensorial exchanges than previously believed.[6] Given the movements and adjustments of plate tectonics and magma, we could even speak of a kind of geological sensing occurring on a planetary scale. Further pushing the idea of sensation to the largest and smallest interactions, we may note that gravity describes attraction between masses, sensed as the pull of bodies, tides, planets, and stars, while subatomic particles interact in manners that physics refers to as "quantum entanglement."

To speak of tidal movements as a "sensing" between orbital masses may seem a stretch, but they do interact and influence each other. We know this because we have expanded our senses through artificial means: Mathematical and linguistic abstractions, precision-machined lenses, chemically classified tracings, mechanically imprinted records, electronically triggered diodes, and digital signal processing—in a word, technology. Extending our sensorium through technology has allowed us to direct attention toward events that occur beyond the thresholds of our perception—that is, toward the background.

Architect Eyal Weizman and philosopher Graham Harman have both argued that objects exist in relationship with other objects through aesthetics, even when the human sensorium has no access to them.[7] Weizman and media theorist Matthew Fuller explain it as follows:

> Aesthetics does not exclusively refer to a property or capacity of humans. It equally refers to other sensing organisms, such as animals and plants, which themselves apprehend their environment. Further, we argue that sensing is also found in material surfaces and substances, on which traces of impact or slower processes of change are

registered, including in digital and computational sensors, which themselves detect, register and predict in multiple novel ways.[8]

This expansion, or redistribution, of aesthetics decenters the human sensorium as our primary mechanism for accessing and understanding the world. That is not to suggest, however, that robots, rocks, trees, and dust are debating the aesthetic value of a sunset. It implies simply that robots, rocks, trees, dust, and sunsets exist in multiple sensorial relations with each other and that these relations can be described as aesthetic, even if humans cannot access them.[9] The processes of oxidation, photosynthesis, metabolism, crystallization, decay, fertilization, electrostatics, and magnetism reflect the interactions of a widely and wildly distributed sensorium. What happens with this redistribution of sensing is that aesthetics is not a specifically human activity but instead a process of entwined attention between entities in the environment. In a way these relations *are* "the environment."

When an aesthetics of attention becomes concerned with how environments sense exchanges outside the thresholds of the human sensory apparatus, questions of sensing and making sense are altered. Walls, floors, and ceilings may be perceived visually as spatial divisions and light-reflecting surfaces. But they are also thermal transformers, vibration resonators, moisture collectors, vessels of mold and decay, extracted materials with embodied energies, and objects of scheduled cleaning, replacement, and repair. Many of their qualities are made sensible to us only through technological mediation, which alters both what we attend to in the environment and how the environment attends to us. Another way to say this is that the environment trains our senses and we in turn alter the environment through design.[10]

The expansion of sensing through technology is not simply a task of deciding to be more inclusive. It's fraught at every level. Technological sensing apparatuses are structured by operations that most people have little access to; with this alienation, a crisis emerges.[11] Anxiety increases as digital sensing is linked to databases where interactions are recorded, compiled, processed, and evaluated—a monitoring structured by market forces that in turn determine how and to what attention is drawn. Bruno Latour describes these assemblies as "black boxes": Clusters of nested technological relations operating through automatism as one.[12] Since their operations are occluded from most people's understanding, black boxes can generate fear of exploitation, loss of critical judgment, and degraded engagement with reality. To believe that the problem disappears once we turn off our devices is to fail to understand how that which consciousness attends to is tangled up with the ways attention structures consciousness. Furthermore, our world is so sensorially interconnected that there is no place to go that is not at some level "sensed." Sensors create images; but more to the point, sensors monitor, model, and render what we engage as the background appearance of reality.

AUTOMATIC ATTENTION

One of the prickliest problems laid out by *aisthēsis* is the coordination of the senses. I see something in the world, but at the same moment I may also hear, touch, and/or smell it. What faculty allows these sensations to become combined? What sense holds them in common? Does sensation happen automatically, or unconsciously, or is it willfully controlled and directed? What happens when sensations conflict with each other or with what is expected of them? Does the quality of a sensation change with greater knowledge? Do animals also make sense of their senses? Do plants? Do rocks? Do machines?

Aristotle engaged these questions of *aisthēsis* by proposing the presence of an inner sense, or "inner touch," that could coordinate the various senses.[13] These arguments are known to us today as *De anima*, or *On the Soul*, which hints at what is at stake.[14] The question of "how we make sense of our senses" lays bare the conflicts between affect and cognition, aesthetics and epistemology, sensual and conceptual, automatic response and directed will. These philosophical questions are of great importance, for they shape the way humans understand their perceptions and then behave. They are tied to the creation of subjectivity and identity. They are also fundamental questions for how art, architecture, and the media are affected by, and in turn affect, the understanding and experience of our shared environments.

There's a conundrum brewing here that raises another term with Greek origins, *automaton*. We tend to associate this word today with technological automation—that is, with "the technique of making an apparatus, a process, or a system operate automatically."[15] In aesthetic discourse it can spark allusions to the uncanny, to inanimate objects becoming animate, or to human behavior becoming excessively repetitive, or automatic. For the ancient Greeks, however, *automaton* had meanings closer to modern notions of autonomy.[16] When used as an adjective applied to a person, it meant "acting of one's own will, of oneself." When applied to events, it meant "happening in themselves, without cause, accidentally or naturally."[17] By implication, this definition grants a level of independence to the elements and entities of the natural world, where interactions occur between things (including human beings).

It is a given that our senses respond to the world in ways that are not fully within our control; the sensations of light, sound, taste, odor, and touch happen to us, and our sensory organs respond in part, if not fully, automatically. Yet directed will, intended interest, and focused attention do affect our perception as an act of a motivated consciousness or an independent subjective identity. How we shift between the reflexive reactions of the sense organs and the cognitive intent of an intellect has never been worked out definitively. Historically the distinction between automatic and autonomous modes of attention was often used to distinguish the animal from the human.[18] In this tradition, knowledge, cognition, and intellect are treated as distinctly human attributes that allow us to master our environments by analyzing them logically and rationally. Claims that humans have a monopoly on motivated sensing have become increasingly untenable as we learn more about the ecologies of the natural world, which sense and interact in much more complex ways than previously assumed. To complicate matters, our sensorium is augmented and expanded by technological sensing and processing. Both alienating and enlightening, this expansion opens access to previously unsensed qualities while also limiting access by black-boxing the processes of sense-making. As an example, our understanding of the current climate emergency is based largely on data collected through a globally dispersed, interlinked technological sensing apparatus where patterns of temperature, flow, moisture, and particulate matter are analyzed and interpreted well beyond the capacities of our biological sensorium. The impact is a kind of global *weirding*, where the results have been disconcerting and decentering yet of fundamental importance for a contemporary understanding of the environment. They are also "technical images."

THE TECHNICAL IMAGE

As developed by philosopher and media critic Vilém Flusser in *Towards a Philosophy of Photography* (1983) and *Into the Universe of Technical Images* (1985), the apparatus of the "technical image" appeared long before the ubiquity of digital images, scanning technologies, and the Internet. It began with photography. *Apparatus* is used here in the sense developed by Michel Foucault: A heterogeneous set of objects, discourses, institutions, and laws that operate at the intersection of power and knowledge.[19] According to Flusser, "One first sees the photographic universe as the product of cameras and distribution apparatuses. Behind these, one recognizes industrial apparatuses, advertising apparatuses, political, economic management apparatuses, etc. Each of these apparatuses is becoming increasingly automated and being linked up by cybernetics to other apparatuses."[20] Yet Flusser's goal in writing a "philosophy of photography" was not to reject images but to explicate how the technical image is structured through language and code, and through this to open a space in which to play against the apparatus, to misuse it toward the "unpredictable," "improbable" image.[21] "For a photograph is not a tool like a machine; it is a plaything like a playing card or chess-piece."[22]

In *Towards a Philosophy*, Flusser laments that the "automaticity" of the apparatus leaves little to no room for human involvement. "All apparatuses (not just computers) are calculating machines and in this sense 'artificial intelligences,' the camera included, even if their inventors were not able to account for this. In all apparatuses (including the camera), thinking in numbers overrides linear, historical thinking."[23] Our postindustrial information society loops images of images—information translated into information—while leaving "the real" deferred into an "eternal recurrence of the same."[24] The nihilism of Flusser's critique shifts with *Into the Universe*. Here he finds that in a world of nondimensional abstractions—data points—the technology of the apparatus is required to "make concrete" the particles and "turn extreme abstraction back into the imaginable."[25] With this suggestion, Flusser offers a glimmer of hope: We can leave linear causality behind. Technical images are dialogical; they send *and* receive information, and they work through probabilities, not truth versus fiction. "Technical images are projections. They capture meaningless signs that come to us from the world (photons, electrons) and code them to give them a meaning."[26] Flusser calls the people who can play with and against the program of the apparatus "envisioners":

> Envisioners press buttons to inform, in the strictest sense of that word, namely, to make something improbable out of possibilities. They press buttons to seduce the automatic apparatus into making something that is improbable within its program. They press buttons to coax improbable things from the whirring particle universe that the apparatus is calculating. And this improbable world of envisioning power surrounds the whirring particle universe like a skin, giving it a meaning. The power to envision is the power that sets out to make concrete sense of the abstract and absurd universe into which we are falling.[27]

An entity that both receives *and* sends information in an exchange akin to sensing *and* imaging or observing *and* speculating, the technical image, as described by Flusser, impacts our thinking on the expanded sensorium. These are not neutral pictures traveling in a single direction from reality to image. Instead, they operate within an "entangled" aesthetics between the human and nonhuman sensoriums. There *is* an alienation in this that is part of the exclusionary fear Flusser identifies in *Towards a Philosophy*; its current manifestation is digital surveillance managed by artificial intelligence. This issue is massively problematic, but the question at hand is, How does one respond creatively once awareness of the apparatus is made clear? Flusser's response does not sound like an argument for increased criticality. "The program" is laid bare not to expose some deeper truth, as he states, the technical image is not a linear causal relation between the world and representation. It thus resists being broken down through an exposure of artifice to identify how a sequence of manipulations distort "truth" for nefarious purposes. For Flusser the possibilities lie elsewhere, in the enchantment of discovery created through play—that is, the enjoyment of attending to small differences in relations between elements, often bending or tweaking repetitive codes and rules, and purposefully suspending the lines between observation and speculation, between truth and fiction. These responses resist "sense-making" as tied solely to the communicative model of information as meaningful language.[28] There is a suggestion that the "button-pushers" can open an alternate aesthetic engagement through creative misuse.[29]

A BRIEF DESCRIPTION OF THE TECHNICAL IMAGE (CIRCA OCTOBER 2022)

Digital sensing and imaging can be defined as the translation of detected environmental energy into numeric information—which means that sensing and imaging are interchangeable. The sensor can be a "camera," but it can also be a satellite, a heart-rate monitor, a keystroke recorder, or a short-range Doppler gaze tracker. The differences between a two-dimensional image and a three-dimensional model, as well as a still photograph and cinema, are also quickly disappearing. We tend to think of cinema as moving pictures, or "movies." But of course the images are not moving; they are simply a succession of images being replaced at a rate that our senses cannot grasp so that we hallucinate motion. The *moved* image—two images of an object from two different locations—can be sequenced to create a sensation of camera motion, but these displaced images can also be used to triangulate the location of a point in space, as with our binocular vision or when birds bob their heads. This moved, or doubled, image of the world is also the basis of photogrammetry. Used for centuries in surveying, the doubled image—"a point in space known through two interrelated projections"—is the fundamental principle of Gaspard Monge's *Descriptive Geometry* (1798), which was the foundational course of the École Polytechnique. It is also the technical basis of interrelated plans and sections in architectural drawing.[30]

A digital image consists of an array of numeric translations of photons of electromagnetic energy—no lines, surfaces, or solids, only red, green, and blue color assignments along rows and columns.[31] Photogrammetry models approximate the location and color of a point in space from multiple images of it. No hierarchical difference between an object and its context is predetermined; everything in the environment becomes evenly captured energetic data, a homogeneous field of colored marks in a matrix, sometimes appearing abstract, at other times realistic. Ideally responding in "real time"—another way of saying that the information is detected and rendered as a continually updated sequence of images, a form of cinema—these models are used to manage the spatial movements of an autonomous vehicle, the targeting of a missile, the location of a suspect, the efficiency of an infrastructure, or the gaze of a consumer. In addition to XYZ coordinates locating points in space, photogrammetry stores RGB color values. If it is less obvious how color would be as useful as spatial information, it is a misunderstanding of the nature of technical images. The images alone do not matter as much as the linked associations created when they are combined with large datasets, cross-referenced, and filtered as a form of "sense-making." They send and receive numeric translations of reflected energy within the environment. RGB data offers statistical information about temperature, moisture, photosynthesis, CO_2 emissions, energy absorptivity, reflectance, wavelength frequency, and chemical residue. These metrics make scanning and imaging services useful to the petroleum industry, climate-change studies, underwater exploration, weather simulations, forensic reconstructions, fauna-migration tracking, and advertising campaigns. As a model made from images, photogrammetry is also critical to the machine-learning algorithms of neural networks, which perform image analysis and manipulation at the granular level.

It is interesting to consider the rapid democratization of neural-networked diffusion models that occurred during the summer of 2022 through the public release of DALL-E and Midjourney. These algorithms are AI image generators that produce "new" image content from natural-language text prompts. Neural networks have been in development over the past half-century for various governmental, policing, and military applications (such as facial recognition, self-guided missiles, autonomous vehicles), and artists and architects have begun to engage with them in the past decade.[32] What is different now are two things. First, user-friendly interfaces allow almost anyone to interact with the image-training set through textual prompts that require no knowledge of coding. (For Flusser this exchangeability of image and text is foundational for all "technical images" and, as we will see below, for conceptual art of the 1960s.) Second, the exponential expansion of the image dataset increases the variety and detail of potential results. Together these two aspects allow the user to feel both creatively engaged *and* surprised by the hyperreal imagery produced. Within four short months of the programs' public release, however, the images being generated had already begun to appear increasingly similar and predictable. They began to appear "gimmicky."[33] The way the algorithm generates images is, after all, by culling large datasets to produce a general middle of highest probability: The largest number of images manipulated by the largest number of users uploaded with the largest number of labels provides the latent space that will be used in the production of the new image. This source imagery has a built-in bias based on the quantity and type of images circulating online, reflecting both the programming and user groups, which now also includes the biases inherent in language as well.[34] Another way to describe this "latent space" is to say it's the homogeneous background of an everyday image world as consumed and created by a specific set of humans and nonhumans through online interactions. We express surprise at the specificity of the generated image, yet the working space of all AI is "generic" in the sense that it seeks to identify aspects "shared by, typical of, or relating to a whole group of similar things, rather than to any particular thing."[35] It is out of this generic homogeneity that it will seek a targeted result to the prompt it has been given. How and where we find interest in the endless production of "meaningless" difference through images is an aesthetic question that is all the more pressing given that these apparatuses are increasingly determining the background of a reality that we consume in a state of distraction.[36]

Clearly an "image" within this system is much more than a picture. The data extracted from sensors is an abstract representation of the environment and the interactions of entities within it. The initial goals of technical sensing are to capture data evenly across the environment—a homogeneous spread of reflected energy, impact vibrations, chemical compounds, moisture content, and so on. This mechanical objectivity is a hallmark of devices that record everything detectable in their environment, unadulterated by human subjectivity.[37] Contemporary technological sensing is an interconnected system of multiple machines performing exchanges in real time and cross-referencing records compiled over years. Within these processes "value" is derived from the patterns, anomalies, and minor differences that provide meaningful information for research objectives in various fields, whether scientific, commercial, governmental, military, or journalistic. Such images operate analogically, equally "real" but of a second order.[38] Second-order abstractions—a text of a text, an image of an image—are often given a prefix to indicate an excess: *Hyper-*.

HYPER-

In the book *Investigative Aesthetics*, Matthew Fuller and Eyal Weizman argue that expanding the attributes of sense and sense-making to nonhuman entities engenders two new categories for aesthetic consideration, which they term *hyperaesthetics* and *hyperaesthesia*.

Hyperaesthetics "emerges in devising forms of integration between different forms of sensation. First, hyperaesthetics becomes particularly palpable through the incorporation of human sensing with a network of devices that monitor, count and measure."[39] *Hyperaesthetics* describes a state of interconnected sensing so intense that traditional anthropocentric aesthetic discourse is insufficient. This is not solely a technological state, for it includes a multiplicity of material and energetic relations: "All bodies of matter and all surfaces are exposed to the environment around them; some impressions linger and register, others are erased and get lost."[40] Attuning ourselves to this extended sensorium, the authors argue, requires a shift in our conceptual framework, a reworking of aesthetic categories, an embrace of technological sensing, and an alternative understanding of *information*. "From the point of view of the description of relations as informational, to hyper-aestheticise is to work with and to intensify, and render differentially sensible, the entry of information into the internal organisation of entities and relations. … Here, 'information' is never disembodied, but always manifest in and as stuff—ideas, chemicals, media, organisms, photographs and so on—all of which transform and translate these translations."[41]

By acknowledging relations between all objects as aesthetic, hyperaesthetics opens alternative avenues of interest and new assemblies of attention "to recognize a multiplicity of different forms of sensation."[42] It also implicitly acknowledges the importance of "images" in the material and energetic construction of reality. "Heat, humidity, kinetic impact, gravity [and] electromagnetic radiation" are all qualities that can be sensed in and from the surfaces of the earth, an expansion of both sensing and sense-making that alters our understanding of the world.[43] The hope is that considering sensing and/or imaging in this manner empowers us to employ and redirect these systems toward alternative functions outside of the economies of prediction and control. In fact these representations and their qualities are not more or less "real" or "fake" than those produced with the biological sensorium; they are images of the world produced from within a *different* sensorium—directing human attention toward previously overlooked relations operating in the background.

Hyperaesthesia occurs when there is so much noise, so much data, that the world ceases to make sense. There is an aspect of violence in this level of excess stimulation. "Indeed, hyperaesthesia can be a component of physical and mental trauma. Trauma over-registers sensation to a degree that sensation does not add information but erases and distorts it."[44] These effects may be the outcome of the battle being waged for our attention, but hyperaesthesia can also be purposefully created as political camouflage, where the inability to determine the difference between signal and noise leads to indifference.[45] We do not know where, how, or even *if* we should pay attention.

It is worth noting that as AI attention-monitoring algorithms increasingly become part of the background of our daily lives, trained through our interactions while training our modes of attention, hyperaesthetics accelerates toward hyperaesthesia. Part of this relates to the fact that the processes of sense-making have become exchanges between nonhuman machines while our attention is analyzed, adjusted, and optimized for reasons outside of our understanding. We also become bored by the struggle to aesthetically engage the deluge of images generated more and more by the generic. As such, hyperaesthesia is a type of commercial camouflage. The small differences in the image background that prick our attention become the valuable patterns that sell us as targeted consumers to corporations. Ironically the capitalist extraction of value through images may not be realized by means of spectacle but rather the boredom of homogeneity.

SERIAL INTEREST

Hyperaesthesia is not new. As many philosophers and psychologists have noted, the world available to our senses is an overwhelming hum of homogeneous stimulation. Meaningful perception requires selective attention. In 1890 William James suggested that it begins with interest:

> Millions of items of the outward order are present to my senses which never properly enter into my experience. Why? Because they have no *interest* for me. *My experience is what I agree to attend to.* Only those items which I *notice* shape my mind—without selective interest, experience is an utter chaos. Interest alone gives accent and emphasis, light and shade, background and foreground—intelligible perspective, in a word. It varies in every creature, but without it the consciousness of every creature would be a gray chaotic indiscriminateness, impossible for us to conceive.[46]

This passage surfaced recently in two books: *How to Do Nothing: Resisting the Attention Economy*, by Jenny Odell, and *Our Aesthetic Categories: Zany, Cute, Interesting*, by Sianne Ngai. Odell writes on how to resist social media, e-commerce, online news, and ultimately the effects of a world in which digital life has reconfigured all aspects of our engagements.[47] What Ngai culls from James is the observation that "if the interesting marks a tension between wonder and reason, increasing in direct proportion to the acuteness of that tension, the feeling that underpins it seems to lie somewhere between an object-oriented desire and an object-indifferent affect."[48]

"The interesting," according to Ngai, is one of the responses that best addresses our current state of constant information exchange in discourse and media.[49] What is "interesting" varies with changing contexts over time; it is contingent and ambiguous, and thus potentially weak as a judgment. Yet in many respects discerning what is interesting entails a crucial aesthetic response, for it describes the feeling when something strikes one's sensibilities as somehow different, important, or distinguishable from within a sea of minor variations.[50] The interesting directs attention toward this, not that, and often toward qualities that appear conceptually empty and require further explanation, thus linking aesthetic feelings to conceptual justifications.[51] The interesting requires repetition, seriality, and the use of language to explicate and articulate exactly what it is that is different. It produces discourse.

Ngai makes a compelling argument for the importance of "the interesting" in the conceptual art of the 1960s and '70s.[52] Formulated around tensions between image and language, conceptual art relies heavily on textual discourse to interpret the work, and the text often becomes the work itself. Photography became a key component of these practices, setting in motion certain links between concepts and aesthetics.[53] For Susan Sontag the photograph captures "the commonplace, the inessential, the accidental, the minute, the transient"—allowing differences to be discerned and interest to be noted and recognized as a comparative tension.[54] When the familiar is captured and reproduced through a technology that stresses mechanical repetition, the generic or typical aspects of the world are exposed to a finer level of discernment. Conceptual art situated these differences in the tensions between "conceptual knowledge and sensory perception."[55] Ngai argues that through this set of relations "conceptual art became the incubator in which the interesting—always already an aesthetic about difference—developed into an aesthetic of information (and more specifically ... into an aesthetic about the technologically mediated dissemination of information). For information was understood by postwar theorists as precisely the basic form of difference."[56]

Bernd and Hilla Becher's depictions of water towers, blast furnaces, and grain silos and Ed Ruscha's pictures of parking lots, gasoline stations, and storefronts both combine photographic realism, serial repetition, conceptual framing, and generic typologies. In these photographic series, the aesthetic effect of interest is generated through attention directed at small differences in the accumulation of the familiar. These works share several similarities: They are typically shot in black-and-white at a medium distance, frontally focused, highly detailed, evenly illuminated, and thematically concerned with places that are usually overlooked as background. These qualities lend the images a documentary sense of mechanical objectivity akin to scientific detachment.[57] There are differences in technique, to be sure. Ruscha's photographs have a seriality that evokes the apparent ease of the snapshot, although it is deployed repetitively, evenly, and comprehensively. The Bechers' series are temporally and spatially disjunctive, its subjects captured in meticulously composed photographs taken with extreme technical precision. Yet the aesthetics of the two series operate in a similar manner: The photographs are not to be appreciated as single images but rather as

Film stills, *Jeanne Dielman, 23 quai du Commerce, 1080 Bruxelles*, directed by Chantal Akerman, 1975.

Film stills, *News from Home*,
directed by Chantal Akerman, 1976.

202   HYPERHOMOGENEITY; OR ATTENTION WITHIN THE BACKGROUND

elements interacting within a larger set. This demands a different mode of attention and temporality. It is through repetition that disruptions emerge—an oddly misplaced window, an unexpected abstraction, an absurd collision of signage. Finding these moments of strangeness within the familiar requires one to pay close attention to *all* of the images and, in the process, notice minor differences lurking within apparent homogeneity. To quote Ngai, the interesting "necessarily arises against a background of boredom, to change against a background of sameness. ... The interesting is thus an aesthetic experience that enables us to negotiate the relationship between identity and difference, the unexpected and the familiar. It also enables us to negotiate the relationship between the possible and the actual, or as Schlegel might put it, between the ideal and the real, and is therefore an aesthetic invested in a kind of realism."[58]

Artists such as Ruscha and the Bechers are "button-pushers" or "envisioners," in Flusser's language. They pervert the apparatus of photography to focus attention on the deviation in things normally perceived as homogeneous. Yet it would be a mistake to consider these aesthetic transformations simply as an increased clarity of meaning. The noise remains. If anything, the background is rendered wilder, more absurd, more unfamiliar. The century-old idea of "defamiliarization"—first developed by Viktor Shklovsky in his essay "Art, as Device"—has become a touchstone for contemporary conversations on realism in aesthetics, popping up in discussions of neural networks, philosophies of the strange and uncanny, Ngai's arguments around "the interesting," and discourse on the films of Chantal Akerman.[59] In lieu of a longer discussion of Shklovsky, I will point out an often overlooked nuance.[60] There have been three English translations of the Russian term *ostranenie*: Defamiliarization (1965), estrangement (2021), and enstrangement (1990).[61] Enstrangement is a neologism, a combination of *enchantment* and *estrangement*.[62] This translation seems to capture much of what Shklovsky was after in his arguments where art should impede automatic responses and resist immediate clarity, elongating and intensifying attention as a renewed sensory experience. Another way to describe these techniques, these devices, is that they create a tension between sensing and sense-making, that their fundamental aesthetic provocation is within notions of realism.

AN AESTHETICS OF HOMOGENEITY

Chantal Akerman has made a unique contribution to the aesthetics of realism in films that hover on the edge of documentary, such as *Jeanne Dielman, 23 quai du Commerce, 1080 Bruxelles* (1975) and *News from Home* (1976).[63] Although it is obvious that *Jeanne Dielman* employs actors, a script, a plot, and a set, even a murder—all elements of cinematic fiction—the fact that we watch the entirety of a meal's preparation, consumption, and cleanup gives it the feeling of a real-time recording. The footage in *News from Home* consists entirely of long takes of New York City streets and subways. It is clearly a record of everyday public space, but aesthetic resonances between objects, details, and colors draw the viewer's attention to fleeting occurrences in the background. Both films raise doubts about the facts they present and play at the tension between reality and its representation, thereby heightening the viewer's perception.

Several recognizable techniques from our previous discussions are used to create these effects: First, the camera faces most scenes frontally and is centered on the set/environment from a medium distance. Second, the camera rarely moves. People come into the frame, are cut off by it, or leave the scene with little acknowledgment by the camera. If the camera does move, it does not seem motivated by either the director or the action; it feels more like an automated device of mechanized surveillance. Finally, the shots occur over an extended duration. They often seem too long for the action they are intended to capture; they seem to offer too much meaningless background. All of these aesthetic devices conspire to make the viewer look at the scenic composition in an altered manner. In *Jeanne Dielman*, for instance, some scenes are spatially composed akin to the perspectives of fifteenth-century paintings; at other times a cluster of objects is arranged like a seventeenth-century still-life. In *News from Home*, the subway columns and passing cars weave taut planar patterns reminiscent of twentieth-century abstraction. Colors and patterns reoccur across objects, environments, and people, both in single scenes and across different scenes over time. This use of color draws entities into constellations, modulating the viewer's attention between foreground and background as well as active and passive events. There are also moments in which background objects behave in seemingly autonomous ways. A hook-hung dish towel is attached to the wall in slightly different locations from scene to scene, while chairs disappear from the kitchen table, and graphic arrows on a matchbox cover point in opposite directions.[64] The repetitive structure of Jeanne's day—her actions homogeneous in their repetition—presents an unsettling stillness that evokes all events as equivalent, yet also directs attention to minor differences which disturb the familiarity and become significant moments.

None of what has been discussed so far touches on issues of undervalued domestic labor, the monetization of sex in prostitution, the numbing perpetuation of social paralysis, and the politics of class and racial identity in public space, among many other themes present in Akerman's work. She does not shy away from social and political issues, but it is through the aesthetics of the films that such conceptual complexities are presented to the viewer. There are dispositions of color and composition that unite the flesh of an actor and a cleaning cloth, the personal realm of a bathrobe and a bath tile, the scarf worn in public to the flower painting at the entry door. The flickering of attention within the background is what allows the political provocations to sit within the realism of the film instead of feeling like univocal statements.[65] This mechanism goes well beyond critical aspects of "raising awareness" and moves toward speculations on how an alternate aesthetics of the familiar could be explored. It is also part of what makes the films so alluring and disturbing: They engage politically through a redistribution of attention.

The phrases "an aesthetics of homogeneity" and "the equivalence of events" originate in Ivone Margulies's writings on Akerman's films, published as *Nothing Happens: Chantal Akerman's Hyperrealist Everyday*. Much of what has been said and will follow owes a debt to her exquisite analysis. For Margulies the aesthetics of homogeneity created by the extended duration of shots, frontal framing, repetition of actions, and equivalency evoked between objects and people hinges on "the interplay between attention and inattention" induced in the viewer.[66] She argues that Akerman pulls the viewer's attention into the background through an aesthetic of minor disturbances within homogeneous repetition, the "automatism" of daily routines and environments.[67] The result is that the intensity of sensation is held within the background, disturbing its relation to the "foregrounded" narrative that one typically attends to when making sense of a filmic plot. Margulies writes:

> Through the unsettling effect of excess description, Akerman approaches an abstract concreteness that unbalances referentiality. There is a sort of metamorphosis: The sharpness of the depiction borders on the hallucinatory. Akerman's hyperrealist style crosses a certain threshold of intensity. An oscillation between recognizing the familiar and being estranged from it is one of the central features of *Jeanne Dielman*. This effect of making

strange through representation is part of the hyperrealist aspect of Akerman's style: The extreme concentration on a certain set of images or gestures over an extended period of time leads to a basic questioning of the conventions sustaining the identity between reality and representation.[68]

News from Home achieves similar effects without intervening physically in the environment. The buildings, streets, cars, clothes, graffiti, and signs of New York City are filmed as they are. The filmic structure is straightforward: Long, frontal, stable shots of the public spaces of the city. The only apparent interventions are cuts between scenes and the disjunction between sound and image as Akerman reads letters from her mother, confusing the focus of attention as they do not correspond with what is taking place on the screen. The visual and sonic sequences compete to create an unstable equivalency of words, objects, and events. In this even haze of distraction, details prick the senses. A patch of color on a shirt matches a bag, which matches a sign, which matches a car. These details may be insignificant, but once noticed they become interesting, and the viewer starts to engage more intensely with the sequences, compositions, and durations.[69] How we as humans make sense of this "aesthetic of homogeneity" is what stimulates a desire to look longer, harder, and differently at the film, and finally at the world around us.

Patterns of meaningless color data are exactly what the apparatus of the technical image is programmed to sense and make-sense of. These are the things that attention-monitoring algorithms capture, quantify, and analyze. Returning to an earlier theme, the hyperrealism of the globally dispersed technical image apparatus produces a hyperaesthetic, a second-order abstraction translating noise into potentially useful information. But are these transactions the only ones of value—the only ones we should care about? Is there another mode of attending to the background through an expanded sensorium that does not reduce "sense-making" to control through the abstractions of capital? What Akerman's films suggest is that the tension that constitutes our mediated world is experienced as an ever-present generic "threat of randomness" operating in the background, where objects and events enter our sensorium accidentally, naturally, automatically.[70] These intrusions create a low-level hum of anxiety, but they also call for an aesthetic engagement that levels the hierarchy between focused and diffuse attention—an unsettling equivalency of events where "the interesting marks a tension between wonder and reason, increasing in direct proportion to the acuteness of that tension."[71]

Akerman's films provide an aesthetic provocation by staging objects and events in the background as autonomous and aesthetically engaged with one another in ways that seem to exist outside the human sensorium. Thus the films invite us to treat the hyperhomogeneous as a field of aesthetic relations to play within and against. It is a form of sensing that does not always make "sense," and when we are no longer able to "make sense of our senses" we may conclude that the world ceases to make sense.[72] Yet this shift in aesthetics gives rise to the possibility of enchantment with a reality made strange—an *enstrangement*—and through this, a renewal of attention and a remediation of care.

1 Matthew Fuller and Eyal Weizman, *Investigative Aesthetics: Conflicts and Commons in the Politics of Truth* (London: Verso, 2021), 33.
2 "Within a magical or 'enchanted' process, language and experience simply fail to connect." Jack Halberstam, *Wild Things: The Disorder of Desire* (Durham, NC: Duke University Press, 2020).
3 Ivone Margulies, *Nothing Happens: Chantal Akerman's Hyperrealist Everyday* (Durham, NC: Duke University Press, 1996).
4 Jacques Rancière, *The Politics of Aesthetics: The Distribution of the Sensible*, trans. Gabriel Rockhill (London: Bloomsbury, 2004), 16–19.
5 The popularity of the word *entangled* can be traced to several sources, but the most influential are perhaps Donna Haraway, *Staying with the Trouble: Making Kin in the Chthulucene* (Durham, NC: Duke University Press, 2016), and Ian Hodder, *Entangled: An Archaeology of the Relationships between Humans and Things* (Hoboken, NJ: Wiley-Blackwell, 2012).
6 Merlin Sheldrake, *Entangled Life: How Fungi Make Our Worlds, Change Our Minds, and Shape Our Futures* (New York: Random House, 2021).
7 Graham Harman, *The Quadruple Object* (Winchester, UK: Zero Books, 2011), and Fuller and Weizman, *Investigative Aesthetics*, 36.
8 Fuller and Weizman, *Investigative Aesthetics*, 33.
9 Harman, *The Quadruple Object*.
10 As Warren Neidich notes, "The history of aesthetics is partly an unconscious dialog between evolving neurobiological structures and the mutating cultural/visual landscape." Warren Neidich, *Blow Up: Photography, Cinema and the Brain* (New York: D.A.P. Publishers, 2003), 73.
11 The Friends of Attention, *Twelve Theses on Attention*, ed. D. Graham Burnett and Stevie Knauss (Princeton, NJ: Princeton University Press, 2022), i–iii.
12 Bruno Latour, *Science in Action* (Cambridge, MA: Harvard University Press, 1987), 131.
13 Daniel Heller-Roazen, *The Inner Touch: Archaeology of Sensation* (New York: Zone Books, 2007), 44–45.
14 Heller-Roazen, *Inner Touch*, 50–51.
15 *Merriam-Webster*, s.v. "automation," accessed June 23, 2023, https://www.merriam-webster.com/dictionary/automation.
16 *Autómatos*, "self moving, self willed"; *autónomos*, "living under one's own laws, independent." Wiktionary, s.v. "automaton," accessed June 23, 2023, https://en.wiktionary.org/wiki/automaton, and "autonomy," accessed June 23, 2023, https://en.wiktionary.org/wiki/autonomy.
17 Ivone Margulies, *Nothing Happens*, 98.
18 Heller-Roazen, *Inner Touch*, 44–45.
19 Giorgio Agamban, *What Is an Apparatus? And Other Essays*, trans. David Kishik and Stefan Pedatella (Stanford, CA: Stanford University Press, 2009).
20 Vilém Flusser, *Towards a Philosophy of Photography*, trans. Anthony Mathews (1983; London: Reaktion Books, 2000), 71.
21 Flusser, *Towards a Philosophy*, 80.
22 Flusser, *Towards a Philosophy*, 78–79.
23 Flusser, *Towards a Philosophy*, 31.
24 Flusser, *Towards a Philosophy*, 76–77.
25 Vilém Flusser, *Into the Universe of the Technical Image*, trans. Nancy Ann Roth (1985; Minneapolis, MN: University of Minnesota Press, 2011), 21.
26 Flusser, *Into the Universe*, 48.
27 Flusser, *Into the Universe*, 37.
28 Claude Shannon, "A Mathematical Theory of Communication," *The Bell System Technical Journal* 27, no. 3 (July 1948): 379–423.
29 The play of "pushing buttons" can be understood as a reference to photography, but there is another path for this discussion that follows the engagement of noise, feedback, technologies of reproduction, and the sample in music: for example, in Igor Stravinsky, Karlheinz Stockhausen, the Velvet Underground, Sonic Youth, My Bloody Valentine, Kraftwerk, Aphex Twin, the Bomb Squad, Dust Brothers, and perhaps the most aptly named button-pusher of all time, Squarepusher. Political and aesthetic issues stemming from the tensions of organized noise are elaborated masterfully by Jacques Attali in *Noise: The Political Economy of Music*, trans. Brian Massumi (Minneapolis, MN: University of Minnesota Press, 1985).
30 Gaspard Monge, *Géométrie descriptive* (1795), quoted in P. J. Booker, *A History of Engineering Drawing* (London: Chatto & Windus, 1963), 88.
31 Hany Farid, *Fake Photos* (Cambridge, MA: MIT Press, 2019), 160–62.
32 The list of artists and architects could include Mario Klingemann, Holly Herndon, Refik Anadol, Mimi Onuoha, Ruy Klein, M. Casey Rhem, A/P Practice, Matias del Campo, and Andrew Kudless.
33 Sianne Ngai, *Theory of the Gimmick: Aesthetic Judgment and Capitalist Form* (Cambridge, MA: Harvard University Press, 2020), 3–4.
34 There have been numerous investigations into bias embedded with AI image and text algorithms. A recent conversation can be found at https://archinect.com/features/article/150354024/ai-is-built-on-datasets-that-are-already-biased-a-conversation-with-felecia-davis, accessed July 31, 2023.
35 *Cambridge English Dictionary*, s.v. "generic," accessed July 8, 2023, https://dictionary.cambridge.org/dictionary/english/generic.
36 Walter Benjamin "The Work of Art in the Age of Its Tech-

nological Reproducibility" (1936), in *The Work of Art in the Age of Its Technological Reproducibility, and Other Writings on Media*, ed. Michael W. Jennings, Brigid Doherty, and Thomas Y. Levin, trans. Edmund Jephcott et al. (Cambridge, MA: Harvard University Press, 2008), 40.
37 Lorraine Daston and Peter Galison, *Objectivity* (New York: Zone Books, 2007).
38 Kaja Silverman, *The Miracle of Analogy, or The History of Photography, Part 1* (Stanford, CA: Stanford University Press, 2015). Silverman's unique and convincing argument has influenced the idea of the photograph as analogous to reality.
39 Fuller and Weizman, *Investigative Aesthetics*, 37. On mechanical objectivity, see Daston and Galison, *Objectivity*.
40 Fuller and Weizman, *Investigative Aesthetics*, 63.
41 Fuller and Weizman, *Investigative Aesthetics*, 58.
42 Fuller and Weizman, *Investigative Aesthetics*, 35.
43 Fuller and Weizman, *Investigative Aesthetics*, 63.
44 Fuller and Weizman, *Investigative Aesthetics*, 83.
45 Paul de Man, quoted in Margulies, *Nothing Happens*, 96.
46 William James, *The Principles of Psychology* (New York: Henry Holt, 1890), 1:402.
47 Jenny Odell, *How to Do Nothing: Resisting the Attention Economy* (Brooklyn, NY: Melville House, 2019).
48 Sianne Ngai, *Our Aesthetic Categories: Zany, Cute, Interesting* (Cambridge, MA: Harvard University Press, 2012), 129.
49 Ngai, *Aesthetic Categories*, 1.
50 Ngai, *Aesthetic Categories*, 130–31.
51 Ngai, *Aesthetic Categories*, 170.
52 Ngai, *Aesthetic Categories*, 144.
53 A short list of aesthetic/conceptual linkages in photography: the lost aura through technological reproducibility (Walter Benjamin), the mechanical seriality of image capture, process, and dissemination (Sianne Ngai), the removal of the hand of the artist (Roland Barthes), the chemical/energetic indexicality of recorded traces of light (Rosalind Krauss), the dematerialization toward information exchange (Friedrich Kittler), the background "noise" of the world made spectral (François Bonnet), the image as analogical reality (Kaja Silverman), the ability for it to be combined with text (Bruno Latour). These are just some of the qualities associated with photography that made it appealing for conceptual art. Each of these qualities spurred discursive innovation; each of these theorists identified an aesthetic tension within the media of photography, directed attention toward it affects, and articulated a conceptual speculation on its implications.
54 Susan Sontag, *On Photography* (New York: Picador, 2001), 111; quoted in Ngai, *Our Aesthetic Categories*, 140.
55 Ngai, *Our Aesthetic Categories*, 165.
56 Ngai, *Our Aesthetic Categories*, 145.
57 On mechanical objectivity, see Daston and Galison, *Objectivity*.
58 Ngai, *Our Aesthetic Categories*, 136.
59 Viktor Shklovsky, "Art, as Device," in *Theory of Prose*, trans. Benjamin Sher (Dallas, TX: Dalkey Archive Press, 1991). See also Matias del Campo, Graham Harman, and Ivone Margulies.
60 I have been guilty of this oversight in the past. See Michael Young, *The Estranged Object: Realisms in Art and Architecture* (Chicago: Graham Foundation, 2015).
61 *Russian Formalist Criticism: Four Essays*, trans. Lee T. Lemon and Marion J. Reis (Lincoln, NE: University of Nebraska Press, 1965) Viktor Shklovsky, *On the Theory of Prose*, trans. Shushan Avagyan (Dallas, TX: Dalkey Archive Press, 2021) Viktor Shklovsky, *Theory of Prose*, trans. Benjamin Sher (Champaign, IL: Dalkey Archive Press, 1990)
62 Danielle Dutton, *A Picture Held Us Captive* (Ithaca, NY: Image Text Ithaca Press, 2022), 10.
63 I started writing this essay in the fall of 2022, and it was wonderful to see both films rise on *Sight & Sound's* list of the greatest films of all time, in December 2022, with *Jeanne Dielman* ranked as number one. Although I admit that I have not been able to reckon with how this recognition affects the arguments of this essay.
64 There is a fascinating film essay that superimposes elevational images of the kitchen in which the behavior of the dish towel can be observed: https://www.filmscalpel.com/regarding-the-pain-of-jeanne-dielman, accessed July 31, 2023.
65 Margulies, *Nothing Happens*, 141–42.
66 Margulies, *Nothing Happens*, 69, 72.
67 Margulies, *Nothing Happens*, 73.
68 Margulies, *Nothing Happens*, 69, 72.
69 Shklovsky, "Art, as Device," 6.
70 Margulies, *Nothing Happens*, 88.
71 Ngai, *Our Aesthetic Categories*, 129.
72 Benjamín Labatut, *When We Cease to Understand the World*, trans. Adrian Nathan West (New York: New York Review Books, 2020).

DRAWINGS NOT FOUND

We'd like to show you some things, but they are gone.

For the past few years we've designed in obsolescence—in the form of "Drawing Fields," a series of fleeting supergraphics exploring the spatial potential of mark making. Each installation utilizes GPS-controlled robots to paint site-specific building-size compositions at a 1:1 scale. The series employs measuring, delineating, and marking to rehearse architecture as a dynamic performance of spatial instructions. The result is a transient spatial practice assisted by a peculiar little robot from Denmark designed to stripe sports fields accurately.

DRAWING FIELDS NO. 02

Our work with robotic painting began at the Ragdale Foundation, in Lake Forest, Illinois, just north of Chicago. We were commissioned to make a temporary performance space, which we situated in a small clearing at the rear of the property, a historic campus designed by architect Howard Van Doren Shaw. Designed with social distancing in mind, *Drawing Fields No. 02* was a temporary venue composed of nothing but brilliant white lines. The pattern was graphically intense yet disarmingly vacant. Its relationship to the site was also odd: positioned askew to the main house, it was tightly nestled in the clearing. So although the drawing was firmly situated, it felt adrift. Oscillating from superimposed to integrated, depending on your vantage point, it comprised hundreds of painted gestures (each roughly four inches wide) resembling stitches in a strange quilt—like the wefts and warps of a larger, unseen pattern. The centrifugal marks originated from an incidental point in space rendered temporarily significant by the cacophony of marks and inscriptions surrounding it. The pulsating graphic was both monumental and momentary. It took two days to paint and lasted two weeks.

Drawing Fields No. 02 during the opening performance, Outpost Office, 2020.

Drawing Fields No. 02 installation with field-marking robot, Outpost Office, 2020.

Cover the Grid with Chicago skyline beyond, Outpost Office, 2021.

COVER THE GRID

Cover the Grid was installed the following summer in a community lot in North Lawndale, on the West Side of Chicago, referred to as WACA (Westside Association for Community Action) Bell Park. For at least thirty years the asphalt surface has defined an essential civic gathering hub for neighborhood residents and organizations. We knew from experience that softscape field painting lasts a few weeks but would last significantly longer on asphalt or concrete, shifting the technique's timescale dramatically. So what kind of mark might we leave on the neighborhood, literally and figuratively, and for how long? How could we facilitate many possible futures rather than prescribe just one? Our questions were provoked by curator David Brown, who sought generative and transitional acts of architecture rather than prescribed solutions for the park. Working closely with collaborators based in North Lawndale, we proposed the installation as a graphic test bed for experimentation, instead of a permanent park, to allow neighborhood residents to consider long-term civic futures. The design provided a provisional landscape for the community to take stock of its needs while planning for the site continued in earnest.

The final installation proposal included a dizzying assemblage of checkerboards, swatches, calibration marks, and color charts scattered across the site. The striping robot delineated the color regions, which were later filled in with an airless sprayer, rendering the site a gigantic coloring book in the scorching Chicago heat. Amid the dense graphic field, identifiable courts of all shapes and sizes emerged for basketball, four square, and hopscotch. Dynamic patterns of crosswalks and visual cues from the nearby elevated Pink Line tracks completed the composition. The pattern lasted about two years. Then, to our delight, it was paved over and replaced with a new park created by others.

FORMATTING AND CALIBRATING

Field painting is an ephemeral technique that can neither achieve permanence nor conform to architecture's expectation of fixity. Freed from the constraints of finality, we adopted a flexible and open-ended design approach. Despite essential differences in programming and context, each "Drawing Field" project typifies methods of formatting and calibration found in design and planning. These conventional preparatory steps entail assessing a found

Cover the Grid pattern detail, Outpost Office, 2021.

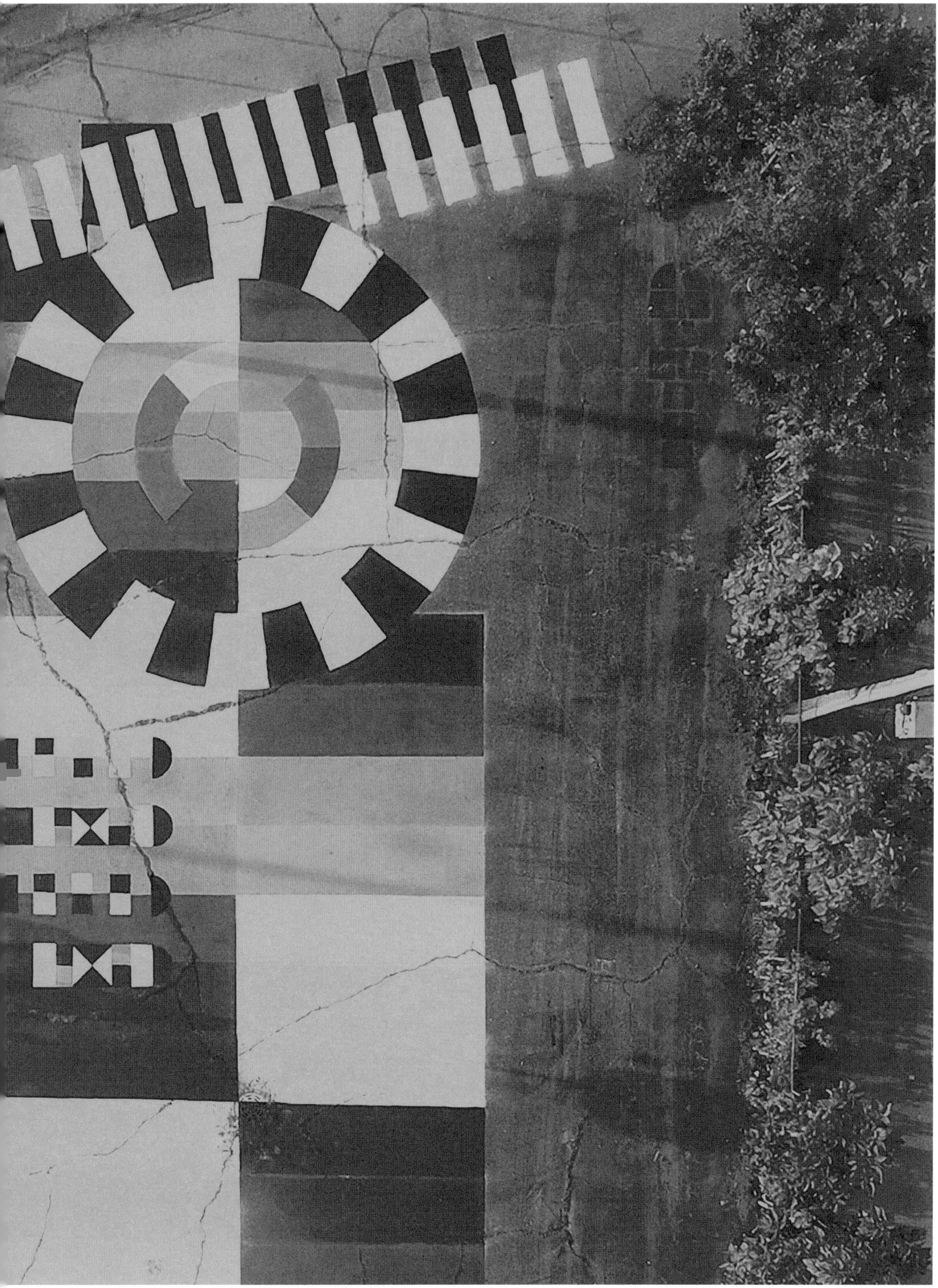

Cover the Grid in Google Earth, accessed September 2023.

condition or site before progressing to more substantial design stages. Typically carried out in pre-design phases, measuring and surveying are primarily automated, anonymous, and distributed. What would it mean to instrumentalize these marginalized processes in new ways and elaborate their effects? How might centering acts of pre-design reveal prosaic processes of formatting and calibration as anything but mundane?

We first considered the paradox of designing blankness—the preparatory composition and construction of empty formats suitable for conveying the replete conspicuousness of design. Although bereft of marks or gestures, a blank drawing should not be dismissed as contentless. Every fresh sheet of paper is a remarkable design object. Various formats and paper standards dictate each sheet's weight, size, and aspect ratio. The constraints of manufacturing, circulation, and standardization prescribe types of blankness: landscape or portrait, A4 or tabloid, 20 or 40 pounds.

Similarly blank digital canvases and empty files are not devoid of properties. They include metadata controlling format, size, resolution, color space, and so on. These technical limits and cultural objects in software shape our relationship to representations and, by extension, to everyday places. Designed for marking sports fields, our GPS-guided robot required specific technical and material formats, the most important being the site. Field-marking robots demand flat, open spaces with no adjacent vertical obstructions and grass trimmed to turf specs. Before our team arrives to install, each location is engineered to produce a suitable landscape of blankness. Acknowledging the robot's limitations, we work with formats, specifications, and standards integral to mediating its relationship with place and space, from standard units of measure and the kinematic limitations of its movements to the satellite network that orients it in space. *Drawing Field No. 02*, for example, included a recursive series of superimposed frames with graphic emblems appropriated from document margins, safe frames, and layouts. These collectively highlighted areas on the Ragdale site properly formatted for field painting—level planes with clear satellite signals. The pattern measures and calibrates its site, manifesting measurement as design.

Anticipating that the majority of the audience would view the first Ragdale event remotely via drone footage, our research employed aerial photo targets, well-known emblems of satellite imaging, surveillance, and mapping. Developed in the 1950s to aid the development of reconnaissance technologies, calibration targets are supergraphics of perpendicular white bars often appearing in complex arrays. The most common configuration is the 5:1 aspect Tri-bar Array, which includes several parallel bars of diminishing scale. Easily recognizable for verification purposes, these patterns are used to control vast territories. Calibration patterns are part of a larger category of what we've come to call anterior graphics—preparatory patterns designed to measure before content is relayed. Television test patterns, another category of anterior graphics, evolved to calibrate picture geometry, resolution, brightness, and contrast. The demise of these once ubiquitous test patterns can be explained by a series of technical achievements (self-calibrating cameras, solid-state components, high transmission rates).

Test patterns might be technically outmoded, but they reinforce the tendencies and performances that underpin our contemporary image culture, predicated on extraction and exchange. Design management tools such as color charts, graphic scales, calibration patterns, and process control patches are necessary to facilitate accurate media transmission. They bridge gaps between agents and actors by providing a datum for comparison and measurement. In our work for *Cover the Grid* we combined charts calibrated to ensure specific aesthetic performances (color charts, calibration patterns, etc.) and templates calibrated for specific bodily performances (courts of all shapes and sizes). Of course we didn't invent any of these graphic elements or templates; our expertise lies in arranging and recombining them in new landscapes of measure. As David Joselit argues in *After Art*, "What now matters most is not the production of new content but its retrieval in intelligible patterns through acts of reframing, capturing, reiterating, and documenting." This approach shifts our focus as designers away from producing gestures and marks toward engaging in how digital objects and their behaviors govern content creation. Field marks are not authorial gestures or forms but traces of orchestrated specifications emerging from analog and digital standardization processes. In many ways they are marks for mediating the standardization of experience. With these works we are interested in what Joselit has described as situations "wherein the worldly entanglements of images—the techniques of their production, the efforts associated with their creation, the mode of their circulation, the historical conditions of their making, etc.—become visible."[1]

PREPARING

As our work with field marking continues, we are exploring material and conceptual temporality with notational performances that rehearse architecture not as a convertible object but as an ephemeral performance. Each installation gives significance to one place at a particular moment, and then it is gone. We contemplate each pattern as the formative moment before a more enduring design might emerge. Embracing the initial tasks of formatting and calibration serves to imbue the resulting design with tropes and techniques of preparation, correlation, measurement, and arrangement. The resulting compositions are expansive open-ended arrays. They resemble the atonal dissonance of an orchestra tuning up as players find their places within the larger body. Yet these reverberations don't resolve toward a singular pitch: instead each installation is suspended in intonation, eschewing resolution in favor of distinctness and nuance. Our approach to these field paintings leaves us increasingly indifferent to simplistic notions of resolution or finality. Architecture is always a preparatory action, speculating on future actions with instructions and specifications. Blurring the boundary between representation and embodiment in architecture, we're rehearsing how to bring a spirit of preparation and generosity to other work. We will continue to mark the earth, drawing at 1:1, not as a representation of the present but as preparation for the future.

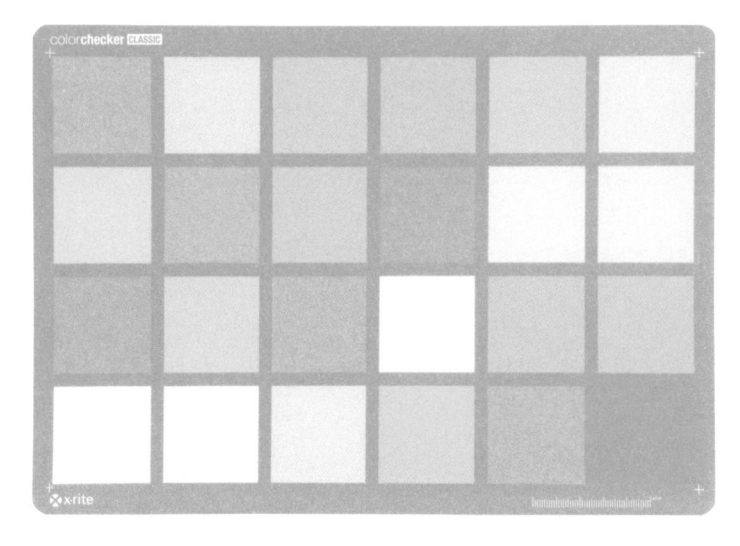

COLORCHECKER COLOR RENDITION CHART, 1976

In 1976 the ColorChecker chart was invented. It is composed of 24 squares, each rendered in matte paint on smooth paper and surrounded by a black border. Each row of colors represents one "problem" of representation. Row 1 includes "natural colors," including spectral simulations of human skin tones, the blues of sky and flowers, and green foliage. The blue flower posed the most significant technical challenge for representation, and the two skin tones demonstrate the bias of its creators. The bottom row reflects six gray tones based on a Munsell color chart. Color charts are an absolute frame for viewing the world that spans digital and analog methods of image production.

We are obsessed with the fraught landscape of color management: CMYK, RGB, RAL, and Pantone, among others. Our work with a robot designed for marking sports fields has introduced fresh challenges of color specification. While the machine can conceivably paint with any "color," this specialized paint (which experienced a shortage in 2020 due to the cancellation of sporting events) is typically available in ten colors, including North Carolina Blue, Syracuse Orange, Wesleyan Gold, and Soccer Yellow. There are more shades of blue than any other color due to the hue's popularity among American sports teams. The single shade of pink is manufactured for breast cancer awareness month, when a pink ribbon is often painted on football fields. For *Cover the Grid* and other field paintings, our color choices were designed by athletic directors, alumni groups, and the NCAA. (And let's be honest, men overwhelmingly lead these groups.)

COLOR STANDARDS FOR FROZEN FRENCH FRIED POTATOES

For $177 you can now own the perfect fry. Or at the very least you can know the precise color of the ideal golden-brown French fry according to the United States Department of Agriculture. As the Pantone website claims, "If there's one thing people agree on the world over, it's that french [sic] fries should be golden brown. But how do we communicate precisely what golden brown is best for what kind of fry? That's where Munsell comes in. Munsell is an approved supplier for the USDA and maintains an ongoing program for USDA food color standards. French fry color standards can be used to program deep fryers to ensure that the right balance of temperature, fat content, and frying duration is achieved."[2]

Page Intentionally Left Blank

The "intentionally blank" or vacat page appears as an orphan adrift in a world of unceasing information. Our digital future will surely leave this anachronistic remnant of printing conventions behind. Emblazoned with the paradoxical label "this page intentionally left blank," the vacant page may be read as a conceptual inquiry into blankness, or it may just be duplicitous. What is a hindrance or nuisance to editors and authors offers a moment of relief and repose for the weary reader. The unstoppable flow of information has stopped. Blankness is the content.

1   David Joselit, *After Art* (Princeton University Press, 2013).
2   https://www.pantone.com/munsell-usda-frozen-french-fry-standard-5-pack.

THIS PAGE INTENTIONALLY LEFT BLANK

ASHLEY BIGHAM, ERIK HERRMANN

Projective drawing, employed to portray three-dimensional information on a flat surface, is a form of camouflage where the picture plane conceals the ambiguity inherent in its illusory depth.[1] Camouflage conceals an object by either reducing its visibility or making it appear as something else. In the case of projective drawing, the positional certainty presented by the picture plane masks the assumptions, doubt, and uncertainty of the illusory pictorial space it conceals. Convention clouds perception so that the true nature of a drawing is bypassed in its reading. In architectural drawings convention ascribes meaning to each line, so without convention alternative views become viable.[2] Dispensing with the reductive notion of the picture plane as a "window" engenders opportunities for the uncertainty of pictorial space to bleed into the measurable space of reality.[3]

Dazzle camouflage was a maritime system developed in World War I. Rather than making ships "disappear," dazzle patterns used strongly contrasting graphic elements as a means of visual disruption to obfuscate their range, heading, and general position, making them difficult targets for German U-boats. Although dazzle camouflage was a wartime response to a desperate situation, it was not developed in isolation from the artistic ideas of the time and was officially invented by Norman Wilkinson, a British maritime artist.[4] The Royal Navy adopted the patterns suggested by Wilkinson and established special camoufleur units to systematically design and test the effectiveness of dazzle patterns. The USS Leviathan [Fig. 2] with a pattern designed by Wilkinson, exemplifies the strategy of breaking up the apparent profile of a ship as well as its lines of perspective, in an effort to complicate range calculations. Following the lead of the Royal Navy, the United States created its own camoufleur units with multiple divisions.[5] In general, camoufleur units consisted of a range of disciplines, including painters, sculptors, architects, stage designers, and a host of trades workers.[6] Two units were created specifically for naval camouflage, a research facility in Rochester, New York, and a design subdivision in Washington, D.C.[7]

Everett L. Warner was an impressionist painter, an educator, and a lieutenant in charge of the design subdivision of American camoufleurs.[8] The unit consisted of a handful of artists who conceived and painted dazzle patterns that were tested on model ships. Once a pattern was found to be effective, the design would be relayed to teams of architects and artists responsible for applying specific patterns to ships in the field.[9] Warner was responsible for describing the processes by which the patterns were developed and demonstrating their effectiveness to facilitate the accurate application of the patterns. For this purpose a number of didactic models were made and photographed to outline the pattern-making process visually.[10] Through trial and error[11] Warner's unit discovered a systematic means of producing effective dazzle patterns. Preliminary work in the process can be seen on the SS West Mahomet, where anamorphic perspective is employed to create a false bow from the vantage point of the photo [Fig. 3]. However, one of the most striking patterns developed by Warner and his team was the pattern painted on the USS Isanti [Figs. 1, 5, 6] where the dazzle pattern not only employs anamorphic perspective, but also uses the apparent displacement of solid geometry in dazzle pattern development. Writing in multiple articles after the war, Warner gave cursory descriptions of some of the strategies used to create effective camouflage:

> We had found that certain patterns and movements of line produced certain effects, and in casting about to learn the reason we realized that it was because these patterns gave the impression of being painted upon the surface of definite geometric solids placed in definite positions in regard to the eye.[12]

> There is nothing really mysterious about the fundamental principles [of dazzle patterns]. They involve for the most part merely a new application of the principles of solid geometry.[13]

This description, along with photos of the process, suggests the manipulation of components that make up projective-drawing systems.[14] Figures 5 and 6 are redrawn examples of Warner's solid geometry process. In this process, Warner shows the geometric solids he references as actual physical solids that exist in front of the ship. Their geometric appearances are then collapsed back onto the ship through a projective-drawing process. In some cases the solids create a reverse perspective on the ship's hull. In other cases the ship model is literally cut up and bent then projected back onto a second hull as a means of perceptual distortion.

The concept of the picture plane is foundational to the system of projective drawing. Not only is the picture plane the physical means through which the drawing is viewed, it is also a threshold separating the bodily space of the viewer from the illusory pictorial space beyond. Projective drawing can be seen as the systematic process of geometrizing pictorial depth so that it can be treated the same as measurable space. Panofsky describes perspective as "a translation of the psychophysiological space into mathematical space; in other words, an objectification of the subjective."[15] However this method of objectification requires a stable system. The picture plane must remain orthogonal to the projectors, and the geometry in pictorial space must not move beyond the picture plane.

If Warner's method of dazzle-pattern production were collapsed into a projective-drawing system, almost all of the elements of the projection system would be disrupted. As can be seen in Figure 6, A perfectly flat picture plane is replaced with the undulating surface of a ship's hull. The geometry to be projected onto the picture plane resides outside of pictorial space and collapses onto the picture plane from real space. The projectors used to project the geometry orthogonally onto the picture plane intersect with the perspectival projectors traced to the station point of the U-boat periscope. This has the effect of bending orthogonal projectors and displacing the picture plane. Lastly, the viewer does not remain orthogonal to the picture plane since a U-boat may come upon the ship from any angle. Therefore the camouflage must perform well from all angles. The resulting projection onto the ship was intended to cause visual ambiguity so that the vessel's bearing and position were difficult to establish.

DAZZLE ANALYSIS

When analyzed as a projective-drawing system, dazzle camouflage inverted the certainty of projective drawing and replaced it with ambiguity, uncertainty, and doubt. Within a drawing system, doubt is detrimental to construction and communication, but for a designer such visual uncertainty often leads to the spawning of ideas. This simple observation has been the root of much of my experimental work.

Over the past four years I have dedicated a portion of my drawn work to what I call "Working Drawings." Unlike architectural working drawings, which enable drawn information to be translated into a material representation, I intend the drawings themselves to do the work—much like dazzle camouflage. The ultimate aim is to enable ideas to be seen in drawings that are not found within the conventional limitation of the projective-drawing system. I have not abandoned the system of projective drawing—a move too easily accomplished—but have sought to expand it. Like the various approaches to dazzle camouflage, the primary method of exploration has been the development of drawing processes that flex and/or displace the relationships of system components in projective drawing (projectors,

Figure 1. USS Issanti. The dazzle pattern painted on the USS Issanti is one of the best illustrations of Warner's block projection method of camouflage design.

Figure 2. USS Leviathan. Dazzle design by Norman Wilkinson, exhibiting strategies of amodal completion, false perspective and object scalar destabilization.

the picture plane, and geometric relationships to both). Because projective drawings are inherently reductive,[16] the ongoing "Working Drawing" series constitutes a search for how they can be used beyond their reductive limitations and fixed conventional meanings without a loss of descriptive capabilities.

A primary starting point in my work was the development of a drawing system by which I could describe the effects of displaced projective-drawing system components. For me this was the equivalent of the modeling systems and photographs Warner used to describe the effectiveness of dazzle patterns. Although I use projective component-displacement strategies similar to those used by Warner, the intent and outcome differ from dazzle.[17] Whereas dazzle patterns sought to disrupt the apparent location of a physical object, I am seeking to develop a spatial association or intuition of an absent physical object through disruptions in pictorial space and drawn visual graphics.

Figure 3. USS West Mahomet. A somewhat distorted anamorphic project of a false bow can be seen in the center of the photograph. USS West Mahomet, dazzle design by Frederick J. Waugh (Behrens, *Ship-Shape*, 200).

Figure 4. Everett L. Warner, center, with model ships for testing dazzle patterns.

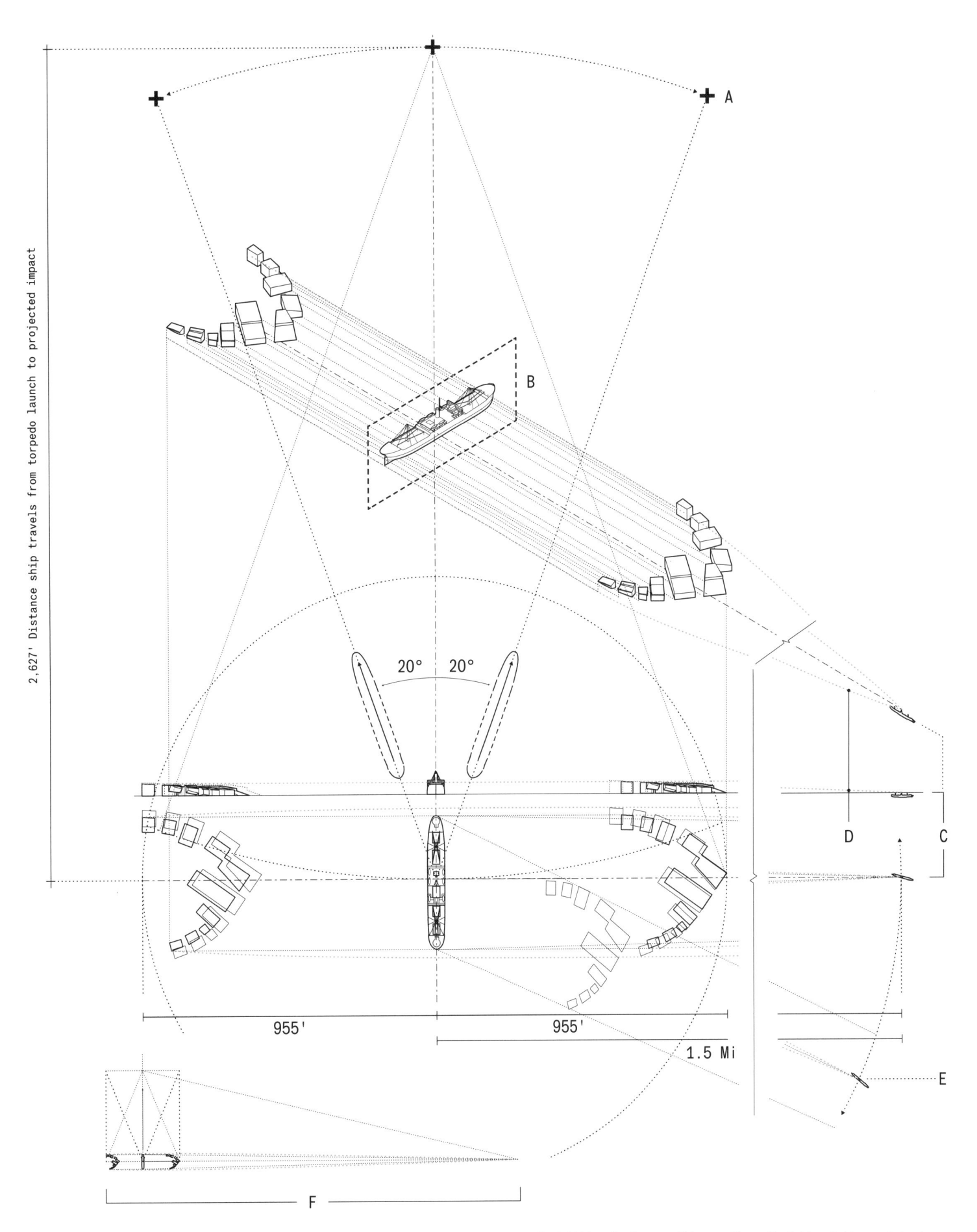

2,627' Distance ship travels from torpedo launch to projected impact

Figure 5. Solid Geometry Derived from SS. Isanti's Starboard Dazzle Pattern. In 1919, an MIT study found an average of 20°-30° error in perceived ship bearing due to dazzle camouflage. To illustrate an instance of perceived displacement of the Warner's block projection method, here the minimum 20° error would place a ship 955' away from its targeted location, if the ship is traveling at 11 knots (typical WWI merchant ship top speed) and a German G/6 Torpedo is fired at a distance of 1.5 miles away (Warner's testing tank distance) at 35 knots. [In this illustration, the average bearing errors presented in the MIT study is used only as a metric to visualize a perceptual error. For more on the original study by Leo S. Blodgett, see Behrens, *Disruption versus Dazzle*, 8].

A   Variability in the possible locations of ship based upon a 20° bearing error
B   Absence of definitive picture plane leading to ambiguity of ship location
C   Station point of U-boat periscope
D   Silver lines indicate the bending of projectors— breaking down the certainty typically present in a projective process
E   Variable station point of U-boat changes apparent projection of dazzle pattern
F   Proportion of dazzle projection displacement at the full 1.5 mile viewing distance.

JEROME TRYON

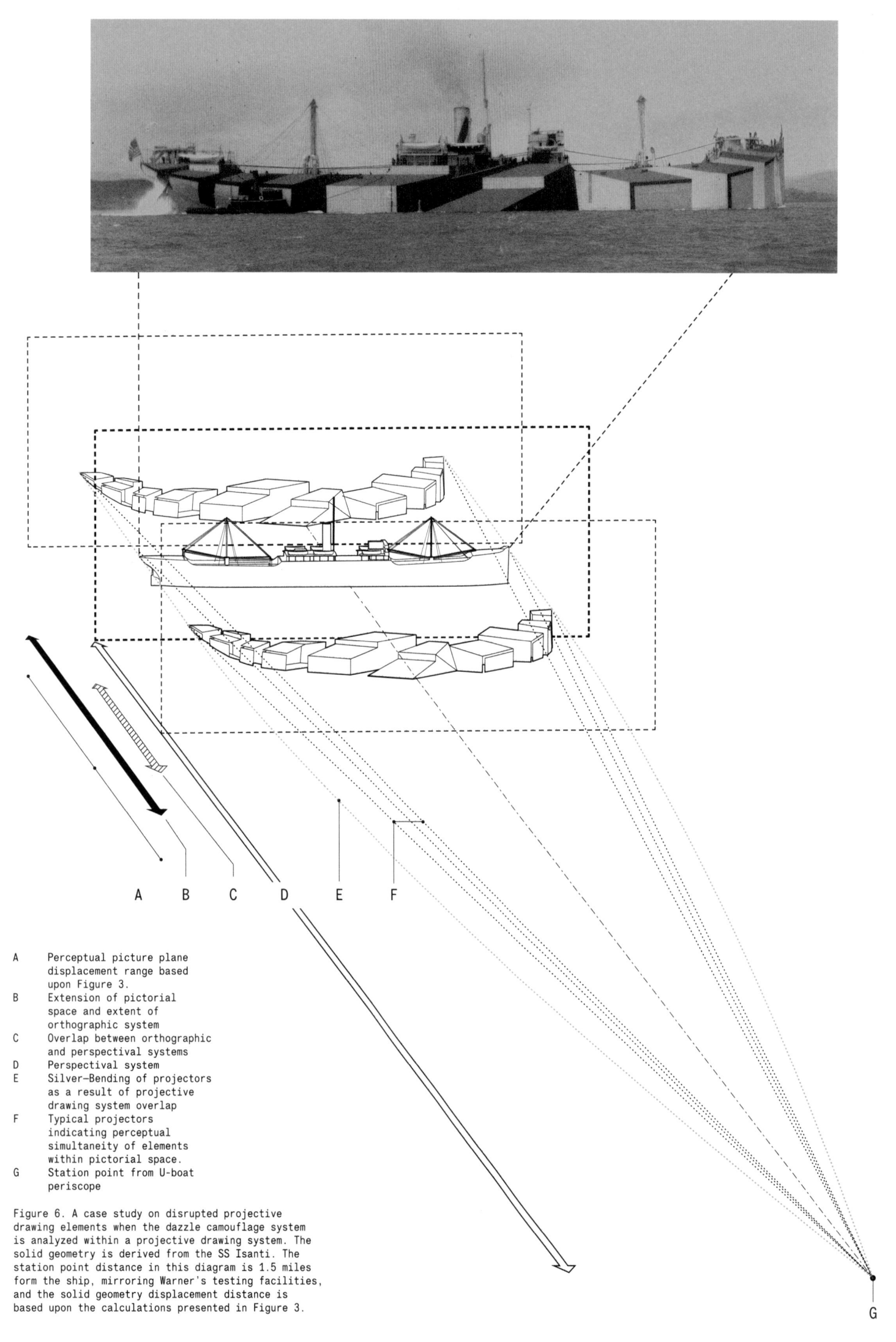

A   Perceptual picture plane
    displacement range based
    upon Figure 3.
B   Extension of pictorial
    space and extent of
    orthographic system
C   Overlap between orthographic
    and perspectival systems
D   Perspectival system
E   Silver-Bending of projectors
    as a result of projective
    drawing system overlap
F   Typical projectors
    indicating perceptual
    simultaneity of elements
    within pictorial space.
G   Station point from U-boat
    periscope

Figure 6. A case study on disrupted projective
drawing elements when the dazzle camouflage system
is analyzed within a projective drawing system. The
solid geometry is derived from the SS Isanti. The
station point distance in this diagram is 1.5 miles
form the ship, mirroring Warner's testing facilities,
and the solid geometry displacement distance is
based upon the calculations presented in Figure 3.

FROM CAMOUFLAGE TO MEMORY: PROJECTIVE DRAWING AND THE ILLUSION OF SPACE

For Warner's photos geometric solids of dazzle patterns were represented in model form and placed some distance in front of the ship's hull. Although the solids were modeled in physical form, they represented a perceived object that would be collapsed onto the picture plane (the ship's hull). This process reverses the typical relationship of geometric projection onto a picture plane and, therefore, conflates pictorial space with measurable mathematical space. Though this inversion disrupts the elements of the projective system, it can easily be described by a conventional plan cut. Similarly if a plan cut can be used to describe the perception of geometry in front of the picture plane, it can do the same for geometry inhabiting the pictorial space behind.

I call this approach to cutting into the perceived space behind the picture plane a "z-cut," as it is a cut in the Z direction of the image and does not necessarily favor either section or plan logic. Z-cuts work on the same conceptual grounds as conventional cut drawings, but with a few conventional updates to accommodate the cutting of perceptual rather than mathematical geometry. Because of the subjective nature of a z-cut, the geometry within the cut can be expected to inhabit different spatial configurations and depths simultaneously.[18] Geometric simultaneity is accounted for by denoting primary and secondary readings within the cut as well as their likely direction of slippage. This methodology allows me to make an objective projection of a subjective reading of a drawing. As a mode of projective drawing, z-cuts relinquish the exhaustive certainty of orthographic drawing while retaining its measurability. Z-cuts are quite similar procedurally to the modeling processes present in Warner's photos but offer more flexibility in the design process.

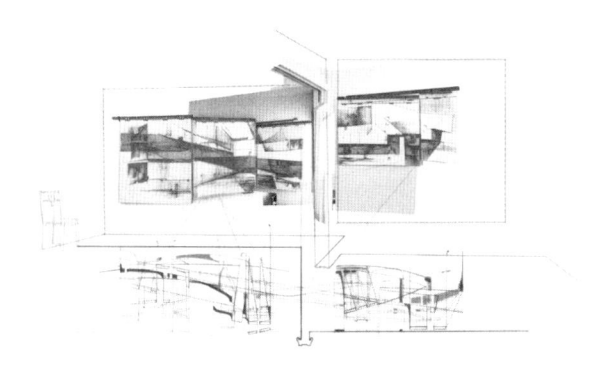

WORKING DRAWING 1

I became interested in using z-cuts as a design methodology where I could design the reading of a drawing's pictorial space before creating the image of that drawing—just as the 3D facsimiles of dazzle patterns were sometimes designed first and then collapsed onto the ship's hull. My first implementation of this process was for a large drawing installation (16 by 4.5 feet): A single image displayed on two offset walls of adjoining rooms that operated as a folded picture plane disrupting pictorial space. Because the image occupied parts of two rooms, it was not visible in its entirety from a single vantage point. To experience the whole image a visitor had to move from one room to the other, engaging the faculty of memory rather than immediate perception.

Because drawings are by nature one-sided, elevations derived from z-cuts do not require a fixed sidedness to the picture plane, so elevations can be projected in front of or behind it without changing the content of the elevation. This has the effect of allowing the perceived location of the picture plane to shift forward and backward in the analytical construction process of the image. As with dazzle camouflage, if the picture plane can be seen as being forward or behind the drawing surface, then the illusive realm of pictorial space can observably enter objective measurable space within the projective construction of the drawing. Yet I was interested in exploring the possibility of mnemonic cognizance of geometry designed in pictorial space, in contrast to dazzle camouflage, where optical disruption was the goal.

WORKING DRAWINGS 2 & 3

For subsequent iterations of the "Working Drawings," I displaced parts of the projective process more explicitly. As a means of dynamic displacement, I constructed operable steel frameworks to house multiple drawings within the same work. To see one of these "Working Drawings" fully, the viewer must move, either in a single moment or over multiple viewings. In either case the drawing, like architectural space, must become an artifact of memory to be seen as a whole.

Rather than using abstract geometry to create abstraction, as in "Working Drawing 1," the later drawings employed seemingly recognizable architectural elements to activate preconceived ideas about space, form, history, and meaning. These fragments of architecture imply strong tectonic and spatial characteristics leading to spatial implications. The drawings were completed from memory, so they contain the distortions and incompleteness of a remembered image while also exhibiting the assumptions and extrapolations created during the nonreferential drawing process. Due to the imperfections of translating a memory into a drawing, the subject matter achieves a degree of separation from any specific historical object, simply becoming a categorical fragment with assumed referential specificity.

Within the total work, the appearance of referential specificity in the drawn portions is important as it allows the representation of the architectural fragment to become an anchor of memory, or a mnemonic reference point grounding the presence of the work. If seen in this way, the presence of the fragment image serves as a type of dynamic icon, its presentation in the flat or very shallow pictorial space pulling it into the space of the operable framework rather than allowing it to recede into pictorial space.

In his discussion of the use of flat pictorial space in religious iconography, Alberto Pérez-Gómez states that "iconic mimesis was neither an essential identity nor a realistic reproduction."[19] Therefore the icon invokes through the visible world the presence of the invisible, which simultaneously enters architectural space while being shielded from representational certainty through the flatness of pictorial depth.[20] While religious icons were meant to invoke the presence of the divine, my work has the less lofty goal of invoking memories of spatial conditions tied to a viewer's former experiences. This type of memory is what E. H. Gombrich labels "the beholder's share."[21] Eric R. Kandel writes that, as in the central idea of Gestalt psychology, "what we see—our interpretation of any element in an image—depends not just on the properties of that element, but also on its interaction with other elements in the image and with our past experiences with similar images."[22] In short, Kandel and Gombrich assert that personal memory affects the way we see images. However within the "Working Drawing" series, the mobility and variable compositional parts of each framework complicate a true "iconic" reading of a work while disrupting the singular state of the beholder's share. This double disruption allows for an interplay between memory, pictorial depth, image, and spatial reality.

WORKING DRAWING 2

In "Working Drawing 2" the large arch was developed as a primary anchor of memory—something over which the images on the folding steel framework could operate, either redacting or completing portions of the total work depending on the disposition of the viewer. However only part of the work could be covered, allowing the primary drawing to maintain referential hierarchy. This hierarchy led to a nondisruptive clarity, diminishing the possibility of productive ambiguity in the work.

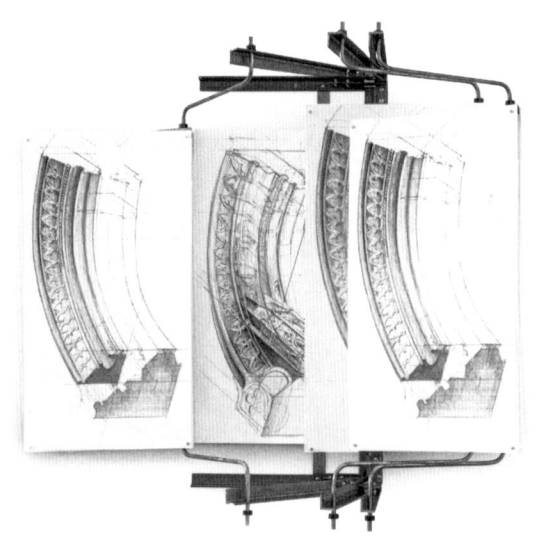

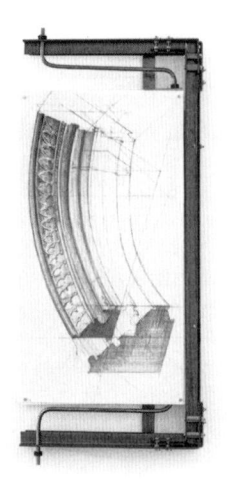

WORKING DRAWING 3

In "Working Drawing 3" less hierarchy is maintained by the fixed image on the wall because the framework holds an equally large image that can be moved to completely obscure or complement the stationary image. Producing a lack of hierarchy in the drawing images was an attempt to allow the operable framework to be perceived more as a part of the composition of the total work and less as a frame. As with "Working Drawing 2," my interest focused on exploring how the operation of the frameworks function over time; by moving the compositions day by day, my exploration sculpted the overall memory of the works. My hope was that the memory images would approach the complexity of the compilation photographs [Fig. 9] since the total work can be perceived only retrospectively in memory. Because the desired holistic representation of the work is a memory image, the completed work is impossible to capture in a photograph, or even a video. Therefore the photos serve only as a type of secondary description of the completed work, not a true documentation.

The hinged movement of the steel frameworks allows the drawings to be viewed at multiple angles, breaking down the expectation of a singular orthogonal viewing angle for the overall work. When the drawings are rotated, the illusory depth of the image is reduced as the measurable space occupied by the drawing is increased. Simultaneously the spatial framework that usually describes the perceived orientation of a geometric volume behind the picture plane becomes visually ascribed to the picture plane itself.[23]

In the dazzle patterns analyzed, the spatial framework and the picture plane were conflated to create the illusion of false proximity as a defensive mechanism for the ships. In a type of inverse relationship, the physical movement of the "Working Drawings" breaks the illusion of false proximity within pictorial depth, causing the conflation of picture plane and spatial framework. This device solidifies the perception of the object as a flat representation in the drawing. Or, stated differently, as the steel framework is operated and produces movement of the picture plane, objects in the drawing can be understood more clearly as allusions to the existence of categorically similar objects rather than illusions of the objects themselves.

Typically associated with Cubism, the flattening of pictorial space to provoke a secondary reading of spatial depth is described by Colin Rowe and Robert Slutzky as *phenomenal transparency*.[24] However this operation depends on a universal frontal picture plane. This is not how I see the flatness in the tiltable picture planes of my work. When tilted forward, the images discourage the reading of a universal frontal picture plane; and, as tilted, they set up an inverse relationship between pictorial and physical depth. The flatness of pictorial depth when the framework is moved into some positions does not lead to phenomenal transparency. Instead two other responses are triggered in the viewing of the work: First, the viewer inevitably tries to employ cognitive mental rotation to correct the distortions of the image, producing conceptual displacement.[25] Second, the viewer employs memory to recognize and categorize what is being seen in terms of what has been seen before.[26] Therefore working memory is employed in the movement of the picture plane, noting its current and former positioning, and long-term memory is employed in categorizing the objects seen in the drawing.

In relationship to projective drawing, the physical displacement of the picture planes by the steel framework expands the overall work, disrupting any reading of a singular frontal picture plane. This is similar to how the undulating surface of a ship's hull complicates a typical picture-plane reading within the dazzle analysis. In both cases the result is an overlap between the projectors from pictorial space and their interaction with a mobile station point in three-dimensional space. In "Working Drawings 2 and 3" the displacement of the projected images bends the projectors, in effect, since the orthographic systems of the hand-drawn elements have a nonplanar transition to the conical projectors of perspectival space [reference Figure 6 of dazzle analysis for an analogous condition]. Serving as the threshold between an uneven transition of orthographic and perspectival projective systems, the steel framework becomes a part of the projective system as an apparatus affecting the picture plane, the spatial frameworks, and the pictorial depth of the work. Each "Working Drawing" is not presented as a whole that can be seen with the immediacy of a single image. In these works I am interested in how drawings can prolong the experience of seeing to extend into time, and in turn transform time into memory.

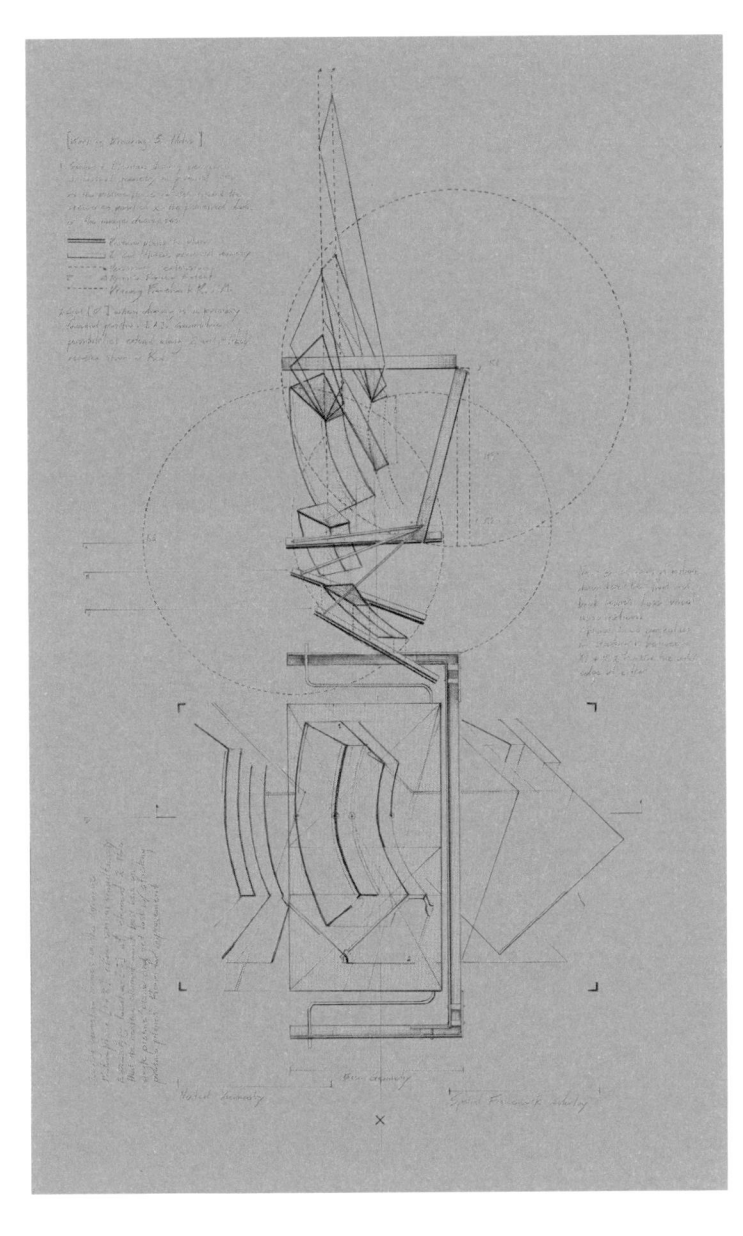

CONCLUSION

At the inception of a new form of drawing, a device or apparatus has often been integral to the medium. The first public demonstration of perspectival drawing by Filippo Brunelleschi was an entire device that included a drawing stand, a mirror, and a hole punched in the drawing.[27] Albrecht Dürer famously created multiple woodcuts outlining perspectival devices involving hinged picture planes, grids, station-point stabilizers, and taut strings as projectors.[28] In the myth of Butades—depicted in the eighteenth-century *The Origin of Painting* (*The Maid of Corinth*), by David Allan—a candle was part of a 3D system used in the collapse of geometry outside of the picture plane onto the 2D surface of the wall,[29] which is not dissimilar to Werner's method of collapsing solid geometry onto a ship's hull.[30] In all of these cases the apparatus disrupts the pictorial space, just like Warner's geometric solids do in dazzle-pattern design. In a similar way I am attempting to use apparatuses and devices as a part of a drawing so that the built apparatus and the drawing are inseparable. Typically as a deeper understanding of the work is produced with the assistance of an apparatus, the apparatus no longer becomes necessary, and the work can be replicated on a singular picture plane. Although this type of spatial collapse is possible in my work, I am more interested in the possibilities present when this collapse is resisted. Unlike the examples given, where the apparatus and drawing are used as a means of proof, in my work the apparatus is the means of exploration.

Although I have outlined strategies and ideas that have both driven and been derived from this series of drawings, the descriptions presented here by no means exhaust the readings or process of the work. First and foremost, the "Working Drawings" series is a method of exploration, a means by which the creative journey takes place with a continually evolving set of approaches for spatial and conceptual discovery. The process is iterative and ongoing. The "Working Drawings" were never intended to be works of art or polemical tools placed within a discursive context. Rather they are the result of a working process of experimentation within the projective-drawing system.

As a system of mathematical logic, projective drawing is well established and has been proven indispensable since Gaspard Monge fully solidified the system of projective geometry, in the late 1700s.[31] Although projective drawing has been proclaimed dead any number of times,[32] its translation into the visual medium of interface between the user and almost all design software has, in my opinion, immortalized its logic rather than secured its death. The inescapability of projective logic and the absolute mathematical precision present in design software creates an unquestioned spatial certainty that I have attempted to move beyond in this work.

The streamlined digital processes that operate on the principles of descriptive geometry are extremely effective for design documentation and construction, but to use the same processes as the sole means of ideation and exploration is like conflating the act of composing with the performance. In closing his extensive work *The Projective Cast*, Robin Evans states, "My purpose here is to show how projection—or rather quasi-projection—breaches the bounds between the world and self, the objective and the subjective."[33] If dazzle camouflage, as I have argued, dissolves and displaces the picture plane, bends projectors, and intermingles pictorial and measurable space, it is one of the breaches that Evans speaks of—a rift in the threshold between the objective and subjective. Through my "Working Drawings" I am looking for an adjacent rift: A space where memory, image, projection, and time intersect, opening up new possibilities for seeing into drawings while allowing the projective system of drawings to surpass their conventional orthographic limitations.

1. As I use the term in this article, projective drawing means the collapse of 3D information onto a 2D plane. Systems of projective drawings are usually broken down into orthographic and perspectival; however, the distinction between these systems becomes interrupted in my personal work and the examples of dazzle camouflage I examine. Therefore, I find it most useful to use the general term projective drawing to describe the overall parent system.
2. Eric R. Kandel, *The Age of Insight: The Quest to Understand the Unconscious in Art, Mind, and Brain, from Vienna 1900 to the Present* (New York: Random House, 2012), Chap. 11.
3. Erwin Panofsky, *Perspective as Symbolic Form.* (New York: Zone Books, 1991), Chap. 2. When using the term *reality* I am following Panofsky's description of reality as "the actual subjective optical impression [of the space we bodily inhabit]."
4. Roy R Behrens, *Disruption versus Dazzle: Prevalent Misunderstandings About World War I Ship Camouflage*, 2018. http://www.bobolinkbooks.com/Camoupedia/DazzleCamouflage/dazzle.html. A notable naval artist, Norman Wilkinson is officially credited with the invention of dazzle camouflage, though John Graham Kerr actually first recommended a similar strategy to the Royal Navy. Kerr's method addressed mainly disruptive coloration and not the perspectival disruption present in Wilkinson's method. For an overview see Behrens, Disruption versus Dazzle.
5. Roy R. Behrens, *False Colors: Art, Design, and Modern Camouflage.* (Dysart, IA: Bobolink Books, 2002), 93–94.
6. E. Malcolm Parkinson, "The Artist at War." *Prologue* 44, no. 1 (Spring 2012). https://www.archives.gov/publications/prologue/2012/spring/camouflage.html.
7. Behrens, False Colors, 94.
8. Behrens, False Colors, 94.
9. Evertt L. Warner, "The Science of Ship Camouflage," in Roy R. Behrens, *Ship Shape, a Dazzle Camouflage Sourcebook: An Anthology of Writings About Ship Camouflage During World War I.* (Dysart, IA: Bobolink Books, 2012), 220.
10. Ibid., 220.
11. Behrens, *False Colors*, 94. Norman Wilkinson visited the United States in March 1918 to present how dazzle patterns worked to President Wilson and the secretary of the U.S. Navy. Warner was his escort during the visit. Although it is apparent that Wilkinson could demonstrate that dazzle patterns worked, Warner implies there was not yet a systematic method of application at that time (Warner, "Science of Ship Camouflage," 204).
12. Everett L. Warner, "Fooling the Iron Fish," in Behrens, Ship Shape, 220.
13. Warner, "The Science of Ship Camouflage," 220.
14. Warner, "Fooling the Iron Fish," 201–2. Warner and Wilkinson both stated explicitly that dazzle camouflage was effective because of its manipulation of perspective. Warner writes, "Reverse perspective was the most important aid to deception which we used at first … but we soon made excursions into solid geometry, and our development of design in that direction constitutes, in my opinion, the American contribution to the dazzle system".(Regarding the disruption of U-boat distance calculations when viewing a dazzled ship, Wilkinson writes, "The mere breaking up of a vessel's form by strongly contrasting colours would not achieve this end without careful study of the perspective and balance of the design" (Wilkinson, Norman. "Camouflage of Ships of War." *Nature* 103 (June 1919): 304–5. https://doi-org.yale.idm.oclc.org/10.1038/103304d0.). In this letter to Nature, Wilkinson was defending himself as the inventor of the dazzle system, effectively differentiating it from the system developed by John Graham Kerr on the grounds of perspective distortion rather than "obliterative colouring," as described by Abbott Thayer, of which Kerr was a proponent. See—Murphy, Hugh, and Martin Bellamy. "The Dazzling Zoologist." *The Northern Mariner/Le marin du nord* 19, no. 2 (April 2009).
15. Panofsky, *Perspective*, 99.
16. Alberto Pérez-Gómez, and Louise Pelletier. "Architectural Representation beyond Perspectivism." *Perspecta* 27 (1992): 21–39. https://doi.org/10.2307/1567174.
17. In this study I am using the following elements of projective drawing: the picture plane, orthographic projectors, perspectival projectors, pictorial space (the illusory space beyond the picture plane), and the perspectival station point.
18. François Bucher, *Josef Albers: Despite Straight Lines, an Analysis of His Graphic Constructions.* (New Haven, CT: Yale University Press, 1961), 12–13.
19. Alberto Pérez-Gómez, and Louise Pelletier, *Architectural Representation and the Perspective Hinge* (Cambridge, MA: MIT Press, 1997), 89.
20. Ibid.
21. E. H. Gombrich, *Art and Illusion: A Study in the Psychology of Pictorial Representation* (Princeton, NJ: Princeton University Press, 1969), 181.
22. Kandel, *Age of Insight*, 304.
23. Rudolf Arnheim, *Art and Visual Perception: A Psychology of the Creative Eye.* Expanded and revised edition. (Berkeley, CA: University of California Press, 1974), 290.
24. Colin Rowe and Robert Slutzky. "Transparency: Literal and Phenomenal." *Perspecta* 8 (1963): 45–54. https://doi.org/10.2307/1566901.
25. Gombrich, *Art and Illusion*, 52.
26. Ibid., 181.
27. Martin Kemp, *The Science of Art: Optical Themes in Western Art from Brunelleschi to Seurat* (New Haven, CT: Yale University Press, 1990) 11, 12.
28. Robin Evans, *The Projective Cast: Architecture and Its Three Geometries* (Cambridge, MA: MIT Press, 1995), 127–28.
29. Robin Evans, "Translations from Drawing to Building." *AA Files*, no. 12 (1986): 3–18. http://www.jstor.org/stable/29543512.
30. Warner, "Fooling the Iron Fish," 195.
31. Alberto Pérez-Gómez, "Architecture as Drawing." *JAE* 36, no. 2 (1982): 2–7. https://doi.org/10.2307/1424613. 3.
32. Mario Carpo, *The Second Digital Turn: Design Beyond Intelligence* (Cambridge, MA: MIT Press, 2017), 99.
33. Evans, *The Projective Cast*, 369.

DOMINO SUGAR FACTORY OR, WHAT IS A REAL PHOTOGRAPH?

Noah Kalina

IMAGE V. PHOTOGRAPH

Perspecta 56 — Your work seems to be constantly ruminating on the nature of images in different ways. In *Newsletter #117: Domino Sugar Factory* you describe your former home, next to the Domino Sugar Refinery in Brooklyn, NY, through images that encapsulate a specific time in your life and that ultimately frame an inevitable change to both the factory and your home, and to yourself. *Newsletter #118: What is a Real Photograph?* asks what is perhaps a rhetorical question in order to examine the process of photography through its analog and digital production.

Perhaps a good place to start, then, is with the question: What is an image, and what is a photograph? People often unintentionally say "image" instead of "photograph," and vice versa. The terms seem colloquially interchangeable, but the implications of both in analog and digital production are significant.

Noah Kalina — I happen to dislike the word "image." Many photographers are used to saying "images." That's been going on for a while. I don't think it really matters. You'd have to be a real purist to insist that "it's only a photograph." I suppose it does relate to what constitutes a genuine photograph because it's essentially just an image on the screen. Perhaps the distinction lies in considering this as a photograph. That might be why I've never liked using the word "image" to describe a photo on the screen, because it feels like you're not taking it seriously since it's not real.

P56 — The use of the word "image" is prevalent in architecture, and not only in terms of visual representation. It takes on multiple, significant meanings when considering the relationships between architecture's ideation, production, and the social realities it ultimately engenders; the multimedial nature of images becomes part of how the world is conceived and consumed. This relationship is something we want to explore with you.

ANALOG V. DIGITAL

P56 — We'd like to delve further into how you perceive analog and digital images today. Have any changes emerged from the distinctions you describe in *Newsletter #118: What is a Real Photograph?*, and how have they influenced your work process? This relates to the time when you were living in Williamsburg and creating the series of photographs "Pictures That Look Like This," with a distinct analog aesthetic.

NK — This is so interesting because it's highly specific to me. I wouldn't say it's influenced by timing, culture, or whatever, but rather the particular period between 2007 and 2012. During that time, my life and career were in a unique phase. Additionally, it's connected to where the internet stood at that point and how people were sharing and creating photos. It still felt like there was a significant presence of legacy media, including print materials and magazines, where the goal was to achieve a print publication because it still had a broader reach. Simultaneously, it's intriguing because I believe these elements haven't entirely disappeared. It's just that my current interests and involvements have shifted. I've grown older and perhaps a bit more fatigued, and I don't engage with as much content as before. I've settled into my own routines regarding how the internet operates and where we showcase our work. I feel that during the period when I created pictures with this particular aesthetic, I named it so because it resonated with the prevalent style of point-and-shoot photography in the mid- to late-2000s. I'm certain this style still exists to some extent.

Although, at that time, it was like the peak-of-ice magazine, with a focus on what they were doing and the gritty, dirty fashion genre that existed, which was not as

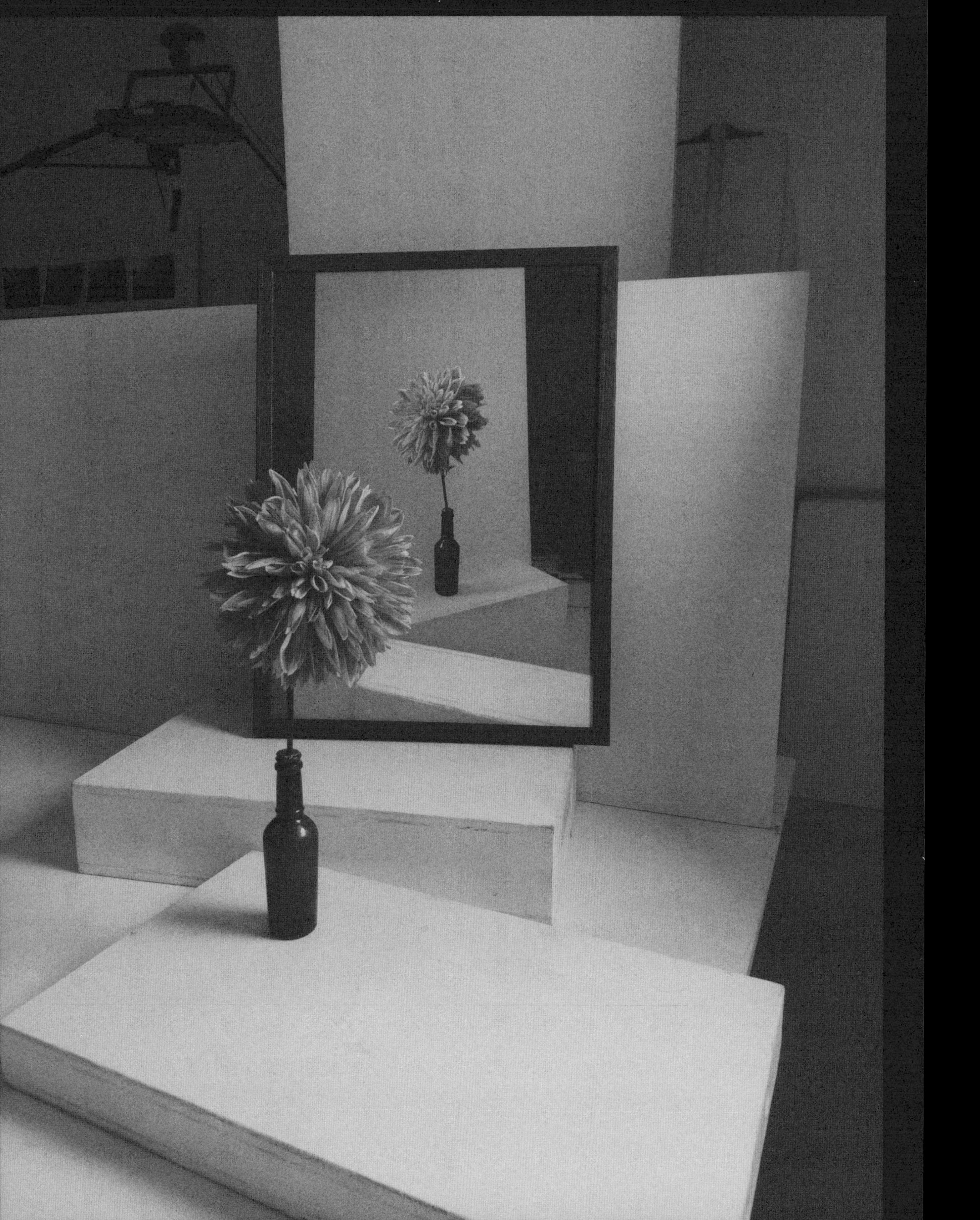

NEWSLETTER #118:
WHAT IS A REAL PHOTOGRAPH?

What is a *real* photograph?

Does the type of camera you use make a photograph more or less *real*?

Is a photograph made with an iPhone camera less *real* than a photograph made with a fifty thousand dollar medium format camera?

Of course not. The tool doesn't determine whether a photograph is real or not.

(All of the photos in this newsletter were made with an iPhone.)

So... When does a photograph actually become *real*?

Is a photograph only a *real* photograph when it becomes a print?

If a photograph never becomes a print, does that mean the photographs in this newsletter aren't *real*?

These days, the vast majority of photographs are made with digital cameras. This means the majority of photography exists in the middle of the spectrum of what's considered digital and physical art.

On one side of the spectrum, you have art that was created entirely on the computer, and its final form is best experienced with the use of a computer. This type of art includes 3D art, pixel art, generative art, etc.

On the other side of this spectrum, you have works that are entirely produced with physical objects, in a physical environment, and the final output is best experienced in real life. Those art forms include painting, sculpture, dance, theater, etc.

Photography is in the middle.

Photography combines both physical aspects (both the tool and the construction of a photograph happen in the physical environment), but the capture and editing process happens in a digital environment.

So does a photograph only become real when it's made into a physical print?

Is the print what makes a photograph *real* because the print is a physical object?

When you look at photographs on a screen, is what you're looking at only a digital representation of a real photograph?

Personally, I think both are real.

What do you think?

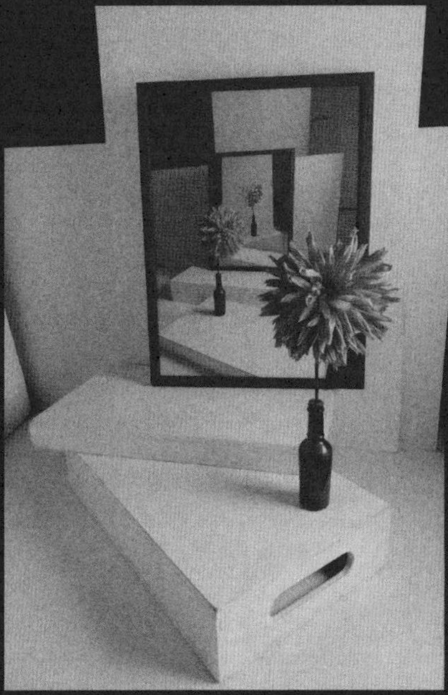
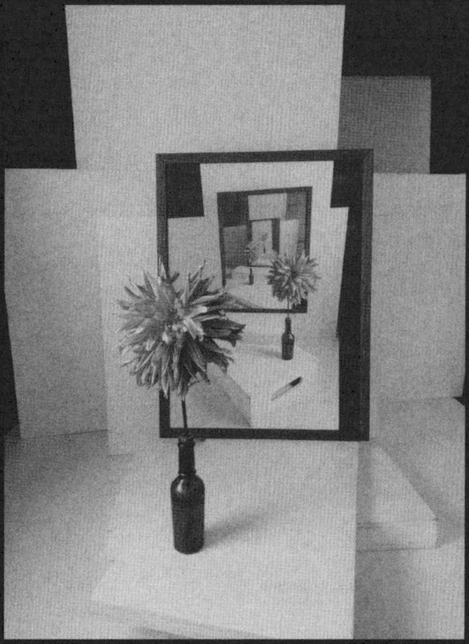
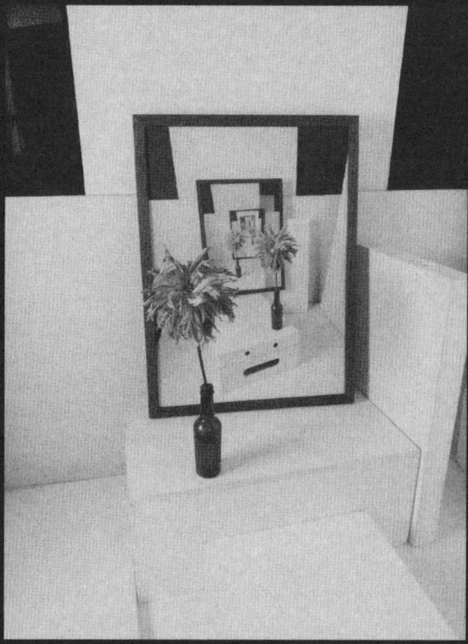
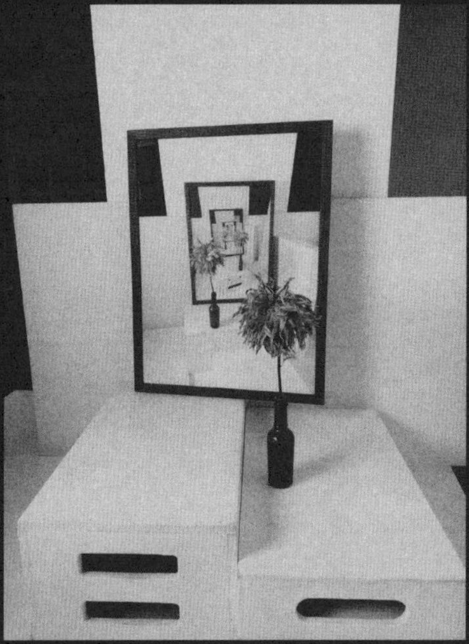
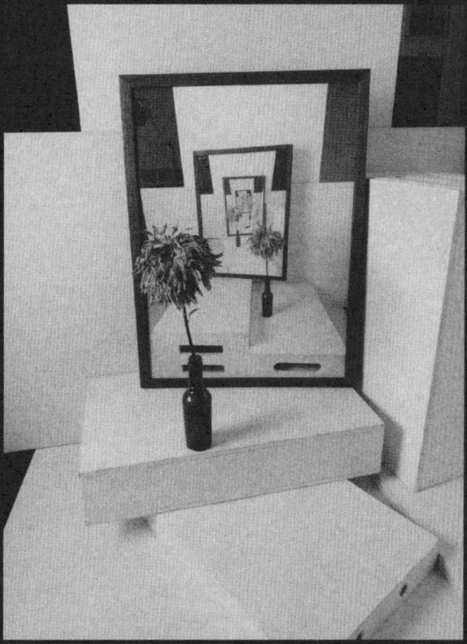
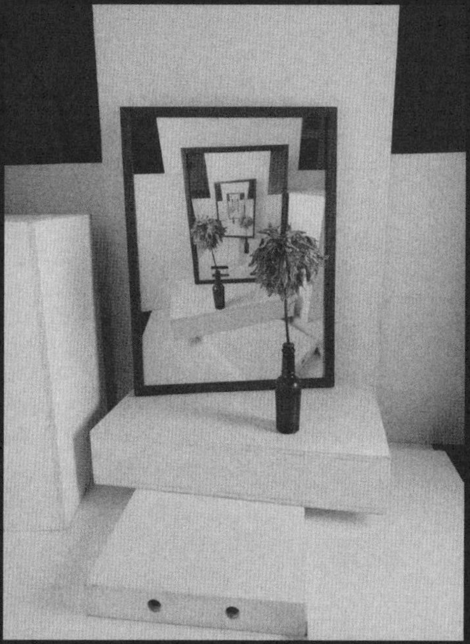
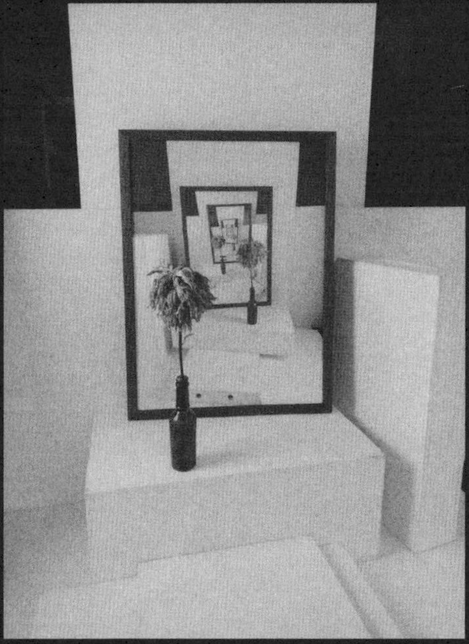

clean as digital photography became. By using that term, I was referring to pictures with such a style, and many photographers were pursuing it during that period, especially emerging from Brooklyn. How does it relate to what constitutes a real photograph? In some ways, I believe you are onto something, because working with analog felt more genuine or authentic, possibly because we used film and produced physical prints. You're correct that these images ultimately ended up on the internet, but they started as analog. I did want to ask you about that, though, what do you consider analog at this point? What does analog mean to you?

P56 Perhaps another way to see it is to question what is truly analog since at least the time of the internet we're discussing.

NK There's a bit of nostalgia at play here. When I was doing it, I was indulging in nostalgia for shooting film, and that was around 15 years ago. It's amusing that it's making a comeback now. Essentially, it's a trend, and it's become quite a significant genre. These photographers aren't just influencers in photography but also influencers in gear. I believe they adopt this role because, ultimately, the only way to sustain as an influencer is by selling the gear you use. They've exhausted all the digital equipment they can promote, so now they're considering film photography, especially if they didn't start with it. I began with film, then transitioned to digital, thinking, "This is the way forward," but what if you started with film and now want to go back? Maybe that's their way of progressing? In a sense, technology was phased out, it declined in quality, and now it's improving again.

It's complex, though, in many respects. From my perspective, I'm not certain if I'm paying enough attention to truly understand the motivations behind these individuals, aside from seeking popularity. I guess they're creating art. They probably are. I'm sure it is. I'm sure it's all wonderful.

PRINT ON SCREEN

P56 Do you think it's purely an aesthetic thing? It's like using a filter, it's about the object and the image of that object. Do you think it's more about that than any interest in the process or because of the fact that, for example, in film, you don't have a pixelated image, but you're instead employing the chemical process of photography to certain effects?

NK It's amusing. It's probably more like the filter is already applied, so they don't have to do it in Photoshop. It could be like that, the natural filter they attempted to replicate solely through Photoshop. Now, it's like the genuine version.

P56 Yes, sometimes you'll see people on Instagram posting a photo of a Polaroid.

NK I do like that. In fact, for a long time, and I still think about it occasionally, I wanted to post only pictures of prints. Some people do that to emphasize that it's actually a tangible object, not just a JPEG on the screen. It can be exhausting or not, I'm not sure. It can also become a matter of aesthetic choices, like how to photograph a print with the right background. Then you start thinking, "I might as well just post the image." People do that with borders too. They add borders around their photos to create a box in between, making it appear as if the JPEG isn't just filling the entire screen on the phone.

P56 Wasn't that one of the first options on Instagram?

NK Yes.

TIME-BASED MEDIA

P56   In fact, one of the main attractions to Instagram at first was the ability to not only share images, but to enhance them with preset filters.

Speaking of which, it's interesting to consider time-of-creation in relation to your famous time-based project. You're up there with some of the first to go digitally viral in the early days of YouTube—we imagine that your feature in *The Simpsons*, in "Homer Takes a Picture a Day for 39 Years," was a significant milestone. Considering the prevailing self-documentation trends today in social media culture, how do you think something like "everyday.photo" has changed in terms of its cultural resonance? Does it mean something different to you, and have other meanings been added to this ongoing project over the course of 23 years?

NK   There's so much here. I feel that many of these things, including everything that has unfolded on the internet, along with all the people responsible for the platforms we now use, like Facebook, Twitter, and others, are relatively new developments that have become deeply ingrained in society. They feel like they've always been around. Yet, it's been less than 20 years for all of these developments, which is basically nothing. It all seems like a matter of luck, being in the right place at the right time to bring these things to fruition because, in retrospect, it feels like all of these things were almost inevitable, even if we didn't realize it at the time.

They just feel special. It's like being among the first, second, or just early adopters, and then you'll find success or recognition. I feel like I happened to be lucky, pursuing photography and starting it when I did. It's similar to digital photography emerging, and me seeing the potential and thinking, "Oh, if I use that to take a photo of myself every day, what a cool idea." Then, fast forward six years later, new technologies were developed, which allowed it to spread and gain popularity. At that time, it was amazing because very few people had seen anything like it, although there were similar projects. Now, it seems like someone else is launching a new project like this every day. There are apps that enable people to create their own versions of these projects. If I were to start these projects today, no one would care. It wouldn't have the same impact as it did back then.

P56   Do you think the enduring relevance comes from the fact that no one else started it when you did, and no one can go back in time to initiate it? This perhaps also ties into another aspect of the question, in thinking of how it has evolved in terms of its archiving.

Your site notes each photo is manually tagged with the people and objects that appear in your life, offering new ways to explore the series as it relates to time. Was this initially born out of necessity? How has your process of taking and archiving these and other photos evolved, as the technology you work with changes?

ON FILTERING

NK   The "tagging" approach played into the concept of rarity traits, especially when dealing with a large number of photos that are only slightly different. The idea of tagging specific unique aspects made certain photos appear rarer. I'm not even sure how many there are at this point, probably over 8,000 or something. Many may appear identical, but then there are some where there are people behind me, though that's only a small percentage. Being able to tag and organize them, and see those specific ones, like 50 out of the 8,000, that have these unique traits makes these photos feel special. Setting aside NFTs and collectability, I do find that aspect interesting in its own right, especially in the context of a highly documented life. It could have been something done just for fun as part of the project, an attempt to achieve that. We did it specifically to give them a sense of being more valuable, which might seem somewhat distasteful but also made sense. Valuable not only in terms of monetary worth but also in terms of their level of interest. When confronted with 8,000 photos, viewers might want to see the highlights, and this tagging system directs them to those highlights, enhancing the overall value of the experience in terms of enjoyment.

P56   This brings us to methods of filtering and how we engage with our digital landscapes. We find it useful to have certain filters, especially those that focus on visuals or specific keywords. Surely writers and other creatives have their equivalents to this, as well.

NK   Yes, they're essentially tags, ways to categorize things. I believe, in some ways, it enhances the project and makes it richer. Perhaps it helps people connect with it better and allows for more in-depth exploration, which can be quite overwhelming otherwise. Regarding the process of managing it, there were two individuals who handled it as their job. Personally, I was physically incapable of doing it, and the thought of doing so is quite bothersome. If I were to start it all over again, it's challenging because there are only so many things you want to do. Isn't simply taking the photo enough? With that project, all I needed to do was capture the image. All the other aspects seemed like too much and unnecessary, diverting from the original purpose. The motivation to delve into that only arose because there was a monetary incentive that made it worthwhile. I had no issue with exploring it further because if it was going to be done, it was certainly intriguing.

NEWSLETTER #117: DOMINO SUGAR FACTORY

P56   In thinking about the facets of your work that are concerned with the passage of time and its effects, how would you describe the relationships you see between the production of images and changes in your environment, in particular the places and transformations you describe in *Newsletter #117: Domino Sugar Factory*?
      The series certainly has an atmospheric quality. However, you also mention that it could become part of a historical record. At times photographers may feel the need to capture something before it's gone if change is imminent. We're curious about what drew you to that building, aside from its proximity to where you lived.

NK   Mostly that, although it's quite iconic. It's not just the waterfront but also the neighborhood itself, unlike some residential buildings or other structures that may unfortunately come and go. This was a massive structure beneath the Williamsburg Bridge, now prime real estate. You were aware of this even then. It was just a matter of time, which is somewhat amusing. That period coincided with the financial crisis, and virtually nothing was progressing. Any proposed development was put on hold. It's interesting because when I lived across the street, I always had the notion that they might knock on my door, kick me out, and commence construction. That was always hanging in the air. It had been known for quite some time that it would transform into something else. However, due to the circumstances of that era, the transformation was significantly delayed. So, one reason for photographing it was its presence, but also because anyone familiar with urban development knows it wouldn't remain unchanged.

P56   It's a landmark building, and they had to keep the exterior intact. We're curious to know how you feel about it? Your primary focus is on photography, but much of your work incorporates spatial elements and structures, and seems deeply intertwined with how you perceive and relate to your environments.

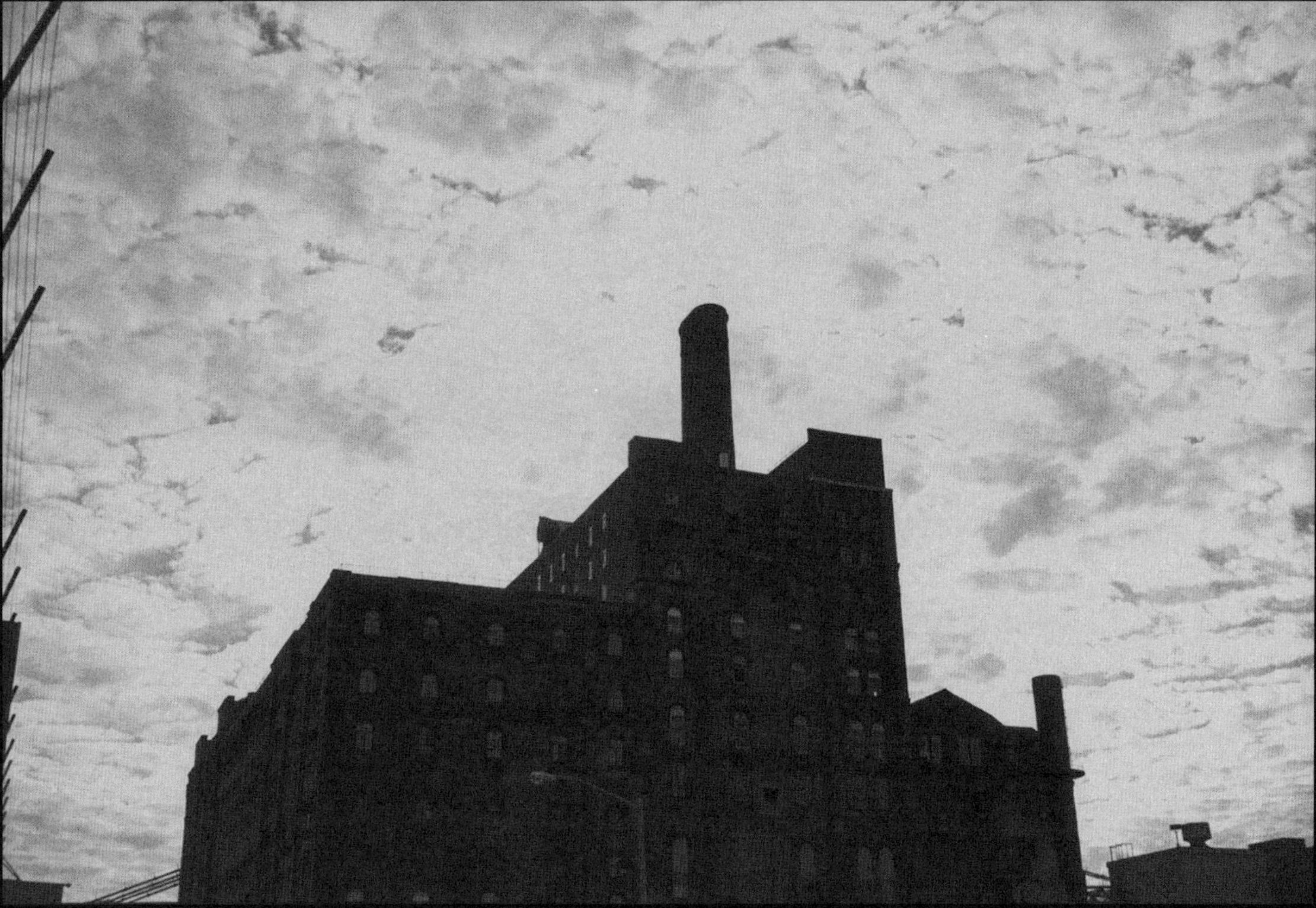

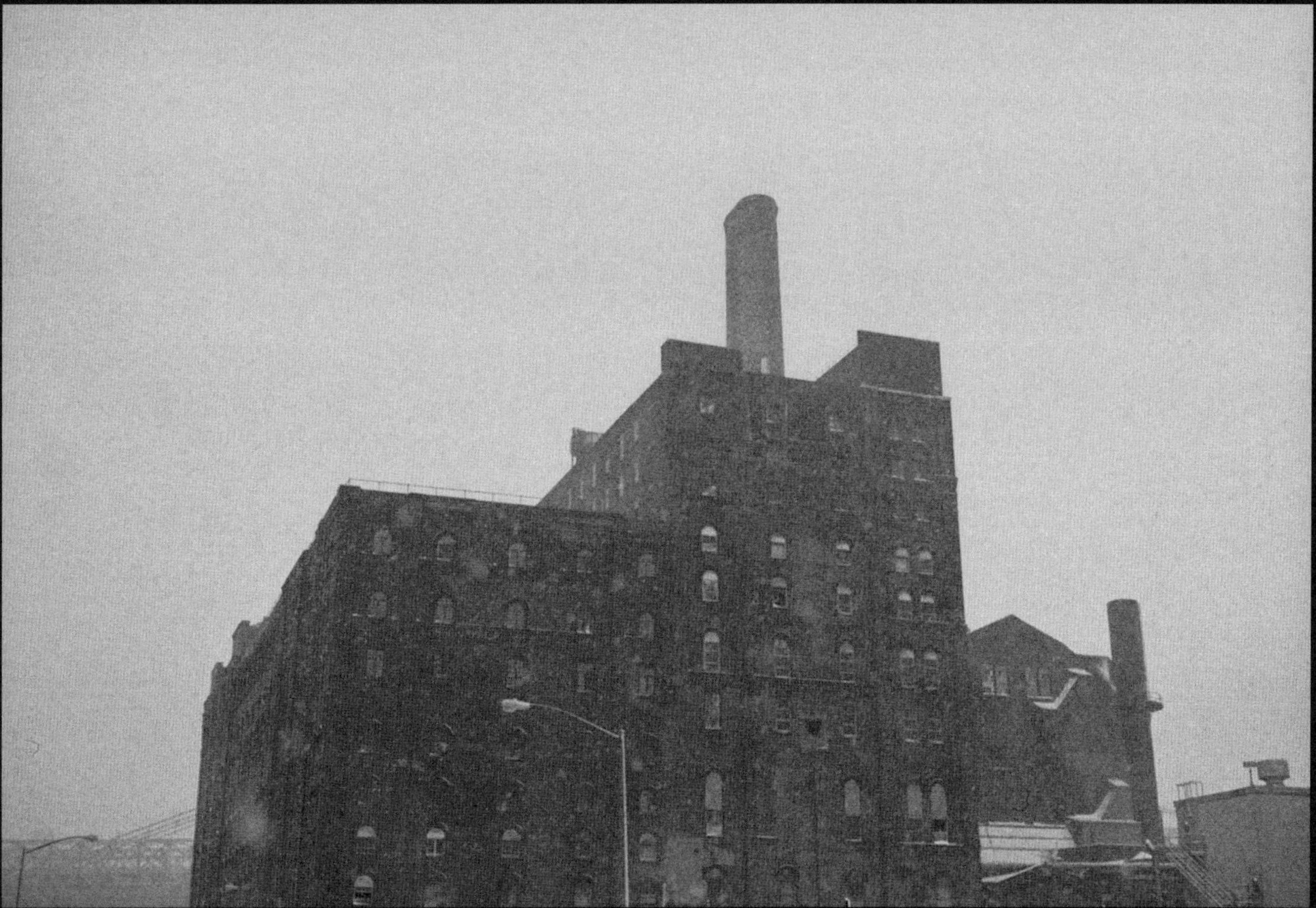

EXCERPT FROM *NEWSLETTER #117:*
DOMINO SUGAR FACTORY

This reminds me. Between 2007 and 2013, I would make photographs with point and shoot film cameras. They were just super casual snapshots. I called that series of photographs "Pictures That Look Like This." They looked like that.
—
Anyway, at the end of every roll of film, I would stand on the corner of S.1 and Kent and look up at the Domino Sugar Factory and make a photo. Since these photos were shot on film, there is no metadata, and I didn't keep records of the dates when I made the photos. All I know is that I made these pictures as often as I could until I moved away in 2013. I made well over a hundred of these photographs over those six years. It was more of a weather and atmosphere study than an overt time-based series, but I figured one day the building would change and these photos would be some sort of historical record.
—
For years the building just sat there. It looked like something was going to happen but nothing ever did. I basically lost interest in revisiting the corner. Between 2015 and 2020, I didn't take a single new photo. But then. Finally.
—
And now, here we are. Alive to see the Domino Sugar Factory begin to take on its last and final form. An adaptive reuse/post-industrial fetishism. This future apartment building is designed to provide only the finest and most luxurious comfort and accommodations for the most discerning upper-middle-class millennial. I immediately went inside the sales office and inquired about when construction would be complete, so I could be one of the first to move in.

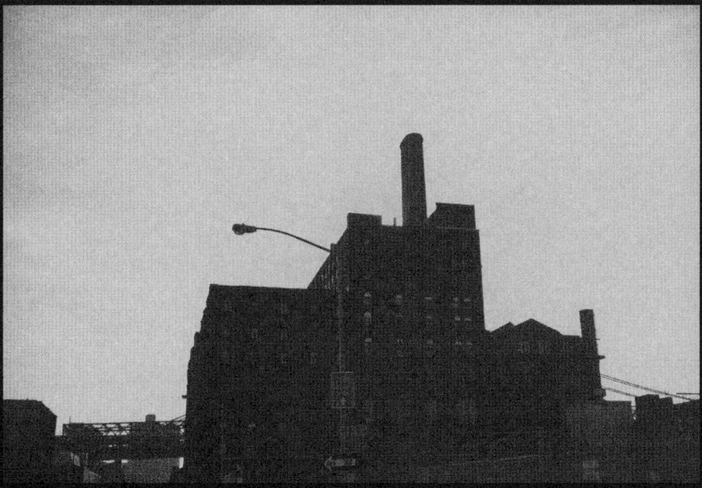
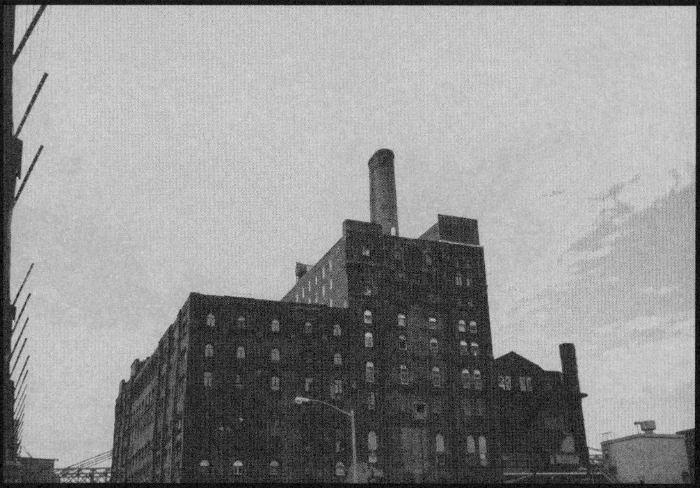
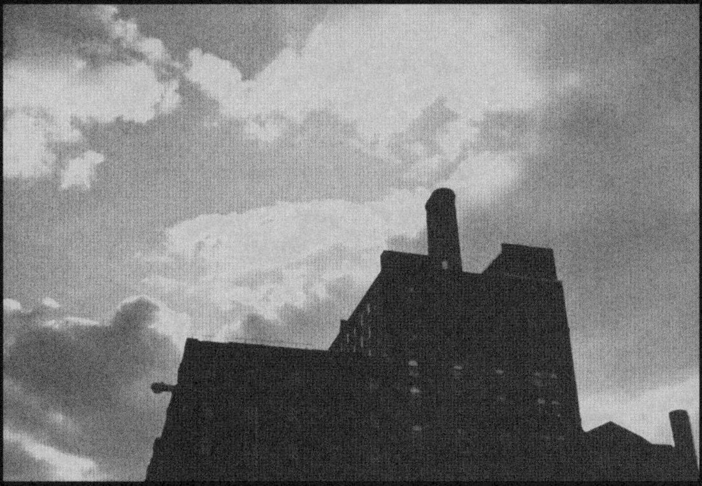
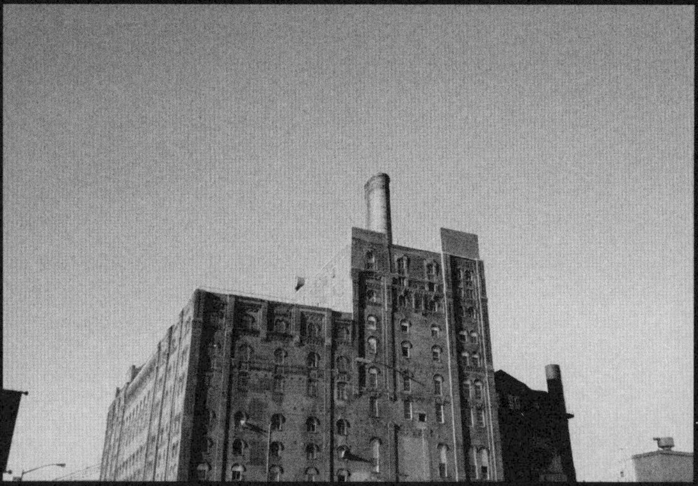
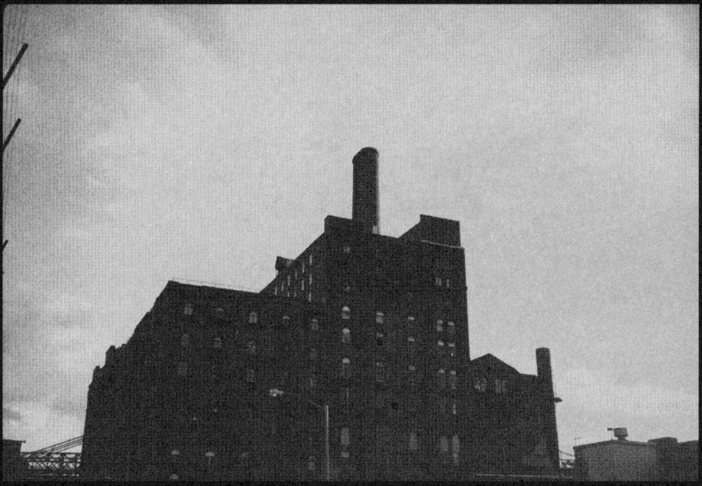
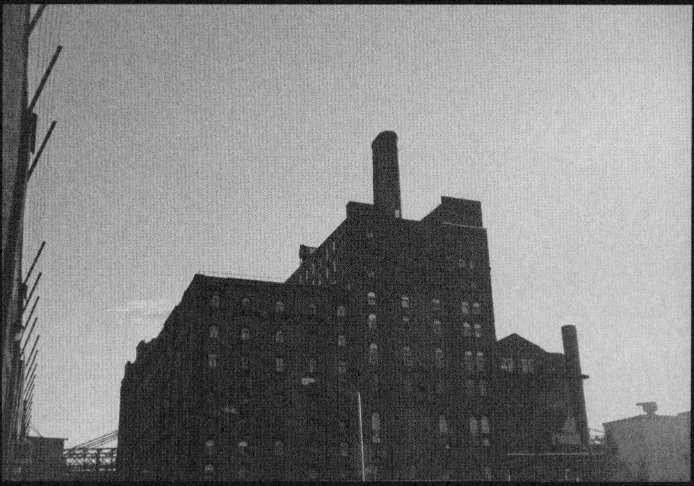
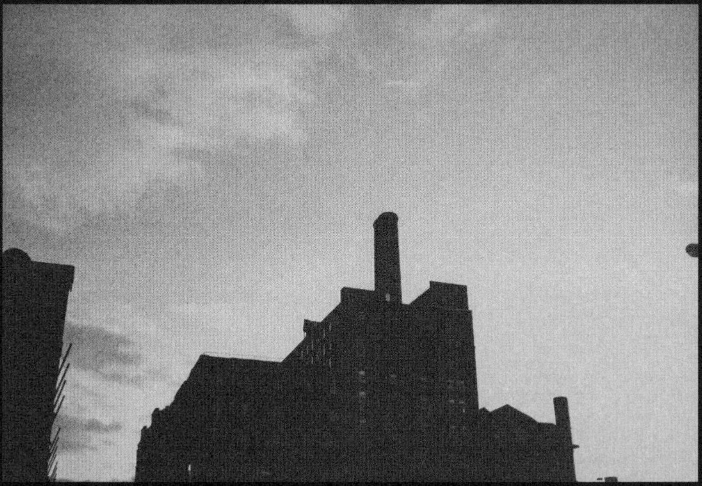
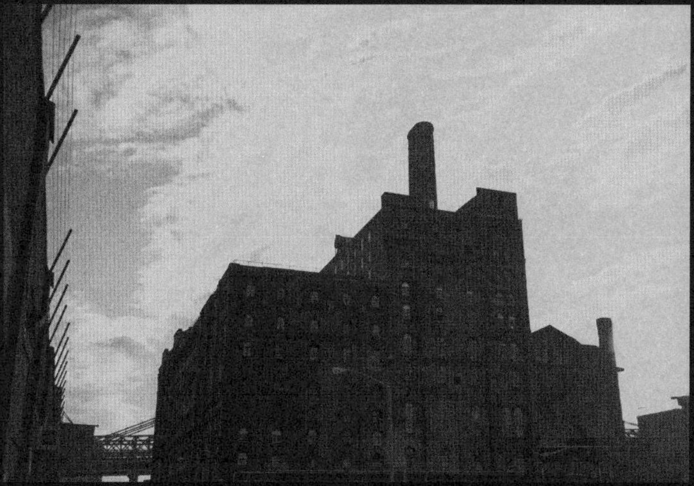

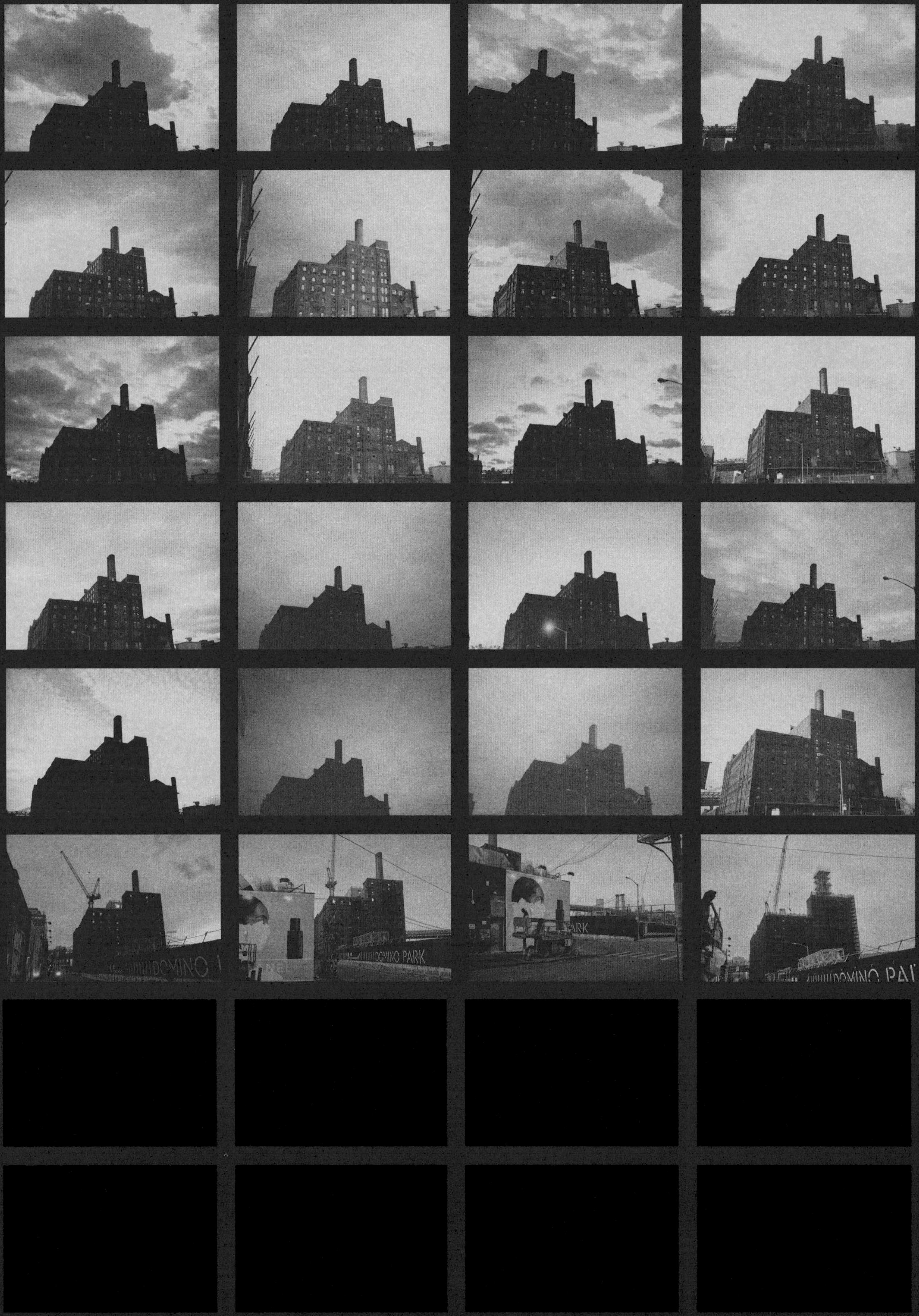
DOMINO PARK

NK It's okay. It almost feels like a joke at this stage, considering how much they altered it. I'm certain they had to preserve its historic value, which is generally a commendable practice. I don't think anyone would object to preserving the original character and not completely erasing history. To me, it seems like those changes are inevitable. What difference does it make? At least we have the photographs. That's part of the reason, at least you have the pictures to remember it by.

P56 Do you have any plans for expanding the Domino Sugar Factory series?

NK When I do go back there, I'll still photograph it. I feel like once those buildings are officially done, maybe I'll photograph those projects because the next cycle of change is not in my life.

ON "IMAGE CULTURE"

P56 We're interested in touching on the idea of "image culture," or how you see the relationship between the circulation of images and the reproduction of the built environment. The way images are produced and shared, and the technologies created to enable this, is always a social and political act. Where would you place your work in this dynamic, or how do you see your photography cast within these cultural currents?

NK In the end, I'd say images can be inspiring and influential, motivating people to take action and contemplate certain ideas. If it weren't for the proliferation of images and how easy it is to share photos …Some things do inspire people to visit places in person, but that isn't my primary motivation. My process is more long-term, deliberate, and focused on accumulating photos over time. However, because those things become popular, they become things that people want to see and understand in real life, beyond me. They want to see how they relate to these projects. That being said, there are numerous both positive and negative incentives behind these developments, which can be overwhelming. These projects are often driven by pure capitalism, contributing to a different realm of motivations and dynamics.

They won't undertake it unless there's a profit to be made. They provide people with enough incentive to make it somewhat worthwhile for them. Criticism doesn't affect them. It doesn't deter them from taking action. It's like an unstoppable machine that keeps moving forward regardless. If you set that aside and focus on a specific corner over time, there's something pleasant, poetic, and calming about it. The motivation is simply to show you something, not solely for monetary gain, which could be considered the purest form of image-making.

I guess that's the thing. There's simply no longer any value placed on real photos. Perhaps this is ultimately the point you're trying to make. It's a shame, but it's also indicative of a generational gap. We just have to come to terms with it. One of my young editors, who's 25, said, "Oh, what are you talking about? That's just the way it always has been. This is just the way it is." I replied, "I guess you're right. For you, it is." We have to move on. It's a common struggle for all of us living on planet Earth.

On August 14, 2014, a Ukrainian government humanitarian aid convoy left Kharkiv bound eastward for Starobilsk, in the Luhansk province. It was intended as a powerful sign of unity in the face of the separatist movement raging in Ukraine. However it would be another government's convoy, approaching from the opposite direction with the same declared purpose, that would receive the bulk of international media coverage. This one had been sent by the Russian government, the very government that had installed the separatist movement in southeastern Ukraine in the first place.[1] Long before its full-scale invasion of Ukraine in 2022, the Russian government was about to turn various stops along the route of its humanitarian aid convoy into a stage for performing "aid theater" for an international audience. A visual, material, and spatial practice that we will define as "scenographic," cloaked in the glaring white fabric of neutrality, was deployed to disguise Russia's covert operations in the Ukraine while the world watched.

For years to come the Russian provision of humanitarian aid to Ukraine—or, more accurately, to the Russian-backed paramilitary forces—would become a concerted, theatrical, and near ritualized effort to shape public perception and influence the narrative surrounding the sovereignty dispute and humanitarian crisis of Russia's own making. Key to the perception of Russia's operation is the concept of "multilateralism," understood as a diplomatic approach in which multiple governments and intergovernmental organizations collaborate to address regional or global challenges such as humanitarian crises for the benefit of everyone involved. Historically this approach was meant to play a significant role in mitigating the risk of a great power abusing its influence in the world. The collaborative provision of humanitarian aid through intergovernmental organizations is a fundamental component of the concept of multilateralism. In this context the visual, material, and spatial appearance of the Russian humanitarian aid convoy to Ukraine represents an effort by the Russian government to disguise its unilateral operation as multilateral. It was formulated to distract international observers from the Russian occupation of Ukraine that was already taking place. The range of techniques employed by the Russian government in the context of its humanitarian aid convoys comprise an effort to exploit internal divisions in Ukraine, subvert Ukrainian unity, and raise questions about the legitimacy of the Ukrainian government and its authority over its people and land. To pursue these covert objectives, the Russian government created a facade of humanitarianism for its intervention in and eventual occupation of Ukraine.

SCENOGRAPHIC PRACTICE

A few days earlier, on August 4, 2014, the Russian Minister of Foreign Affairs, Sergey Lavrov, had sent an official request to the United Nations (UN) and three other intergovernmental organizations—the International Committee of the Red Cross (ICRC), the Organization for Security and Co-Operation in Europe (OSCE), and the Council of Europe (CoE). All three of these organizations operate under their own mandates but play complementary roles as part of a rules-based UN-centric international system that has promoted compliance with human-rights and humanitarian law amid the complexities of armed conflicts and humanitarian crises. Russia requested to organize a joint humanitarian operation together with these organizations, yet their responses are inconspicuously absent from the government-funded and -controlled Russian media outlets.

On August 11, 2014, Vladimir Putin went ahead and announced that Russia would send a humanitarian convoy to Ukraine, supposedly in cooperation with representatives of the ICRC.[2] According to Putin, the details were to follow. Rather tellingly, the Russian president announced his intent in a call with European Commission president José Barroso rather than in the presence of his Ukrainian counterpart. Speaking to a European Union (EU) representative played into the narrative Putin had carefully framed for his domestic audience. Between 1999 and 2004 the EU expanded significantly into Central and Western Europe, and he had repeatedly framed the its eastward enlargement as the latest threat to Russia's existence. In 2014 Ukraine signed

Figure 1. Greater polity-scale map of the Russian MChS HADR Convoy 1.

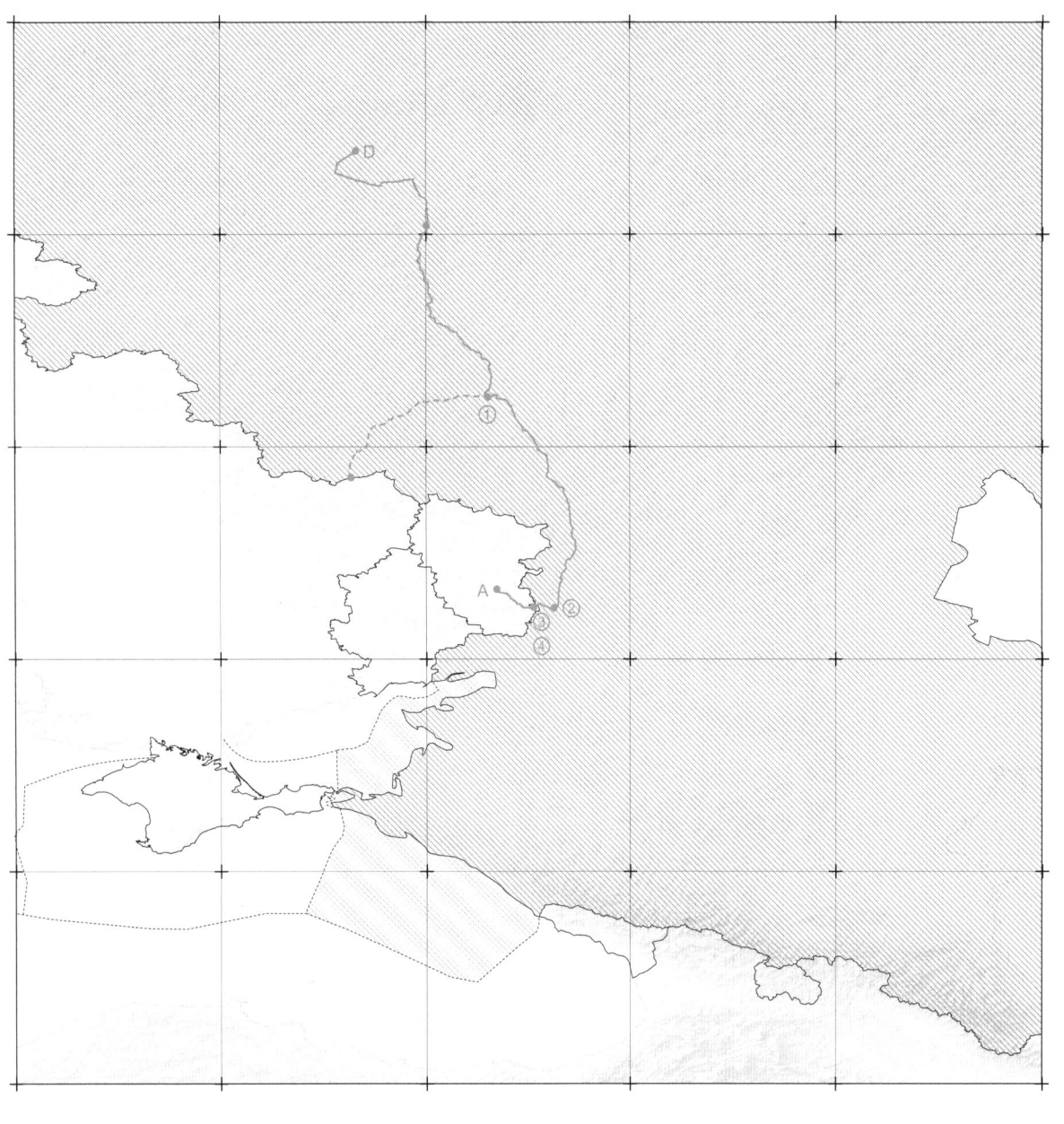

D   Departure Ground Force Base, Alabino (12 Aug, 2014)
① Stop 1 Ground Force Base, Voronezh (12 Aug, 2014)
② Stop 2 Ground Force Base, Kamensk-Shakhtinsky (14 Aug, 2014)
③ Stop 3 Border Checkpoint, Donetsk (15 Aug, 2014)
④ Stop 4 Border Checkpoint, Izvarino (Izvaryne) (22 Aug, 2014)
A   Arrival and Return, Lugansk (Luhansk) (22 Aug, 2014)

● MChS HADR Convoy 1 Stops
— MChS HADR Convoy 1 Route
-- MChS HADR Convoy 1 Proposed Route

☐ Disputed Areas
---- Boundary Lines

a politico-economic association agreement as a framework for cooperation with the EU. In his call with the Russian president, Barroso warned against Russian intervention in Ukraine under a humanitarian pretext—a detail that was absent from the Russian government's press release. The Ukrainian Foreign Ministry later reacted by clarifying that the Ukrainian government would accept humanitarian aid only if it was to be delivered under the auspices of an intergovernmental organization such as the ICRC.[3] The ICRC in turn stated that to comply with international law it would first have to receive an inventory, logistical details, and security guarantees for a humanitarian aid convoy.[4]

Instrumentalizing the Appearance of the Convoy.
Over the next few days Russia would use the visual and material appearance of its humanitarian aid convoy to make grandiose declarations about its aid to Ukraine in an effort to create a positive public perception of its intentions. By presenting itself as a benevolent actor, Russia sought to gain international sympathy and portray itself as a protecting patron of Slavic language and culture as well as the Russian Orthodox Church. By August 11 few details had been agreed upon, let alone arranged, with any intergovernmental organization. Yet the next day the Russian Minister of Foreign Affairs announced that a column of trucks carrying humanitarian aid had already departed from a ground force base in Alabino, in the Moscow province, in the early hours of the day.[5] Photos released by Russia's TASS news agency captured early-morning scenes with rows of trucks covered with white tarps illuminated by the light of the moon. Against a backdrop of trees lining the horizon, these scenes evoked a sense of awe.

In the context of armed conflicts, the color white is widely recognized as a sign of protection. It is meant to signify that an object and the associated person are not to be attacked because they are unarmed and desire to negotiate or give aid. More generally white is the color of neutrality, impartiality, and independence. Several of the convoy's trucks featured flags mounted on the white cabs, alternating between those of the Moscow municipality, the Moscow province, and, controversially, the Red Cross.

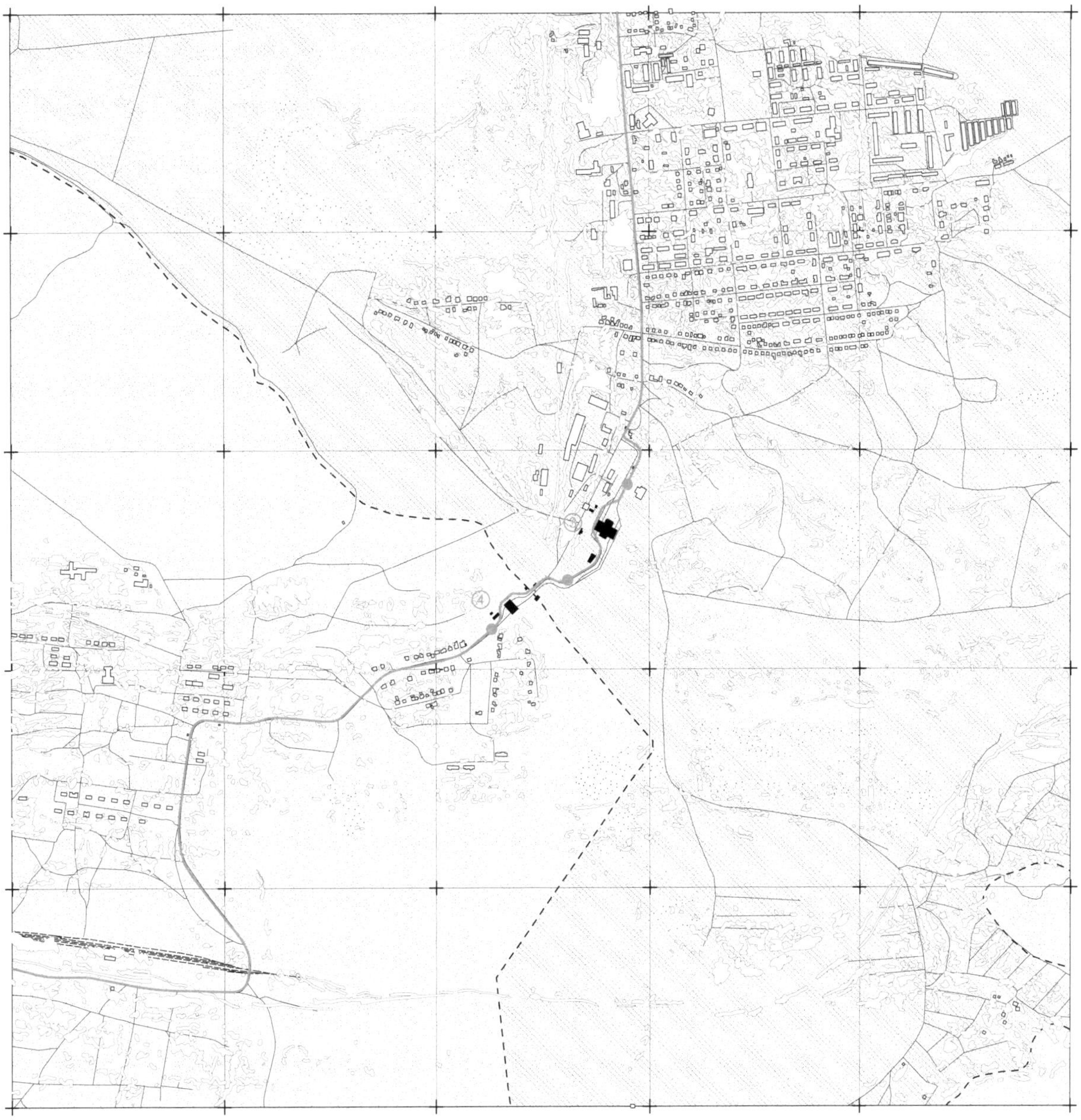

Figure 2. City-scale map of the Russian MChS HADR Convoy 1.

③ Stop 3 Border Checkpoint, Donetsk (15 Aug, 2014)
④ Stop 4 Border Checkpoint, Izvarino (Izvaryne) (22 Aug, 2014)

● MChS HADR Convoy 1 Stops
— MChS HADR Convoy 1 Route

-- Boundary Lines
☐ Built Fabric
— Roads

This white convoy was organized by the Russian Ministry of Emergency Situations (MChS, or EMERCOM).[6] While the convoy continued to move south toward Ukraine, the Russian government was still negotiating with its Ukrainian counterparts and the ICRC regarding the modalities and conditions for the operation to be recognized as humanitarian aid.[7] At the time the Russian government was reported to have agreed to its trucks using Ukrainian vehicle registration signs as well as carrying representatives of the ICRC, OSCE, and Ukrainian government once inspected by and moving through Ukraine.[8] Another condition the Ukrainian government insisted on, in accordance with international law and the ICRC's approach to humanitarian operations, was for the convoy not to be accompanied by a military escort. Lacking any Russian federal-level government insignia, with only those of a municipality or province, and enhanced by the flag of an intergovernmental organization, the white convoy looked like a multilateral rather than solely Russian effort. Yet it was not fully authorized by the Ukrainian government or the ICRC, even though it carried its flag. Already on the move, it sought to gain an advantage in the negotiations in which decisions still needed to be made.

Instrumentalizing the Route of the Convoy

Subsequently Russia would continue to conceal and confuse observers by changing the proposed route of the convoy. This continued to make it difficult for Ukraine and the international community to ascertain the true nature of Russia's actions. By the end of August 12 the convoy had reached a Russian ground force base in Voronezh, where it stopped for refueling.[9] Photos released via TASS showed rows of white trucks parked in an open field that stretched out for a long distance and MChS staff standing near the trucks. This waypoint represented a junction between the E38 highway, leading west toward the Kharkiv province, and the M4 highway, leading south toward the Luhansk and Donetsk provinces in Ukraine. The Ukrainian government expected the convoy to turn west from Voronezh toward

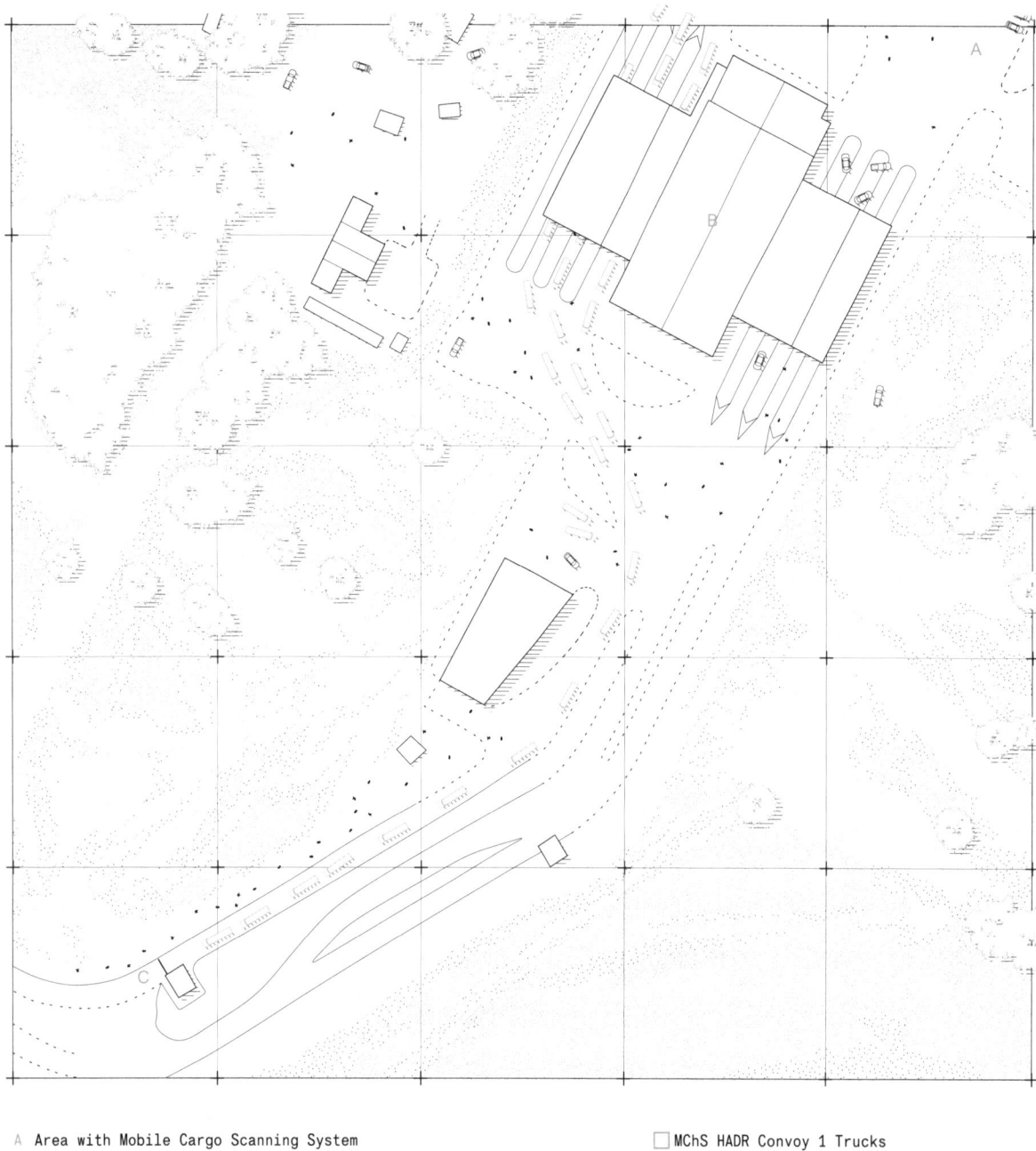

Figure 3. Landscape-scale site plan of the Russian MChS HADR Convoy 1 Stop 3 at the Border Checkpoint in Donetsk (15 Aug, 2014).

A Area with Mobile Cargo Scanning System
B Main Building
C Exit Booth with Priest

☐ MChS HADR Convoy 1 Trucks

☐ Built Fabric
---- Roads

the Pletenevka border checkpoint in the Kharkiv province. The Ukrainian government had requested Pletenevka to be the Russian convoy's point of entry into Ukraine. A key condition in the ongoing negotiations had been for the convoy's designated point of entry to be under the control of Ukrainian authorities rather than any Russian-backed separatist authorities of paramilitary forces.[10] At this point the ICRC still had not received the logistical details and security guarantees it had originally requested other than a vague inventory.[11]

In the limelight of world opinion—with the attention of the media already firmly set on the apparently neutral, impartial, and independent convoy of benevolent white trucks bound for Ukraine—the Russian government sought to pressure the Ukrainian government into making concessions. Given the uncertainty, however, the Ukrainian Minister of Internal Affairs, Arsen Avakov, eventually stated that the Ukrainian government would not allow the Russian convoy to enter.[12] The convoy was then reported to have stayed in Voronezh for most of the day, which suggested that the Russian government may have considered further negotiations and possibilities. Instead the Russian convoy changed the point of entry it had initially agreed upon with the Ukrainian government.[13] It continued south along the M4 highway, which was a route the Ukrainian government had wanted to avoid all along. Instead of the Kharkiv province, the Russian convoy now moved directly toward the Luhansk and Donetsk provinces, where the Russian-backed separatist movement had been raging for months. With its convoy on the move again during the unresolved negotiations, the Russian government sought to exploit the psychology of urgency, gambling that international media attention would amplify the stakes and lead to swift recognition of the unauthorized convoy. As humanitarian aid trucks traveled through the grassy fields of western Russia, journalists followed. In his work for BBC News following the convoy's journey, British journalist Steve Rosenberg would report how the Russians kept the Ukrainian government uncertain about the mission's intentions.[14]

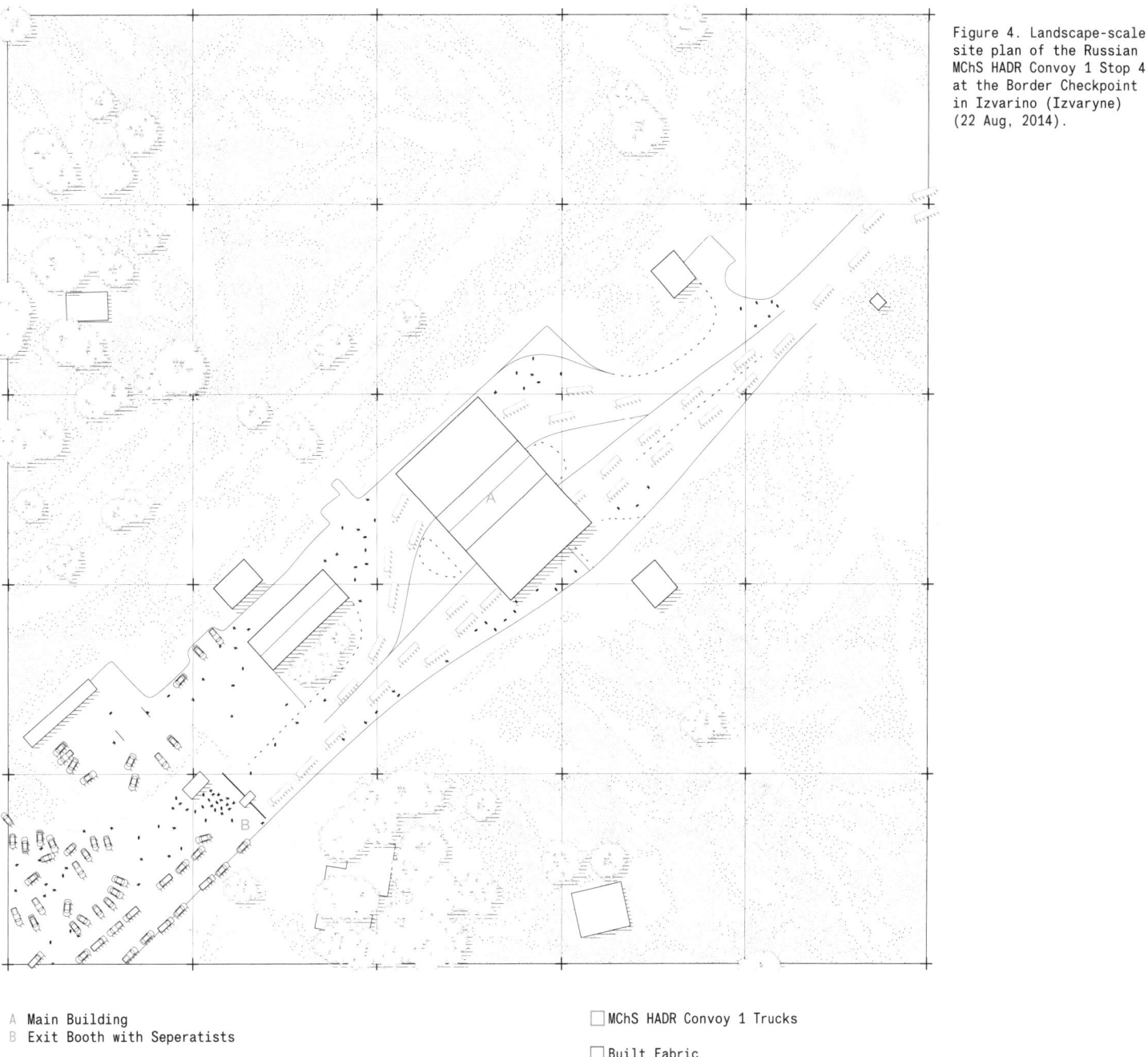

Figure 4. Landscape-scale site plan of the Russian MChS HADR Convoy 1 Stop 4 at the Border Checkpoint in Izvarino (Izvaryne) (22 Aug, 2014).

A Main Building
B Exit Booth with Seperatists

☐ MChS HADR Convoy 1 Trucks

☐ Built Fabric
— Roads

Instrumentalizing the Inspection of the Convoy

In the days that followed, Russia would allow only limited access to the convoy for sham inspections. This was intended to augment the illusion of transparency, cooperation, and compliance with international authorities and norms. Although various individuals and organizations, such as journalists of various media outlets, would be provided with some form of access to "inspect" the convoy along the route, access for the Ukrainian government to inspect the convoys upon entry was ultimately hindered. By the end of August 14 the convoy had reached a ground force base in Kamensk-Shakhtinsky.[15] This was where the Russian MChS first invited journalists, the Ukrainian government, and representatives of intergovernmental organizations to inspect the convoy in person the day after.[16] Rosenberg would report that many of the trucks journalists had been shown were in fact nearly empty.[17] Over the course of the next few days the OSCE's observer mission, mandated with promoting politico-economic security in Ukraine, would report on movement and activities at the border, closely following events tied to the Russian humanitarian aid convoy.[18] By August 17, sixteen of a reported total of 280 trucks had moved from Kamensk-Shakhtinsky to a closed parking lot located 100 meters from the entrance to the Donetsk border checkpoint in the Rostov province of Russia. Opposite the checkpoint, across the border, was the Izvaryne border checkpoint in the Luhansk province of Ukraine. For weeks this point of entry, chosen by the Russian government, was under the authority of Russian-backed paramilitary forces. This is evident from photos of the Izvaryne border checkpoint published by the Russian government-funded and -controlled media outlets weeks before the convoy arrived on the opposite side of the border. On the Ukrainian side, paramilitary forces had put up pro-Russian flags and even mockingly changed the "Ukraina" (Ukraina) sign on the checkpoint building to read "Ruin" (Ruina). The latter is inconspicuously absent from Russian media reports.

During the day a Heimann Cargo Vision (HCV) mobile cargo scanning system provided by the Russian Ministry of Finance (Minfin) Federal Customs Service (FTS) also arrived at the scene; a feigned sign of the Russian government's goodwill and complicity in the supposedly multilateral process. Like a theater prop, the mobile cargo scanning system was an example of the Russian government highlighting aspects of the scene in a very visible way for the eyes and camera lenses of the journalists on-site. It provided the illusion of seemingly expedited inspection and clearance while doing little to actually comply with the conditions that had been set out by the international representatives in the first place. The Ukrainian government and the ICRC had still not received the logistical details and security guarantees they had originally requested. In other words, the preconditions under which the Ukrainian government would have granted entry to the Russian convoy had not been met. Yet according to the Russian government, it continued to provide opportunities for the Ukrainian immigration and customs officers as well as ICRC representatives to inspect and clear the convoy at the border. However, given the separatist movement raging in southeastern Ukraine at the time, the invited representatives would point out repeatedly the struggles to actually access, let alone inspect and clear, the humanitarian aid cargo. On August 20, 16 trucks moved to the Donetsk border checkpoint for verification under the auspices of ICRC from the closed parking lot outside.[19] The day after another sixteen would be moved from Kamensk-Shakhtinsky to the border checkpoint grounds for verification.[20] By the end of August 21, after having been in the vicinity of the border checkpoint for a week, the customs check and clearance of cargo formalities had only been completed for 32 trucks in the humanitarian aid convoy. It was at this time that the OSCE representative reported a significant deterioration of mobile Internet connectivity and a total loss of fixed Internet connectivity in the vicinity.[21]

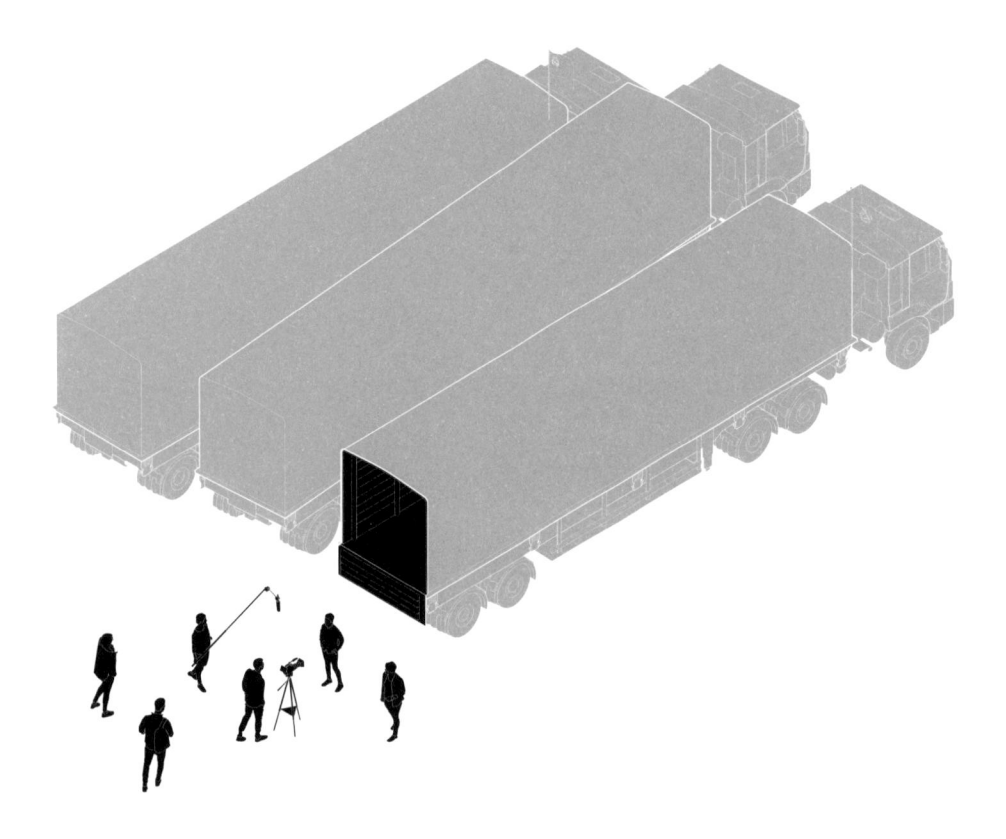

By August 22, as it became evident that the ICRC representatives would refuse to escort the convoy citing the ongoing lack of sufficient security guarantees, the Russian government decided to move its entire convoy without authorization from the Ukrainian government. At noon trucks started crossing into Ukraine. 34 trucks had been checked and cleared at that time, but at least another 100 uninspected trucks would follow without authorization. In photos from the events a priest can be seen blessing the humanitarian aid trucks passing through the border checkpoint gate into Ukraine—a sign of the close relationship between the Russian government and the Russian Orthodox Christian Moscow Patriarchate (MP). Over the years the MP has provided justification for their blessings of built objects, including offensive and defensive military objects, often in the name of protecting the Russian people and their language, culture, and beliefs. In this case the blessing of the convoy helped divert attention away from the Russian government.

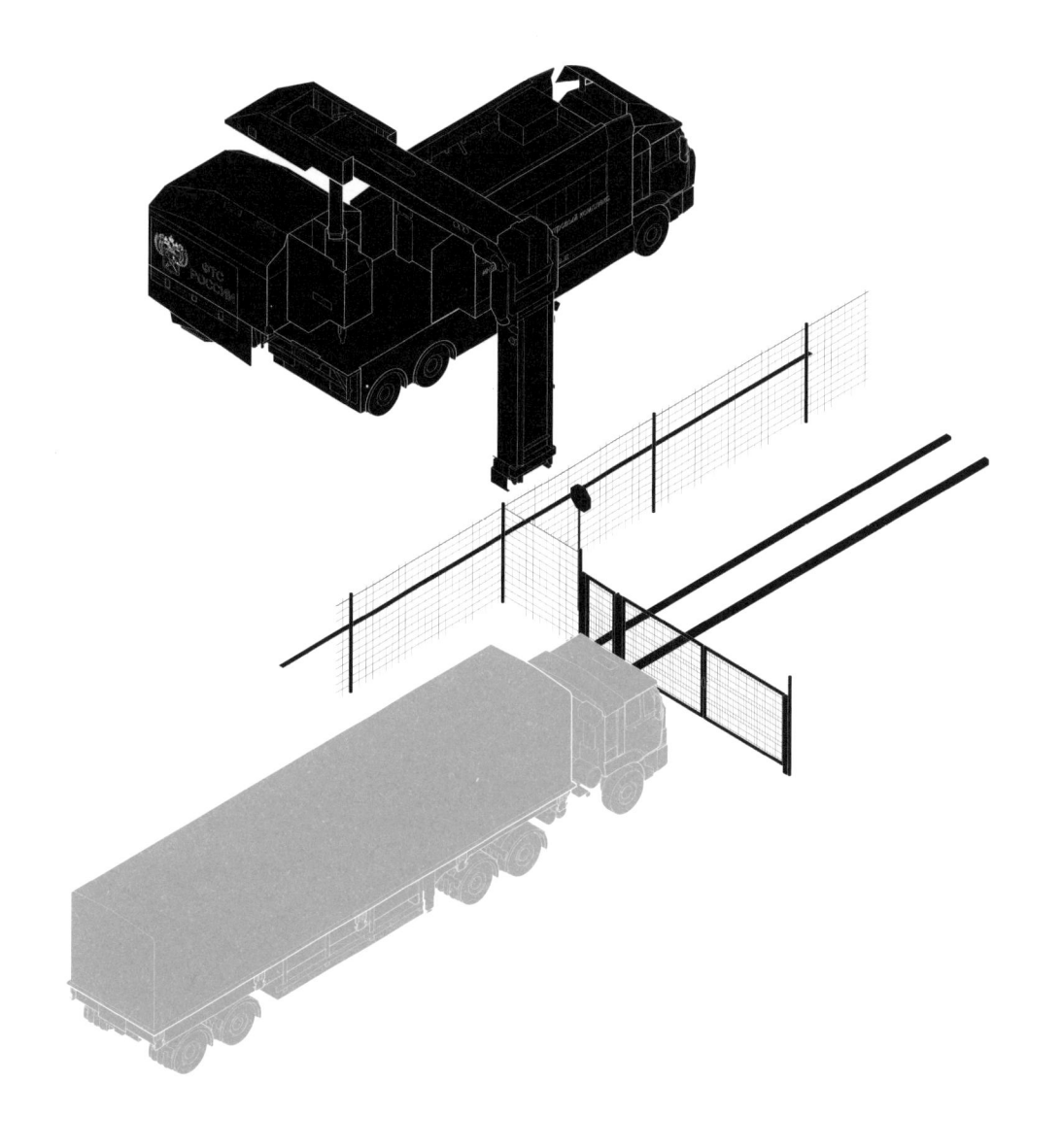

Like the Red Cross flag, signs of institutions such as the Russian Orthodox Christian Moscow Patriarchate may also be considered off-limits or protected under humanitarian law amid armed conflicts and humanitarian crises. For example, the Geneva Conventions provide protections for cultural objects. Similar to how it had used the Red Cross flag, the Russian government instrumentalized Christian signs and objects to reinforce the narrative that Russia was acting as a responsible and compassionate protecting power in crisis-stricken Ukraine. In photos from the events, vehicles can be seen passing by a booth at the Izvaryne border checkpoint on the Ukrainian side. Upon closer review, however, it is clear that this booth still had many of its windows broken from the violent takeover by the Russian-backed paramilitary forces weeks prior. Similar to how it had invited journalists to "inspect" the convoy to augment the illusion of transparency, cooperation, and compliance with international authorities and norms, the Russian convoy crossed into Ukraine via a checkpoint that appeared to be in use but was actually held by Russian-backed separatist authorities.

Opposite the booth where the convoy passed a flag had been raised, bearing arguably the most popular military-patriotic symbol in Russia due to its inconspicuousness: the so-called "Awareness Ribbon of Saint George." This ribbon, with a bicolor pattern of three black and two orange stripes, has traditionally been used to raise awareness for the European theater of operations against the Nazi

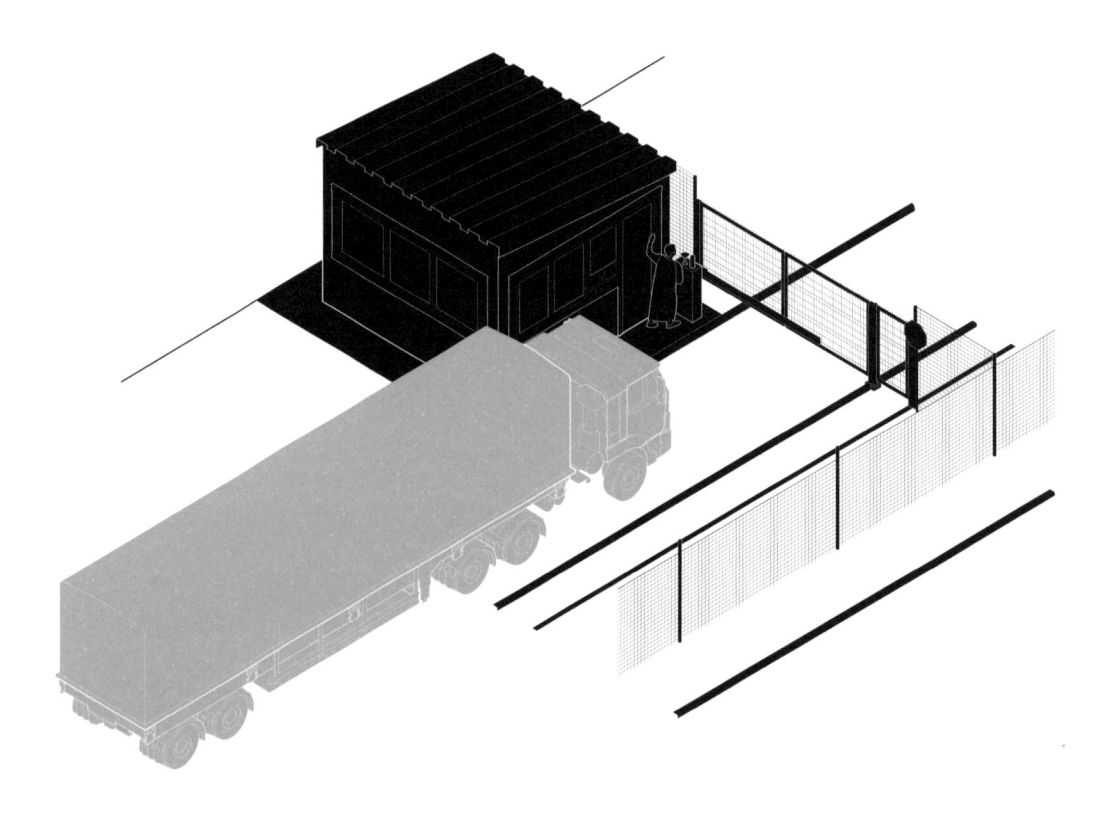

German Empire in the Second World War. It commemorates the veterans and victims of the war. With a distinct orange triangle shape on the upper left, this particular version of the ribbon referred to the National Liberation Movement (NOD), which over the years has advocated for the "restoration" of Russia's sovereignty. The potency of this symbol lies in its ability to recall multiple episodes in Russian history since the bicolor pattern has been a component of many military awards since the time of the Russian Empire. However, particularly in areas that had formed a part of Russia's former empire or union, the aforementioned symbols have become very controversial due to their association with an ultranationalist and imperial-colonial expansionist Russian sentiment. By employing symbols referring to its past victories against Euro-Western threats, the Russian government has sought to legitimize a new present.

The coverage of this and subsequent MChS humanitarian aid convoys to Ukraine fails to acknowledge how they relate to a more generally established practice rooted in the past. In other words, this contemporary case has its origins in a very long genealogy. Historically political communities such as nation-states have employed a "scenographic" practice that has allowed them to stage their authority over people and land. There is a long history of symbolic objects that connect the periphery or edge of a politically organized community with its center—in this case people whose ethnicity, language, culture, and beliefs are of Russian origin but who live outside Russia with Moscow. Via the predetermined movement of the humanitarian aid convoys the Russian government seeks to demonstrate its influence by going further into its sphere of influence.

INTERLUDE: CONTEXT

To violate the sovereignty of another polity under the guise of a humanitarian intervention is not a technique limited to recent history. Interventionism and the belief that humanitarian intervention is in the best interest of Indigenous local people, who will supposedly benefit from it, has a long and dark historical genealogy. Empires have been founded on cultural beliefs such as the British "white man's burden," the French "mission civilisatrice," and the American "manifest destiny" and way of life, claiming that it is their civilizing mission or honorable duty to modernize, Europeanize, and Westernize Indigenous people. The belief that people of particular ethnographic-linguistic origins are supposedly superior to others has provided a basis for the justification of these hegemonic powers' claims to authority and privilege. This imperial-colonial belief system continues to this day, providing ideological justification for a government to portray itself as a savior with the honorable duty to protect and even liberate others.

There is a relatively recent Western historical precedent for the events in Ukraine. In 1999 a Euro-Western military alliance intervened in an Eastern European polity based on humanitarian justifications. In the preceding years an Albanian-backed separatist movement in Yugoslavia had sought to transform the Serbian autonomous province of Kosovo-Metohija within the Yugoslav constituent republic of Serbia into a self-governed polity. With the eventual outbreak of full-scale war between Yugoslav Serbia and the separatist movement, the Big Five great powers, former allies in the Second World War represented as permanent members on the UN Security Council, were deeply divided over how to address this sovereignty dispute and humanitarian crisis. Russia had close ties to Yugoslavia and was opposed to any intervention. Given this deadlock in the council, the United States decided to unilaterally bypass the council by swaying the US-led North Atlantic Treaty Organization (NATO) to intervene instead. Although unilateral in effect, the intervention was given a multilateral appearance through the complicity and rubber stamp of the NATO military alliance.

In the aftermath of the military intervention in Yugoslavia, various intergovernmental organizations and governments with close ties to the United States sought to reformulate the "right to intervene" in international law to justify what happened retroactively. In 2001 the International Commission on Intervention and State Sovereignty (ICISS) even went so far as to advocate for the value of the "right to intervene" to be higher than the concept of sovereignty itself. ICISS argued that sovereignty should be dependent upon a government's responsibility to its people. In other words, as a social contract between a government and its people, the sovereignty of a government would be deemed illegitimate if it is unable to protect its own people from any crime against humanity. As such, ICISS proposed a shift from a "right to intervene" to a "responsibility to protect" (R2P), which was later endorsed by UN Secretary-General Kofi Annan at the UN World Summit of 2005. By 2008 Kosovo had formally declared its independence. Two years later the UN International Court of Justice (ICJ) would rule that Kosovo's declaration was not in violation of international law; in exercising the right to self-determination Kosovo was not obliged to apply to the Yugoslav Serbian authorities for permission to declare its independence. Until now only a part of the world's governments represented in the UN have recognized Kosovo as an autonomous and self-governed polity. Yet many European and Western intergovernmental organizations and governments have continued to applaud and justify NATO's intervention as a humanitarian act in response to Yugoslav crimes against humanity in the autonomous province. Meanwhile many other governments around the world, including Russia, have called out NATO on its violation of Yugoslav sovereignty under the guise of humanitarianism.

Yet NATO has set a dangerous precedent: Given that NATO got away with effectively redrawing the map of Eastern Europe without the approval of the UN Security Council, it comes as no surprise that Russia has modeled its recent actions on the Kosovo intervention. In its effort to play the game of great powers, Russia has emulated the language of hegemonic Euro-Western governments. This process of acculturation entails the spread of and adaptation to concepts and ways of life propagated as supposedly exceptional and superior to those of limitedly recognized or unrecognized self-governed polities. Russia's claims to sovereignty are legitimate only if its target audience sees and recognizes them as such, in the so-called process of "nation-building," through which a politically organized community is recognized by the "international community." This often involves the construction of an identity through practices of power projection and sovereignty acquisition and the associated symbolic paraphernalia: insignia and flags, folkloric songs and tales, culinary dishes, calendrical holidays and time, standardized weights and measures, monetary coins and notes, country-of-origin labels, vehicle registration signs, postal stamps, as well as passports. Through repetition and endorsement from international communities, these practices and their associated paraphernalia have become recognized as customary. Once a practice becomes customary, it takes on heightened symbolic meaning and becomes more widely accepted.

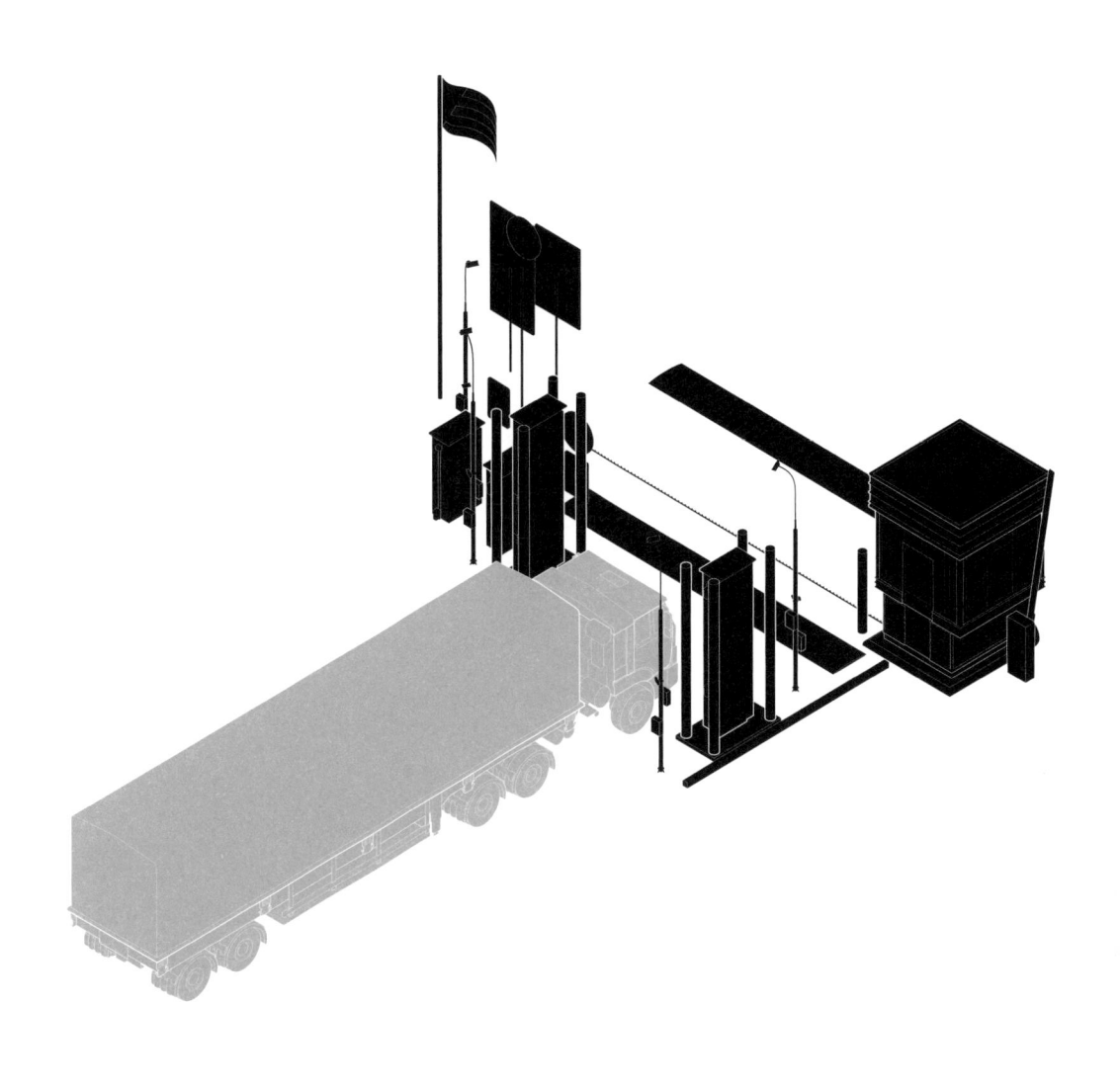

REPETITION

After its first convoy crossed the border into Ukraine to deliver cargo, the Russian MChS would continue to send humanitarian aid to Luhansk and Donetsk on a nearly weekly basis. More and more new convoys were sent, accompanied and documented by a circus of excessive media coverage.[22] After one year 36 Russian convoys had reached Ukraine.[23] The standard humanitarian aid convoy would depart from the MChS Rescue Center in Noginsk, stop for refueling in Voronezh, and travel onward to the MChS Rescue Center in Rostov-on-Don, where it would be on display for journalists.[24] From there it would cross the border into areas held by Russian-backed paramilitary forces—the Luhansk province in Ukraine, via the Russian Donetsk border checkpoint, and the Donetsk province in Ukraine, via the Matveev Kurgan checkpoint. The Russian government would later state that it had always "notified" the Ukrainian government of its incoming humanitarian aid convoys and that the Ukrainian government always had the "opportunity" to inspect them.[25]

Given this concerted, highly repetitive effort, it is hardly surprising that a collateral event was held by the Russian-backed authorities of the so-called "Lugansk People's Republic (LNR)" for the arrival of the 36th convoy, marking the first anniversary of the deployment.[26] The leader of the LNR, Igor Plotnitsky, remarked that people had gathered at Yarmarochnaya Square in Lugansk to demonstrate once again their "unity" and "inseparability" as a "single whole." On this occasion Russian MChS employees were awarded badges to commemorate the first convoy in 2014. Plotnitsky expressed his hope for the memory of the first convoy to be passed down from generation to generation. The Russian-backed LNR authorities then presented to the MChS employees a folkloric song titled "White KAMAZ Anthem," named after the manufacturer of the trucks in the convoys, composed by Yuri Dersky to verses by poet Vladimir Zaitsev, and performed by musician Anatoly Lavrentiev, of the Luhansk Philharmonic Society. Later, on the occasion of the 50th convoy, the LNR authorities would present a CD audio recording of this emblematic song in addition to a postal stamp produced in collaboration with the LNR Pochta postal service.²⁷ In the context of nation-making, the repetition of a near-ritualized performance fosters a sense of unity and identity among a community.

Today in Ilovaysk a life-size replica of a heavy-duty vehicle fashioned after the KAMAZ truck stands on a plinth, placed at an angle for dramatic effect.²⁸ Painted in white, the truck is inscribed with a series of insignias and a sign that reads "Humanitarian Aid from Russia." In nearby Izvaryne another memorial features a sign depicting the white KAMAZ truck mounted on a metal scaffold to render it into three-dimensional form.²⁹ Angled similarly to the plinth in Ilovaysk, it bears an image that is perspectival. Next to the sign is another, also mounted on a metal scaffold, with a text reading "Thank you, Russia!" Both of these built objects, and their portrayal in the international media, convey precisely how the actors behind them wish to "officially" represent these memorials.

Recognized by most of the international community as still being a part of Ukraine, Ilovaysk and Izvaryne have effectively been occupied and administered by the LNR since 2014. According to Russia, the memorials in Ilovaysk and Izvaryne, both constructed in 2015, represent a "responsibility to protect" its "fellow nationals" or "compatriots" in the face of "ethnic cleansing, genocide, and other crimes against humanity." In this case *compatriots* refers to people whose ethnicity, language, culture, or beliefs are of Russian origin or association and live outside Russia without Russian citizenship. Yet for media outlets in Ukraine and many other European and Western governments these memorials represent the invasion of Ukraine under the guise of a humanitarian aid operation in response to a crisis that Russia has manufactured to advance its own agenda.

This article has been partially supported by the University of Toronto (UofT), Daniels Emerging Architect Fellowship research fund and a UofT A&S School of Cities (SofC) Research Award grant. The author would like to thank the Vertical Geopolitics Lab (VGL) Research Assistants Darien Timur Mirzoev, Michelle Li, and Liane Werdina for assistance in the production of the visual component of this article.

1. "Premyer DNR: Sredi Opolchentsev nakhodyatsya okolo 3-4 tys Dobrovoltsev iz Rossii," *TASS*, August 28, 2014, http://www.tass.ru/mezhdunarodnaya-panorama/1404553.
2. Russian Presidential Executive Office, "Telefonnyy Razgovor s Predsedatelem Yevrokomissii Zhoze Manuelom Barrozu," August, 11, 2014, http://www.kremlin.ru/events/president/news/46433; "Peskov: Gumanitarnuyu Pomoshch' Ukraine okazhut nezamedlitelno posle soglasovaniya vsekh Nyuansov," *TASS*, August 11, 2014, http://www.tass.ru/politika/1373152.
3. Ukrainian MZS, "Zayava MZS Ukrayiny shchodo napravlennya Humanitarnoyi Dopomohy do Luhanskoyi Oblasti," August 11, 2014, http://mfa.gov.ua/news/2134-zajava-mzs-ukrajini-shhodo-napravlennya-gumanitarnoji-dopomogi-do-lugansykoji-oblasti.
4. ICRC, "Ukraine: Urgent Need for Aid in East," August 11, 2014, http://www.icrc.org/en/doc/resources/documents/news-release/2014/08-11-ukraine-east-civilians-plight-concern.htm; "Krasnyy Krest zhdet ot RF detalnuyu Informatsiyu dlya nachala Gumanitarnoy Operatsii na Ukraine," *TASS*, August 11, 2014, http://www.tass.ru/mezhdunarodnaya-panorama/1374095.
5. "Avtokolonna s Gumanitarnoy Pomoshchyu Zhitelyam Yugo-Vostoka Ukrainy vyyekhala iz Podmoskovya," *TASS*, August 11, 2014, http://www.tass.ru/obschestvo/1374303.
6. "Dostavka Rossiyskoy Gumanitarnoy Pomoshchi na Vostok Ukrainy: Khronologiya," *TASS*, November 19, 2015, http://www.tass.ru/obschestvo/1390550.
7. "Financial Times: Kreml' soglasuyet s Kiyevom mesto Vkhoda Gumanitarnoy Kolonny RF na Ukrainu," *TASS*, August 12, 2014, http://www.tass.ru/politika/1374393.
8. "Lavrov: Moskva poluchila Notu ot MID Ukrainy o gotovnosti prinyat' Gumanitarnuyu Pomoshch' ot RF," *TASS*, August 12, 2014, http://www.tass.ru/politika/1376262.
9. "Avtokolonna s Gumanitarnoy Pomoshch'yu RF dlya Zhiteley Yugo-Vostoka Ukrainy pribyla v Voronezh," *TASS*, August 13, 2014, http://www.tass.ru/obschestvo/1376789.
10. "Kiyev uvedomil Moskvu ob Usloviyakh, pri kotorykh vozmozhna otpravka Gumanitarnoy Kolonny, i nadeyetsya, chto Rossiya ikh uchla, otmechayut v MID Ukrainy," *Interfax-Ukraine*, August 11, 2014, http://interfax.com.ua/news/political/217888.html; "Ukrayina chitko poyasnyla Rosiyi, yaku Humanitarku propustyt'—MZS," *Ukrainska Pravda*, August 11, 2014, http://www.pravda.com.ua/news/2014/08/11/7034574.
11. "Krasnyy Krest poluchil Uvedomleniye RF o Dvizhenii Gumanitarnogo Konvoya k Granitse s Ukrainoy," *TASS*, August 12, 2014, http://www.tass.ru/mezhdunarodnaya-panorama/1375381.
12. Arsen Avakov, "V Zdanii MVD na Komandirskikh Etazhakh, da i v Tselom po Upravleniyam—pustynno," *Facebook*, July 29, 2014, http://www.facebook.com/arsen.avakov.1/posts/676279482462161; "Ukraina ne uvedomlyala Rossiyskuyu Tamozhnyu o Zakrytii Punkta 'Shebekino-Pletenevka'," *TASS*, August 13, 2014, http://www.tass.ru/mezhdunarodnaya-panorama/1378000.
13. "Humanitarna 'Dopomoha' z Rosiyi napravlena v Ukrayinu v obkhid Kharkivskiy Oblasti," *Ukrinform*, September 9, 2014, http://www.ukrinform.ua/rubric-other_news/1695783-rosiya_raptovo_zminila_kurs_konvoyu_do_ukraiini_1963468.html.
14. "Ukraine Crisis: Russia Aid Convoy Heads South," *BBC News*, August 14, 2014, http://www.bbc.com/news/av/world-europe-28783587.
15. "Ukraine Crisis: BBC Finds Russian Aid Trucks 'Almost Empty'," *BBC News*, August 15, 2014, http://www.bbc.com/news/av/world-europe-28799627.
16. "Sotrudniki MChS predlozhili Krasnomu Krestu proverit' Gumanitarnyy Gruz dlya Vostoka Ukrainy," *TASS*, August 14, 2014, http://www.tass.ru/obschestvo/1381022.
17. "Ukraine Crisis: BBC Finds Russian Aid Trucks 'Almost Empty',"; "V Gumanitarnoy Kolonne Obyasnili Polupustyye KAMAZy: Oni Slishkom Novyye," *NEWSru*, August 16, 2014, http://www.newsru.com/russia/16aug2014/kolonna.html.
18. OSCE, "Spot Report by the OSCE Observer Mission at the Russian Checkpoints Gukovo and Donetsk, 22 August 2014: Russian Humanitarian Aid Trucks Departed from the Donetsk Border Crossing Point without ICRC's Escort," August, 22, 2014, http://www.osce.org/om/122927.
19. OSCE, "Spot Report".
20. OSCE, "Spot Report."
21. OSCE, "Spot Report."
22. "Dostavka Rossiyskoy Gumanitarnoy Pomoshchi na Vostok Ukrainy: Khronologiya," *TASS*, November 19, 2015, http://www.tass.ru/obschestvo/1390550.
23. "Dostavka Rossiyskoy."
24. MChS, "Intervyu TASS o tom, kak formiruyutsya Gumanitarnyye Kolonny na Donbass, sobirayetsya Gruz i kto yego raspredelyayet," October 27, 2016, http://mchs.gov.ru/deyatelnost/press-centr/intervyu/1444234.
25. MChS, "Intervyu TASS."
26. "Pervyy Gumkonvoy MChS RF privez v Respubliku Nadezhdu i Veru – Plotnitskiy," LNR Lugansk Media Centre (LITs): August 20 (2015), http://lug-info.com/news/pervyi-gumkonvoi-mchs-rf-privez-v-respubliku-nadezhdu-i-veru-plotnitskii-5910; "Luganchane vospeli Belyye KAMAZy Gumkonvoya MChS RF," LNR Lugansk Media Centre (LITs): August 20 (2015), http://lug-info.com/news/luganchane-vospeli-belye-kamazy-gumkonvoya-mchs-rf-5927.
27. "Glava MChS LNR vruchil Pamyatnyye Podarki Rossiyskim Spasatelyam 50-go Gumkonvoya," LNR Lugansk Media Centre (LITs): March 24 (2016), http://lug-info.com/news/glava-mchs-lnr-vruchil-pamyatnye-podarki-rossiiskim-spasatelyam-50-go-gumkonvoya-foto-11872; "'Pochta LNR' vypustila Khudozhestvennuyu Marku, posvyashchennuyu 50-mu Gumkonvoyu MChS RF," LNR Lugansk Media Centre (LITs): March 29 (2016), http://lug-info.com/news/pochta-lnr-vypustila-khudozhestvennuyu-marku-posvyaschennuyu-50-mu-gumkonvoyu-mchs-rf-12023.
28. TV-Sphera, "Belyy Kamaz Simvol Mira i Nadezhdy,: YouTube, 2019, accessed November 2023, http://www.youtube.com/watch?v=vfG9h-D6gaXU.
29. "Vlasti LNR otkryli Pamyatnyy Znak 'Spasibo, Rossiya!' na Granitse s Rostovskoy Oblastyu," LNR Lugansk Media Centre (LITs): December 30 (2015), http://lug-info.com/news/vlasti-lnr-otkryli-pamyatnyi-znak-spasibo-rossiya-na-granitse-s-rostovskoi-oblastyu-foto-9585.

The "Ghost Army" was a top-secret World War II unit staffed by an unusual group of people. Instead of infantrymen, tankers, and artillery, it was composed of painters, designers, and architects. Among its ranks were artists Ellsworth Kelly, Art Kane, and Bill Blass. Their mission was to conduct large-scale deception operations. The Ghost Army fabricated and deployed inflatable tanks and mock combat materiel to spoof Nazi reconnaissance operations, used giant loudspeakers to create illusions of nonexistent tank divisions moving through the countryside, and arranged for phony generals to appear in unexpected places. Through trickery and deception, the unit aimed to create an alternate reality in the service of strategic military goals.

PSYOPS are designed to make people see what you want them to see, perceive what you want them to perceive, and believe what you want them to believe. They are most effective when specifically shaped for a particular person or group, and are crafted to exploit well-known features of human perception, belief, emotional life, and group dynamics.

Our world of recommendation algorithms, generative-AI models, gamification, and the ferocious quest for engagement is a world of ubiquitous and relentless "influence" operations. We are racing through the world of "surveillance capitalism" into an era of "PSYOPS capitalism."

I. UNIDS

For the last several years, I've been undertaking the most technically challenging photography series I've ever attempted: A project to photograph objects of unknown origin in orbit around the earth.

There are roughly 350 objects in orbit around the earth whose origins are unknown. These fall roughly into two categories: 1) Objects that the US Air Force tracks on radar and publishes orbital data for; 2) Objects that both amateur astronomers and foreign sources track and observe, but that the US military does not acknowledge, presumably because these unknown objects are classified.

The term "unid" is a term that amateur astronomers created to describe objects that they have observed in orbit, but whose identity they have failed to establish. In the first part of this text, I provide an overview of what we know about these objects, and review some attempts to identify them and their purpose. In the second part, I'll describe some of the techniques I've used in my attempts to photograph them.

What are Unids?

The short answer is, nobody knows. The longer answer is that for some objects, somebody probably knows something about some of them, but they're not saying. Or, that also might be wrong and actually nobody knows.

Some background: The US Space Force's 18th Space Defense Squadron, located at Vandenberg Space Force Base[1] on the California coast north of Santa Barbara, is tasked with operating the US' Space Surveillance Network. This is a global network of powerful radar systems, classified telescopes, space-based surveillance platforms, and other sensor networks. The squadron's job is to identify and keep tabs on tens of thousands of objects in orbit around the earth. Over the course of their work, they regularly track and observe nearly 350 objects whose origin and identity are unknown. The 18th SDS catalogs these as "well tracked analyst objects."

The "well-tracked analyst objects" are described by the surveillance squadron as "on-orbit objects that are consistently tracked by the U.S. Space Surveillance Network that cannot be associated with a specific launch. These objects of unknown origin are not entered into the satellite catalog, but are maintained using satellite numbers between 80000 and 89999." (In the military satellite catalog, satellites are cataloged sequentially, i.e. the rocket that launched Sputnik is catalog entry #1, Sputnik is entry #2, etc.)

So what are these objects? The best answer is that, well, nobody knows. A more fine-grained answer involves some informed speculation. It is unlikely, however possible, that some of these objects are natural phenomena such as wayward asteroids. Undoubtedly, most of these "unknowns" are unidentified

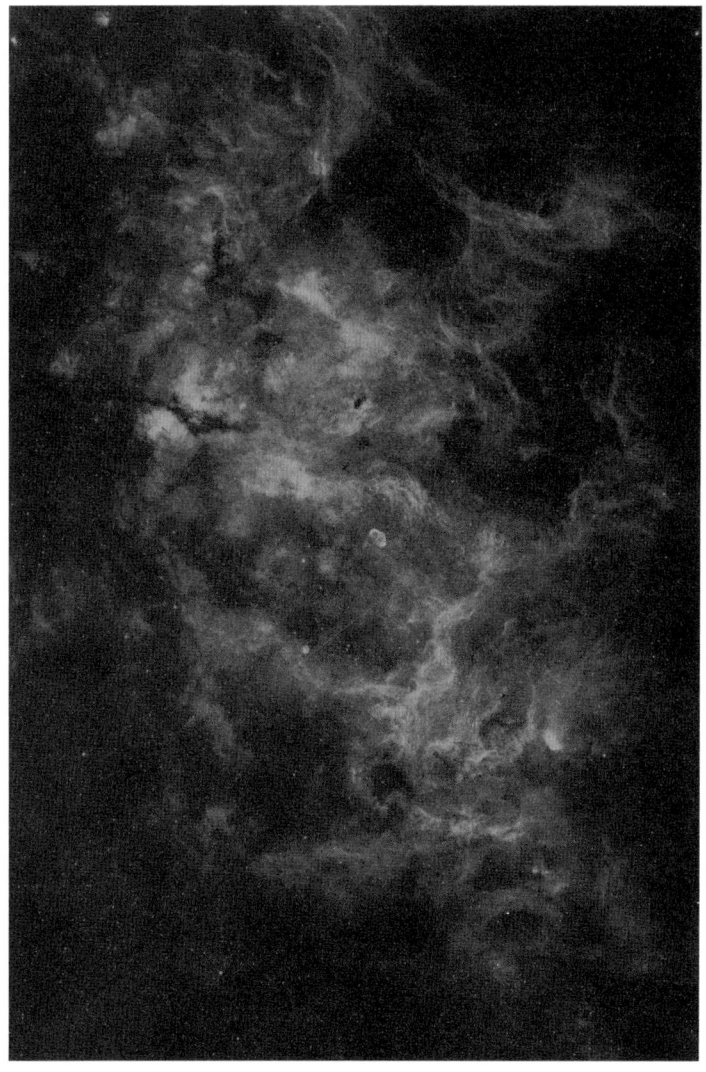

UNKNOWN #89161 (Unclassified object near The Revenant of the Swan), 2023. Silver gelatin LE print, 80 × 54 inches.

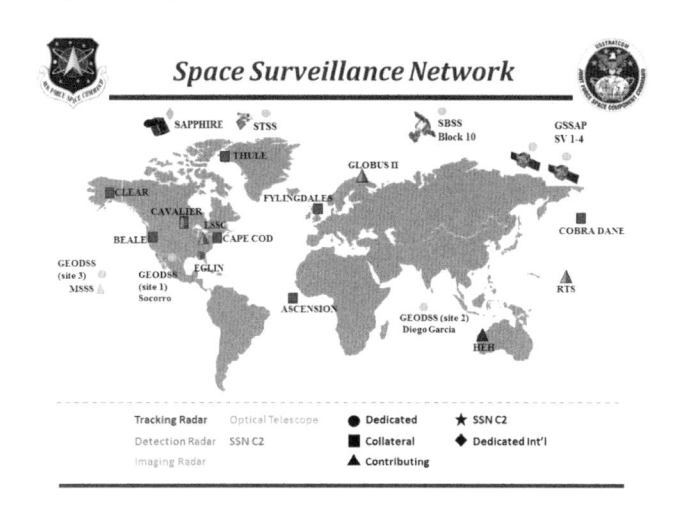

```
Unidentified - TO BE ASSIGNED
1 82891U          19274.97211782 +.00000236 +00000++40169-4  9992
2 82891  97.8262 340.4146 0014238 192.8285 167.2566 14.77392039103911
Unidentified - TO BE ASSIGNED
1 82939U          21305.97543406 -.00000116 +00000--78523-2  9997
2 82939 086.3573 310.0542 1886417 292.7704 048.5108 08.75629108323084
Unidentified - TO BE ASSIGNED
1 84006U          22230.06235828 -.00000089 +00000++00000+  9997
2 84006  23.7246  50.0003 6131819  14.0642 357.3454  2.16231398 57994
Unidentified - TO BE ASSIGNED
1 84353U          22157.1200206+.00000353 +00000++00000+  9990
2 84353  18.8985 279.1353 6683612 272.4086  18.7931  2.037266041915
Unidentified - TO BE ASSIGNED
1 85205U          22230.48154229 +.00000122 +00000++10863-3  9999
2 85205  82.9573 134.6974 0038197  79.5215  46.9552 13.76490932439570
Unidentified - TO BE ASSIGNED
1 85410U          20016.12638888  .00000006  00000- 00000+  9996
2 8541 80.0053  91.4245 0009717 273.382201.61913.14633027     10
Unidentified - TO BE ASSIGNED
1 85412U          20016.34702987  .00000012 +00000- 00000+  9991
2 85412  88.910 82.4227 001013287.140204.57013.55759361     14
Unidentified - TO BE ASSIGNED
1 87730U          22234.79320754 +.00000069 +00000++56451-4  9994
2 8773 82.9432  47.6587 0031023 128.3305 232.0646 13.74210671419417
Unidentified - TO BE ASSIGNED
1 87934U          22234.40224825 +.00000053 +00000++40448-4  9992
2 87934  82.9356 112.5085 0031253 152.3913  24.1539 13.72830243438503
Unidentified - TO BE ASSIGNED
1 89177U          22231.34219058 +.00000062 +00000++50806-4  9994
2 89177  82.9179  87.0619 0031057 272.6767  87.0834 13.73436645896661
```

Orbital Elements for Unknown Objects, Paglen Studio.

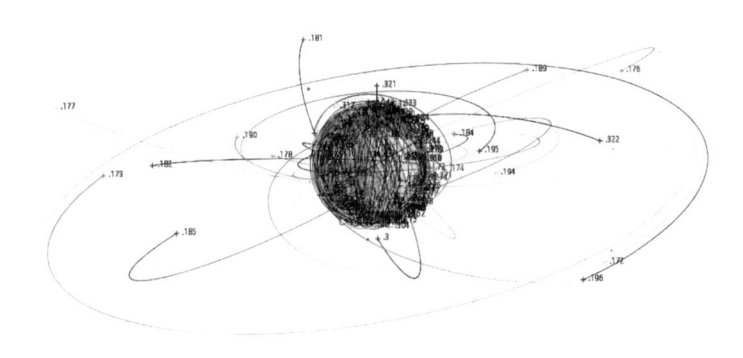

Visualization of Unknown Object Orbits, Paglen Studio.

debris from satellite launches in places or times where the Air Force's tracking capabilities are limited. But the story is almost certainly far more complicated.

The US' National Reconnaissance Office (NRO) has a history of building satellites that attempt to disguise themselves as pieces of debris. This was the case for example with a spacecraft called "USA 53" (deployed from the Space Shuttle in 1990) that faked its own explosion, and again in 1999 when another "stealth" satellite deployed a balloon-like structure as a decoy. The Russian military has engaged in similar tactics, most recently with a spacecraft called Kosmos 2499, which behaved as if it were a debris object but which was almost certainly a satellite designed to attack other satellites. (Kosmos 2499 was mysteriously destroyed in early 2023, creating a small debris field.)

Analyzing Unids

The only publicly available analysis of the "well-tracked analyst objects" that I'm aware of comes from a PhD dissertation written by space-security researcher James Pavur at the University of Oxford. Pavur took a novel approach to the analysis of these objects. He created a dataset of known satellites, and another dataset of known debris objects, and then trained a machine learning model on each. His idea was to build a classifier that could distinguish between a "generic satellite" and "generic debris object." Pavur then used those models to analyze the orbit of Kosmos 2499, a satellite that pretends to be a debris object. His model correctly predicted that Kosmos 2499 was a satellite, not a piece of debris. Pavur then ran his model on the entirety of the "well-tracked analyst objects" data and discovered something remarkable: The model predicted with high confidence that a non-trivial number of unknown objects behaved, in fact, like spacecraft.

Almost immediately after the publication of his dissertation, Pavur was tapped to work for the Department of Defense and is unable to speak about his current work. However, Pavur did provide me with a copy of the models he used in his analysis and I'm conducting a review of them to see if there's more to learn about "analyst objects" from his work.

There are, however, a few limitations to Pavur's approach. Firstly, Pavur's classifier wasn't designed to detect station-keeping maneuvers. Operational satellites in low-earth orbit are affected by small amounts of atmospheric drag in the upper atmosphere that slowly bring them back down to earth. To counter this, a satellite has to periodically "boost" itself back into its desired orbit using small thrusters located on the spacecraft. Satellites in higher orbits are affected by the gravitational influence of the moon, and from the uneven nature of Earth's gravity field.[2]

The Plot Thickens...

In addition to objects in the 18th Space Defense Squadron's publically available data, there are two additional sources of information about unknown objects. The first is a hybrid Russian civilian/military tracking program called "ISON" (International Scientific Observer Network), and the second is a database of classified objects maintained by a network of amateur satellite observers, unofficially known as the "See-Sat" group. Both of these groups have identified a handful of unknown objects in orbit whose existence is classified by the American military—in other words Top-Secret unknown objects.

So, to recap: There are many hundreds of unknown objects in orbit around the earth, many of which are tracked and acknowledged by the US military. Researchers who've analyzed these objects have concluded that a non-trivial number of them display characteristics more consistent with spacecraft than debris objects, although these results require further study. What's more, there are more than a dozen other objects that are also "unknowns" but whose existence is classified and whose orbits are undisclosed.

Photographing Unids

Photographing these objects is extremely difficult in every way, but can be done using good data, accurate modeling, and very specific optical equipment.

Step 1: Get the Data

The first thing one needs to photograph unids is a good source of data. I use two sources: Two-line elements (a file format for describing satellite orbits) for "well-tracked analyst objects" are readily available by creating an account with "The Space Force," on their portal for satellite information at space-track.org. This database provides a list of unclassified data. To retrieve data about classified unknown objects, the best source is a website maintained by satellite observer Mike McCants, who collates observations from amateur satellite observers and publishes orbital elements based on those observations. Those elements need to be downloaded and filtered for both "unknown" objects and "ISON" objects.

Table 9.5: "Analyst Objects" Most Like Satellites

NORAD Catalog Identifier	Satellite Classification Confidence
85412U	0.980
87934U	0.962
84006U	0.960
87730U	0.957
82939U	0.945
89177U	0.928
82891U	0.911
85410U	0.910
84353U	0.903
85205U	0.895

We find that our model flags *2014-28E* as a disguised satellite from the very first TLE entry in Space-Track.org - six months faster than existing monitoring techniques did. It does so at a > 91% confidence, which equates to 2.55 total anomaly detection alerts per year under the conditions simulated in Section 9.4.5. This suggests that essentially any implementation of our system — whether or not it assumes defender access to astrometry equipment — would have identified Russia's claim that *2014-28E* was space debris as dubious.

Excerpt from James Pavur's dissertation "Securing new space: on satellite cyber-security" (2021).

Classified Unknown Objects in Earth Orbit, Paglen Studio.

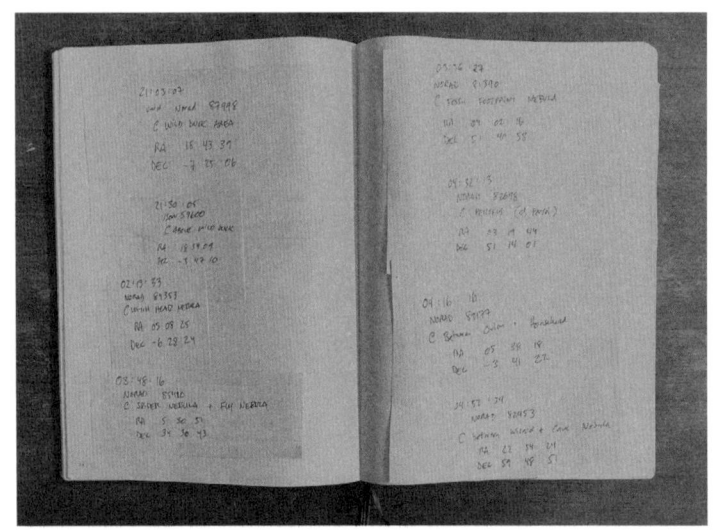

Caption (middle image): Production and research documentation, Paglen Studio.

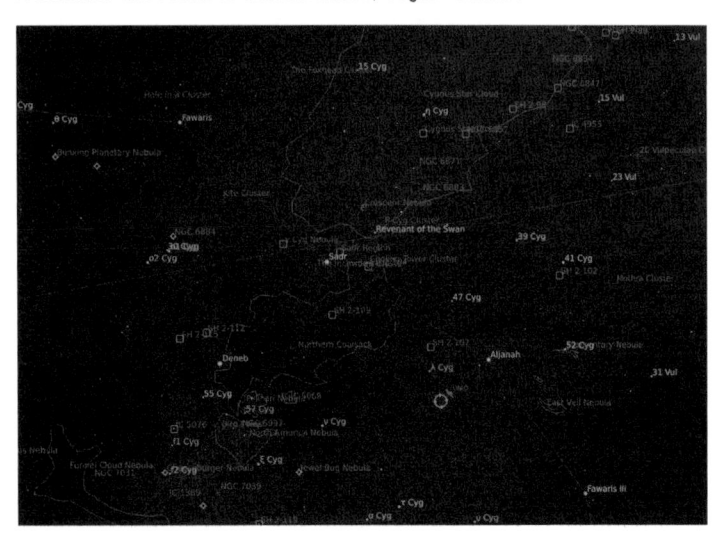

Caption (bottom image): Using the modeling software, I can make predictions about when and where in the sky I might find a particular object.

Step 2: Model the Orbits

Then I import that data into two different virtual planetarium software environments. (I use two in order to ensure that my predictions are accurate across multiple models and that I haven't made a mistake). The first software I use is Stellarium (this is a superb piece of free astronomy software). To check my work, I load the same data into a second modeling program called Heavensat.

It takes the better part of the day to model these orbits, and to select a series of targets for a given evening. Once I've selected the objects I want to image, I write a script for the evening in a software package I use to control the telescope, mount, and camera. The script tells the telescope to point to a particular point in the sky at a very precise moment, then instructs the camera to start making exposures before, during, and after the predicted pass of the unknown object. If I do everything correctly, I am able to capture the light-trail of the object as it passes through the telescope's field-of-view.

Step 3: Equipment

The main difficulty in choosing an appropriate telescope for photographing unids is sourcing a telescope that can collect as much light as quickly as possible. Because unids tend to be both very faint and fast-moving, I use the "fastest" telescope that I can. In my case, that means a Rowe-Ackermann Schmidt Astrograph (RASA) astrograph.

The RASA design is designed above all for speed, but it sacrifices ease and multifunctionality to get there. The design is a variation on a Schmidt-Cassegrain Telescope that replaces the secondary mirror with a camera sensor. The advantage of this is that the telescope can collect far more light much faster than a telescope with a secondary mirror. There are, however, many disadvantages. First, the removal of the secondary mirror means that there is no possibility of including an eyepiece in the design—there is no way to look through the telescope and it can only be used with a specialized camera. Secondly, at f/2 the critical focus zone (known as "depth of field" in 'normal' photography) of the telescope is smaller than half the width of a human hair. This translates into extreme technical difficulties in positioning the camera sensor accurately, as slight imperfections in how the camera sensor is placed in its housing during the manufacturing process create optical anomalies that have to be manually compensated for. This process is not fun.

On any given night, I'm aiming for triple-redundancy: for each image I am using three separate telescopes to collect as much light as possible and to mitigate against any mechanical failures (which happen often).

When I've successfully photographed the light-trail of a unid, I task the telescopes with collecting additional data from that region in the sky to fill out the photograph. Each exposure ends up being about 10,000 seconds worth of data or about 3 hours, much of which is shot with an infrared filter to highlight the various stelliferous and gaseous regions in the sky that are invisible to our eyes.

The night sky looks very different to infrared-sensitive equipment than it does to unaided eyes. Hydrogen, sulfur, and oxygen emissions reveal great cosmic clouds, stellar remnants, and galactic structures that recall Gustav Dore's etchings of the Divine Comedy. Their names refer to ancient myths, stories, and ancestral star-gazers. Many of the stars in the sky have names so ancient that their origins of those names, and the stories they once referred to, have been long forgotten.

Gustav Dore, *The stormy blast of hell with restless fury drives the spirits on*, ca. 1890.

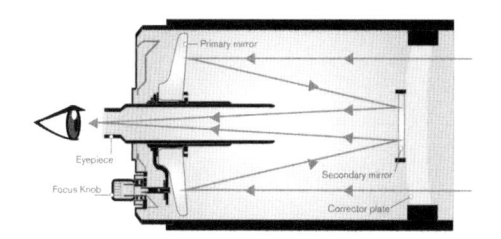

Schmidt-Cassegrain Telescope

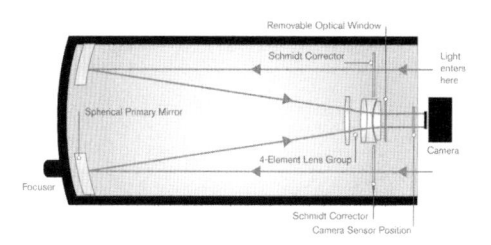

Rowe-Ackermann Schmidt Astrograph

I have spent countless days and nights studying the unknown objects, plotting orbits, measuring light curves, and analyzing their movements over time to see how their behavior may have changed over the years. I've tried to learn anything and everything I can about their shape, size, and mass, the relative stability of their orbits, and the question of whether they receive energy from any non-natural sources. Some of the numbers are surprising.

But every analytical technique available supplies only tiny variations

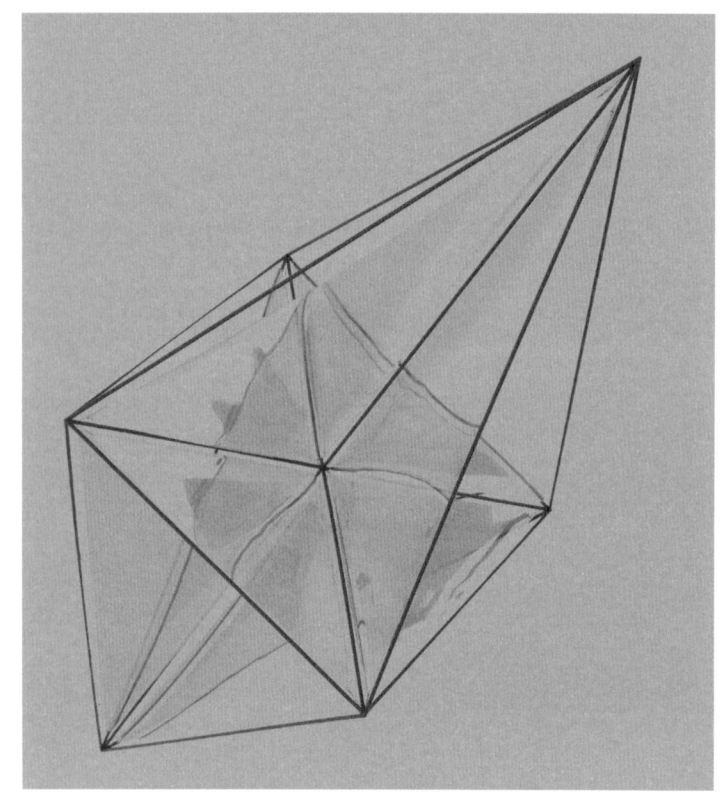

PALLADIUM Variation #4, 2023. Stainless steel, mirror foil. 23 ⅝ × 70 ⅞ inches.

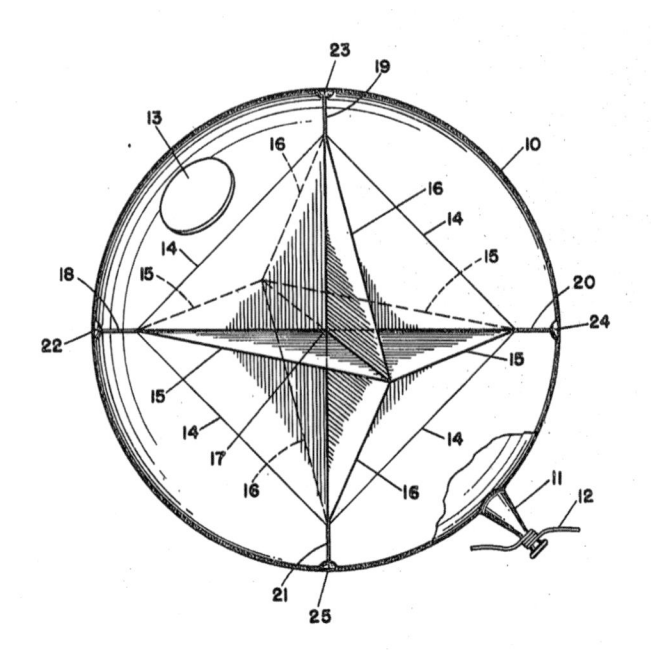

on a simple fact: The identity of these objects is "unknown." Given this, I ask myself where my desire to "identify" them comes from. Where does my unconscious desire to place these objects into received categories come from? Why does my subconscious seek the comfort of pre-existing language and concepts in the face of these unknowns?

II. PALLADIUM VARIATION #4

In late October, 1962 an American fighter jet out of Key West screamed south towards Havana Bay. The reaction was almost immediate: The Cuban military scrambled a pair of interceptors and raced north to meet the intruder. Just as the American jet neared the coastline, it banked north, flying impossibly fast and remaining just out of Cuban pilot's visual range. In the meantime, out of nowhere, a handful of unidentified aircraft of varying shapes and sizes appeared just outside the bay…

There was one problem. None of it was real. The plane was an electronically-generated "ghost." The UFOs were a collection of specifically-calibrated balloons launched from an American submarine, carefully designed to appear on radar screens as something wholly different than what they actually were.

Palladium Variation #4's lightweight, mirrorized, faceted structure is inspired by a history of objects built by military and intelligence agencies to spoof adversarial sensor systems. Objects like these are part of a broad category of military capacities called "Electronic Warfare."

Electronic Warfare (EW) is a huge field with many aspects to it, but a large part of it has to do with developing technologies that allow someone to remotely influence or control adversarial sensor systems and hardware. The idea is to make those systems "see" what you want them to see and "do" what you want them to do.

There are a wide range of applications in EW including remotely disabling rival sensors, making objects appear, disappear, or behave erratically, and conjuring all sorts of digital illusions.

A small subset of the field has to do with building unusual objects—structures that to human eyes might look like a balloon or basketball, but that look to a radar operator like a fleet of bombers or a misbehaving UFO. The concept is related to stealth technology (creating shapes that are "invisible" to radar), but much broader, namely creating objects that look like a huge range of things to sensor systems.

I often think about the relationship between the postwar aerospace industry and minimalist art. Undoubtedly, minimalist artists were inspired by the faceted shapes and then-exotic materials that emerged from advanced military research and development programs. But the philosophy of materials and shape descended from the Palladium programs are altogether different. They are not so much about the specificities of the objects-as-such. Quite the opposite. They are objects designed to dramatically amplify the different points-of-view that disparate observers and forms of seeing bring to them. They are adversarial sculptures, designed to weaponize the underlying assumptions built into different visual apparatuses.

III. BECAUSE PHYSICAL WOUNDS HEAL…

One genre of "outsider art" I'm most interested in is the unit patches and other emblems that military special operations groups and "black" units wear on their uniforms. These can be rare glimpses into some of the niches of military culture. One of the sculptures in my new body of work is inspired by designs made by PSYOP units…

Because Physical Wounds Heal…, 2023. Mixed Media, 50 × 50 inches.

The latin inscription on the sculpture is a translation of a slogan widely used in PSYOP units: "You've just been fucked by PSYOP. Because physical wounds heal." A second message on the sculpture's outer ring is available for viewers to attempt to decode.

YOU'VE JUST BEEN FUCKED BY PSYOPS
★ BECAUSE PHYSICAL WOUNDS HEAL ★

PERSUADE CHANGE INFLUENCE

310TH
A3
NIGHTMARE
SOMNIA NON PROHIBERE

304th PSYOP COMPANY
MIND BENDERS

PSYCHOLOGICAL OPERATIONS
SUADERE MUTARE DIRUERE

4TH PSYOPS GP.
CONFUSION TO THE ENEMY

YOU'VE JUST BEEN SMUG'D BY ANYA
BECAUSE PHYSICAL WOUNDS HEAL

I don't care about this particular psyop
Honestly

Throughout their history, PSYOP units have conducted missions such as Operation Wandering Soul, which involved making audio recordings of "ancestral ghosts" that were played from loudspeakers in patrol boats and helicopters during the Vietnam war. In the 1980s, the Air Force Office of Special Investigations worked with Richard Doty to generate deception campaigns intending to manipulate and monitor UFO investigators.

Here's the basic "generic" PSYOP crest. The figure of the horse is common in PSYOPS iconography. It has two meanings. The "knight" chess piece moves in a circuitous fashion and can attack from behind enemy lines. The second is a reference to the myth of the Trojan horse. The lightning swords are represent the ability to strike quickly.

Another figure commonly associated with PSYOP is the ghost. This references the "Ghost Army" of World War II, a group that conducted large-scale deception operations using inflatable tanks and materiel, loudspeakers and radio broadcasts, fake "generals," and other ruses designed to make things appear that weren't there. The "Ghost Army" was staffed by painters, designers, and architects including artist Ellsworth Kelly and fashion designer Bill Blass.

The ghost logo is still very much in use, sometimes in connection with the figure of the horse.

Things get lively pretty quickly when you start looking at PSYOP iconography… Here's the logo for the 304th PSYOP company based out of Sacramento, CA.

Here's a patch for the 609th Air Operations Center, based at Al Udeid Air Base, Qatar, and Shaw Air Force Base, South Carolina. The slogan here is along the lines of "to sweat, to change, to destroy…" The artwork is taken from a popular youtube meme.

And of course we find the usual grim reapers and other D&D imagery.

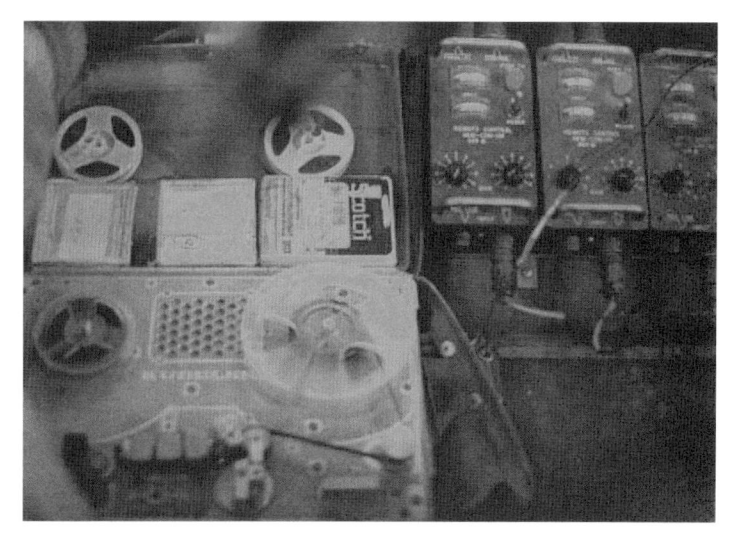

In 2011, the Army tried to change the name PSYOP to MISO (Military Information Support Operations). SecDef Robert Gates said "the term PSYOP tends to connote propaganda, brainwashing, manipulation, and deceit" and thought it was a bad look. The rank-and-file revolted—they didn't like having the same name as a bowl of soup. In 2017, the Army changed it back to PSYOP.[3]

People have had a lot of fun making meme designs around PSYOP…

Of course, the art of PSYOP isn't primarily about making patches, and it's not a coincidence that artists have been involved in it from the beginning.

In the past decade, online psychological operations have become ubiquitous. The documents leaked by Edward Snowden included information about a British unit called the "Joint Threat Research Group," which hired prominent psychologists to aid its online efforts to destroy their target's reputations and

We want to build Cyber *Magicians*.

Doty, 2023. (Still from video), Single channel video projection, black and white, stereo mix, 66 min (loop).

to manipulate online communities and discourse.

The JTRIG slide deck describes the dynamics that contribute to sociality, a sense of belonging, a sense of purpose, and explains how to weaponize those dynamics in order to fracture targeted individuals and communities. It also goes into the relationship between the physiological, psychological, and cultural dimensions of perception and shows how those too can be weaponized. The deck describes techniques utilizing everything from magic tricks to a belief in UFOs in order to persuade targets to believe or act in one way or another.[4]

IV. DOTY

As part of his training to join the Air Force Office of Special Investigations (AFOSI), Richard Doty was taught how to recruit spies, conduct and resist interrogations, run surveillance operations, and organize and manage deception and disinformation campaigns. After graduation, he was assigned to Kirtland Air Force Base in Albuquerque, NM.

During his active years in the late 1970s and 1980s, all sorts of strange, cutting-edge projects were taking place at the airbase. There were experimental laser systems, nuclear weapons programs, highly classified "stealth" aircraft, and other advanced technology demonstrators. Bizarre light shows, unearthly radio transmissions, and impossible-to-explain events became a mainstay in the base's vicinity. Civilian UFO researchers took notice and began to investigate the goings-on at Kirtland.

Using his training in counterintelligence, deception, and spycraft, Doty would recruit people from the UFO community to act as informants for the Air Force, and to assist him in crafting and spreading disinformation among their ranks as part of his mission to protect Air Force assets.

Doty concedes that the field of UFO research is filled with charlatanism and disinformation, but nonetheless insists on the reality of the phenomenon. Over the course of his intelligence work, Doty describes being "read into" a top-secret program having to do with the US Government's relationship to the UFO phenomena.

V. CYCLOPS

Cyclops is a networked performance, collaborative narrative, and alternate-reality-game designed to be played by groups of people working together across the word. Set in the late 1960s and early 1970s, the game begins with a series of audio tracks. Some tracks are musical compositions, others are filled with odd voices reading letters and counting numbers, others still resemble nothing more than noise and static. Each track is, in fact, a puzzle of increasing complexity. As players work together to solve them, a narrative about early research into psychological operations, mind-control experiments, and an alternative history of the internet age begins to emerge. Over the course of the game, players come across a collection of artworks that are specifically created for Cyclops players. To find these artworks, players must identify and follow up on clues provided within the game. Cyclops is a world within a world.

This essay is a print version of a series of posts supporting works from the exhibition *You've Just Been Fucked by PSYOPS* at Pace Gallery, New York.

CYCLOPS, 2023.

1 I'm sorry I really have a hard time saying or writing the words "Space Force."
2 Gravitational anomalies are areas on Earth where the local gravity field is stronger or weaker than the global average. These variations can be caused by differences in the density of the Earth's crust, the presence of large mountain ranges or ocean trenches, and variations in the distribution of the Earth's mass. One of the most well-known gravity anomalies is the "Indian Ocean Geoid Low," which is a region of low gravity field strength in the Indian Ocean. This anomaly is primarily due to the large mass of the Himalayas to the north and the Earth's equatorial bulge. Gravitational anomalies affect satellites by subtly altering their inclination over time, and by causing them to drift longitudinally.
3 #https://www.armyupress.army.mil/Journals/Military-Review/Online-Exclusive/2018-OLE/Mar/PSYOP/
4 For more recent examples of the relationship between PSYOPS and aesthetics, consider the infamous "Ghost in the Machine" video produced by the 4th PSYOP Group: https://www.youtube.com/watch?v=VA4eONqyYMw. And for a critical reading of how the aesthetics and politics of PSYOPS is all-too-real, check out these essays by @gunseli_yal and and @ja_ak_rtgr. https://www.punctr.art/because-physical-wounds-heal/. https://www.dazeddigital.com/life-culture/article/58042/1/were-entering-an-age-of-psyop-realism-but-what-does-that-mean. And for a deeper dive into the wheels-within-wheels logic of possible PSYOP media, see https://youtu.be/JFlB2lVPoWo perhaps an example of where the logic of PSYOP is going…

51.4 °C e=0.95

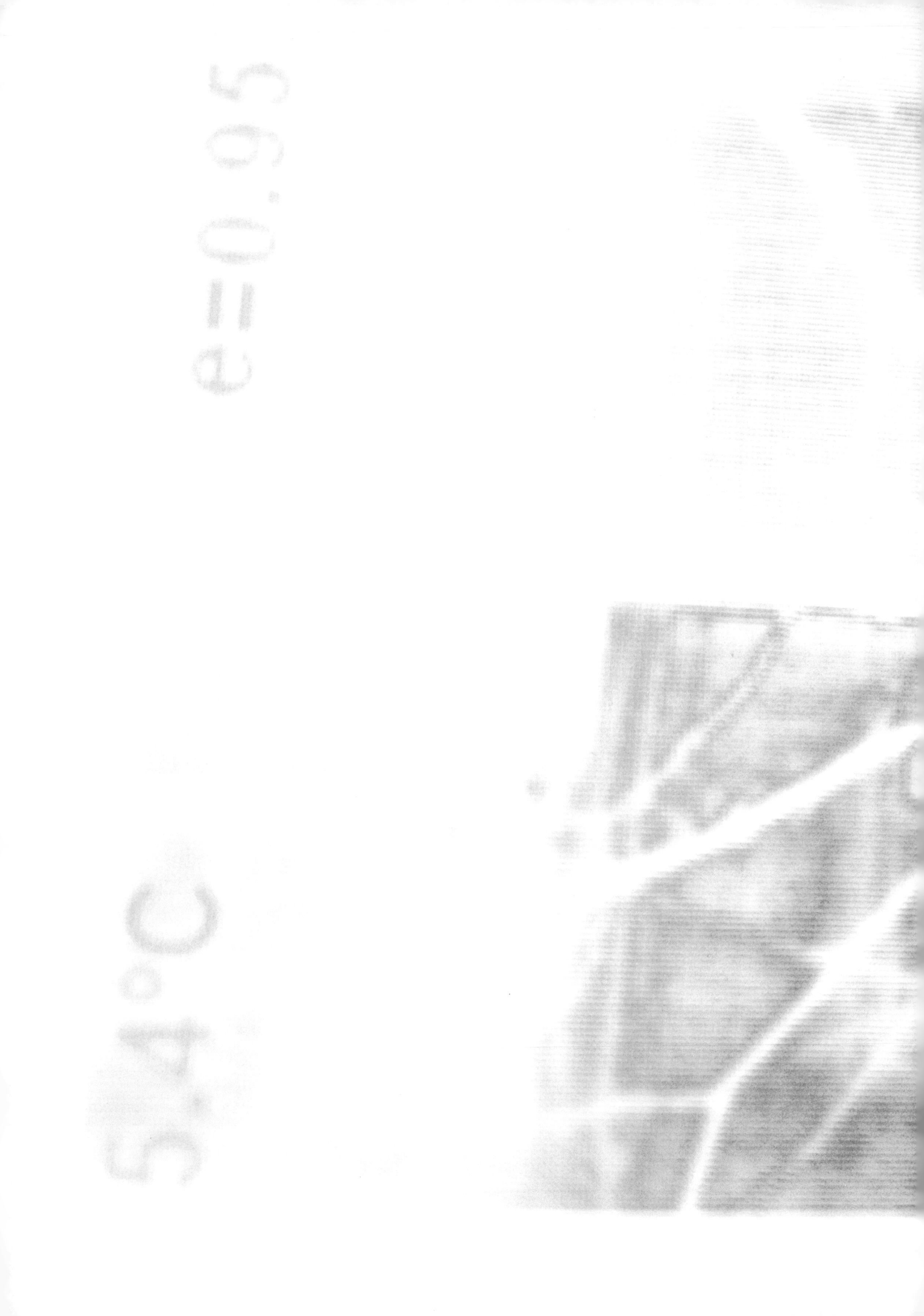

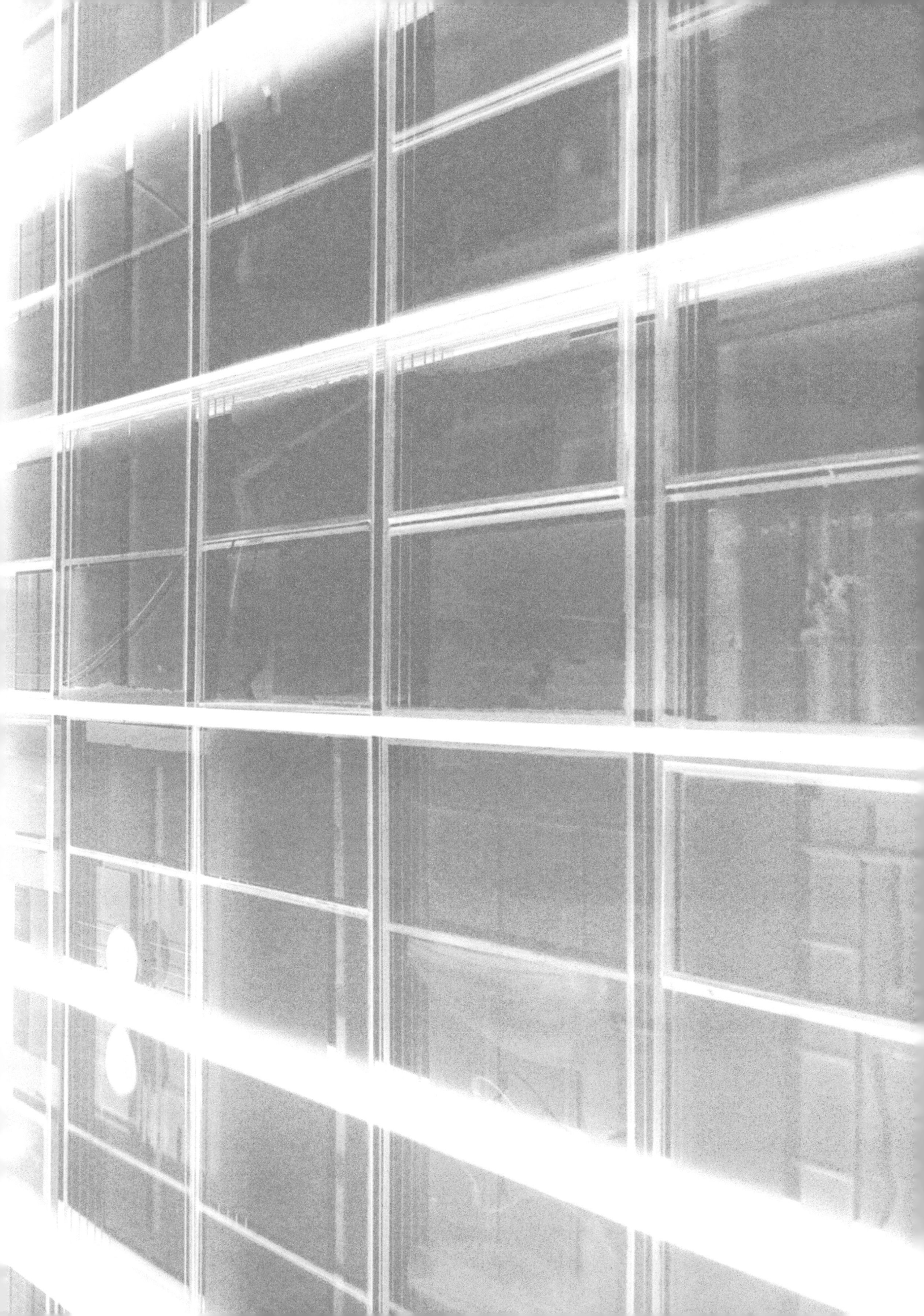

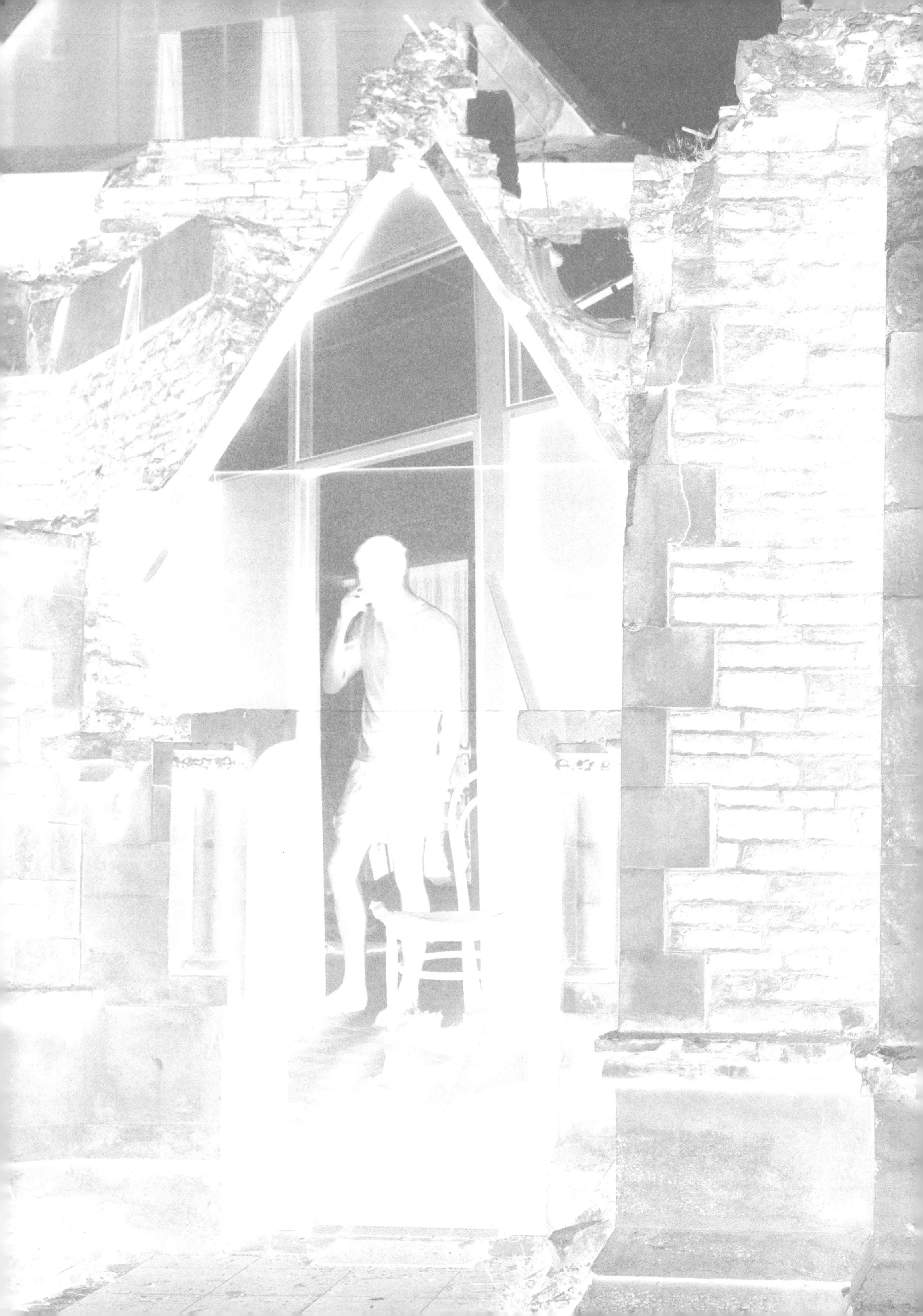

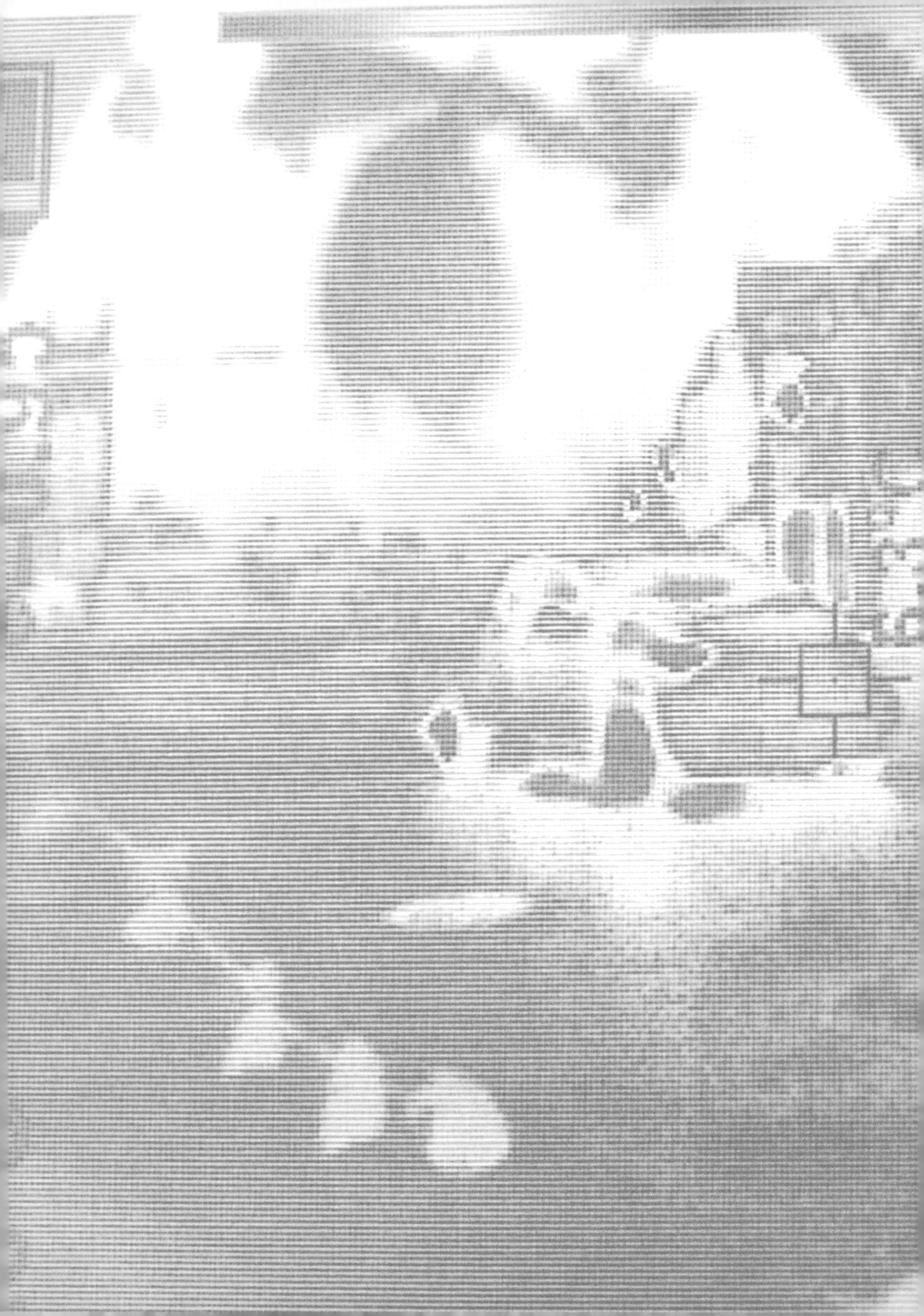

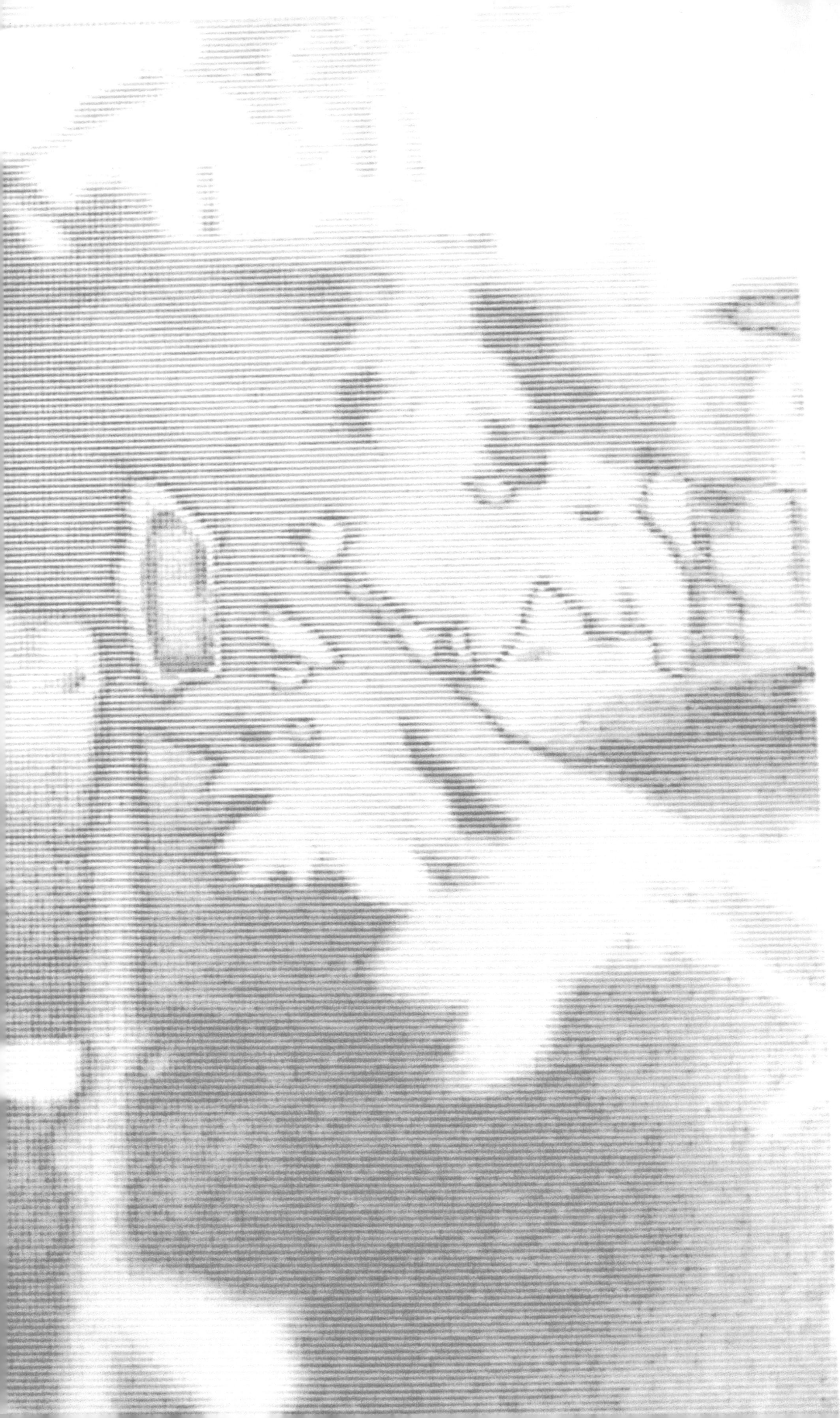

CONTRIBUTORS

APRDELESP, XAVIER NUENO GUITART

APRDELESP (since 2012) is an architecture office based in Mexico City: A practice-as-research on space and its appropriation. Some of their best-known case studies are the Mexican Pavilion at the 18th International Architecture Exhibition La Biennale di Venezia (2023), Lodos (2021), Feria Material (Vol. 8, Vol. 7, Vol. 6, Vol. 5, Vol. 4, and Vol. 3), Estación Material, (Vol.2, Vol.1), Parque Experimental El Eco (2016), MUEBLES SULLIVAN (2013), and CAFÉ ZENA (2012). They won the public competition make the Mexican Pavilion at the 18th International Architecture Exhibition La Biennale di Venezia (2023), have been selected as one of the winners of Housekeeping, the Architectural League Prize for Young Architects and Designers (2021), and won the "Pabellón Eco" competition for Museo Experimental El Eco (2016). They have exhibited their work at ArtCenter College of Design (Pasadena, United States), Lodos (Mexico City, Mexico), The Architectural League of New York (New York, United States), and Kirkland Gallery—Harvard Graduate School of Design (Cambridge, United States). They have published the books *A Manifesto on the Appropriation of Space: a Methodology for Making Architecture* (2019) and *Notes on Winnie-the-Pooh's house-tree* (2019).

Xavier Nueno Guitart received his PhD from Harvard University. He writes about the history of knowledge in its multiple scientific, artistic, sensorial and technological forms, from antiquity to the present. His wide and diverse field of study has led him to collaborate with artists, architects, cooks and activists on books, short films and exhibitions. He is co-author of *Napa(s): To Persist in the Unfinished* (2018) and *Chaque Mercredi Caracas* (2020). He currently conducts his research at the Laboratory of History and Theory of Architecture, Technology and Media at the Ecole Polytechnique Fédérale de Lausanne (EPFL) in Switzerland. His most recent book is *El arte del saber ligero: Una breve historia del exceso de información* (2023).

ASHLEY BIGHAM, ERIK HERRMANN

Ashley Bigham and Erik Herrmann are co-directors of Outpost Office and assistant professors of architecture at The Ohio State University's Knowlton School of Architecture. Their practice designs installations, events, and buildings that challenge architecture's core tenets of permanence and accumulation by proposing provisional, open-ended, and contingent environments. The work of Outpost Office has been exhibited internationally, including at the Chicago Architecture Biennial, Art Omi, and the Wexner Center for the Arts. The practice has been in residency at MacDowell, Ragdale, Loghaven, and Headlands Center for the Arts. Their recent work includes houses that are too small and too big.

ESTHER M. CHOI

Esther M. Choi is a multidisciplinary artist and scholar whose work explores how concepts of identity and nature have been shaped by the aesthetics and narratives of Western cultural worldmaking practices. Her work draws from art and architectural history, decolonial and postcolonial theory, critical environmental studies, and feminist science and technology studies. Choi's socially-engaged projects include *Office Hours* (2020–), a knowledge sharing project by and for BIPOC cultural producers; *Le Corbuffet* (Prestel, 2019), a Fluxus-inspired, James Beard-nominated cookbook that poses questions about canons, interpretation, and cultural value; and *Public Service* (2023–), a web series featuring BIPOC artists, designers, and scholars in conversations about catalyzing change in the culture industries—and beyond. Her writing has been published in *Artforum*, *Art Papers*, *Harvard Design Magazine*, and *e-flux*, in addition to edited volumes and exhibition catalogs. She is the co-editor of *Architecture at the Edge of Everything Else* (MIT Press, 2010) and *Architecture Is All Over* (Columbia University, 2017). Choi's work has received support from The Ford Foundation, Canada Council for the Arts, Richard Rogers Fellowship, and The Graham Foundation, among others. She was a 2022 Getty/ ACLS Postdoctoral Fellow and is an Associate Professor, Adjunct, at The Cooper Union.

FEMINIST ARCHITECTURE COLLABORATIVE

feminist architecture collaborative (f-architecture) is a three-woman* architectural research enterprise aimed at disentangling the contemporary spatial politics of bodies, intimately and globally. Their projects traverse theoretical and material registers to locate new forms of architectural work through critical relationships with collaborators across continents and an expanding definition of Designer. They think, write, and design about blood, teenage dreaming, sovereignty, fakeness, and protest—among other supposedly extra-disciplinary fixations.

f-architecture is a winner of the 2019 Architectural League Prize. *Como-Clinical Interiors of Beirut*, their exhibition on the architectural reproduction of virginity in the Lebanese capital, opened at VI PER Gallery in Prague in 2018 and has been re-staged by the Architectural League of New York, and at the NTU Institute of Science and Technology for Humanity in Singapore, where they were shortlisted for the 2019 Global Digital Art Prize. In January 2020, they were Artists-in-Residence at The Lab at Darat al Funun in Amman, Jordan, during which time they produced the exhibition *Paper Machine* (آلات ورقية). Their writing and work have appeared in *Harvard Design Magazine*, *e-flux architecture*, *The Funambulist*, *Real Review* and *Log*, among other publications, and at institutions including Morgan Library and Museum, Studio-X Amman, Universität der Künste Berlin, FRAC Centre-Val de Loire, and UN-Habitat. f-architecture is a former member of the GSAPP Incubator @ NEW INC, the incubator initiative of the New Museum of Contemporary Art in New York.

*Virginia Black, Rosana Elkhatib, and Gabrielle Printz co-founded f-architecture in 2016. They maintain their wily practice and their deep friendship in Brooklyn, New York.

MARIANELA D'APRILE, DOUGLAS SPENCER

Marianela D'Aprile is a writer and the deputy editor of the *New York Review of Architecture*. Her writing on art, architecture, literature, and politics has been published widely, including in *The Nation*, *Jacobin*, *n+1*, and *The Architectural Review*. The first essay she co-authored with Douglas Spencer was published in *The Avery Review* in 2022. From 2018 to 2021, she served on the National Political Committee of the Democratic Socialists of America. She lives and works in New York City.

Douglas Spencer is Pickard Chilton Professor of Architecture at Iowa State University. He is the author of *The Architecture of Neoliberalism* (2016), *Critique of Architecture* (2021), and, forthcoming, *Architecture and the Ends of Capitalism* (2025). His writing on architecture theory, labor and critique has also been published in *ARCH+*, *Avery Review*, *Harvard Design Magazine*, *Log*, *New York Review of Architecture*, *Radical Philosophy* and in numerous edited book collections.

THEO DEUTINGER, CHRISTOPHER CLARKSON

Theo Deutinger is an architect, urbanist, and curator. He is founder and head of The Department (TD), a practice that combines architecture and urban design with analytic research. With his office he works at all levels from global planning to architecture to graphic design and curatorial works. Deutinger is known for his theoretical writings on the transformation of European urban culture and his publications such as the *Handbook of Tyranny* and *Joy and Fear*. His work has been shown at the Stedelijk Museum in Amsterdam (2017), Storefront for Architecture in New York (2019), and the Swiss Architecture Museum in Basel (2020) among others. He lives and works in Austria.

Christopher Clarkson was born in South Africa and is currently based in the Netherlands. He is in his final year of graduate studies in Architecture at the Delft University of Technology within the Borders and Territories group. Besides this Christopher Clarkson works as a freelance editor, photographer, and curator. His publications include several essays in the student and faculty-run journals *pantheon//* and *Bnieuws*, and together with Theo Deutinger and Pia Prantl he is the co-author of "Ministry of Ethics: The Department of Ethical Design" (2022). Additionally he was the proofreader for "Repository, 49 methods for writing urban places" (2023) edited by Klaske Havik et al, and carried out research for Theo Deutinger's latest book *Joy and Fear* (2023).

DESIGN EARTH

DESIGN EARTH deploys the speculative architectural project to make public the climate crisis. They are authors of *Geographies of Trash* (2015); *Geostories: Another Architecture for the Environment* (3rd ed. 2022), *The Planet After Geoengineering* (2021), and *Climate Inheritance* (2023). DESIGN EARTH are recipients of the United States Artist Fellowship and the Architectural League Prize for Young Architects + Designers, amongst other honors. Their work has been featured internationally, including at Venice Architecture Biennale, Bauhaus Museum Dessau, the San Francisco Museum of Modern Art, Milano Triennale, Matadero Madrid, and the Museum of Modern Art in New York City, where their project "After Oil" is in the permanent collection. DESIGN EARTH was founded and is led by Rania Ghosn and El Hadi Jazairy. Ghosn (Beirut, b. 1977) is Associate Professor of Architecture and Urbanism at the Massachusetts Institute of Technology. Jazairy (Algeria, b. 1970) is Associate Professor of Architecture and Director of Master of Urban Design degree program at the University of Michigan. The DESIGN EARTH project team for "Elephant in the Room and Other Fables" is Rania Ghosn, Monica Hutton, El Hadi Jazairy, and Anhong Li.

DAVID FREELAND, BRENNAN BUCK

Brennan Buck is a principal at FreelandBuck in New York City and a senior critic at the Yale School of Architecture. His writing on technology and representation within the discipline of architecture has been published in several books and journals including *Log* and *Project Journal*. Prior to teaching at Yale, he was assistant professor in Studio Greg Lynn at the University of Applied Arts, Vienna. He has worked in the offices of Neil M. Denari Architects and Johnston Marklee & Associates in Los Angeles and Walker Macy in Portland, Oregon. Brennan is a graduate of Cornell University and the UCLA Department of Architecture and Urban Design.

David Freeland is a principal at FreelandBuck in Los Angeles and design faculty at Southern California Institute of Architecture. Prior to SCI-Arc he taught at Woodbury University where he was instrumental in developing the FabLab and teaching fabrication and computation. Freeland has worked with architecture offices in Los Angeles and New York including Michael Maltzan Architecture and Peter Eisenman Architects. He holds a B.S.Arch from the University of Virginia and an M.Arch from the UCLA Department of Architecture and Urban Design.

LINDA GORDON

Linda Gordon teaches history at NYU. Her study of 20th century social movements, including a discussion of the 1930s American fascist groups, will be published by Norton in early autumn 2024. Her most recent book is *The Second Coming of the KKK: The Ku Klux Klan in the American Political Tradition* (2017). She is one of a very few historians who won the Bancroft prize for best book in American history twice, for *The Great Arizona Orphan Abduction* (1999), the story of a vigilante action against Mexican-Americans, and *Dorothea Lange: A Life Beyond Limits* (2009). More of her work is available at lindagordonhistorian.org.

NOAH KALINA

Noah Kalina was born and raised in Huntington, New York and attended the School of Visual Arts in New York City. Ten years ago he built a studio in Lumberland, New York where he is now based full-time. His work has been exhibited nationally and internationally and is in numerous personal and public collections. His work has been commissioned by the Museum of Modern Art, Google, Samsung, Gucci, and Disney, and has made editorial work for the *New York Times Magazine*, *Wired*, and *Dwell* among many others. Noah has published two books, *Bedmounds* (2019) and *Tiny Flock* (2020), and was the main photographer for the international bestseller *Cabin Porn* (2015). His ongoing (now over two decades) self-portrait project, *Everyday*, was parodied on *The Simpsons*.

DANA KARWAS

Dana Karwas is the Director of the Center for Collaborative Arts and Media (CCAM) at Yale University and is a Critic at the Yale School of Architecture teaching courses related to mechanized perception and space architecture. At CCAM her Ultra Space research explores earthly reference frames for understanding the body in space. The research is inspired by the work of Shusaku Arakawa and Madeline Gins, who consider the body as a part of its architectural surroundings. The Ultra Space initiative is integrated into her Yale School of Architecture courses and CCAM workshops, including *The Mechanical Artifact*, which is taught in collaboration with Ariel Ekblaw *Manipulations* taught in collaboration with Sarah Oppenheimer, and *Bodies in Space* taught in collaboration with Harshita Nedunuri. Her Ultra Space research is shared with wider audiences through the annual CCAM Ultra Space symposium.

Karwas is a fellow at the Aurelia Institute, a nonprofit space architecture R&D lab, the NYU Tisch Collaboratory, and at Branford College at Yale University. She has taught interdisciplinary art and architecture courses at New York University and Columbia University.

ANDREW ECONOMOS MILLER

Andrew Economos Miller is a designer and educator who uses the trash pile as a tool for the deconstruction of architecture as an imperial labor form. They are interested in heterogeneous materiality and the intentional demolition and reconstruction of the built environment toward new ends. They were the 2022–23 Schidlowski Emerging Faculty Fellow at Kent State University with their exhibition, *Refuse//Repose*. Their writing has been published in *Disc*, *Log*, and *Paprika!* and their work has been featured in exhibitions at A83, Kent State University, and the Yale School of Architecture North Gallery. They received their Bachelor of Science in Architecture from Ohio State University and a

Master of Architecture from the Yale School of Architecture. They have worked professionally in New York City and Columbus, Ohio as an architectural designer and editor. They are currently teaching at Kean University in Union, New Jersey and working in practice in New York City.

M.C. OVERHOLT, ALEX WHEE KIM

M.C. is an architectural writer and researcher based in Philadelphia. She is a graduate of the Master of Environmental Design (M.E.D.) program ('21) at the Yale School of Architecture and is currently pursuing her doctoral degree in the History and Theory of Architecture at Weitzman School of Design. Her scholarly work—which can be found in venues including *Public Culture*, *Platform*, *Imago: Studi di Cinema e Media*, and the forthcoming edited collection *Living Room* (edited by S.E. Eisterer)—uses queer, trans*, and feminist of color frameworks of analysis to reread interlocking histories of architecture, science, and embodied subjectivity. In particular, her developing dissertation examines the influence of 20th-century American sexology on architecture, arguing that, through this interaction, an ecological conception of sex was forged that positioned the built environment as a primary influencing factor in the production of so-called "deviant" sexual behavior. M.C. has presented her research at venues including the Society of Architectural Historians Annual International Conference, the Urban Humanities Network (un)Conference, the University of California Santa Barbara, and the University of São Paolo Faculdade de Arquitetura e Urbanismo. She is also co-editor for *Perspecta* 57 alongside Alex Whee Kim, Sarah Kim, and Brian Orser.

Alex Whee Kim (he/him) is a designer and writer from California. His research generally focuses on the role of games and other participatory media in the history of political and spatial practice. He is also interested in technologies of management, the history of the "modern-colonial," and Cold War-era discursive networks. His doctoral research traces the genealogy of war gaming media and imperial geographical pedagogy, their relationship to games-based approaches to architectural design and urban planning in the 1960s and '70s, and the development of computational thinking and crisis management. His writing—often collaborative—has appeared in *Imago: Studi di cinema e media*, *Places*, and *Disc*. He has been a coordinating editor of *Paprika!* and is a co-editor of the forthcoming *Perspecta* 57. Alex has a B.Arch from Syracuse University and an M.E.D. from Yale.

TREVOR PAGLEN

Trevor Paglen (b. 1974) lives and works in New York, NY. As an artist, filmmaker, investigator, technologist, and theorist, Paglen asks questions around vision, perception, materiality, and aesthetics. His wide-ranging oeuvre includes work on artificial intelligence and computer vision, aerospace technology, secrecy and conspiracy, experimental landscapes, speculative fiction, nuclear histories, notional archaeology, psychological operations, and the Weird.

Paglen has photographed secret military bases from enormous distances, tracked classified satellites and objects of unknown origin in earth orbit, led underwater tours of internet infrastructure, created a radioactive sculpture for a nuclear exclusion zone, profiled an Air Force disinformation specialist, built numerous AI and computer vision models, performed with the Kronos Quartet, written several books, and launched two sculptures into space, among other things.

Ultimately, Paglen poses the following question: How can we learn to see the world at a moment in time where accelerating technologies, politics, and cultures come up against the limits of reason and perception?

LUKAS PAUER

Lukas Pauer is a licensed architect, urbanist, historian, educator, and the Founding Director of the Vertical Geopolitics Lab, an investigative practice and think-tank at the intersections of architecture, geography, politology, and media, dedicated to exposing intangible systems and hidden agendas within the built environment. At the University of Toronto (UofT), Lukas is an Assistant Professor of Architecture, Inaugural 2022–2024 Emerging Architect Fellow. There, his contribution at disciplinary intersections is reflected in his engagements as a Faculty Affiliate in Urban Studies at the UofT A&S SofC as well as a Faculty Affiliate in Global Affairs and Public Policy at the UofT Munk CERES. From the Architectural Association in London, he holds a PhD AD on political imaginaries in architectural and urban design history with a focus on how imperial-colonial expansion has been performed architecturally throughout history. Pauer holds an MAUD from Harvard University and an MSc Arch from ETH Zürich. Among widespread international recognition, he has been selected as an Ambassadorial Scholar by the Rotary Foundation, a Global Shaper by the World Economic Forum, and an Emerging Leader by the European Forum Alpbach—leadership programs committed to change-making impact within local communities.

NINA RAPPAPORT

Nina Rappaport is an urbanist, curator, critic, and educator. She is publications director at the Yale School of Architecture, where she edited the magazine *Constructs* for 24 years. Currently, she also edits a book series and the school's exhibition catalogs.

As director of Vertical Urban Factory, she focuses on the intersection of production spaces, economies, and the factory worker as an advisor to city agencies. She is author of *Vertical Urban Factory* (Actar 2015 and 2020) and curator of the 2011 eponymous on-going traveling exhibition. She co-edited *Design for Urban Manufacturing* (Routledge 2020) and *Hybrid Factory/Hybrid City* (Actar 2023). She has written essays in the publications *Lifelines* (Politecnico di Torino 2022), *Production City* (AD 2021), *Industrious City* (Lars Muller 2020), *Twisted* (Actar 2019), *Harvard Design Magazine* (2019), *City Made* (010 2018), *The Built Environment* (2018), and *Encountering Things* (Bloomsbury 2017), as well as for *Praxis*, *Perspecta*, *Scapes*, and *306090*. Her other focus on the role of structural engineers as designers resulted in the book *Support and Resist* (Monacelli 2008).

She is coordinator of the history and theory program at the School of Public Architecture at Kean University and has been a Visiting Professor at Politecnico di Torino and Università degli Studi di Roma La Sapienza. She has received NYSCA, Graham Foundation, and NYC grants. She is on the steering committee of the Western Queens Community Land Trust, on the program committee of the Design Trust for Public Space, and a founding member of Docomomo US and the New York/Tri-State chapter.

DAVID SADIGHIAN

David Sadighian, Assistant Professor of Architecture at Yale University, researches and teaches the history of architecture, infrastructure, and material culture in the Atlantic World since the eighteenth century. He completed his PhD in the History of Art and Architecture at Harvard University, where his dissertation examined the global circulation of design methods taught at the Paris École des Beaux-Arts during the Age of Empire, ca. 1870–1914. David's work situates the history of design at the nexus of colonialism, migration, capitalism, and political thought, bridging the disciplines of art and architectural history with global history, sociology, and related fields. Support for his research and studies has been provided by the Social Science Research Council (SSRC-IDRF), the American Historical Association, the Krupp Foundation, the David Rockefeller Center for Latin American Studies, the Graham Foundation for Advanced Studies in the Fine Arts, the Deutsches Forum für Kunstgeschichte (DFK Paris), and UCLA's Center for 17th and 18th Century Studies. Having published his work in several journals and edited volumes, David was also the co-editor of *Perspecta* 44 "Domain" (2011).

MATTHEW SOULES

Matthew Soules is an Associate Professor in the architecture program at the University of British Columbia's School of Architecture and Landscape Architecture and founder of Matthew Soules Architecture. He has been visiting faculty at the Southern California Institute of Architecture and visiting Associate Professor at the Harvard University Graduate School of Design. His most recent book is *Icebergs, Zombies and the Ultra Thin: Architecture and Capitalism in the Twenty-First Century* (2021). He is co-founder of Architects Against Housing Alienation (AAHA), an activist collective that represented Canada at the 2023 Venice Biennale of Architecture.

JEROME TRYON

Jerome is a critic at the Yale School of Architecture and holds a B.Arch from the University of Oregon and a M.Arch from the Yale School of Architecture where he received the William Wirt Winchester Fellowship, the school's most prestigious award. He has also been recognized by the ICAA with the Rieger Graham Prize for a fellowship at the American Academy in Rome, The Sir John Soane's Museum Foundation Graduate Fellowship as a Soane Scholar, the Cavin Family Traveling Fellowship, and the Olson Kundig Travel fellowship. He has worked in the offices of Olson Kundig, MICA (formerly Rick Mather Architects), and Knight Architecture.

Jerome's current work and research focuses on memory's role in shaping perception and the way both memory and perception intersect with architectural space. He operates a practice that explores the adjacencies between art and architecture. His projects encompass work at all scales and media—from drawings to architectural objects.

MICHAEL YOUNG

Michael Young is an Associate Professor at The Irwin S. Chanin School of Architecture at the Cooper Union and founding partner of Young & Ayata. He is the recipient of the 2019–20 Rome Prize from the American Academy of Rome. He is the author of *The Estranged Object* (2015) and *Reality Modeled After Images* (2022). Young & Ayata have received the Progressive Architecture award, the Design Vanguard Award, the Young Architects Prize, the AIANY Honor Award, a first-place prize for the design of the Bauhaus Museum in Dessau, Germany and a first-place prize for the New Agricultural Management Institute, Gyeongsangbuk-do, S. Korea.

IMAGE CREDITS

The editors greatly acknowledge the permissions granted to reproduce the copyrighted material in this publication. Every effort has been made to trace the ownership of all copyrighted material and to secure proper credits and permissions from the appropriate copyright holders. In the event of any omission or oversight, all necessary corrections will be made in future printings. Unless otherwise noted, all images are courtesy of the author(s).

ESTHER M. CHOI

Fig. 1, 2. Louverture Films.
Fig. 3. © Roz Chast/The New Yorker Collection/
The Cartoon Bank.
Fig. 4. © Artforum.
Fig. 5. © Art Resource New York.
Fig. 6. Library of Congress, LC-DIG-ppmsca-09855.
Fig. 7. © Getty Images.
Fig. 8. Creative commons: Tate Museum.

ANDREW ECONOMOS MILLER

All images courtesy of the author and Norman Foster Foundation, Madrid.

THEO DEUTINGER, CHRISTOPHER CLARKSON

All images courtesy of the authors.

M.C. OVERHOLT, ALEX WHEE KIM

All images courtesy of the authors and Maria Baranova.

DANA KARWAS

Fig. 1, 2. © 1997 Reversible Destiny Foundation. Reproduced with permission of the Reversible Destiny Foundation.
Fig. 3, 4. © 2023 Reversible Destiny Foundation. Reproduced with permission of the Reversible Destiny Foundation.
Fig. 5, 6, 7. © 2023 Reversible Destiny Foundation. Reversible Destiny Foundation Archives.

DAVID FREELAND, BRENNAN BUCK

All images courtesy of the authors and Maria Baranova.

NINA RAPPAPORT

p. 94. Library of Congress.
p. 96, 97. Konrad F. Wittman, Camouflage Laboratory, Department of Architecture, Pratt Institute, 1942.
p. 98. Burbank Historical Society.
p. 100. Lockheed Martin.
p. 102. Architectural Record.

DAVID SADIGHIAN

Fig. 1. Homes Sweet Homes (London and New York: John Murray and Transatlantic Arts, 1946; first published in 1939), p. 38.
Fig. 2. London, The British Museum, Accession Number 1948,0214.971.
Fig. 3, 4, 5. France, Private Collection.
Fig. 6. Providence, Brown University Library, Anne S.K. Brown Military Collection.
Fig. 7. Paris, Bilbiothèque nationale de France, département Estampes et photographie, FOL-VE-1368.
Fig. 8. Collection Comte de Rosebery.
Fig. 9. Paris, Musée du Louvre, département des Peintures, service d'etude et de documentation.
Fig. 10, 11. France, Private Collection.

DESIGN EARTH

All images courtesy of the authors.

MARIANELA D'APRILE, DOUGLAS SPENCER

All images courtesy of the authors unless otherwise noted.
p. 135. Wikiarquitectura.
p. 136. Carsten Janssen.
p. 137. Smarthistory.
p. 137. dalbera, Wikipedia.
p. 137. Atlas of Places.
p. 137. © Ezra Stoller | Esto.
p. 137. CultureNow.
p. 137. Bundesarchiv, Wikipedia.
p. 138. © Gili Merin.
p. 138. © Fondazione Prada, photo by Bas Princen.
p. 139. © Felix Loechner.
p. 140. © Santi Caleca.
p. 140. © Iwan Baan.
p. 141. © Yongjoon Choi.
p. 141. © Amazon.
p. 142. Fendi.
p. 142. Neom.

MATTHEW SOULES

All images courtesy of the author unless otherwise noted.
p. 146. Halkin Mason, courtesy of Rafael Viñoly Architects.
p. 146. Paul Raftery.
p. 147. Graham Turner, courtesy of Redux Pictures.
p. 147, 149, 151. Josimar Dominguez.
p. 149, 150. Lőrinc Vass.
p. 152. Tim Franco.

FEMINIST ARCHITECTURE COLLABORATIVE

All images courtesy of the authors unless otherwise noted.
p. 158. Sliman Mansour/Wikiart.
p. 163. Antonio Faccilongo.

LINDA GORDON

Fig. 1. Library of Congress, LC-USF34-002328-C.
Fig. 2. Bureau of Agricultural Economics, BAE 083-G-44065.
Fig. 3. Library of Congress, LC-DIG-fsa-8b33499.
Fig. 4. Library of Congress, LC-USZ62-19804.
Fig. 5. Library of Congress, LC-USF34-016013-C.
Fig. 6. Library of Congress, LC-USZ62-118393.
Fig. 7. Library of Congress, LC-USF34-019499-E.
Fig. 8. Library of Congress, LC-DIG-fsa-8b33791.
Fig. 9. Library of Congress, LC-DIG-fsa-8b34016.
Fig. 10. Library of Congress, LC-USF34-020033-C.
Fig. 11. Library of Congress, LC-DIG-fsa-8b34211.
Fig. 12. Library of Congress, LC-DIG-fsa-8b29637.
Fig. 13. Library of Congress, LC-USF34-019904-E.

APRDELESP, XAVIER NUENO GUITART

All images courtesy of the authors unless otherwise noted.
p. 190. Nippon TV.
p. 191. Meta.
p. 191. The Walt Disney Company, 21st Century Fox.
p. 192. Taller de Arquitectura—Mauricio Rocha.
p. 192. Wikipedia.
p. 194. Co-Star Astrology.
p. 194. Junya Ishigami.

MICHAEL YOUNG

All images courtesy of the author and the Chantal Akerman Foundation, Brussels.

ASHLEY BIGHAM, ERIK HERRMANN

All images courtesy of the authors.

JEROME TRYON

Fig. 1. U.S. National Archives.
Fig. 2. Bureau of Ships Collection, U.S. National Archives.
Fig. 3, 4, 6. U.S. National Archives.

NOAH KALINA

All images courtesy of the author.

LUKAS PAUER

All images courtesy of the author.

TREVOR PAGLEN

All images courtesy of the author unless otherwise noted.
p. 251. 18th Space Defense Squadron, Wikipedia.
p. 255. © Celestron.
p. 255. © SOTK2011/Alamy Stock Photo.
p. 258. Mountain Tactical Institute.
p. 259. Psywarrior.

COVER IMAGE

CYCLOPS, 2023. Image courtesy of Trevor Paglen.

INTERSTITIAL IMAGES

p. 9. Advanced Spaceborne Thermal Emission and Reflection Radiometer (ASTER) image of Pakistan flooding, 2010.
© NASA/GSFC/METI/ERSDAC/JAROS, and U.S./Japan ASTER Science Team.
p. 10. Multi-frequency, multi-polarization spaceborne radar image of seasonal sea-ice cover in the Weddell Sea, Antarctica, 1994. © NASA/Jet Propulsion Laboratory—Caltech.
p. 12. ASTER image of the Andes along the Chile-Bolivia border, 2000. © NASA/GSFC/METI/ERSDAC/JAROS, and U.S./Japan ASTER Science Team.
p. 14. ECOsystem Spaceborne Thermal Radiometer Experiment on Space Station (ECOSTRESS) image of Namib Desert, Namibia, 2018. © NASA/Jet Propulsion Laboratory—Caltech.
p. 16. ASTER image of Namibia sand dunes, 2012. © NASA/GSFC/METI/ERSDAC/JAROS, and U.S./Japan ASTER Science Team.
p. 18. ASTER image of Rub' al Khali sand dunes, Saudi Arabia, 2000. © NASA/GSFC/METI/ERSDAC/JAROS, and U.S./Japan ASTER Science Team.
p. 84. Metahaven, *Bats on a Bus*, 2023. Embroidery on bus seat fabric. © Metahaven.
p. 86. Architecture Office, *Big Will and Friends*, 2016.
© Ioana Tuscan.
p. 88. Rachele Didero, *Cap_able*, 2016. © Marcello Chiesa, Marta Morini, Eugenio Chironna, Ana Alice Alves Santos.
p. 90. Carmen Argote, *Me At Market*, 2020. © Kara Leigh Kirk.
p. 92. Sarah Sze, *Fallen Sky*, 2021. Stainless steel. © Sarah Sze.
p. 180. Lhoist Lime Quarry, Marble Falls, Texas, 2023.
© Google, Airbus, CAPCOG, CNES/Airbus, Maxar Technologies, USDA/FPAC/GEO.
p. 182. Lhoist Lime Quarry, Marble Falls, Texas, 2023.
© Google, Airbus, CAPCOG, CNES/Airbus, Maxar Technologies, USDA/FPAC/GEO.
p. 184. Circular patterns from center pivot irrigation systems in crop land near Garden City, Kansas, seen from space. Courtesy of Wikipedia.
p. 186. Teton Springs residential development, Utah, ca. 2012.
© Google, Airbus, CAPCOG, CNES/Airbus, Maxar Technologies, USDA/FPAC/GEO.
p. 188. Circular patterns from center pivot irrigation systems in crop land near Garden City, Kansas, seen from space.
© B.A.E. Inc./Alamy Stock Photo.
p. 262. Giguel Maybach, *Sentinel*, 2021. Domestic and urban scenes rendered through thermal camera interface, New Haven, Connecticut (land of the Quinnipiac, Paugussett, Wappinger, et al.). Courtesy of the artist.
p. 264. Taller Frida Escobedo, *El Otro*, LIGA 06, 2012.
© Rafael Gamo, Courtesy of Taller Frida Escobedo.
p. 266. Mike Hewson, *Homage to the Lost Spaces*, 2012. Digital print on exterior of earthquake damaged building, 130 m². © Mike Hewson.
p. 268. Juan Campanini Josefina Sposito, *Fachada en la calle Dr. Erazo*, LIGA 37, 2023. © Arturo Arrieta.
p. 270. Giguel Maybach, *Sentinel*, 2021. Domestic and urban scenes rendered through thermal camera interface, New Haven, Connecticut (land of the Quinnipiac, Paugussett, Wappinger, et al.). Courtesy of the artist.

ACKNOWLEDGMENTS

Perspecta 56 was brought into being through the inspiration and efforts of many individuals, and we wish to dedicate the issue to their earnest and diligent collaboration.

We are endlessly grateful to professor Joel Sanders, whose encouragement and leadership in the Post-Professional Master of Architecture program expanded our understanding of the complexities and intersections operating within the built environment. The initial concepts for *not found* emerged over the course of our studies with professors Sanders, Sunil Bald, Ana María Durán, and Aniket Shahane. We are also indebted to professors Keller Easterling, Joan Ockman, and Alan Plattus for their insight and provocations that helped to shape our conception of the critical issues within the theme.

We thank members of the *Perspecta* board for their continuous support, generous critique, and trust in our editorial vision: Emanuel Admassu, Barry Bergdoll, Deborah Berke, Brennan Buck, Keller Easterling, Nontsikelelo Mutiti, Alan Plattus (BA '76), Ife Vanable, and especially Ali John Pierre Artemel (M.Arch '14) for his inestimable assistance on every detail related to production. We'd also like to express our deepest gratitude to all of the authors, whose work gave meaningful scope and urgency to the issue's questions. The exchange involved in developing the essays was a wonderful and deeply enriching experience for us.

Translating the editorial concept from statement to publication was a veritable collective endeavor engaging multiple hands and voices. Graphic designers Mike Tully and Cat Wentworth deepened the significance and experience of *not found* through their incisive design concepts while also creating a space and language for a true creative partnership. Cathryn Drake edited the texts with inexhaustible attention and commitment to each author's intentions and produced the tone that connects and amplifies the meanings in every contribution. At Grafiche Veneziane, Filippo Ranchio embraced the design ambitions of *Perspecta 56* with unflinching resolve, and we thank the entire cooperative for the extraordinary efforts to make printing possible. We are also grateful to Emily Simon and Kate Elwell, of MIT Press, for their dedication and patience in guiding us through the intricacies of distribution and keeping the project on track.

We owe special recognition to the friends and classmates whose sincere criticism and encouragement was a constant source of motivation. Hojae Lee provided us with essential insight into the initial application phase. Jack Rusk, Takuomi Samejima, Janelle Schmidt, and Rukshan Vathupola gave us invaluable notes on our editorial direction. Saba Salekfard's counsel was integral in the beginning stages of production, and Meghna Mudaliar generously reviewed and commented on endless details and statement iterations. Alper Turan provided us with unwavering sustenance and advice from beginning to end.

Coincident with this issue's exploration of the obscure dynamics underlying the built environment and the practice of architecture, we want to commend the Yale School of Architecture for its enthusiastic endorsement of our editorial stance toward fair compensation. *Perspecta* has long operated with an exceptionally limited printing budget that did not allow remuneration for the labor of its editors, designers, and contributors aligned with professional standards. We especially praise Dean Deborah Berke's commitment to updating the budget for *Perspecta* so that all of those involved in its production will be compensated beginning with this volume. Our gratitude extends as well to the editors and writers of past issues, who planted the seeds of this outcome over the years.

This vital publication exists thanks to the ongoing generosity of current and past donors: Tom Beeby from the Richard H. Driehaus Foundation; Marc Appleton (M.Arch '72); Hans Baldauf (BA '81, M.Arch '88); the Austin Church III (BA '60) Family Fund; Fred Koetter and Susie Kim; Cesar Pelli (DHFA '08); Robert A.M. Stern (M.Arch '65); Jeremy Scott Wood (BA '64, M.Arch '70); F. Anthony Zunino (M.Arch '70); and the Robert A.M. Stern Family Foundation for the Advancement of Architectural Culture.

Most of all we'd like to thank our families and friends for their support and understanding during the long process of editing *Perspecta 56*. Your thoughtfulness was never *not found*.

PERSPECTA 56: NOT FOUND
The Yale Architectural Journal

    EDITORS
Guillermo Acosta Navarrete
Gabriel Gutierrez Huerta

    COPY EDITOR
Cathryn Drake

    DESIGNERS
Mike Tully
Cat Wentworth

    PRINTER
Grafiche Veneziane, Italy

    PAPER
Munken Lynx Rough

    TYPEFACE
Executive, Optimo
Executive Mono, Optimo and Cat Wentworth

    PERSPECTA BOARD
Emanuel Admassu
Ali John Pierre Artemel (M.Arch '14)
Barry Bergdoll
Deborah Berke
Brennan Buck
Keller Easterling
Nontsikelelo Mutiti
Alan Plattus (BA '76)
Ife Vanable

    DIRECTOR OF COMMUNICATIONS
Ali John Pierre Artemel (M.Arch '14)

Perspecta, The Yale Architectural Journal is published in the United States of America by the Yale School of Architecture and distributed by the MIT Press.

Distributed by the MIT Press
Massachusetts Institute of Technology
Cambridge, Massachusetts 02142
mitpress.mit.edu

©2024 Yale University

All rights reserved. No part of this book may be reproduced in any form by any electronic or mechanical means (including photocopying, recording, or information storage and retrieval) without permission in writing from the publisher.

ISBN: 978-0-262-54781-9
ISSN: 0079-0958